PARADOX POLITICS

People and Power in Idaho

a 2nd edition

Randy Stapilus

Ridenbaugh Press

Ridenbaugh Press

P.O. Box 843, Carlton, OR 97111
www.ridenbaugh.com

Printed and bound in the United States of America
First Edition 1988
Second Edition 2009

Revised edition ©2009 Ridenbaugh Press

Library of Congress Cataloging in Publication Data

Stapilus, Randy, 1955-
Paradox Politics
Bibliography
Includes Index

1. Idaho-History. 2. Idaho-Politics and Government.
I. Stapilus, Randy. II. Title.
JK7516 1988 979.6 88-090516
ISBN 978-0-9824668-0-3 (softbound)

Front cover photo by Randy Stapilus
Back cover photo by Frank Lundberg

Contents

Introduction   7

Acknowledgements: Without Whom   11

Chapter 1 Combatants   14

Tour: The North Country   27

Chapter 2 Wild lands   38

Chapter 3 Sagebrush rebels   49

Tour: The Southwestern Valleys   61

Chapter 4 Use it and/or ...   67

Chapter 5 Democrats: Booms & Busts   73

Chapter 6 Republicans: Sorcerers' Apprentices   94

Chapter 7 Painful Realignment   118

An Aside: East to Zion   144

Chapter 8 Out of Control   158

Chapter 9 Sunnyslope and the Supply Side   179

Chapter 10 Showdown in 1980   192

Tour: Middle Mountains   209

Chapter 11 Back to the Future?   213

Chapter 12 One-percenters and Their Friends   234

Chapter 13 At the Arid Club   249

Tour: The Magic Valley   264

Chapter 14 The Rise and Swan Falls of Idaho Power   268

Epilogue   285

Appendix/The Winners   288

Notes   291

Introduction to the 2nd edition

For those who have suggested, for an uncomfortable number of years, that Paradox Politics be updated …
(Or: If you're thinking of buying this book, you need to read this first) …

Paradox Politics: People and Power in Idaho was conceived in early 1987 and birthed a year and a half later – more than 20 years ago, and at the time it broke some ground. In an entirely different way, I'm hoping this new edition of the book will break some ground as well.

Take yourself back to 1988 –a whole different world in so many ways. No Internet, no e-mail (other than for a handful of computer geeks).

Idaho was different then, and certainly its politics was. Steve Symms was one of the senators, and Cecil Andrus the governor. Politics in the state was competitive in a way it has not been since.

There was also little in print, in the form of books, about public affairs in Idaho. The only biography or autobiography by or about a recent Idaho public official then available concerned former Senator Glen Taylor, who left office in 1951. I was a political reporter at the time for the *Idaho Statesman* in Boise (and had been writing politics for about a decade) and undertook the book partly out of frustration that the pieces of the Idaho political puzzle had never been set down in print. Like everyone else, I had to pick them up item by item, slowly, learning over years what my teachers had learned over years.

There may, in hindsight, in fact have been something useful in that … *Paradox*, which brought together the running narrative of Idaho politics, and a few related topics, for the last half-century, did seem to bring some people up to speed on Idaho faster than they could have done otherwise. It received a cordial response – I was gratified to see – around the state. It won a state library association award as book of the year for 1988. It was named by the Idaho Centennial Commission as one of the state centennial books in 1990. It received a batch of nice reviews, especially pleasing since many of the reviewers are not known for pulling punches. When that blunt-spoken curmudgeon and lifetime student of Idaho Perry Swisher gave it a thumbs up, I felt confident the book hit reasonably near the mark in telling its story.

And so much for all that. For me, the years since have seen a departure from the news media and into publishing of various sorts, especially monthyly publications including the *Idaho Public Affairs Digest* and the *Snake River Basin Adjudication Digest*. (*Paradox Politics* was supposed to be a one-shot for Ridenbaugh Press, but life does take its unexpected turns.) *Paradox* has sold well for a book of its kind, well enough to be called a local best-seller, though that still translates to a microscopically smaller scale than the books that come with 30%

discounts at Barnes & Noble. Through the years, I've been asked regularly whether *Paradox* will be updated with a new edition. I've invariably waffled in my reply, for a number of reasons.

For one, *Paradox* was a bear to organize in the first place, and a revision to bring events up to date, to 2009, would be even tougher. Politics, and the nature of Idaho, has been so different in this last decade that it almost doesn't fit *Paradox* at all. The period from the late 80s up to now (and possibly the next few years as well) make for a story all their own, and I have begun mapping out plans for writing another book about it

For a second, I have been doing updates. In 1990, specifically with the idea of expanding on and updating *Paradox*, Ridenbaugh Press published its second book: The *Idaho Political Almanac 1990*. We published updated political almanacs through 2002. We expect to resume some of that effort late in 2009.

There's a third: *Paradox* is no longer the only long book-form explication of recent Idaho politics and public affairs. A raft of such books have been issued in recent years, most of them in the form of biographies or autobiographies. Books by or about Robert Smylie, Frank Church, Cecil Andrus, James McClure, Phil Batt, Don Samuelson, Perry Swisher, J.R. Simplot and others – not to mention two new histories of the Idaho National Engineering & Environmental Laboratory – all have appeared in the last few years, since *Paradox* was published. (And I wholeheartedly recommend them all to anyone interested in Idaho public affairs. I'd like to think that *Paradox* helped kick-start some of that action.) It's like the joke of the dancing bear – that people were so taken with the dancing bear not because it danced so well, but because it danced at all. *Paradox* remains alone in as a neutral (i.e., non-participant's) account, but it is no longer the only dancing bear on the stage of recent Idaho writing on politics.

Still, there are some compelling arguments in favor of – doing something – with *Paradox*.

For one thing, it's still out there, and for the moment stands as written all those years ago, even when its author isn't standing in the same place. People are still using it as reference, although – while the history pretty much up – Idaho politics in the years since has taken directions that are drastically different from those described here. It is increasingly becoming a history book, as opposed to a study of current affairs (which it was in 1988), but it *should* continue to be useful.

For another thing, I know more now than I did then.

And for one more thing, the first edition is nearly out of print. And in some way, shape or form, I'd like to keep it out there.

So by way of a short statement of intent:
This version does not change the original book text. (Most of the photos, too). None of it has been conveniently revised to match later conclusions or events. (We did correct typos that cropped up in the original production process, however.)

What's new is a bunch of footnotes, by way of updating and correcting – making the book maybe a little more useful to a generation later. Reference notes are, as in the original, in the back of the book; all the footnotes you see here are new to this edition. They offer additional information, updates and new interpretation, and in a few cases corrections to errors in the original. (If there are more errors, someone please let me know.)

The object is *not* to bring to the story of Idaho and its politics fully up to date. It *is* intended to help bring the subjects referred to here up to current context, so that a reader in this millennium will have a better handle on how these events relate to more recent times. And to reflect, in a number of cases, a better understanding of some of the people, places, events and trends reflected in the book.

Paradox remains book about politics in Idaho during the half-century or so up to 1988; but it now also includes more information and commentary based on what I didn't know, or didn't understand, or hadn't happened yet, in the period from there to here. And in a number of cases, this new edition tells you "whatever happened to" a number of the key players in the original story.

Reviewing these chapters, and writing these updates, I had to reflect on just how much has changed. And you'll see a number of those reflections here. And some amendments to earlier thinking.

So this revision, by itself, may provide a useful look at where Idaho has not only been, but where it come.

At least until the next book comes along …

Randy Stapilus
May 2009

Introduction: The Paradox of Idaho

When they take away our guns, how we gonna shoot liberals?
— Idaho bumper sticker

Not long ago someone described Idaho's news media people as the state's highest-paid migrant work force. Maybe so. At least, TV news anchors and newspaper reporters are the most visible and obvious of Idaho's migrants.

But they are not out of character for Idaho: the whole state is thinly rooted.

The Idaho Legislature, that stable of community pillars, is in fact a revolving door. After the 1988 elections barely one tenth of the 126 legislators will have more than a dozen years of legislative experience; most will have four or less.

So certain lobbyists – those who know what they are doing – have power. And key legislative staffers – notably the razor-sharp and witty Legislative Council Director Myran Schlechte, who has held his sensitive job for a quarter-century – have had far more impact on Idaho law in recent years than any single legislator.[1]

When Idaho became a state in 1890 it did not have even half as many people as Ada County does today. Most newcomers were immigrants; Idaho seldom has produced enough jobs to keep its children in-state. Only in the Silver Valley mining country, on the Indian reservations, and in scattered farm lands in the south, do substantial populations go back more than a couple generations.

That is one fact about Idaho the outsiders miss.

Occasionally, Idaho gets national attention. Maybe because of an earthquake.

Or a herd of Mud Lake farmers bashing jackrabbits.

Or a political race involving Frank Church or Steve Symms or George Hansen or Cecil Andrus – all elected to high office in 1974. That kind of election – a political paradox – drives national pundits crazy. Why does Idaho do such strange things?[2]

---

[1] Schlechte retired in 1993, and the Legislature hasn't been the same since. His impact on the lawmakers was enormous; the effect is more diffuse now, the impact spread among more legislative staffers.

[2] But not any more. It is said that sometime not long before his death in 1984, Church – who had narrowly lost his Senate seat in 1980 – opined privately that apart from Cecil Andrus, no Idaho Democrat would win a major elective office (governor or congressional seat) for the rest of the century. If he did say so, he was prescient, for none have, though many have tried. Idaho politics in 2000 is far more monochromatic than it was in 1988.

Let's go further. Forget for a moment about the people Idahoans elect to front for the state. Consider the internal contradictions.

It is a state of open political processes. In few states can an unknown, unconnected, unwealthy person go so far so quickly in politics or other public activities.

Yet it is also a state of tight personal networks that can throw elections at the drop of a telephone tree. In decades past elections could be – and were – orchestrated by political mechanics like Republican Lloyd Adams and Democrat Tom Boise. Now the clout has gone to apolitical organizations ... sort of.[3]

Power in Idaho comes from controlling a concentration of resources (such as timber or silver), voting blocs (such as union members or Mormons) or money (the ratebase of Idaho Power Co. or the public employee pension fund). In modern times no person or organization has had a firm handle on all three. The last one that came close – Idaho Power – has seen its Statehouse clout gently diminish in the eighties.

Aside from a Democratic swing in the Great Depression, Idaho has been basically Republican since statehood. Yet since the Depression, Republicans have controlled the five major offices (the congressional delegation and the governorship) and the legislature for just one two-year period, in 1951 and 1952.[4]

Idahoans cherish not just rugged but aggressive independence. As a group they display a cheerful political perversity: they'll lead you to the water's edge of absolute victory, but will not let you drink. Just ask the Idaho Republican Party.[5]

Politicians who understand this can do well in Idaho, whatever their party or philosophy. The unwillingness to turn over government to a single group is a mark of a healthy society. But there are down sides to the lack of roots.

When I came to Idaho in 1973 and wanted to learn about the state's mountains and streams, I could pick out a wheelbarrow full of books. But on the whys and wherefores of Idaho, of who the people are, of why they think and act as they do, of the consequences of their thoughts and actions, the well was empty.

The biographies of Sen. William E. Borah and Gov. C. Ben Ross brought Idaho politics at book length up to 1940. The biography and autobiography of Sen. Glen Taylor, which came out later in the seventies, advanced pieces of that history up to 1956. Biographies of Sen. Frank Church, which will appear by 1990 or so, will extend that

---

[3] "Apolitical" was the wrong word, but it has remained true that organizations which are not overtly political can have a huge effect on Idaho politics.
[4] True enough in 1988, but no longer. Republicans held all five major offices continuously from 1995 to 2009, when Democrat Walt Minnick won the 1st District House seat. From 2006 to 2008 they held all congressional and statewide seats.
[5] Uh, well, up until the 00s, at least. That cheerful perversity seems to have gone by the boards.

time a bit. (The fine Forrester Church book, *Father and Son*, was a reminiscence, not a political biography.)[6]

But none of those biographies have given (or, in the case of the Church works, probably will give) more than a cursory nod to the sweep of Idaho politics.

And none of the most intriguing figures — Lloyd Adams and Tom Boise, to name two — in Idaho politics has figured significantly in any book-length study.

Until now.

Adams and Boise, the two most influential people in the last 50 years of Idaho politics, are nearly anonymous today. (Adams did write, but never completed, his memoirs. I have obtained one fascinating draft chapter. The assembled papers would be a treasure and a revelation; perhaps their custodians will one day have them edited into book form.) The next two most influential political Idahoans, Verda Barnes and Gwen Barnett, also are little known to the public.[7]

Yet Idaho probably would be more different today without any one of these four people than without any one of its better-known citizens.

This book is an attempt at setting this in context, at showing how the people and events in Idaho's public life in the last half-century fit into place and make Idaho what it is today.

Parts of *Paradox Politics* — some incidents, observations, and documents — are new in the sense that they have not been public knowledge until now. Some of the more than 50 people I interviewed who once were unable to candidly discuss certain events, felt freer with the passage of years. One, an hour into talking about a controversy several years in the past, stopped, startled by a realization. "You know," he said, "this is the first time I ever told the truth about this."

Some kinds of truth are hard to express at all.

In this book, some politicians will be called "liberals" or "moderates" or "conservatives," and this calls for explanation (if not apology). These words are the bane of political reporting: they mean too much and too little, and their meanings change over time. By way of loose definition, in most times and places in this book, a "liberal" is more inclined toward government social activism and larger budgets

---

[6] As noted in the revised introduction, there's now a shelf-full of books available on recent Idaho political figures. They include biographies or autobiographies of Frank Church, James McClure, Robert Smylie, Cecil Andrus, Phil Batt, Don Samuelson, Perry Swisher, J.R. Simplot, the Compton White family, and others. You can Google them, and I recommend doing that. They're not listed in the references section here because, simply, they weren't around when this book was written in 1988. Some of them are, however, referenced here and there in the footnotes.

[7] Does that assessment of political impact hold up? There's a temptation now to throw Governor Robert Smylie into that mix of four. But maybe the choice was a good one. Barnett may be the least known of the group today, but she was instrumental in the crafting of a fully conservastive Republican Party in Idaho in the 60s – a development powerfully impacting state politics to this day. Smylie's tradition of moderate Republicanism, on the other hand, has almost completely evaporated.

and programs for the needy; a "conservative" is inclined toward tight restrictions on government budgets and on taxes and more often voices support for business; and a "moderate" fits in between, taking pieces from both perspectives.

But there are many exceptions. And it can be said (and often has been) that Idaho has had few New York-style liberals, and none who have consistently won high office. Anyone who puts Frank Church or Cecil Andrus in that category doesn't understand either man's record. And yet describing each as a "liberal" became the only way I could sensibly describe how they fit into Idaho politics.[8]

But these philosophy words are the only blunt tools available for showing – without getting too ponderous about it – how groups formed and how the pieces fit together. They're primitive tools, but until someone invents better ones, they'll have to do.

My point is not to create a revisionist view of Idaho's public life. I couldn't; this is the first telling of that story.

If it prompts a further look at, and more informed debate about, Idaho's future, it will have served a large part of its purpose.

June, 1988
Boise, Idaho

---

[8] What was uncomfortable about these words back in 1988 has turned into flat impracticality in the nineties era of Republican super-dominance. The Idaho political lexicon is in dire need of an overhaul, when almost everyone – all save the tiniest sliver of activists – involved seriously in Idaho politics is a self-described "conservative." That includes the lone Democrat elected to major office in 2008, Walt Minnick: Even Republicans have typically labeled him "conservative."

Without whom . . .

It seemed so simple to lash together a few thoughts on the how and why of Idaho politics. I'd covered the subject as a reporter and editor for the last dozen years. Wasn't that enough?

Nope. Not even close.

No one person's perspective could do anything approaching justice to a subject so multifaceted (hence the decision, in many places in this book, to let participants speak for themselves). Many people gave freely of time, effort and memories. All of the hundreds of people (at least) who have shared their knowledge of Idaho with me over the years contributed, one way or another.

The core of this book came from research undertaken for it in 1987 and 1988. That included interviews with more than 50 people who have been involved in recent Idaho politics; examination of tens of thousands of pages of archival and other records; and review of miles of newspaper and magazine microfilms.

The names of the key interviewees follow; the dates indicate the occasions of primary interviews.

Cecil Andrus, elected governor 1970, 1974, 1986; interior secretary 1977-81; state senator; Orofino logger. Jan. 22, 1988

Phil Batt, lieutenant governor (1979-83), legislator (1964-88), Wilder farmer. March 14, 1988

Jim Bruce, chairman, Idaho Power Co.; former deputy attorney general. Dec. 4, 1987

Carl Burke, Boise attorney; long-time campaign manager for Sen. Frank Church. Jan. 29, 1988

Don Chance, leader of the Idaho Property Owners Association which spearheaded the One Percent Initiative. April 27, 1988

John Corlett, long-time political editor of the Idaho Statesman newspaper, an Idaho political reporter since the mid-thirties; since 1975 a Statesman columnist. Jan. 12, 1988

Floyd Decker, executive director, the Association of Idaho Cities; key player in downtown Boise conflict. Feb. 18, 1988

Dick Egbert, legislator between 1940 and 1980; sheep rancher in Tetonia. Oct. 16, 1987

John Evans, governor 1977-87, rancher, banker, lieutenant governor (1975-77), state senator, Malad mayor. Oct. 15, 1987

Jim Goller, aide to Jim McClure, GOP strategist; since 1987, member of the Northwest Power Planning Council. Jan. 7, 1988

Bill Hall, editorial page editor, Lewiston Morning Tribune since 1965; briefly, a staffer for Frank Church. April 19, 1988

George Hansen, congressman from Idaho 1965-69, 1975-85. Four times a candidate for U.S. Senate. June 1, 1988

Richard Hendricks, GOP official, campaign strategist and aide to George Hansen. He died in December 1987, weeks after his last interview with the author. Oct. 18, 1987

Jim Jones, attorney general, candidate for Congress (1978, 1980), staffer for Sen. Len Jordan. Feb. 18, 1988

David Leroy, lieutenant governor (1983-87), attorney general (1979-83), Ada County prosecutor (1975-79). Jan. 5, 1988

Don Loveland, Cassia County assessor, state legislator and member, State Tax Commission. Nov. 27, 1987

Harry Magnuson, Wallace businessman. Jan. 14, 1988

Charles Moss, Pocatello city manager (1970-85), since 1987 a state administrator. Nov. 17, 1987

Laird Noh, Kimberly farmer, farm organization leader, and state senator since 1980. March 29, 1988

Anthony Park, attorney general (1971-75). Feb. 24, 1988

Jack Peterson, executive director, Idaho Mining Association, and a leading Idaho economist. Jan. 9, 1988

Martin Peterson, state administrator; director, Association of Idaho Cities; staffer for Frank Church (1968-71). Nov. 20, 1987

John Porter, veteran Rexburg mayor, newspaperman and Democratic leader. April 22, 1988

Vern Ravenscroft, legislator, ran for governor (as both a Democrat and a Republican), state Republican chairman. Jan. 22, 1988

Mary Lou Reed, state senator, local government official in Coeur d'Alene. Oct. 22, 1987

Harold Reid, 28-year state representative, specialist on taxes, Craigmont farmer. Jan. 19, 1988

Mark Ricks, Rexburg farmer, state senator, and a regional leader in the LDS Church. March 16, 1988

Ray Rigby, Rexburg attorney and state senator. May 19, 1988

Jim Risch, Boise attorney, Ada County prosecutor and since 1982 state Senate president pro tem. Dec. 3, 1987

Don Samuelson, governor (1967-71), state senator. Oct 23, 1987

Erwin Schwiebert, legislator, ran for Congress. Jan. 7, 1988

Allan Shepard, justice, Idaho Supreme Court, since 1968; attorney general (1962-68); legislator. May 9, 1988

Robert Smylie, Boise attorney, governor (1955-67), attorney general (1947-55). Dec. 4, 1987

Carol Stacey, manager, Nickel's Worth advertiser in Coeur d'Alene; community activist. Oct. 22, 1987

Perry Swisher, newspaperman, legislator, candidate for governor (1966) as an independent; Pocatello city councilman; Idaho Public Utilities commissioner. Nov. 30, 1987

Lloyd Walker, Twin Falls attorney, state Democratic chairman (1962-65), candidate for governor (1966, 1970). April 12, 1988

Compton I. White, Jr., Clark Fork businessman; congressman (1963-67). April 18, 1988

Joe Williams, state auditor since 1958, Ada County Democratic leader. Feb. 26, 1988

Others included Walter Yarbrough, a Grand View rancher and 11-term state senator; Myrna Sasser, who has worked for Frank Church and the Idaho Democratic Party since 1959; Louise Shadduck, Coeur d'Alene, an aide to

Sen. Henry Dworshak and Congressman Orval Hansen, a department director in the Smylie and Samuelson Administrations, and Republican candidate for Congress in 1956; Lillian Inscore, Moscow, widow of J.R. "Jap" Inscore, a top Democratic organizer; Myran Schlechte, director since 1963 of the Idaho Legislative Council; Jay Shelledy, publisher of the *Idahonian* newspaper in Moscow, formerly a reporter and editor of the *Lewiston Morning Tribune*; John Greenfield, a Boise attorney and a former state Democratic Party chairman; Jim Hawkins, businessman and since 1987 director of the Idaho Department of Commerce; Byron Johnson, a justice on the Idaho Supreme Court; Max Hanson, a state legislator and candidate for governor in 1958 and 1966 and for the U.S. House in 1974; Marguerite McLaughlin, a Democratic state senator from Orofino; Frank Lundberg, a consultant and former aide to Gov. Evans; Bob Drummond, a Coeur d'Alene art dealer and former board member on the Coeur d'Alene Athletic Roundtable; Tim Tucker, a Democratic state representative from Porthill.

Andrus, Jones, Schlechte, Smylie, Risch, Leroy, Decker, Park, Goller, Shelledy, Ravenscroft, Martin Peterson, Schweibert, Magnuson and Swisher each reviewed portions of the manuscript and provided helpful suggestions.

Others who provided valuable review and editorial assistance included David Morrissey of the *Albuquerque Journal* in New Mexico (formerly an Idaho news reporter); James Weatherby of the Association of Idaho Cities; Tom Knappenberger, Paul Beebe and Charles Etlinger of the Boise *Idaho Statesman*; Dan Myers of the Pocatello *Idaho State Journal*; Steve Ahrens of Boise Cascade Corp. (formerly a political editor, from 1975 to 1982, of the *Idaho Statesman*); Gary Richardson of the Idaho Public Utilities Commission staff; Larry Taylor of Idaho Power; Larry Swisher (Perry Swisher's son), a former Idaho newsman currently working as a Washington-based columnist on Northwest affairs; Jean McNeil, a former Idaho public television reporter; Pat Costello, a Boise attorney and former newsman; and Mike McPeek, a Boise attorney and a former reporter for the *Idaho State Journal*.

Thanks to Katie Higgins and Tom Menzel, and Craig Carter, for help with design and related matters.

Special thanks to Jean Wilson of The Book Shop in Boise, for her excellent advice and for suggesting the title.

My especially grateful appreciation, for their extensive and thoughtful — and essential — help with the whole manuscript, to Lindy High and Ralph Nichols, and Pete and Irene Stapilus.[9]

---

[9] Updates here are in order. Quite a few of these people have died since 1988, among them Don Chance, John Corlett, Harry Magnuson, Vern Ravenscroft, Richard Egbert, Richard Hendricks, Don Loveland, John Porter, Harold Reid, Don Samuelson, Dick Egbert, Jim Goller, Walter Yarbrough, Louise Shadduck, Allan Shepard, Lloyd Walker, Compton I. White, J., and Joe Williams. David Morrissey, one of the key editors of the original edition and a good friend of many years, died in 1996. And the Book Shop of Boise – a critical institution in development of Idaho books, without which support *Paradox* probably wouldn't have been published at all – announced its closure in September 2000. People and circumstance have changed over the years from the descriptions above; some of that will be addressed in the pages ahead.

1 | The Combatants

"Main floor," the elevator's muffled female voice murmured to Cecil Andrus.[10]

He was in the only talking elevator in Idaho.[11] It startles people, as this elegant European-style resort does, planted amidst forests, lakes and woods.

Andrus was used to it. He was here often in the months of campaigning that ended six days ago with his election to a third term as governor. The Coeur d'Alene Resort had, since opening in May 1985, pulled a host of conventions that attracted politicians like moths to light. Tonight one hundred Idaho politicians – winners all – were here, drawing lobbyists with them.

Outside, Lake Coeur d'Alene was glazed with ice and light snow cover; the forests behind it looked unreal in the still winter air. The mountains around the lake town were blanketed with snow, glistening when the moon peeked through the clouds. The scene was breathtaking, but pity the drivers who paid it much attention. They did not have an easy time getting here. The three highways south from Coeur d'Alene were slick with ice. Highway 95 north to Sandpoint was treacherous, east-west I-90 barely passable, the under-used airstrip north of town hardly better.

For many legislators, Coeur d'Alene and the North Idaho Chamber of Commerce Tour were routine. They were used to socializing in the hospitality rooms on the shore of Lake Coeur d'Alene, the bus rides to the mines at Kellogg and Wallace, the ski resort at Sandpoint, and the local Chamber chatter. It was part of the cycle, like summer, winter and Election Day.

For freshmen, it was inspiring, electrifying, confusing.

For Cecil Andrus, the Monday night attraction, it was a test.

Andrus could be chatty, a joker, a fine story teller – when he chose. He could also be cool and regal. He walked straight as a flagpole, tall and imposing, with speed and spring to his step. He had a piercing gaze and a voice that commanded attention, especially when he kept it low. He could walk into a room, dominate it, and deliver an ad-libbed speech that held his audience where he wanted it.

These were not natural gifts. In his first term in the state Senate, he was liked and respected but was more an afterthought than a key player. He honed his skills, sometimes the hard way. Like some politicians, he survived mistakes. Like few, he learned from his

---

[10] This scene was set in November 1986, less than a week after that year's general election. It resulted in the election of Democrat Cecil Andrus to a third term as governor, and returned the Idaho Legislature once again to Republican control.
[11] It's not the only talking elevator in Idaho any more. Boise has had several of them in some of the towers that have gone up since this was written.

CECIL ANDRUS *was in his third term as governor in the late 80s. He would be elected to one more.*

mistakes. He still made some, but not many – and rarely the same one twice.

Tonight Andrus carried a talisman from one of those lessons.

He stepped briskly off the elevator, across the long tan lobby with the lounge and piano on one side and gift shops on the other, toward the banquet room.

Press aide Marc Johnson, walking with him, carried copies of the speech.

But the evening's real symbol, a two-foot switch, was in Andrus' hands. A whipping switch? No, no – not tonight.

Andrus had an olive tree in the back yard of his house in the east foothills of Boise. He could harvest nothing edible from it. But one day he came up with the idea of pruning a branch and offering it as a token of peace to the Republicans with whom his predecessor, fellow Democrat John Evans, had warred so often.

Getting the branch to Coeur d'Alene wasn't easy. First he cut it too big and couldn't fit it into his baggage. He discovered olive branches are thorny. He tried recutting it and fitting it into his brief case. That wouldn't work. He trimmed it again and finally bent it around the corners of his suitcase.

Now, walking into the banquet room, he held it like a trophy.

He offered it not just to legislators but also to the lobbyists and corporate heads or almost-heads. Taken together they represented a sizable chunk of what passed for the power structure of Idaho. Andrus would have to deal with all of them.

Power in Idaho comes from control or influence over an important resource like timber or water, a block of money like the state pension fund or budget or the annual rate base of the Idaho Power Co., or a chunk of votes. That power was diffused. But the people in this room could deliver a lot of it.[12]

Andrus was good at mixing; he worked magic one-on-one. He could walk up to a conservative Republican who'd had a "Cease Mining, Cease Logging, Cease Farming, Cece Andrus" bumper sticker on his pickup the last eight months. Slap him on the back. Shake his hand. "Well Fred, how are you? Pheasants still hopping?" No philosophical brickbats, just something personal. And in minutes, Fred was eating out of Cece's hand.

Soon he saw someone he needed to talk to. Jim Risch, president pro tem of the state Senate, was nursing a drink near the head table, and Andrus took long strides over to him.

They knew each other, but not as well as they might have. Andrus and Risch were long-distance ships who passed in the political night. Andrus resigned as governor in January 1977 just as Risch settled in as Senate majority leader.

Risch now had been pro tem – the top Senate leader – for four years and had become a power center of Idaho government during the ten years Andrus was out of elective office. They had worked opposite sides of the fence; Andrus popped up in campaign brochures for Risch's Democratic opponent, Larry La Rocco. Now they had to work together.

Andrus' campaign and business offices, which faced each other across Bannock Street in Boise, were only a couple of hundred yards from Risch's white-and-reflecting-glass law building. The day after the election he walked to Risch's office, stopping to uproot a "Leroy for Governor" yard sign in front. "He brought it in and said, 'You're not going to be needing this any more'," Risch recalled. "We both acknowledged how we tried to cut each other's throats during the election, and that was behind us."

On Friday, before heading north for the tour, Risch was interviewed on Boise Channel 7's *Viewpoint* program. "The governor-elect," he said, "is a person with whom I have worked in the past and who has the ability to talk with people, to give and take and to reach some consensus without necessarily having to go to the press and bang on the table and whine and cry about the opposition." Risch drew a

---

[12] From 1997 to 2002, Ridenbaugh Press compiled annual lists of the most influential people, and influential organizations, in Idaho – and they seem to give the lie in part to this analysis. In part, that's because natural resource industries are relatively less important in Idaho than they were, and others – mainly high tech manufacturers, some of them nonexistent in 1988 – have gained influence.

breath, perhaps recalling his years of combat against Gov. Evans. "So, I'm looking forward to that."

It sounded upbeat, and now as they sipped drinks Andrus told Risch he appreciated the compliments. He had read them in the paper and had looked forward to seeing Risch say them on television. There he was foiled: The program, scheduled for Sunday afternoon, had been pre-empted at the last moment.

Andrus knew Risch's shark-like reputation and his clout – which might increase next session. House Speaker Tom Stivers had not run for re-election, so the next session's House leader would be new and probably look to Risch for guidance. Risch certainly would be in charge again in the Senate. The election for pro tem hadn't been held yet, and Risch faced a potential challenge by Sen. Phil Batt, a Wilder Republican. Batt had been pro tem a decade ago – when Risch became majority leader – and since had been lieutenant governor and a candidate for governor. Batt was as respected and personable as anyone in the Senate. But he never got a serious beachhead to regain his old leadership job and would abandon the try days after the tour broke up. The outcome was evident even tonight. Risch dined publicly with half a dozen Republican senators, some of whom could have been swing votes.

Feldmarschall

The how and why of Risch's strength was harder to pin down; as with Andrus, it came mostly from personality. He wasn't drawing on an old-boy network; he was an urban lawyer in a Senate dominated by rural farmers, businessmen, and retirees. He was years younger than most other senators. Nor did Risch have Idaho roots, though his background may be more typical of many eighties Idahoans than that of the ranchers and miners with generations of Idaho history. Risch was a "backeasterner," a native of Wisconsin, where a lot of Republicans were progressives. Risch's father was a telephone company accountant, not the sort of background from which an Idaho pioneer/master-the-land/individualist ordinarily springs full-blown. But Risch had some of that in him early on: not for him a corporate life in the crowded east.

He wanted to work in forestry. A student at his high school had gone to the University of Idaho in Moscow for a forestry degree. A guidance counselor steered Risch to him; Risch liked what he heard and went west. "It was probably as much as anything because of this kid," Risch said. "I don't remember his name."

As he fell into Idaho so, once he had his degree in forest management, he fell into the law.

Jim Risch – *I wasn't really ready to leave college, and it just seemed like an interesting thing to do. And again, that was fortuitous. I owe that to [law school* *dean] Phil Peterson. I went to see him about it. I went to sign up for a master's in business, an MBA, and shortly before school started I thought well, you know, maybe I'd like to go to law school. And I really had not had much contact with law although my uncle was a judge, and there are several people in our family who are attorneys, but I really hadn't thought that much about it.*

Anyway, shortly before the semester started I went up to see Phil Peterson. He said, certainly you can go to law school, you fill out the usual forms, you take the LSAT [law school admission] test in the spring and then the next fall you can go to law school. I said, "No, no, no, you don't understand, I want to go to law school this semester." He said, "You've got to be kidding me. We've got a waiting list, etc., etc. There's no way I can get you into law school this semester." So I said, well, that was fine. I bought my books and started going to school for two or three days in the MBA program. So anyway, about three days into school Phil Peterson calls and says, "Hey, I got an opening up here." He said, "I like the looks of your transcript and why don't you come on up and start school." So I went up there and started going to school.

I still have nightmares because nobody, nobody, goes to law school without taking the LSAT test. I have never taken the LSAT test. And I still have nightmares of Phil Peterson coming in and picking up my diploma for not taking the LSAT test.

He called me up last year during the legislature, and we were 48 hours away from adjourning. He said, Jim, you've got to help me. He says, we have a bequeath that is coming to the university and the lawyer who is handling the estate says that it can't go to the university because we have these university foundations and trusts that are being managed by the university itself, and the statute only allows banks and what-have-you to manage it. He says, we need to amend the statute. I says, "Phil, we're 48 hours from closing this down." He says, "I know you can do it." Anyway, we now have a law ...

He took to the law like an elk to woods, as he did later to politics – though his introduction to it was even less considered. Risch had not been much involved in politics, but he soon found he had to be. Quickly.

A law professor helped him land a job at the Ada County prosecutor's office, a good place for the politically ambitious. Next to attorney general, the job of

Ada County prosecutor is the best spot in Idaho for a lawyer to impress the public and powers that be. Some former Ada prosecutors – most seemed to get the job at a young age and hold it only a few years – became wealthy or prominent in politics or law. The Ada prosecutor who hired Risch, an Idaho native named Wayne Kidwell, became state Senate majority leader. Kidwell was succeeded as prosecutor by Ellison Matthews, and Risch became Matthews' chief deputy. In 1970 Matthews started to run for re-election and then, after the primary election, decided he wanted out and declined the Republican nomination. That pushed Risch into the race; if he didn't run, the new prosecutor might install a new chief deputy.

JIM RISCH *talks with fellow legislators on the floor of the Senate, as the end of the 1988 session approaches.*
(Photo/Randy Stapilus)

The name on the ballot would be chosen by the Ada County Republican Central Committee on Sept. 1, 1970. The county had not elected a Democratic prosecutor in decades, so the committee's decision among four contenders was the key.

Jim Risch – *That's where I really got my feet wet in politics, in that race, and I tell you that for somebody from the outside stepping into an internal deal like that ...*

[Because Risch was chief deputy] I was the candidate to beat, so they were all running against me. They decided what they would do is vote low-man-out, which obviously would give an edge to them. So we had gone around and visited most of the precinct people. Vicki [his wife] and I went around - I was married by then - and talked to all these people. There were 90 precincts at the time, and they never had more than 20 people at a meeting. We were hoping for a low turnout because I had some good, fairly hard-core people who were on my side.

When we got there I told Vicki, "I'm going to count the ones that are here I know I've got. And when they call the roll you count how many are out." There were eight precincts that weren't filled, and the reason there were only eight precincts that weren't filled is that they had just had a fight between Bob Watson and Peggy Bunting to be county chairman, and it was a knock-down drag-out. So ... everybody was there with the exception of maybe one or two. There were, like, 80 people there, and I had 33 or 34 votes in the bag. I told Vicki, "We ain't gonna make it."

He did, on the first round. He hasn't lost a race since.[13]

---

[13] He *did* lose his Senate seat – just two months after *Paradox Politics* was originally published (and about six months after this section was written). What happened? He was accused of being arrogant and remote from the voters. The Democrat who ran against him, Mike Burkett, was also a Boise attorney but in personality a friendly, aw-

Two years later, in 1972, Kidwell left the Senate to run – unsuccessfully – for Congress. Risch thought of running to replace him in the Senate but decided against it. In 1974 he did run against Kidwell's successor, an insurance salesman named David Eskelin, and beat him in the Republican primary. That same year, Kidwell was elected attorney general. (Risch protege David Leroy, a Lewiston native, later became Ada prosecutor, attorney general, lieutenant governor, and ran unsuccessfully for governor against Andrus in 1986.)

Risch was more cautious than Kidwell, who seemed to have a political death wish and twice lost races for Congress he might have won, or Leroy, who faced one of Idaho's most popular politicians when he took on Andrus. Risch was, above all, a pragmatist. Senators and congressmen were stuck back east in Washington, far from the hunting and fishing lands Risch came to Idaho for.

People who saw him in three-piece suits doubted Risch could be comfortable outside of a courthouse or statehouse. In fact he lived on a semi-ranch south of Boise and spent his free time hunting and fishing. Governors were locked into a full-time job with no opportunity to make money or contacts out-side as a state senator could do. He developed his niche to perfection. Helped by Vicki, one of the best political operatives in the state, he never has had a really close shave for re-election.

He stayed in the Senate, never making a serious misstep, although he stepped over bodies now and then.

In 1976 Batt moved up from majority leader to president pro tem, and Risch wanted to replace him. So did Larry Craig, a Republican senator from Midvale first elected with Risch in 1974, and who would be elected congressman in 1980. In 1976 Risch had a tough re-election campaign against Democrat Pat Dorman, and only after he won in November could he work on the leadership race. A day or two after the election, Risch got a letter from Craig asking for his support for majority leader.

Jim Risch – *I said, now wait a minute. I can do that. So I called Phil Batt up and he says, you're crazy. Larry has been running the re-election committee for the Senate, see, and he was unopposed [in the general election]. He was running*

---

shucks, down-home country boy. (There may be little coincidence in Risch's presentation of himself as a rancher in more recent elections.) Burkett was re-elected in 1990, opted out of the Senate in 1992, and lost a bid for attorney general in 1994; some years later he returned for several years to the Senate. Meanwhile, Risch became a great political comeback story. He sat out for a while after his 1998 loss, then lost a primary election (his first-ever primary loss) before being appointed to the Senate by new Gov. Phil Batt in 1995. He started up the leadership ladder again but slipped in 2000 when he lost a Republican caucus contest for Senate pro-tem (his first-ever leadership loss), and then only narrowly won his Republican primary that year. In 2002 he ran statewide, for lieutenant governor, and defeated an incumbent Republican (Jack Riggs) and a Democrat (Bruce Perry) in the fall. He served as governor for seven months in 2006 after the resignation of Dirk Kempthorne, then ran for lieutenant governor again. The patience and forbearance paid off. In 2008, he was elected to the U.S. Senate, winning both primary and general election easily.

around handing out money and everything to the candidates. I said, well, I'm going to give it a try. He said, you're wasting your time.

We went on the North Idaho tour and I put the arm on a couple of people and picked up [Nampa Sen.] Leon Swenson - he was a key person - but it just didn't look good. We came back and Batt and I were talking. I said, how am I running? And he said, you're running better, but you're still not going to make it.

He did. Risch became a master at reading senators, divining what they wanted, appealing to them. In 1978, after Batt became lieutenant governor, Risch ran again for majority leader. Word spread that Craig would oppose him, but "by then I knew how to do this. So within two days I had that thing nailed down."

Batt's successor as pro tem was Sen. Reed Budge, a crusty Republican from Soda Springs, one of the Senate cattlemen known collectively as Sirloin Row. He had served in the Senate since 1967 and was well-liked by the old guard. But Budge preferred managing the Senate offices and leaving control of the legislative work to Risch, who swiftly took over. He became a key source of information and decision-making in the Senate, and lobbyists and campaign contributors went out of their way to work with him and heed his advice. His influence grew, crystalline, quickly.

The process was not always smooth. One year a legislator from the House, an amateur artist, drew a caricature of "Feldmarschall von Risch" in full Nazi regalia. During sessions when Republicans had only a small voting majority Risch had a reputation of being an arm twister. Senate Democrats publicly called him Napoleonic, arrogant and abrasive; some Senate Republicans said so privately. Senate onlookers long remembered the day in 1980 when a respected freshman senator emerged from a Republican caucus meeting teary-eyed and changed his key vote to join the rest of the caucus. (And later decided not to run for re-election.) Onlookers nodded knowingly: Risch is at it again.

But that wasn't the whole story. His harshest critics admitted he was uncommonly smart and one of the best debaters in the Legislature. Risch was one of the sharpest wits in the Legislature, and he had plenty of friends. Two of them were Democratic minority leaders Ron Twilegar, a fellow sometime attorney, and Kermit Kiebert, with whom he liked to hunt elk in Northern Idaho.

Risch said that he would have been happy to stay majority leader and didn't especially want to become pro tem. In fact, with Budge as pro tem, Risch ran the show and wasn't stuck with administrative grunt work. But after the 1982 election rumblings started: word was that Risch might take on Budge.

At the North Idaho tour that fall, several Republican senators pounded on Risch to stage a coup. "They were getting beat up on in the press because of Reed," he recalled. "Everybody loved Reed. But the state was moving, the Legislature was moving and particularly the Senate was moving, and Reed wasn't moving. And you know Reed. He was very inflexible in his political philosophy, which I admired the man greatly for. You talk about purist ... But there were a lot of people that felt we needed a different image."

Beating Budge, breaking up a team in place for four sessions, meant a new alliance with junior urban and moderate Republicans. It meant generational change. Risch's backers ran a quiet campaign, gathering votes one by one. Risch never announced he was going after Budge's job until the votes were locked up.

It happened in a caucus at the Owyhee Hotel in downtown Boise. It was more a surprise to Budge, who thought he had votes to spare, than to legislature-watchers outside the room. Budge was in near-shock for weeks. He was experienced in the ways of the Senate, a careful vote-counter whose oft-spoken admonition was to "know the players." This time Budge didn't know them well enough or, at least, didn't know the freshmen and sophomores as well as Risch did. Senators he was sure of had signed on with Risch, seemingly at the last minute. Budge felt betrayed – not by Risch, but by senators who had indicated they would support him and didn't. (Budge retired in 1986, and died the next year.)

Risch did not reshape politics; rather, he saw what was there and acted accordingly. He was not a miracle worker. Again and again, opposing tax increases or changes in the voter-passed One Percent Initiative, he did what his conservative district seemed to want. When that became impractical he would compromise.

It would happen again in 1987.

Logger Sophisticate

Andrus could not know that yet. He did know they would clash on school financing, and picked the olive branch knowing it.

He and Risch looked like opposites. Risch was short, dark, quick-talking, younger in appearance than his 44 years. Andrus was tall, white-haired but balding, and looked more than 55, but seemed younger because of his considerable energy. They had in common fine political skills and a background in timber (Andrus was a former logger; Risch studied forestry).

And neither was an Idaho native.

Andrus was born and raised around Hood River, Ore., and attended Oregon State University at Eugene for a couple of years. He joined the Navy and spent time in Korea. Discharged in February 1955, he had a wife, a young daughter, $300 and need of a job. His father and some business partners were setting up a timber mill operation called Tru Cut Lumber Co. in Orofino, Idaho, and offered him $600 a month to work there. Andrus jumped at it. His wife Carol wanted to live in a larger city like Eugene or Spokane; Orofino was 40 miles from the nearest city of any size – Lewiston – and 200 miles from Spokane.

"Heck, it's just outside of Spokane," he told her.

A politician was born.

Cecil Andrus – *The economy was a single based economy ... purely lumberjacking. There were several divisions in Orofino: Yellow Dog, Whiskey Creek, Little Canada, Jingle Town, the various areas within the town. They all had their own personalities, some of them their own ethnic groups. But the common denominator was lumbering, logging, trucking of wood products. The population was about the same as it is today. There used to be an old joke that it was a very stable population because every time a baby was born, a man leaves town. Except we don't use that joke much anymore.*

On a typical Saturday night, there were about three honky tonk bars around the town, and there'd be peace until 11 p.m., and be a little more tense until 1 a.m., and it was not unknown to have a group go out in the alley to test somebody's mettle late at night. If it was a warm summer night they used to last longer than they did when it was cold and rainy. It was a typical North Idaho logging town, not one bit different from a St. Maries or some of the others.

It is a little more diversified today because with Dworshak Lake there's more tourism, fishing, boating, and the prison is a big thing because it gives a stable payroll into the area. There used to be nine saw mills, small mills, like the one I worked at, and others in that area. Now there's one ...

I'd go up to work on the week, drive home on the weekend, before I found us a place to live. I took pictures of the new swimming pool, the new elementary school – which looked good as long as you got close enough that you didn't let too much of the other stuff show in the picture - and the VFW building. And I said, "Yeah, it's just outside of Spokane. You want to go shopping, just go down to Spokane."

I had rented a little apartment in the basement of a house, and we decided to find a different place. We arrived there after dark. I had my wife and baby daughter in the car, so [Carol] couldn't really see the country. I made the mistake of showing her Main Street on the way up to where I rented this place. And she was shaking her head, and I was thinking that was the end of the marriage right there. But she adapted very well.

Orofino then was half a century old, a former trading town for nearby mining camps. Its perch on the Clearwater River saved it when the metals ran out; the miners who went north to the Silver Valley were replaced by sawmill operators. As housing boomed in the fifties, so did Orofino: millers like Andrus moved in and the town grew by half. The rest of Clearwater County grew little.

The timber people were Democrats. From 1944 to 1958 they outvoted the Republican merchants and the ranchers on the Weippe plain, and carried the county in every race for president, Congress and governor but one (moderate Republican C.A. Robins, the first Northern Idahoan ever elected governor, won there in 1946 by 64 votes). Ray McNichols, later a federal judge, practiced law there and ran the Democratic organization. McNichols was plugged into the powerful Tom Boise organization in Lewiston, a machine with reach throughout Northern Idaho, capable of swinging statewide elections and altering the course of the Legislature.

Andrus was naturally sociable. He joined civic groups and was commander of the Veterans of Foreign Wars Post 3296, the social center for young World War II and Korean War vets. But politics turned him off.

One day in 1956 Glen Taylor, a former Democratic senator running for another term, hit town. Taylor had been a vaudeville singer and actor, and it showed in his campaigns. He drove to downtown Orofino, stopped in front of the Sports Club, jumped atop a platform on the roof of his station wagon, picked up his guitar and started singing. Andrus watched and thought, "My God, is that what politics is all about? Thank you, no thanks."

Yet Andrus was pulled in, inch by inch. His eldest daughter was approaching school age and the local school was nothing to write home to Oregon about. The Republican state senator from Clearwater County, Leonard Cardiff, said the state should use average daily attendance by students to figure how much state money each district should get. Andrus thought that was crazy: it would hurt smaller school districts and those split by mountains or other rough terrain.

He hashed it over with his friends down at the VFW club. Then one of them said, "We ought to take you up and introduce you to the county chairman."

Andrus met McNichols one day after work. Andrus did all kinds of work then, from helping run the mill to cutting timber in the woods to fixing machinery. A lot of it was messy.

Cecil Andrus – *I had on leather boots and black pants, a work denim shirt, black suspenders and a hard hat, and we go upstairs above the old bank building where Ray's old law office was located. I walked in; I had come off work.*

I didn't know it but Ray had a brand new rug in his office. I had grease on the bottom of my boots and I made about three steps toward his desk and you could see the [grease] and I went, "Oh my God, Mr. McNichols, I'm terribly sorry about your brand new rug." And he'd invested too much money in it, and his secretary was busy cleaning it up; of course, she wanted to get me out of there, so she started cleaning the grease up out of that carpet. And [later] McNichols said, yes, that was the first time I met Cece Andrus.

They became friends. Andrus was so impressed with McNichols he thought of him as material for high office, like the Senate. McNichols, it turned out, was an early supporter of Frank Church. But he had plans for Andrus, too.

Republicans did better in state legislative races than they should have in Clearwater County: since World War II the county had elected them to the Legislature more than it did Democrats. The county's senator in 1960, Republican mill owner Cardiff, had held the office since 1952. Another Republican had held it four years before that. In 1960, Cardiff decided to retire.

So in the spring of 1960 Democratic organizers like McNichols scavenged for a runner for the jinxed seat. They fastened on Andrus, a committeeman in the Riverside precinct.

One night the Andruses made the bumpy 40-mile drive to Lewiston to listen to a Massachusetts senator named John Kennedy. "I was very much captivated by him, the man, his vision, his strange accent and speaking style," Andrus recalled.

Andrus was a logical prospect for McNichols and others, but when they suggested he run, he turned them down. Politics? Naah.

Word spreads fast in small towns, and the Andrus tidbit soon reached the Orofino Republicans. One of them, Bob Oud, walked up to Andrus and told him he had made a wise choice. "We'd have beat the heck out of you," he said.

The taunt got under Andrus' skin and on his nerves. Within hours he was at the Clearwater County Courthouse, filling out forms, paying his filing fee. Andrus whipped? No way.

He was 28 and running against the mayor of nearby Pierce, X.E. "Bus" Durant.

Andrus described himself in his ads as "a small businessman with a desire to better our community and state, with particular interest in the advancement of our education system." He got help from the Orofino Democratic establishment, but he could see right away he had to hustle to win. Andrus tried to knock on every door he could in a county full of extremely remote doors. His textbook, which he sometimes carried along, was a little AFL-CIO book on practical politics. But instinct told him to do what a professional would advise: leave no stone unturned and never quit working. He began to enjoy it.

He enjoyed it more when he won 12 of 15 precincts in Clearwater County in November 1960, and was sworn into the Senate.

It was an unusual freshman Senate class. Jim McClure, a future U.S. representative and senator, joined the state Senate then. It was also the first year for Don Samuelson, a future governor, and Bill Roden, a future majority leader and eventually the top lobbyist in the Statehouse. It was the first year, too, for William Dee, soon to be the state's leader of conservative Democrats.

Andrus was the youngest of all.

He was understated, listening and learning amid the bluster and thumping of egos. His peers in the Senate liked him; still a bit startled to be there at all, Andrus had little inclination at first for conflict. His first speech was on a subject of local concern: protecting state forests from Christmas tree thievery.

He became involved with statewide issues as the political bug sank deeper into his system and he won a second and a third term. He crusaded on state self-insurance and on the Old Soldiers' Home, a tatty, unsound old building in Northwest Boise where porches were falling away and ceilings falling in. A new Home was built. Andrus became noticed. In 1966 he ran for governor in one of the turning point elections in Idaho history. He lost then, but four years later ran again and won.

They called that 1970 campaign the "White Clouds" race.

The White Clouds in the Sawtooth Mountains are uncommonly beautiful and potentially profitable. The American Smelting and Refining Company (ASARCO) planned an open pit mine to extract a molybdenum near the peaks. Republican incumbent Gov. Don Samuelson was identified with the plan; Andrus opposed it.

"The most important long-range issue is the protection of our magnificent Idaho environment," Andrus said in August 1970. "We must not allow irreplaceable natural resources to be destroyed for temporary economic gain. We cannot tolerate the abuse and destruction of the White Clouds."[14]

No one before had made an environmental issue a major campaign keynote. Or at least, no one had made it work.

It worked for Andrus. Never mind the years spent logging or peddling insurance or spent on tax and budget issues. Andrus had a reputation as a super-environmentalist that would not shed.

There was a time, after he went to Washington as Secretary of the Interior, when pundits back home said he couldn't be elected dogcatcher. Six years after his chores at Interior were done, six years of mending fences and building bridges and raising money and charming the socks off everyone in sight, Andrus was re-elected governor. But it was a far cry from 1974, when he won with 71 percent of the vote. On election night in 1986 Andrus was behind. Not until early Wednesday morning did he catch up and win by 3,635 votes – a third of his margin in 1970.[15]

Andrus' demeanor in Coeur d'Alene, a few nights later, betrayed none of this. He was full of cheer. He told the legislators and lobbyists, "Naysayers tell you that partisanship always gets in the way of progress. I don't accept that. We need not choose up sides and face our future across that partisan line. If we choose, and I think we must, we can break the old pattern."

That old, ingrained, Idaho pattern is one of conflict.

Idaho, they say, is what was left after they made Montana, Washington, Utah, Oregon, Wyoming and Nevada. That isn't literally true – Wyoming and Utah became states after Idaho – but it seems so. Idaho is one of the most varied of states; conflict is inherent. Idaho survives by settling conflict or suppressing it. And it seldom stays suppressed for long.

---

[14] The White Clouds have remained largely untouched, though they became a substantial environmental and political issue again in the late 90s.

[15] However, in 1990, Andrus was re-elected with 68.2% of the vote, leading the way on what was the strongest Democratic year since 1958. He announced soon after that win that he would not run for re-election again in 1994, and hasn't run for office again since. He has stayed active in politics, endorsing and working for many candidates, including new Congressman Minnick.

Tour | The North Country

David Leroy – *I grew up in Lewiston and recall acutely the healthy suspicion all of us Northern Idahoans had of anything south of the Salmon River, which more often than not was well-founded, particularly in politics. And the sense of alienation can't really be learned by somebody who has spent all their time in the state's capital. Often, it can't be attacked or assuaged by much of anything anybody says.*

North Idaho – *A State of Mind* – bumper sticker
Southern Idaho – *A Mindless State* – another bumper sticker

Some Idaho roads close all winter. Highway 95, the only land link between Northern Idaho and the south, can be treacherous in those months. Little wonder Idaho is so split that North Idaho separatist movements spring up.

But only two roads close every night. Customs offices at the north ends of Highways 95 and 1, at Eastport and Porthill, are darkened from 11 p.m. to 7 a.m. There are no late-night crossings for hundreds of miles around.[16]

Porthill and Eastport are not metropoli. Porthill is a few houses secluded in woody hills and, down a gravel path, a few businesses near customs offices. It once had a population of 1,500, when it was last stop for the Great Northern Railroad and a main stop on a steamboat line from Nelson, British Columbia, to Bonners Ferry. Now Porthill has bar business for the border traffic. It and Eastport vote mostly Republican.

The mountains here in Boundary County are bracing but not rugged, a Washington coast without ocean. In a valley sliced by the Kootenai River sits Bonners Ferry, the commercial center which seems larger than it is (2,100 people) and prosperous despite timber reversals. Timber is two-thirds of the economy; 740,000 of the county's 822,000 acres are forest. Remoteness, not the fine scenery, brought people here. There are retirees, mostly political conservatives, and fringe stragglers getting as far from it all as they can without leaving the country.

Loggers and small unions usually keep Boundary Democratic. In the 1986 Senate and governor's races, which were close statewide, Boundary County went two-to-one for the Democrats. Many of the Republicans are deeply conservative and haven't built bridges to enough people to create a new majority.[17]

---

[16] The Kings Gate crossing on U.S. 95 now is open 24 hours, every day.
[17] No longer true. Boundary County, in the 2000s, votes solidly Republican.

Little Boom

Bonner County, a few hilly miles south, has boomed and changed. In 1970, when Sandpoint resident Don Samuelson was governor, just under 16,000 people lived here, about as many as 10 years before. By the late eighties the population was up to 26,000. Sandpoint , the county seat and center – and Idaho's own retirement and vacation spot – kept pace. While Sun Valley, McCall, and Coeur d'Alene got the press, a lot of Idahoans played at Lake Pend Oreille.

Sandpoint is connected to civilization (Coeur d'Alene and Spokane) by one of the best highways in Idaho. It has a good ski resort, Schweitzer Basin. If Bonners Ferry looks like small towns did before the days of mass market franchises, Sandpoint is an eighties town, complete with outsized shopping mall.

A timber base made Sandpoint a traditional Democratic bastion with a strong party organization. But an early warning signal came in 1960 when veteran state Sen. Glenn Bandelin, a Democratic leader, was beaten for re-election by Republican Samuelson. On balance Bonner stayed Democratic but by the mid- eighties, with the boom in the local economy, rising salaries, and influx of new business people, Democrats considered it a touch and go place.

Jim Goller – *They still say they're Democratic, but they'll go with issues more. They got very upset with [Gov.] John Evans because they thought he should have helped get the wilderness question settled. I think organized labor has less influence up there. There's also a large Southern constituency up there, from the Civil War days.*

The premier Democrat here in the seventies and eighties was Jim Stoicheff, who once lost a state senate race to Samuelson but won legislative contests consistently after that. Stoicheff is a school teacher utterly without pomposity, a lunch-bucket Democrat as financially conservative as any Republican. His newspaper columns are humor pieces lampooning both himself and the Statehouse. He doesn't look like a politician, with his out-of-fashion clothes and a car that seems unlikely to make the 450 miles south to Boise.[18]

Southeast of Sandpoint is the old rail, timber and mining town of Clark Fork, home of a family of Democratic congressmen. This is where Compton White, Sr., made a small fortune after a storm blew over a tree on a patch of ground he owned, uncovering a rich vein of silver underneath. He was also fortunate to be the Democratic nominee in the first congressional district in 1932, the Roosevelt sweep year, and he would serve in the U.S. House 16 years. Later, his son, Compton White, Jr., would serve there four years in the sixties.

---

[18] Stoicheff was still in the House in 1999 when he died. A much-loved statehouse personality, he served as House Democratic leader for much of his House tenure.

But after defeats that took them out of office, both returned to Clark Fork. The younger White, active in local civic affairs for many years and a member of the Clark Fork City Council – since leaving Washington – for almost 20 years, oversees the family business and works out of a small office building that his father built decades ago. Southwest along the old Great Northern rails and Pend Oreille River lie old logging camps and new construction. Oldtown (abutting Newport, Wash., on an invisible border) and Priest River grew fast in the eighties, each prosperous enough to support a weekly newspaper. Some of the hilly, lake-studded land south of Oldtown has resort potential – Spirit Lake has a small lake downhill from an old-West town – but little has been developed. Logging usually means Democratic votes, here as elsewhere.

As the Pendulum Swings

At Rathdrum, as woods thin, farming and ranching become more important. South and east, tourism and land development dominate. Kootenai County has swung wildly as for years it absorbed and expelled influences, changing political shape like an amoeba.

The boomlet in Bonner was a blip compared to the clamor of Kootenai . In 1960 Kootenai's population was under 30,000; in the eighties it approached 70,000. As elsewhere when growth (or decline) is sudden, people get fearful and extreme.

For decades into the sixties, Kootenai and its key city, Coeur d'Alene, were chiefly a place for timber cutting, processing, and hauling. Early in the century, Coeur d'Alene went through a radical-left phase, and in 1911 swept a socialist ticket into city hall. (The socialist mayor elected in 1911 was John T. Wood, who later underwent a complete reversal and was elected a congressman in the fifties as perhaps the most right-wing major office-holder in Idaho's history.)

But after that, into the sixties, Kootenai was Democratic. Its politics were those of pragmatism, allied to Lewiston party machinery and - after World War II - led by the local businessmen who met at the Athletic Roundtable.

Harry Magnuson – *About 1940 Farragut Naval Station started. That brought a big influx into Coeur d'Alene, and 70,000 sailors up there on Lake Pend Oreille. That started a change in Coeur d'Alene.*

In those efforts there were some leaders in the community. They sort of came together, the new generation of people, and got a club in the basement of the Desert Hotel in Coeur d'Alene. It was called the Athletic Roundtable. They made a social club out of it. Their efforts were to help some local causes and University of Idaho athletics. And they had slot machines, 50 slot machines down there at the Athletic Roundtable. They made a lot of money on those slot machines. This went on during the forties and fifties. It was very successful ...

They become involved in good community things, and they had a lot of influence. They worked for specific projects, specific types of legislation, specific types of candidates.

The slot machines went out in 1954, but the momentum carried them on about 20 years more. About 1967, the Roundtable needed some money and they came to me. I was close to all of them, and I bought the Desert Hotel and rented it to them; it was just a deal so they could free up some cash. We had a fire about 1971 or '72; the damn hotel burned down to the ground. The Roundtable then moved up the street about a block from the Coeur d'Alene Resort, and they made a new location. Damn thing never worked. When it was down in the basement it was the hottest spot in the world; when it moved up people just never took to it ... Finally about four years ago they gave up the ghost. Hagadone bought the thing. They call it the Silver Moose Bar now.

The Roundtable was plugged into Silver Valley mining interests, utility and business interests in Spokane, and Idaho Democratic and Republican organizations. When St. Maries physician C.A. Robins was elected governor in 1946, the Roundtable was prepared to buy a governor's mansion in Boise until a reluctant (and embarrassed) legislature agreed the state would pay for it. The Roundtable had money; in its slot machine days it raised more than $100,000 a year. Membership peaked at more than 1,500.

For years the Roundtable provided the leadershp and money and timber unions the votes. But timber became less dominant in the seventies as tourism blossomed in Coeur d'Alene, on the northern shore of the like-named lake. Boaters and water skiers migrated there; the city's location 30 miles from Spokane didn't hurt. Businesses blossomed north of town, near the interstate.

Then conservative retirees flooded in. In the forties they were few, some wealthy like Bing Crosby, who had a house at ritzy Hayden Lake. In the sixties and seventies came the masses.

Most notorious and uncharacteristic were the white supremacists who set up camp in secluded woods near Hayden Lake. Richard Butler, a Southern California expatriate, founded the Aryan Nations and built a fortress complete with school, guard post, and living quarters. Arms were abundant. Dobermans slept in the parking lot. When Butler went to Hayden to pick up mail he sometimes stopped for coffee across from the post office, and regulars there were stunned to see the piles of checks he got.

In the mid-eighties, jarred by prosecution and dissension, the Aryans went into decline, which pleased the locals. The Aryans' main effect was to make their neighbors more self-consciously tolerant. Beyond that they had little effect on politics; those who ran for office were buried by the voters.

Genuine change was signaled by Kootenai's 1968 support for Republican Rep. Jim McClure; it had voted Democratic before. In 1972 Kootenai Democrats were hit with surprise losses. Then in the late seventies Kootenai became a home to a property tax revolt. The county turned Republican and elected some of the most conservative legislators Idaho has ever had.

In the mid-eighties reaction set in. Voters moved to the middle; with the Aryans bringing so much attention to the area, they had little use for extremism. They elected some Democrats again, and moderate Republicans. Liberal Sen. Mary Lou Reed helped pull together a strong Democratic organization and in the mid-eighties the parties once more were closely competitive.

No one idea, organization, or industry dominates Coeur d'Alene. But one man overwhelms the public landscape.

Duane Hagadone, who inherited the *Coeur d'Alene Press* and a few other holdings, is essentially a self-made man, and remade Coeur d'Alene in the process. He collected properties – especially a big apartment complex and the massive Coeur d'Alene Resort – until a good chunk of the town was his. Some thought Coeur d'Alene seemed like a company town. A person might work at Hagadone's Resort, read Hagadone's daily newspaper, listen to Hagadone's radio station, live in Hagadone's apartment complex and shop in stores Hagadone's construction company built.

For all that, and while Hagadone backed candidates for office who helped him out, he seldom intervened directly in Democratic or Republican politics. But he is a power locally. Dignified and silver-maned, projecting the visible spark of an entrepreneur, he personally – rather than some hired gun – attends meetings and lobbies officials to push his projects. In 1988 those included a golf course on the lake and a dog track west of town. The golf course became an issue on the state land board, and Gov. Andrus went head to head with him. But when the smoke cleared, Hagadone got his golf course. He is the big fact of public life in Coeur d'Alene.[19]

Mary Lou Reed – *The whole concept of planning is that a community or county is capable supposedly of choosing its own future and to say that this is what we want to be, this is our image, this is our place ... So who is in control is central to the Hagadone question. It's not whether what he is going to do is going to benefit the community. It's, what does the community want?*

The development of the golf course has been primarily real fear on the part of the citizens that access to their swimming area is going to be cut off. To some extent it died down because he was willing to assure people that he would let people swim out there if they look out for flying golf balls ...

There's one city council candidate who's running on that issue [in 1987, against the development]. It will be interesting to see how well he does.

He lost.

---

[19] At this writing, he is mainly retired and living in southern California, but retains his business interests and clout in the Idaho Panhandle.

The Silver Valley

In Idaho, I-90 runs from the sleazy border village of State Line on the Washington border 70 miles to Lookout Pass on the Montana line. It is a center of gravity in the Panhandle: more people live within 10 miles of it than in the rest of the five northern counties. To the west is timber and tourism, to the east is mining at Kellogg, Wallace, Osburn and Smelterville.

The Silver Valley seems of a piece; in fact, it's a patchwork. There are a few tiny anti-union Republican enclaves. Kellogg and Wallace, the big towns, are twins to outsiders but brisk Valley rivals. Wallace is county seat and administrative center; most of the mines are here, and this is home to management. Kellogg was where the miners lived. It was a company town, the company being Bunker Hill mine and smelter, a powerful force within the mining industry and influential in Boise as well. For years it was the first- or second-largest single employment site in Idaho.

The old Silver Valley was for decades synonymous with metals extraction and production and intense labor-management conflict. These were rough and tumble towns where gambling was in the back room of the bar and the "houses" around the corner and up a flight of stairs. "Wallace," Robert Smylie said, "is the only place I ever had a minister tell me that you had to have houses of ill repute in order to protect the ladies of the town ... It was part of the old mining syndrome, I think. It had something to do with the fact that Shoshone County was an independent judicial district with its own judge. And if you try to do anything up there law enforcement-wise from the state level, what happened was that you'd get enjoined by the local district judge. Then you'd have to go to the Supreme Court and get it undone." The Valley was so far away, state officials figured, why bother?

Politics here – more than anywhere in Idaho - was like big-city rust belt politics, where union strength was the key and where Democrats almost always won. Labor's turn-of-the-century history was radical and stayed so for years. "When [conservative Republican] Henry Dworshak first ran for the Senate, he carried Shoshone County," Perry Swisher recalled. "Shoshone was available. It required striking a deal with the mine owners and the old mine and smelters coalition. The mine metals and smelters' workers union had some of the most sophisticated political leadership in the state ... It was absolutely cold-blooded."

The reliably Democratic days of the sixties, seventies, and eighties may be changing. The 1981 shutdown of Bunker Hill, one of the great mines of the world, wiped out more than 2,000 jobs, and other mines also have closed or scaled back. After an interlude of flailing, businessmen in Wallace and Kellogg by the mid-eighties moved solidly toward turning mining towns into tourist mining towns like Park City,

Utah, or Silverton, Colorado. They got a boost in 1987 when Congress – via swift moves by Sen. Jim McClure – approved money for a gondola ski project in Kellogg. As the economy changes, so will politics.

The other fact of Shoshone political life was Harry Magnuson. His is a classic Northern Idaho story of business and political skill and iron determination. He started in Wallace as an accountant – albeit, a Harvard Business School- trained accountant – and gradually picked up mining and other interests. His energy was unusual for so small a town, and his wealth multiplied. "I think I've owned everything in Wallace that's worth saving," he said – such as the newspaper, department store, motel and other businesses. He is a Republican willing to back Democrats, as he did Cecil Andrus for governor and John Evans for senator in 1986.

His influence in the Valley matched Hagadone's in Coeur d'Alene; nowhere else in Idaho in the eighties did single individuals have such local clout.[20]

It was enough to stop the federal government, the Idaho Department of Transportation, and Interstate 90 dead in their tracks. He is why, at Bank and 7th Streets in Wallace, travelers pause at I-90's only stop light between Seattle and Boston.

Harry Magnuson - *I'm solely responsible for that stoplight.*

They started to plan the freeway in the early sixties, or even before that ... They were going to put this thing through one side of town, just level it out. They didn't have much room to level too much out. You've got a couple railroad lines, you've got a freeway, you've got a town, you've got a stream and a few other things and you try to get it all together. They bought several buildings. They got rid of the old hotel and they were going to get rid of many more buildings. They had the freeway starting to come from both ends. I could see it there in the west, putting that damn big ribbon of concrete up there.

This was something that had been in the back of my mind for some time. I'd always been so damn busy in life and I just couldn't come to grips with it. But the thing got close enough and it was either then or never. My emotions ran away with me again.

I always got the best attorney. I got Scott Reed, who was an environmentalist in Coeur d'Alene. He was an enigma to the mining industry, but he was the best one. So I went down and said, "Scott, you got to help me out." We filed suit against the highway department, the federal government and everybody in the world. We came down to Boise in 1970 and Judge [Ray] McNichols listened to that stuff for about a day and a half. And he said, reluctantly, I have no other alternative. I have to suspend the project ...

It's taken them 17 years to get their goddam papers together. They've become much more conscious of the aesthetic, economic, people impact ... Finally we got together about five years ago. We had to do something, and we worked together. A freeway anywhere isn't a good solution for a small historic community but you had

---

[20] And his clout remained substantial until his death in January 2009.

*to do something. Plus the fact that I'd run out of legal options. So we got the best
deal and went home.*

Farmer, Logger, Town and Gown

South from Cataldo the country bumps and rolls past smallish
cattle ranches and great stands of timber. At St. Maries (population
2,800) the battle is won by the trees. St. Maries and the towns in its
orbit, Plummer and Tensed, are logging and mill towns rising or falling
with that industry. Vast acreages of timber land here and south in
Latah County have been privately owned for decades, snapped up by
railroads and nineteenth century timber barons before much of
Northern Idaho became national forest.

Benewah County is Democratic because of the loggers and the
Coeur d'Alene Indian Reservation to the west. This area likes
conservative Democrats like C.C. "Cy" Chase, the St. Maries car dealer
elected to the state Senate for a couple of decades.

To the south Bovill, Helmer, Deary, and Troy in Latah County
also are timber towns. Only Troy has had a range of businesses;
highly-regarded wine has been made there, and it has a prosperous
bank. While Benewah gets moderation from its single reality – it is of a
piece – Latah is made up of starkly different parts.

Latah is Democratic in the eastern logging towns and in parts of
the southern farming valley on the Potlatch River (in Kendrick though
not in Juliaetta, which has a deep Republican tradition). It is
Republican in the western rolling wheat fields. And there's a wild card:
the University of Idaho at Moscow, Idaho's biggest school. People get
along here remarkably well. A split state like Idaho could do worse
than to study Latah County.

A student wit once said that without the U of I, Moscow would be
known as the gateway to Troy. But Moscow is also a farm center and
has grown gracefully, absorbing university, farm and commerce
influences, and becoming politically competitive.

It got that way because of Jasper "Jap" Inscore, builder and owner
of the Hillcrest Motel in Moscow . A North Carolina native, he moved
to Idaho as a boy and grew up in the logging country of Benewah
County. He ran businesses there and got involved in Democratic
politics before moving to Moscow in 1957. (He never ran for public
office.) Latah then was the only Republican county in Northern Idaho.
Inscore, aided by Tom Boise, built a Democratic organization which
made Latah competitive, as it still is. He was a power statewide, a
critical early backer of Frank Church and - in 1966, breaking with Tom
Boise to do it - Cecil Andrus. At his funeral in 1971, Andrus was a
pallbearer, Church an honorary pallbearer, and former Congressman
Compton White, Jr., officiated. Unlike Boise or Lloyd Adams, Inscore
practiced politics as an avocation, not a livelihood. Like them he
spread cash and influence where it would matter, shunned publicity,

and usually spoke softly and gently. At his funeral White said he once heard Inscore threaten to punish his dog for misbehaving by unplugging its heating pad.

South of Moscow are miles of wheat fields and little Genesee, a quiet farm town now, a wild place early in the century when it was a rail stop for cattle shippers. It was important because of the sharp drop-off to the south, where the Snake and Clearwater Rivers cut deep gorges and early settlers built Lewiston . Highway improvements took the white knuckles out of driving up and down Lewiston Hill, but they did not diminish the drama of watching the town below, sprawled on the confluence of the two big rivers.

Logger Valley

Lewiston the city has grappled with splits as wide as the rivers, the widest being whether it was even one city.

It was one of the first Idaho cities. For years it, like Boise, had an age-old charter and could not annex outside ancestral limits. Outskirts called Lewiston Orchards, south of town, grew as big as Lewiston proper and city fathers thought the area should be annexed. Bill Hall, who became editorial page editor of the Lewiston Morning Tribune as emotion on the issue peaked, went door to door with pro-annex petitions. He recalled that a local Kiwanis Club and irrigation district were as close to local government as the Orchards had. (The area had no street signs until the Kiwanis put them in.) Many in the Orchards did not want to pay city taxes, and the battle went on for years.

When the Orchards were annexed in the late sixties some city council members welshed on a promise to resign to make way for new members from the Orchards. In the uproar that followed, Orchards people took over the council and offered the citizenry a vote: should the place be de-annexed or stay in the city? Not only Lewistonians but Orchardites wanted the larger city. Despite rumblings lasting into the eighties, the union was preserved.

Lewiston's early influences were loggers and miners; it became rigidly Democratic in the Depression and stayed that way. The *Tribune*, which was for decades until the late sixties the only even moderately liberal newspaper in Idaho, was a strong influence in that direction. (It has been run for about a century by the Alford family, which long meshed civic involvement with newspapering. One of its early executives, Albert H. Alford, was a Democratic House speaker in 1897.) In the quarter century up to the mid-eighties, Lewiston elected fewer than a half-dozen Republicans to any public office.

The Nez Perce Indian Reservation south of town added to Democratic margins in Nez Perce and in little Lewis County. But the biggest reason for the Democratic margins here is the huge Potlatch mill on the Clearwater River east of town. Its strong unions gave Democrats a fine base.[21]

Cecil Andrus – *Separate the mill owners from the mill workers. If you look at Potlatch, you can't exactly call the Potlatch [executives] a Democratic organization, not the corporate structure. But I could always look at them and say, "But yeah, it's my folks going through your gate out there. You can beat me up all you want, but I'm going to get 80 percent of the votes." And I always did.*
... If you saw the blue collar worker, that's what we were, those were Democrats. In the timber industry you had a lot of migration, a lot of Michiganders coming to the Orofino area; they were all Iron River, Michigan- type Democrats. It has changed, some of that. But we were the working types, rolled up our sleeves, wore the black jeans.

It was home base to Tom Boise, long Idaho's most influential Democrat. Some of the deals hatched with his Republican counterpart, Rexburg attorney Lloyd Adams, changed Lewiston forever.

Perry Swisher – *It was a lashup between Lloyd Adams and Tom Boise that made it possible to get boats on the Snake River plain in formation for the Port of Lewiston, to create the port district. It took an amendment to the [Idaho] constitution to make that possible. In the alliance that was struck, Adams quite typically looked at the food processing industry down there [in Southern Idaho] and he thought these people might want to form port districts ... We linked that Snake River plain of Adams' with the creation of the seaport at Lewiston. The two paths diverged but what got the South to vote for the port in the North was the concept of moving agricultural products.*

On the Camas Plain

In southern Lewis County and northern Idaho County, land rises and turns back into wheat fields like Latah 's. This is the Camas prairie, a great wheat producer. The central town, Grangeville (3,600 people), boomed in the fifties' timber prosperity but slowed later. It is evenly-split politically, as is Idaho County generally. Loggers, many of the farmers (that being unusual for Idaho) and the insular German Catholic town of Cottonwood – with its little college and convent, Idaho's most religion-oriented town outside the east – historically are Democratic. Those margins shriveled in the eighties as the timber industry automated.[22]

---

[21] But no longer. In the 90s it elected mostly Republicans to the Idaho Legislature – all Republicans, since 1998 – and has been competitive at the courthouse as well. The driving issue: the environment, especially on breaching the Snake River dams that make possible the Port of Lewiston.

[22] Idaho County turned solidly Republican in the 90s, electing Republican legislators since, though Democrats have had (since 2004) better luck in winning races at the courthouse.

South of Grangeville is White Bird Hill, the true line between northern and southern Idaho. The Salmon River 30 miles south, where northern Pacific Time becomes southern Mountain Time, is the formal line. White Bird is the obstacle.

For decades White Bird Hill road was full of hairpin switchbacks, making it a breathtaking challenge. It was improved in the seventies but heavy trucks and cars with weak horsepower still find it a strain. And drivers can still be surprised at the climatic differences on the hill; air and ground can be warm and dry on one side, blustery and snowy on the other.

So it is politically.

2 | Wild Lands

No one could have guessed so much would result from that lazy afternoon in 1959 when a Republican Idaho governor, a Kentucky senator, and a New York banker sat down to talk.

It was supposed to be just another fishing weekend on the Teton River. The Teton Dam, which 17 years later would collapse, flood cities, and be roundly cursed, was years from construction. The river was cool and pure and the fish were jumping.

Robert Smylie, who had been re-elected governor a year earlier, was taking it easy. He spent the weekend at Victor at a cabin owned by Harley Markham, a close friend and then Republican national committeeman. He was fishing with freshman Kentucky Sen. Thruston Morton, like Smylie a Republican moderate.

They got a call from Roland Harriman, who was at Ashton 50 miles north near the huge Railroad Ranch at Island Park, who wanted to join them. So Smylie, Morton, and Harriman whiled away Sunday afternoon sitting in the yard by Markham's cabin.

The Railroad Ranch

Ronald Harriman – banker, rancher, leader of civic organizations – was actually a less renowned brother. The Harriman family fortune was on a par with any; when Averell Harriman ran against Nelson Rockefeller for governor of New York, the press called it "the race of the millionaires." Averell, a chairman of Union Pacific Railroad, had a big impact on Idaho. In 1932, to lure more passengers on his trains in Western states, he decided to create a big, modern resort. By Christmas 1936 the lodge at Sun Valley was open for business, and a hot spot for wealthy idlers. The Democratic rail chairman would be pleased to learn that it also would become a Democratic island in a Republican sea.

Roland's contribution was different. That Sunday afternoon he spoke of his love for the Railroad Ranch near Yellowstone Park, 4,700 acres of pine trees and meadows where elk, trumpeter swans, and sandhill cranes lived happily. It was a part of him, and he didn't want an overeager relative slicing it into subdivisions. Idaho was his second home. New York already had a Harriman park; why not Idaho? Harriman proposed that after his death the state get the Ranch and other nearby property and turn it into a park.

Robert Smylie – *I was born and reared in Iowa, and there they had let everything like that get away from them. They had to go out and almost reconstruct them from scratch. Someplace along in the twenties there was some damn governor smart enough to – they didn't really establish them, they designated them as state park areas. Anybody that had a swamp or was on a river bank or had a piece of rock sticking out of the prairie, could probably get it designated as a state park.*

As recently as [Idaho Gov. Len] Jordan's term, it took six meetings of the Land Board to decide if we could accept having Lucky Peak [Dam, near Boise, as state park land] down there below Discovery Park. That was going to be too much of an undertaking ... I think the reason for it was, if you're living in the middle of a park, why do you have to build one?

Smylie liked Harriman's idea but he wanted to think about it. Three weeks later he wrote Harriman in New York, saying he wanted the Ranch but that the offer should depend on the state first creating a professional park department.

There were legal issues and such matters as reimbursing Fremont County for taxes lost when the private land went public. But the big issue was that Idaho had no parks department, and taking care of the Ranch meant making one from scratch.

In the first 70 years of statehood, vast tracts were set aside as national forests or Bureau of Land Management territory. But the state did little.

In 1961 Idaho had only three state parks: Ponderosa near McCall, Heyburn near St. Maries, and Mary Minerva McCroskey near Plummer, all managed by sundry state agencies. (Heyburn was named after Idaho Sen. Weldon Heyburn, who disliked the concept of state parks and thought them an embarrassment.) As a practical matter it had two: McCroskey was a lush strip between Plummer and Washington state but was hard to reach and never developed. Even in the eighties it wasn't listed in state park brochures, so as to keep tourists from stumbling in and hurting themselves.

For two years Smylie and the Harrimans worked in secret on the park proposal. In December 1961, a few weeks after they came to terms, Smylie announced the deal. Politicians love to overstate accomplishments, but Smylie definitely understated this one. It marked a revolution in Idahoans' attitudes about their public land.[23]

In 1959, before word of the Railroad Ranch deal got out, Smylie asked the Legislature for a parks department. The Legislature, Democratic then, wasn't cooperating. Smylie said later that the Democrats had eight or nine jobs in the state lands department – run by the then-Democratic land board – which might be shifted to parks,

---

[23] He understated it in his autobiography, *Governor Smylie Remembers*, too, devoting less space to it there than it received here (although I got most of the details from Smylie). In somewhat more compressed form, he told there about the same story as is told here. But he passed over most of its implications.

"and they thought they were all going to get the shaft if I got a new department. That was understandable."

Democratic Weiser attorney and then-state Sen. James Donart explained it to Sen. Frank Church this way:

The political story behind this is that for the past four years and for the next four years the governor has had to work with certain constitutional boards in the state that have been comprised of Democrats. Among others is the State Land Board. The State Land Board, of course, hires the state land commissioner who has under his control the state parks. The machinery is presently there to set up a career professionally staffed state park department in its literal sense. The Smylie interpretation of a "Career Professional Staffed Department" means one created and appointed by him ...

In 1961 the effort failed again. In 1963 Smylie got the Legislature to approve the contract with the Harrimans but still could not push his parks bill through. That finally happened, along with so much else, in 1965.

The impact was immediate. Within two years, six new state parks sprang into existence, and more were added by the mid-seventies. As the state's population and tourism industry exploded in the sixties, the parks fed both tourism and migration into the state.[24]

It was one of several bursts of growth in the latter Smylie years, like budgeting for the massive building programs on the Capitol Mall (in 1963), a new penitentiary (also in 1963), and creation of a water resource agency (in 1964). But this park growth was different. It was synergistic, part of a revolution in Congress at the same time.

Church and the Great Outdoors

Frank Church and the outdoors didn't seem to go together.

He looked more natural and at home in a three-piece suit, like the lawyer he had been and would be again, and the U.S. Senator he was for 24 years. Put him in a cowboy outfit pumping hands at a county fair and he seemed out of place. Church was urbane in his precise use of word and metaphor, in his measured, cordial manner. His legislative specialty was foreign affairs.

But he did not ignore Idaho's out of doors.

In his early Senate years, Church got on the development side of lands bills. In 1956 he flew over what later would be named the Frank Church-River of No Return Wilderness area, where cobalt was then mined. Church promised that if elected he would make sure a threatened shutdown would be averted. And he did.

---

[24] The expansion of the state park system was steady for some years, slowed after the 70s, but has continued. Two state parks were designated in 1999, and Smylie's precedent for cutting deals to obtain state lands has continued. The most notable recent example is Gov. Phil Batt's work in bringing the Magic Valley's Box Canyon into the state system.

Church asked not whether a dam should be built at Hells Canyon, but rather who should build it. Like most Democrats he supported a single big public power dam at the site, while most Republicans supported Idaho Power Co.'s request to build three smaller ones. Idaho Power prevailed. Church did push through the Senate a string of bills for dams elsewhere around Idaho, only to see most of them die in the House. He and fellow Sen. Henry Dworshak succeeded, however, in getting several dams built, including Bruces Eddy (later called Dworshak Dam), Fremont Dam (later called Teton) and Spangler Dam (on Mann Creek near Weiser).

How times change.

In the mid-fifties few people suggested preserving Hells Canyon as is. By the mid-sixties Church, who had called for preserving some central Idaho wilderness rivers and land, concluded that no dams should be built north of Hells Canyon on the Snake River. But vast hydropower potential still lay in the hundred miles of river north of Hells Canyon Dam, to where the Snake left Idaho at Lewiston. Builders considered another dam – or more than one – at three sites: Nez Perce (just below the mouth of the Salmon River, blocking both the Salmon and the Snake), High Mountain Sheep (nearby, but damming only the Snake) and Appaloose (to the south, closer to Hells Canyon Dam). Sen. Len Jordan, Dworshak's successor, who lived for years on a ranch close by the Snake near the dam sites, favored Nez Perce. In 1964 the Federal Power Commission actually approved construction at High Mountain Sheep.

Then the U.S. Department of Interior challenged its sister agency, the FPC, in court, claiming the dam would wreak too much environmental damage. The case went to the U.S. Supreme Court, and in a landmark 1967 ruling written by Justice William O. Douglas (an ardent conservationist), it said the FPC "must hold more hearings on the subject of whether any dams should be built at all, not just which one." That completely changed the rules of the game.

In 1968 Church and Jordan agreed on a 10-year dam-building moratorium, and it became law. They beat back efforts the next year by Oregon Sen. Robert Packwood to end the moratorium. And in 1972 they hatched the plan to preserve 101 miles of the Hells Canyon-to-Lewiston Snake River stretch. Idaho Governor Andrus, Oregon Gov. Tom McCall, and Washington Gov. Daniel Evans, jointly declared opposition to building any new dams on the lower Snake. A bill was introduced in 1973, backed by the odd quartet of Idaho Sens. Church and James McClure and Oregon Sens. Packwood and Mark Hatfield, all of whom had quarreled over Hells Canyon for years. It later passed Congress and was signed by President Ford in 1975.

Wilderness

Idaho has long been heavily federal. Most of the national forests, open to timber cutting, were established early in the state's history. Bureau of Land Management territory, also open to some private uses, had also been stable a long time. The 3.3 million acres in the federal wilderness areas – Idaho, Sawtooth, and Selway-Bitterroot – which existed in Idaho early in the sixties had been set up between 1931 and 1936. Timber and mining industries grew up around a stable system of multiple use, of extracting resources from federal lands.

In November 1959, Church attended a Lewiston hearing on water development of the Salmon and lower Snake rivers, which he later said greatly influenced him. Afterward, he spoke of the Snake as the state's "working" river, where the dams should be, and of the Salmon, the "River of No Return," as a river to be protected. Church introduced bills to preserve the Salmon and, early in 1960, suggested carving a Sawtooth National Park from the Sawtooth Primitive area. That never happened, though it was talked about seriously for years. When a similar idea was proposed in the mid-eighties by Republican Congressman Larry Craig, it was hooted at by some of the same groups of people who backed Church. But by the late eighties, it had not died yet.

In September 1961, after years of burbling under the surface, a bill to set up a national wilderness system got to the Senate floor. Church was floor manager. It created the system from federal holdings "with little or no commercial value"; Idaho holdings included the Selway-Bitterroot area and Sawtooth Primitive Area. The bill passed the Senate 78-8, and went to the House, where it fell into the hands of another Idahoan.

First District Congresswoman Gracie Pfost, a Democrat, chaired the House Public Lands Subcommittee. In November she held a hearing at McCall on the wilderness bill. Armies of opponents – 106 speakers, 300 written statements – descended. Three times as many speakers opposed the bill as supported it.

The town of McCall saw its future on the line. Its days as a tourist town mainly were in its future; its north-south highway was yet too rugged. McCall, Cascade, and Donnelly were timber towns, tied to the national forests.[25] Eighty-five percent of Valley County is national forest, a bigger portion than any other Idaho county. People here often gave Republican politicians the edge, but they had voted for Church in 1956 and for Pfost in her last two races. Now that support was on the line, too. Pfost, for one, was careful to say in McCall that she was neutral on the bill and was just gathering information. A lot of Democrats spoke against it; more might have but for Church's support of it.

---

[25] If you're looking for a moment when rural communities who had been voting for conservative Democrats began to realign, you could do worse that these meetings in 1961 and 1962 – though, as Church's re-election showed, the effect was not yet fully felt.

Church said the bill was misunderstood, that it would not take timber areas out of production or halt existing grazing. Mineral prospecting could go on, including some commercial mining.

Years later, in a speech, Church would recall how it went:

"Senator, why are you in favor of converting our Western forests into wilderness playgrounds for Eastern millionaires?"

Church said Idahoans used the wilderness more than others.

"That's not the point, senator. Maybe some just-plain people do enjoy the wilderness. Still, they're not the majority. Most of us want to drive through the woods and find places to park our campers ..."

"'Well, fine,' I would reply. 'We're spending a fortune building forest highways, developing campgrounds, marinas and other recreational facilities. By the time we're done, 90 percent of our public lands will be accessible to the majority who want to take their vacation on wheels. But what about the people who don't? Are we to leave nothing for them, no escape from the pavement, the crowds, the billboards, the costly resorts? This country is big enough to leave some of its land alone as a sanctuary for those who, from time to time, feel the need to get away from it all. Otherwise we'll turn this country into a cage."

Multiple users

Many people were concerned about losing timber cuts or mining rights. Mining interests wanted a survey of proposed wilderness areas so they would know what precious or strategic metals would be barred from access. Farmers and cattlemen worried that more federal land controls might lead to control over water as well – a fearsome prospect at a time when diversion of water from the Snake River to California and Arizona was discussed seriously.

War had begun. It would outlast Church, Pfost and almost all the early contenders. It would go on more than two decades.[26]

Republicans rubbed their hands with glee. Wilderness seemed a great issue to pummel Church with in the campaign of 1962.

Church maintained from the beginning that while the critics were more vocal, most people wanted wilderness. He pointed out that for years moneyed interests defeated legislation in the Statehouse regulating dredge mining, but in 1954 the voters approved it by initiative.

Republicans lined up a year before the November 1962 election to take Church on. The primary winner was Jack Hawley, a Boise attorney who had beaten Church exactly 10 years before, when they were contenders in Ada County for the Idaho House. The night

---

[26] Needs noting here: From 1984 for a quarter-century, no new wilderness was added in Idaho. But in 2009, the Owyhee Canyonlands was designated wilderness (Senator Mike Crapo was instrumental in that) and additional wilderness in central Idaho seemed to be in the cards.

before the 1962 election Church's father-in-law, former governor and then-federal judge Chase Clark, warned that farmers were mad at him, ranchers were mad at him, timber men were mad at him, and mining interests were mad at him. "I would like to know how you expect to get elected," he said.

Church won. And in 1964, after setbacks, a revised wilderness bill was signed into law.

It was a big achievement but still left fuzzy the status of thousands of acres of land in the middle of Idaho. That continuing wilderness debate would go on, often boil over, and on one occasion help unmake one governor and make another.[27]

White Clouds

No one lived in the remote place call the White Clouds, east of Stanley Basin and north of Ketchum. White clouds really are there, around the rickety peaks that look like sharks' teeth, where Castle Peak rises 11,820 feet. Mountain goats and bighorn sheep climb the precarious peaks and graze around the 54 high glacial lakes.

To this place in the summer of 1968 came helicopters bearing research crews from the American Smelting and Refining Co. (ASARCO), looking for an alloy called molybdenum, used by the space program to toughen steel so it could withstand tremendous heat. The prospectors told ASARCO executives that millions of dollars worth of molybdenum lay around the White Clouds Mountains. ASARCO promptly filed mining claims and asked the Forest Service to let it build roads. The service said federal law didn't allow it to reject a properly-filed mining request. Early in 1969 ASARCO announced contractors for White Clouds work and predicted 350 new mining jobs, 500 in spinoff businesses.

Reaction set in that spring when the Forest Service held required hearings on the road permit. Testimony was ferocious. Industry spokesmen, convinced the development would do little harm, clashed with conservationists who predicted the whole region, including critical fish runs, would be damaged by the development.

Because this had to do with federal lands it was a federal issue, and the congressional delegation got involved. Sens. Church and Jordan and Congressman Orval Hansen suggested including the White Clouds in the proposed Sawtooth National Recreation Area, a designation which would give the Forest Service a freer hand in regulating mining. That plan passed the Senate, but by midsummer 1969 Congressman McClure, a master of deft legislative maneuvering, succeeded in bottling it up in the House Interior Committee. There matters stayed

---

[27] Not much mentioned (only implied) in *Paradox*, but Church's environmental activism was only beginning in the early 60s. He would push through more wilderness areas later, and was instrumental in the designation of the River of No Return Wilderness, later (after he left the Senate) partially renamed in his honor.

on the federal level: a standoff. ASARCO had no road permit, but neither had its opponents succeeded in barring the company from the White Clouds.

Then Gov. Don Samuelson entered the scene, saying Idaho needed to use its resources where it could. "They aren't going to tear down mountains," he was quoted as saying at one hearing. "They are only going to dig a hole." Then he took after the Forest Service for delaying the grant of a road permit to ASARCO.

He got attention. He got even more when the chairman of the state parks board, Ernest Day, resigned. "I don't see any sense of being part of a team which doesn't have enough regard for our resources to better differentiate between uses," he said.

The dispute got national attention in January 1970, when *Life* magazine ran an article, "Whose Wilderness?", powerfully recapping the White Clouds issue, from an environmentalist standpoint for a national audience. Cards and letters of complaint flooded Samuelson's office and the Forest Service. In July the service banned crawler tractors and other earth-moving equipment from the White Clouds area. Then the congressional delegation set another round of hearings, and a bill calling for a national park in the Sawtooths was introduced. The issue blew up again, three months ahead of the 1970 election for governor.

Samuelson said he wanted the decisions made on "facts and not emotion." He was widely reported as simply favoring open-pit mining in the White Clouds; he would say later that his stand was distorted, only that mining near the White Clouds, if it could be done without great harm, should be studied.

Don Samuelson – *They said that I wanted to go in and destroy the White Clouds. There's no way ... That was an empty basin where this mine is, outside of the White Clouds. It was on the outside; there was nothing but sagebrush on the outside of it. There was a shallow little frog lake that was involved in the thing, and it was just a little shallow doggone deal right there on one side of it. It didn't have any fish in it. It was so shallow it froze out every year and it didn't amount to anything.*

What the Forest Service had been planning to do was to put a road right up into that area so people could hike in. And this was what ASARCO wanted to do, to improve the road and make it wide enough so the public could get up there, and put in a parking area. What they had planned to do was use all the waste from their mines and dig a tremendous big dam down below where they were working, and when they finished mining that deposit, there would be a huge lake ...

Samuelson's office was deluged with letters and little cut-out coupons saying, "We urge you to reconsider your support of ASARCO's open pit mine, mill and tailings pond in the White Clouds. Please don't allow Eastern mining interests to exploit and ruin Idaho's prime scenic and recreation area." Samuelson's form responses did not include a specific stand on the White Clouds, expressing only support for "orderly resource development in areas suited for multiple use."

While the governor kept trying to make his position clear, his Democratic opponent, Cecil Andrus, had no such trouble. Andrus said simply that he wanted no mining in the White Clouds. And he tried something new: tying a single environmental issue to "quality of life," giving coherence to Andrus' stands.

In June 1970, Central Surveys Inc. of Shenandoah, Iowa, surveyed Idaho opinion and concluded that "the majority of voters object to mining in this [White Clouds] area, and they also have a clear understanding that Gov. Samuelson favors the mining. Most voters apparently have not yet come to grips with this inconsistency when they give support to the governor."

Don Samuelson – *I didn't worry too much about it because the only place where it was, was right there in that little Boise [group] ... I figure I've been an environmentalist all my life. I've fought the Forest Service. I'm a fly fisherman, and I've run into so many places where they would slash and leave and run the cats into the creek and dump brush in the creeks and stuff and tear the whole damn drainage up. I've fought that all my life, that sort of thing. But I've felt there had to be balance.*

But White Clouds clearly had become a statewide uproar.

Oct. 15, 1970 Mr. George Hartzog, Jr.
Director, National Park Service
Dear Mr. Hartzog:
Rumors have reached my ears that you are scheduled to speak in Idaho the latter part of October. My understanding is that the meeting is in Pocatello. I know neither the nature of the meeting nor the sponsoring organization, but I thought I should advise you that you are walking into the middle of a very delicate political situation.
As you are probably aware, there is a very hard-fought race underway for the office of governor of the state of Idaho. The Sawtooth-White Clouds proposals are very much involved in the on-going debate in the campaign. I certainly would not want to see you inject the National Park Service into the middle of a partisan wrangle. Even if you do not speak on the subject, I am sure you will be asked questions about it by the press. While I hesitate to say it, and hate to think it, I'm afraid you have been drawn into the midst of a partisan battle which it would have been better for you to have avoided. I can't suggest appendicitis, but a pain in the stomach is sometimes better than a pain in the neck.
James McClure
Member of Congress

Samuelson did start to discuss the environment. More and more of his campaign ads were geared in that direction.

Client: Re-elect Governor Samuelson

Station: KBOI, KID-TV, KIFI-TV, KMVT
Length: 60 seconds
Start date: July 21
Music - MQ774
(Gov. at Water Scene)
GOV: I want to make and keep two things clear ... air and water.
(Series of scenes depicting clean air and water)
ANNCR: Yes! Clean air and clean water in a clean state. That is a firm pledge of Gov. Don Samuelson. Most of Idaho is clean and beautiful. Major attention of Gov. Samuelson's administration is being centered on those areas afflicted with water and air pollution problems. Through the Environmental Division of the Department of Health and through the Idaho Air Pollution Control Commission, Idaho is meeting pollution problems head-on and is winning the fight.
(Water scenery)
GOV: Let's make two things clear ... air and water.
(Gov. at Water)
ANNCR: Nature endowed us with a beautiful state. It's everyone's job to keep it that way. If you believe -
(Gov. against Sky)
- as Gov. Samuelson does, that clean air and water are prime necessities for providing the good life in Idaho, then re-elect the man you can trust to get the job done. Re-elect Gov. Don Samuelson. — television ad script

But Samuelson didn't have the image of a pollution fighter, and when business expansion came easy and mining jobs were considered less precious, talk about helping the state's economy seemed less urgent. The White Clouds were not the only reason he lost, but they were a visible symbol.

Cecil Andrus — *How do you know? We won by 10,000 votes. Don Samuelson was for the miners and mining it and I was opposed to it. That issue very clearly was an overriding issue. But if that were even [if Andrus had gained no votes from it], you could say funding of education was an overriding issue. I had the IEA [Idaho Education Association] with me because of the budgetary restraints on education, Samuelson's position versus mine. That's probably worth 10,000 votes. The moderates in the Republican Party weren't for Cecil Andrus but they were saying, "Well, we'll vote for Andrus this time to get rid of Samuelson, then go kill Andrus next time" ...*

That was worth 10,000 votes. So which 10,000 votes do you want to point to as the deciding factor? Without any of the three I might have been dead.[28]

As it was, the environmental issues helped make Andrus the first Democratic governor in Idaho in 24 years.

---

[28] His point should probably have been taken more seriously by the string of Democrats seeking office in the years since on environmental platforms, with the implicit idea that: "Andrus did it." As Andrus suggests here, the reasons for his 1970 win are far more complex than some people would like to imagine.

Steamroller

In 1966 Church helped push through the Wild and Scenic Rivers Act, in 1974 the Sawtooth National Recreation Area bill, in 1975 the Hells Canyon bill, in 1977 the Gospel-Hump Amendment, in 1978 the St. Joe River wild and scenic designation amendment, and in 1980 the River of No Return Wilderness Act.

None of it happened without a fight. But it did happen, and the elected officials who backed the changes kept getting re-elected. Andrus, whose reputation as an environmentalist outstripped his actions, was re-elected by a nearly record-breaking vote in 1974. Church won re-election in 1968 and 1974, and when he lost in 1980 wilderness and related issues were not a big reason.

But that did not mean countervailing forces were not present – or powerful.[29]

---

[29] The matter of natural resource politics does deserve, on reflection, an additional set of comments before this chapter ends.

For one thing, the 1980 Senate race between Church and Steve Symms did turn, as one of its factors, on federal control of land in Idaho. That was only one issue among several playing key roles in that race, but it was high-profile in the couple of weeks leading up to election day. Given the closeness of the result, it can't be said on the basis of that election that conservation issues are an election loser in Idaho, but they were shown to be far from a rallying point.

Two other elections since then are worth some reflection.

One was a 1996 ballot issue in which environmental interests asked voters to repudiate a nuclear waste deal Gov. Phil Batt had arranged with the federal government. The voters instead strongly backed the deal. In truth, that can reasonably be seen as a pro-environment vote, since the deal Batt had cut (which at this writing appears to be working well in its goal of moving waste out of Idaho) was intended to improve the state's environment. But it was presented to the voters as being inadequate, and the voters brushed off the objection.

The other was an Idaho Supreme Court race in 2000, in which a decision awarding water rights to federal agencies for wilderness areas led to a statewide uproar and the first ouster of a Supreme Court justice in half a century. That was a choice between wilderness areas and private water rights, and the latter easily prevailed. (Granted, that issue wasn't the only one in the divisive race, but it was crucially central.)

3 | Sagebrush Rebels

Vern Ravenscroft was born in 1920 on a ranch near Buhl in the middle of what then was mostly desert land covered with sagebrush. Ravenscroft's family – conservative Democrats from West Virginia – came to this place in 1910, and stayed.

The farm economy was horrible in the early thirties, and many farmers were driven out of business. Those who survived worked long hours of heavy lifting and ripping out sagebrush, installing irrigation, and made scant money. This treeless, arid land sprang to life once the water was brought in, but it was hardly populated until then. The first buildings in Buhl went up about 1910. Twin Falls barely existed. The settlement on the north side of the Snake River came later.

What made reclamation possible, albeit not easy, was the federal Carey Act of 1894, which gave massive land transfers to private farmers and incentives for Eastern moneymen to invest. The Ravenscrofts eventually cleared and planted about 340 acres. It was tough work; Ravenscroft remembers hiring out during the Depression to pitch hay for 50 cents a day.

He got a degree in forestry from the University of Idaho, then spent nine years as a traveling forester for the Extension Service, experimenting with woods. He developed a commercial prospect, passed the hat, and in 1950 set up Penta-Post and Treating Co. in Tuttle. Ravenscroft also ran a farm and became executive director of the Idaho Carey Act Development Association.

But ever since his days on his college debate team he had thought of becoming governor. So he was ready for politics when local Gooding school issues turned his switch on.

Vern Ravenscroft – *That was home base, where my granddad [Turner Lee Ravenscroft] had a political identity. The story was that he moved into Gooding County one day and joined the Democratic Central Committee the next. That was just about right. Back in those days you could vote for all the Democrats or all the Republicans just by making an "X" at the top of the ballot, and then you vote for everybody down the line. The standing joke was that it only took him three seconds to vote.*

"Mr. Republican in the county," Ravenscroft said, "was a fellow who also ran the school district and a dozen other things, a pretty competent type of guy, a local patriarch": Emerson "Smokey" Pugmire of Hagerman. He was a county commissioner 22 years, mayor of Hagerman 17 years, a veteran on the Hagerman School Board and a leader of the Gooding County Republicans. He had lived in Hagerman since 1926, and had run a growing service station-hardware-trucking business there since 1944. Pugmire died in October 1964. "It was a local fiefdom, and well run," Ravenscroft recalled. But Ravenscroft joined a group of upstarts and won a seat on the Hagerman School Board, where he served eight years, and cracked the fiefdom. He had political ambitions, and looked ahead to the next step.

Vern Ravenscroft – *Gooding County has always been maverick. They're a conservative county but they'll elect a liberal Republican if they happen to like him, and then they'll elect a Democrat if they dislike a particular Republican.*

They had an incumbent [state representative] who had been in for two or three sessions, but he didn't represent Gooding County as much as he represented the Republican hierarchy. He came home one election and woke up to the fact that he had voted for a school formula bill that took money away from every school district in the county. And being on the school board, I suddenly had all kinds of pressure to run for the legislature. I beat the incumbent. In fact, I beat a former legislator for the nomination on the Democratic side and then beat an incumbent for the seat. That was the election of '62.[30]

He stayed 12 years. He ran, unsuccessfully, for governor in 1970 as a Democrat and in 1978 as a Republican and for lieutenant governor in 1974 as a Republican. He became state Republican chairman in the mid-seventies. But the farm days never left him.

Ravenscroft eventually set up in Boise as a consultant and lobbyist, mainly for water development and irrigator interests. He went to work on irrigation and hydropower projects, some almost immediately controversial.

One of his projects became a statewide controversy.

Seeds of Rebellion

There are about 53 million acres of Idaho. Around 200,000 of those acres – a third of a percent – are urban.[31]

Most of the rest is resource land, woods and pastures and rangelands where much of Idaho makes its living, or lands with no commercial use. About 16 million acres are in private hands. Close to two-thirds, 34 million acres, is federal; all but about a million of those acres are run by the U.S. Forest Service and the Bureau of Land Management. Policies that might seem arcane in Washington carry enormous wallop in Idaho.

Those policies stayed fairly stable for decades as ranchers, farmers, and feds found ways to accommodate each other. But in the sixties

---

[30] Back in those days, Gooding County – like several other rural ranch counties – had a conservative Democratic tradition. Democratic wins in places such as Owyhee, Custer, Valley and Washington counties were not unusual through the 1950s. Ravenscroft's eventual shift to the Republican Party was emblematic of how those areas and others – rock solid Republican for a third of a century now – made their change.
[31] This percentage may have doubled since 1988, with the growth in the Boise and other urban areas.

and seventies the feds became more active, slapping more laws and court decisions on how the land could be used.

As recreation area and wild and scenic rivers laws fell into place, battles shifted in the seventies to the lands that ranchers, timber cutters, and others had been using. BLM's role as owner, not just interim manager, of vast tracts became formal with the Federal Land Policy and Management Act (FLiPMA, in jargonese) of 1976. It outraged people who had accepted the fiction that BLM lands eventually would go to private owners. That had been unlikely for decades; now FLiPMA nailed it down.

FLiPMA had another sweeping impact. It said what could be done on public lands but did not say specifically what ought to be done. That policy setting was left up to regional federal officials who started taking heat for decisions they had never had to make before and would rather not have to make at all.

Then Jimmy Carter was elected president and appointed Cecil Andrus secretary of the interior. Their policies, Ravenscroft recalled, were "very, very restrictive, extremely regulatory and in some instances uncalled for. It was more a matter of attitude than specifics."

It hit home especially in the cattle industry. Nationally, cattlemen mostly use feed lots for stock, but Idaho has so much pasture land – mostly federal – that they use it more heavily.

Cattle are a half-billion-dollar-a-year business in Idaho, and cattlemen historically have had outsized influence in Idaho politics. "Sirloin Rows" of senators and representatives often dominated the legislature. Until the seventies Idaho cattlemen were split politically, but in the Carter years Idaho's cattle community moved into the Republican fold. These are rugged individualists who want to make their own way and be left alone.

They hated implications that some out-of-stater cared more about the land than they did. Sheepman Dick Egbert, who remained a Democrat, recalled one encounter during a flyover of the Targhee National Forest. He wound up telling a Sierra Club spokesman, "You tell me how much you love it. I was born in a log house right out here. My mother loved the mountains. She had a high regard for the mountains. And she taught me to look at those peaks, and they were just ingrained in my soul. Next to my mother's eyes probably those peaks were some of the first visions I had locked in my memory."

Richard Hendricks – *That was strictly the attitude: We've been here longer than the Forest Service, and those trees are ours, and those hills are ours and those deer are ours.*

You can see it when you go up into Leadore. I went up there one night on behalf of the congressman [George Hansen]. The Forest Service had a meeting in a log building with a pot-bellied stove. The service was there versus the rancher and farmer.

One old man looked like he'd just walked through the swinging doors of the Longbranch Saloon. I'll bet he was 75. And he stood there with his old sheepskin

*coat around him and a red bandanna around his neck, and a cowboy hat on him.
He was just about that big around and his shoulders were that big. And he had
leather gloves on. He listened for about an hour. He just sat there.*

*Finally, he said, "I'd like to say something." And everybody turned and there
was that grizzled old character. He said, "My granddaddy came on that land in
1880. The Forest Service didn't come till 1914. That's my land and what I do
with it is my business and none of the Forest Service's business. Be advised that if
any of you step on there, I'll kill you."*

*He turned around and walked through those doors and walked off. Nobody
said a word for probably four or five minutes. It was just — death. I believe he
meant it.*

It wasn't a one-way street. The more experienced Forest Service
and BLM officials made friends and sometimes bent a regulation here
or there to get cooperation. It was a delicate relationship, with the
local feds serving almost as mediators between Washington and the
farmers and ranchers on the land.

That is why FLiPMA and wilderness planning created such an
uproar: they overloaded the system. In the case of wilderness planning,
eight million acres were at stake. Head honchos, not sub-regional
offices, made those decisions. Local compromising wouldn't work.
Worse, the planning never seemed to end.

It started early in the seventies and was supposed to climax in 1973
with release of the Forest Service's Roadless Area Review and
Evaluation (RARE) study. Environmental groups took it to court,
partly on grounds that not enough public comment went into it. The
court told the Forest Service to do it over, this time with more public
participatory gusto.

And there was plenty of gusto in RARE II.

Oct. 1, 1984
Gov. John Evans:
*... I guess is the main concern I have is that all the so called politicians say
"give us your input" and we do, but it is like we are completely ignored, all they can
say is that we should compromise. WHY SHOULD WE COMPROMISE?
We choose to live in an area like this because we want to, but not so that some rich
flatlander can come visit for a week and watch the natives run around.*

*Why should we be locked up more than we already are? Multiple use is the best
use, or doesn't anyone really give a damn about what the people who live here year
around think. It is like beating your head against the wall, except that after you do
that long enough, people start getting frustrated and then violent. Everyone in this
part of the Country has had ENOUGH of big city and big Government.*
Thank you.
Charlie Burns
[Mayor of Challis]

In September 1978 the Forest Service RARE II road show came to
the high school in Soda Springs, a sedate cattle-timber town of 4,000.

The cattle were fed and the timber cut on federal lands. Several hundred thousand acres within shooting distance of Soda were wrapped up in RARE II; more than a third of Caribou County was Forest Service land. The response was predictable.

About 250 people filled most of the seats in the auditorium. Environmental group speakers were present and accounted for about half the testimony. But the electricity during the three-hour session came from the locals.

The Forest Service people stayed cool. One spokesman said they were only exploring options – "A" through "J" – from opening the land completely to turning it all into wilderness, where no mechanized equipment is allowed, where no roads can be built, where man can venture but not stay.

Another spokesman said he was only trying to "isolate the areas on which we have consensus."

The ranchers weren't buying.

One pointed out that timber cutting is allowed in many forest lands. "You're setting aside this timber. Now how are you going to get it out without any roads?"

Another said that some roads – dirt paths traversed by pickups and four- wheelers for hunting or sheep running – had been shut down. "Are you going to open them up again?"

"We'll evaluate that on a case-by-case basis," service spokesman Sonny O'Neill said. "Some were closed because of erosion."

The ranchers booed. And hissed.

O'Neill said, "I know we're a little off the subject, but we'll try to get back on it –"

Catcalls. The ranchers were talking right up their dusty alley: transgressions, perceived or real, by the Forest Service. They were angry, less interested in planning than in brass tacks.

Another rancher: "Will the people who live near the forest determine what will happen to it or is it a case of the whole population of the United State determining that?"

Cheers. A rancher shouted, "Don't walk around the answer."

"I don't know the answer," O'Neill said.

Between the lines they were saying the whole thing was out of their control, that faceless forces far away who never saw the forest would impose a decision that could kill them economically.

As one speaker said: "Most problems I have are those caused by the federal government. I'd like to see it revert back to the state and have the state take care of it the way they see fit."[32]

---

[32] Although resource policy seems to have moved toward the back burner, relatively, in Idaho politics in recent years, very little in this arena has actually changed. The disputes over public lands and the roads running through him certainly have continued, and roared to life in 1999 when President Bill Clinton announced a new roadless area initiative. Some other issues, such as wolf reintroduction and protection, have stayed as hot as ever.

The Rebels

Vern Ravenscroft – *I was outgoing president of the Southwest Idaho Development Association [in the late seventies]. That entity still had dreams of developing land from Boise to Glenns Ferry, and with the proper management of water and so forth and without the Swan Falls problem, you could do it. It doesn't make economic sense today, and I'd have to be the first to say so. Anyway, that was the thrust.*

We had supported the Birds of Prey preserve when they were talking about [designating] canyon lands from Grand View past Swan Falls down toward Homedale, near the river, or back a mile and a half or so. That was fine. Then the Carter Administration and the BLM came in with this environmental impact study and were proposing running it almost out to I-84, vastly expanded. It killed any [development] potential for the foreseeable future, of any kind. It was an economic problem to Southwest Idaho and had an economic impact from Twin Falls to Payette.

The Southwest Idaho Water Development Association felt that was a big enough problem and had enough steam behind it politically, that we weren't big enough [to handle it] ... There was membership all the way across the valley. Idaho Power was an active supporter. The membership was from roughly Bliss, Hagerman, Buhl, Gooding, as far as Weiser on the upper river. A pretty broad-based group. But when you got into something as political as the Birds of Prey designation, and with some of the industries that were there not wanting to get too obvious, and the need to solicit the cattlemen who had their own organization, and implications on grazing rights on the Birds of Prey designation, and the Farm Bureau had their own organization that was interested in the issue, it was determined to form a broader coalition, a membership made of organizations, an umbrella.

Being the outgoing president of the Southwest Idaho Development Association, it fell my lot to being elected chairman of the umbrella. And when they got around to naming themselves, and wondered what the dickens to call it, somebody suggested Sagebrush Rebellion, Inc.

Which is the first time in the history of man they ever incorporated a rebellion.

It started in Nevada, where the 1979 legislature passed a bill declaring state control over millions of acres of federal land there. The idea spread to other western states. In Alaska they called it the "Tundra Rebellion."

In the 1980 legislative session Sen. Dane Watkins, an Idaho Falls Republican, said Idaho should follow Nevada's example and claim the BLM lands. He didn't get far, but the idea caught on.

In April 1980, Sagebrush Rebellion Inc. filed suit in federal court to keep Interior Secretary Andrus from expanding the Snake River Birds of Prey Natural Area. The expansion, Ravenscroft said then, impinged on people who held and expected to farm desert land under the Desert Land Entry and Carey Act programs. It was an odd beginning for a group intent on turning land over to the state: Its first action was an argument that one federal action should be blocked because it conflicted with another.

Technically, the Rebellion was aimed only at BLM lands, which were about a third of the federal lands, and not at Forest Service or other territory. But the ownership principle obviously could be taken further, and there it ran into opposition.

It was the last big issue of the wild 1980 Senate race between Democrat Church and Republican Congressman Steve Symms. Church, sponsor of key wilderness legislation for two decades, despised the Rebellion, considered it a blind for forces of rape and ruin that wanted forest lands put on the auction block. Barely a week before the election, Church unleashed blasts at Symms over the Rebellion. Church's campaign manager, Carl Burke, recalled, "Most Idahoans were in favor of wilderness protection and preserving the forests, and they were for open use. Which ran counter to the prevailing notion, which was that most Idahoans at that time were for increased development."

One of Church's campaign brochures said, "I mean to keep these lands open to all the people. If the special interests are ever permitted to take charge, then we'll all discover what a 'lockup' really means, as the public lands – your lands and mine – disappear behind barbed wire fences and 'No Trespassing' signs."

Then Utah Sen. Orrin Hatch, on a campaign swing for Symms through Southern Idaho, was quoted as saying a Sagebrush bill then in Congress would give states control over millions of acres of national forest land. Symms said he interpreted the bill differently, and loud debate continued. Prospects of state ownership or sale of BLM lands did not shock Idaho. The prospect of forest sales did. Here was the balancing act: Idahoans don't want federal controls but neither do they want their land subdivided and turned into miracle miles. What's more, they don't want outsiders controlling that land and keeping them off of it.

Somewhere on election night, as troops of Rebels (including Symms) were elected, the Rebellion lost its momentum.

Two weeks after the election Nevada Sen. Paul Laxalt, who may have been the top national Sagebrush Rebel, described the Rebellion as actually just "a symbolic thing." Backers like Idaho Sen. McClure said the Rebels should follow the old advice on Vietnam: withdraw and declare victory.

And they did.

Idaho was one of the few western states whose legislature never did pass a Sagebrush Rebellion law. One reason probably was that although many land users agreed they didn't much like federal policy, they couldn't agree on what policy would be better, or that the state's land department would do a better job. Some saw too that state management be an expensive proposition.

In the summer of 1981 McClure, the new chairman of the Senate Energy and Natural Resources Committee, said "you've got to have very strong feelings in order to make that massive a change of policy ... I don't think there's that intensity of feeling now because people are confident this administration is going to do right."

Victory?

Even so, federal policy on Idaho lands stood almost still in the Reagan years. One reason was James Watt, appointed by Reagan to succeed Andrus as interior secretary, more effective at creating firestorms over quirky statements than at changing anything. Another was the U.S. House; its environmental committees were on guard. And, unlike the early seventies, when Idaho grew like a dustball, expansion was running out of gas. Farmers did not want to irrigate more land and cattlemen did not want to graze more cattle. With a slowdown in changes in federal rules, farmers, ranchers, and local feds rebuilt their balancing act.

Frank Lundberg – *What struck me years ago was how much the environmental groups and livestock groups have in common, if they'd quit calling each other names.*

An example of that is the Idaho Rangeland Committee, a voluntary group where everybody walks out on a parcel of land, everybody who has an interest in it, whether it's Fish and Game or the Idaho Conservation League or whoever, and talks about it and discovers they can reach an agreement.

The Challis Stewardship programs are another, the same type of cooperative decision-making. That's under Section 12 of the Public Range Improvement Act of 1978. Senator Church put in that it provided for experimental programs in various parts of the country where the land would be, in essence, managed by a committee ... I knew it was going to work when after one meeting one of the cattlemen invited everybody back to the ranch for a volleyball game. You had the BLM and the cowboys playing volleyball together. You knew then it was working.

And there are signs Idahoan's views on the feds may change.

Jack Peterson – *We've always had a great stabilizing effect by the number of federal employees in Idaho, in public lands, national forests, fish and wildlife, USDA activities. They have had a large work force and a major capital investment in Idaho to maintain their facilities. With the dawning of the Gramm-Rudman era, that employment force has been significantly reduced, the amount of federal dollars invested in the management and rehabilitation of Idaho's public lands is declining dramatically ...*

For example. In the Sawtooth National Recreation Area – the first NRA in the nation I believe, 1973 was when that law was passed – we had a giant management team. We had people in the Stanley Basin, in the Sawtooth Valley, in Ketchum where they built a big beautiful headquarters north of town. Last year they could not get funds for one permanent ranger up in the Stanley Basin. They closed that beautiful ranger station. All the SNRA's summer activities are

managed by volunteers, with the exception of the supervisor and his immediate staff.
That's Gramm-Rudman.

It would seem to me that two things would happen.

One, that cattlemen's groups, sheepmen's groups, logger, mining groups, should
suddenly become advocates of an increased level of participation by the federal
government in the management of its own lands. If you get a declining quality of
management and the availability of personnel, where can you get answers about a
grazing fee, a natural resource calamity, a landslide or whatever? Your costs of
operation go up because you have to find these people, have to ferret them out in Salt
Lake City or Boise rather than down the road ...

And two, it would seem to me that the historical adversarial relationship
between western natural resource users - cattlemen, loggers, sheepmen, miners - and
the Forest Service and BLM should come to an end.

Slowly, too, the whole economy of the area is changing, and
attitudes toward the feds inevitably will change as it does.[33]
In March 1986 economist Jack Peterson gave farmers, cattlemen,
and other attendees of an Idaho agriculture conference one vision of
their future. After making several assumptions about power rates and
national tax policy, he said:

... in the 21st century, everything you have traditionally known and were sure
would never change with regard to western water, has changed. In that new
environment, only the most technologically sophisticated and economically efficient
producers will survive. Among those the only survivors will be those who also have
sophisticated management and marketing skills. In other words, what we have
before us in 2010 is a brave new world that will be quite unlike that which we
have known in the past.

Irrigation in the Snake River Basin will have significantly changed ... The
federal government will have asserted their "Federal Reserved Water Rights" and
will be charging for reserved federal water, which they began in 1986 when they set
a precedent in charging the city of Orofino $60,000 a year for diverting water from
the Dworshak Reservoir for domestic purposes. As noted earlier, farmers will pay
from $10 to $20 per acre foot ...

In the 21st century when you look across the Snake River Plain for the vast
acres of feed grains and alfalfa produced for feeding livestock, you won't find them.
What you will find is large drip- and gravity-irrigated acreages of truck farming,
grass and vegetable seed producers, sugar beets, potatoes and vineyards. The shift to
less and less red meat and dairy products in the American diet will not only have
continued but have resulted in beef and dairy production in the United States
reaching all time lows per capita. Vegetable and cereal grain consumption and
production will have dramatically increased as will lamb and fish consumption.
Livestock feedlots will be converted to broccoli forests and asparagus farms.

---

[33] Haven't much, as it turns out. Even as Idaho has become increasing urban and
suburban, anti-Washington feeling has remained strong. In part, however, that
continues to be generated from rural areas where federal policies on land access,
timber cuts, environmental (Superfund) cleanups and other issues persist.

Peterson recalled the reaction by cattlemen and others: "They were stunned. No one argued. Several came up and said, 'You know more about our industry than we do, because those are the trends we're seeing and we don't even want to talk about it'."

Leader of the Delegation

Jim McClure
(photo/Randy Stapilus)

And then there was the nature of McClure, after 1980 Idaho's top lands man in Congress.

He was an active senator but no crusade leader; soft-spoken, more easily described as intelligent and precise than colorful. Yet by 1980 his Senate seat was unassailable. He got to there not by building an emotional bond with Idahoans but by coming across as a small-town guy, and by making the right moves. He was not consumed by ambition but he faithfully returned its calls.

McClure came from Payette, one of a clutch of small farm towns on the Idaho-Oregon border isolated from everything but each other. Conservatism was ingrown, and conservatives had few political problems. When in 1950 he came home from the University of Idaho at Moscow with a law degree in hand, and ran for county prosecutor, he barely had to campaign. "That was simply a matter of the youngest, newest lawyer in town becoming prosecutor because no one else wanted it," he said later.

He served six years as prosecutor; later, most local governments were his clients at some point. He got involved in the local Chamber of Commerce, the American Legion, the Highway 95 Association (which has, on and off, been important in Payette), and other groups. Then in 1960 opportunity beckoned again.

The three-term state senator was Vernon Daniel, a former law partner of former U.S. Sen. Herman Welker. Local Republicans thought he was vulnerable and recruited McClure to take Daniel on in the primary. It was a sweaty little fight. With hard work and organization McClure beat Daniel by 137 votes out of 1,309 cast.

McClure loved the state Senate. Years later, when he had moved on to Washington, he would say that in some ways the legislature was more fun because things moved, things happened. McClure was one of the movers. Future governor Don Samuelson, whose state Senate years coincided with McClure's, recalled relying on McClure for help. In the 1965 session, one of the best in the state's history, McClure was assistant majority leader.

Payette voted against Welker, a close friend of Wisconsin Sen. Joe McCarthy, in 1956, but liked his conservatism. McClure followed the Payette pattern. With other conservatives like friend and Washington County Republican Sen. Harold Ryan (whom McClure later would get appointed to a federal judgeship) he pushed for a loyalty oath for state employees (later ruled unconstitutional) and the "Liberty Amendment" to do away with income taxes.

Don Loveland recalled from his days in the Senate with McClure that "he had the best feel for legislation, how it would work in actuality, of anyone ... Part of that came about, I think, because he had been the county attorney. He had been close to local government. He didn't stampede."

McClure also had luck and one of the best operatives in Idaho, Boise businessman Jim Goller, who managed his 1966 campaign and worked on his staff afterward. McClure knew the rules and sometimes, despite his country-lawyer demeanor, he slipped little time bombs into otherwise innocuous bills. He was a legislative subversive; some said "sleight of hand" was a McClure trait.

In the U.S. Senate McClure combined a conservative's distaste for federal regulation with a desire to develop energy. In the mid-seventies, when the energy crisis hit, McClure was one of the few senators who already had made a specialty of energy. While Frank Church blasted multinational corporations (such as major oil companies), McClure was more sympathetic. He was an ally of Southern oilpatch Democrats but stayed independent enough to avoid being typecast: he drove an electric battery-powered car to work.

He seemed more comfortable in the loyal opposition than in the majority, or as chairman of Energy and Natural Resources. He was only the third Idahoan to chair a full Senate committee.

"I had to develop the consensus around bills that would produce enough votes to get them passed," McClure said in 1986, when Democrats recaptured the Senate. "That meant I had to work with a larger number of points of view ... It's a little harder to move into the majority than it is to be a critic. Even a constructive critic doesn't have to produce the final result."

McClure had some successes: raising the amount of oil in the Strategic Petroleum Reserve and increasing operations at the Idaho National Engineering Laboratory. He pointed with pride to overdue reclamation reform and dam safety legislation.

A spate of wilderness bills did move in 1984, but not the long-delayed Idaho bill. Years of effort on that one got him nowhere. McClure never could reach an agreement with the Democratic committee in the House.

And yet in 1987, with Democrats controlling both chambers and a Democratic former interior secretary as governor back in Idaho, McClure hoped for an agreement. And he got it.

Out of the Wilderness

Andrus said in his 1986 campaign that he wanted to negotiate with McClure on a wilderness bill. They did. The Idaho wilderness bill they released in December 1987 could have come as a shock to the people who knew only those men's reputations. It could not have surprised anyone who knew their backgrounds.

In the state Senate, Andrus and McClure were among those who took bill books home at night to pick at the flaws other senators might miss. McClure kept at it in Congress, chipping away at technical detail while others contented themselves with broader strokes. In the governor's office Andrus pored over budgets, burrowing into details other governors might get from staff reports.

So it was with wilderness. McClure was supposed to be tight with the timber companies and development interests, and Andrus with the environmentalists. But they talked about it after Andrus became governor again in 1987. For months they did research, amassing volumes of data. What they released in December, at a joint press conference in Andrus' office, was a jumble of details, not a philosophical statement.

Because a jumble of details, however thoughtfully developed, had no built-in constituency, it got criticism from everywhere. In 1988 it was in jeopardy.[34]

---

[34] And it promptly – swiftly – died. The failure of this serious proposal by the state's two top politicians has discouraged any similar comprehensive efforts since, and only occasionally have members of the Idaho delegation – Rep. Larry La Rocco briefly in the 90s, and Rep. Mike Simpson a few years after that – have made even piecemeal efforts. Not until the late 00s did serious wilderness legislation again start to make real progress.

Tour | The Southwest Valleys

South of White Bird Hill are many mountains and few people. For one hundred miles south civilization comes in drips and drabs, clinging where people can make a living doing a little of this and a little of that. Many of them are small businessmen, not corporate employees, an independent lot who sneer at government and often like what they hear from Republican politicians.

Riggins (population 500) is, as its name suggests, shored up by river-runners and outfitters who take flatlanders on wild trips down the Salmon River. Riggins was a sawmill town until the Salmon River Lumber mill burned in April 1982. After that its economy turned on small tourism businesses and retirees who settled on the riverside, and Riggins turned more Republican.

Farming, logging, and tourists are mainstays around McCall, New Meadows, and Tamarack. South of McCall past Donnelly and Cascade runs the Long Valley, 40 miles of cattle ranching. Like most cattle ranchers people here tend to vote Republican. Adams and Valley counties' do too, but aren't rigid about it. County seats at Cascade (Valley) and Council (Adams), and a few other spots, are more Democratic than the rest of their counties.[35]

Farm Country

South of New Meadows – a little crossroads town catering to truck traffic – come more mountains and small timber towns, then rolling farm lands at Cambridge and Midvale. That landscape prevails to the south, the land getting richer closer to the Snake River. All of this is Republican but for islands of competitive cities and towns.

Washington County is the least Republican, meaning that Democrats sneak into office now and then. The reason is Weiser, the county seat, a lively town of 4,600 known for its National Old Time Fiddler's Contest and Festival each June. It has unusual variety of businesses, including one that codifies ordinances for local governments. Washington County politics are an exaggerated Valley

---

[35] Even in 1988, Valley County merited more mention, though not for its politics. Valley is one of Idaho's beauty spots, which is what prompted the big Tamarack ski area development in the 00s (after being sought after for two decades). Valley has grown rapidly, but Tamarack' crash in 2008 raise fresh doubts about its future. Recently in the mid-00s, politics at Valley – long ago conservative Democratic, then for decades reliably Republican – has been shifting again, with Democrats pulling better numbers here than in decades. They're still some distance, though, from outright winning over the county.

and Adams politics, with Democrats often surging a dozen percentage points better in Weiser than in rural precincts like Midvale and Cambridge.

South are the quiet farm towns Payette (5,500 people) and Fruitland (half as big), as conservative and Republican as any places in Idaho. Payette has a well-knit Republican organization that produced Sen. Herman Welker in the fifties and then Sen. James McClure, who by the mid-eighties had been in Congress more than 20 years. Party labels are important here. The mayor of Payette for many years, and still in 1988, was Democrat Dick Butcher. He was prominent in city association circles statewide and easily won on nonpartisan ballots. But his prospects in a 1988 run for the state Senate, as a Democrat, were unclear.

Payette was founded as a rail town, but what really mattered was the 100,000 acres of irrigated farmland started before the turn of the century. Like most irrigation farmers, the people here are deeply conservative. Former Gov. Smylie recalled that in the sixties Payette's high school was housed in churches for seven years because voters wouldn't pass a bond issue for a new school. "Now, that's pretty far out," Smylie said.

To the southeast, across a flat valley, is Emmett, seat of Gem County, a farm center that is also home to milling operations when the economy is up. Most people here are Republicans, but Gem has a quirky Democratic past. It was a hard-core holdout for leftist Sen. Glen Taylor and sometimes threatens to break the Republican farm pattern. By the late eighties it hadn't, but that could change if Democrats find the right candidate.[36]

Canyon

Nearby Canyon County is the richest and most densely settled Idaho farm country. It was one of the first irrigated places in Idaho; the biggest lake in Southwest Idaho - Lake Lowell, site of a national wildlife refuge - was built for reclamation. The people of Canyon, the second most populous county in Idaho (about 90,000), are spread out. The two large cities, Nampa (27,400 people) and Caldwell (18,000) have less than half of Canyon's population. The farmers are Republican, as is the county.

That's the image, but it isn't the whole story. Phil Batt, who won elections here from 1964 to 1986, describes two political Canyons: Nampa and the rest. Like all of Canyon, Nampa is founded on farming. And it has a religious conservative base in the Nazarene church community, bolstered by Northwest Nazarene College.

But Nampa is Canyon's Weiser or Cascade; plenty of Democrats live here. The city has big manufacturing plants, like U and I Sugar,

---

[36] Apart from a brief flirtation with Democrats around 1990, Gem has remained solidly Republican.

Carnation, and Pacific Press Publishing. It has been a major railroad town and remains an important stop. Its union population is smaller than Lewiston's or Pocatello's, but enough to diminish Republican wins. It was why Batt got a surprisingly low 54 percent from Canyon when he ran for governor in 1982 (while pushing Right to Work). Nampa also has Idaho State School and Hospital, an institution for the severely developmentally disabled. Many Nampa city politicians have been political moderates.[37]

Caldwell is more conservative and Republican, but that could change. It is a place of extremes, where rich and poor converge, and of unpredictability: this is where a jury exonerated the Top Theater, the only Idaho theater then showing triple-X rated movies, of obscenity. Conservative religious influences are less obvious here. (Nampa has Northwest Nazarene College; Caldwell the Presbyterians' College of Idaho.) Like Nampa, Caldwell has a manufacturing base at the huge Simplot food processing plant west of town. Caldwell also is as close as Idaho has to a Hispanic center, and groups like the Idaho Migrant Council have unified many migrant workers. They and labor could make a Democratic machine in Canyon, but that hasn't happened. Canyon has been a hard county for either party to organize well, perhaps because the people are spread so evenly across the landscape.

Canyon Republicans have taken hits for electing their share of weak officeholders, the bane of any one-party area. But it has fielded strong statewide vote getters. Steve Symms, a congressman and senator, is a Canyon product. And Batt served with distinction in state government since the early sixties. Both were farmers from large, well-known families in western Canyon, where conservatism reigns strongest.

Batt got involved in politics in the early sixties through a Wilder club, "people who were just meeting socially anyhow, bridge clubs and so on. It was quite active; we had speakers in. I remember when we had John Birch-type speakers in, some anti-communist types, various kinds. I'm not sure we had any liberals." The club got John Batt to run for the House and, when he found it not to his liking, got brother Phil to replace him. That's normal Canyon politics. Symms, who never had a high profile in politics until he ran for Congress, was active in Republican booster groups in the sixties.

South across the Snake is Owyhee County and the small farm town of Marsing. So devoted is it to farming that Marsing has had a Spanish-language movie theater for migrant workers. (An old booster

---

[37] Nampa has grown ferociously in the years since this was written. It is now in many ways a high-tech center, with some food processing on the side. It is – as of the mid 00s – the second largest city in Idaho, with population growing so far it could reach 100,000 in the next decade, depending on economic growth (which there as elsewhere slowed drastically in 2008). Some Democratic strategists now see Nampa as a prospective growth area for them, because of the urban population in the center of town as well as the large Hispanic population. The elections of 2010 and 2012 may indicate whether that comes to fruition. For the moment, however, Nampa has elected mostly conservative politicians to local as well as legislative offices.

brochure said Marsing is "Where Crops are Tops.") But politics here is the politics of Anglo ranchers who vote Republican. Nearby Homedale, three times as large (2,200 people) is about the same: quiet, calm, contered on farming.

Owyhee is the county least touched by time. It last changed early in the century when the mines at Silver City and Delamar played out and shut down. In 1934 the county seat moved from Silver City, in the mining south, to Murphy, a wide spot in the road — it has one parking meter, in front of the courthouse — in the ranching north, settling the issue of rancher or miner control. Murphy's virtue was its location between the populous ends of the county, the Homedale-Marsing west and Bruneau-Grand View east. (The east is marginally more Republican.) Owyhee elected many Democrats early in the century and in the Depression, and conservative Democrats were strong for decades. Their numbers diminished as many became Republicans in the seventies. In the eighties, the one successful Democrat was Sheriff Tim Nettleton, whose family led the local Democrats. Owyhee was reliably Republican in the seventies and eighties.

South of the Snake River ranches lie vast mountains and desert so remote that only a few people desiring serious solitude — some deadly serious about it, as Claude Dallas showed when he shot two Fish and Game wardens here — live there.

The prototype Owyhee politician is Walter Yarbrough, a Grand View rancher and conservative Republican elected to the state Senate 11 times until his defeat in 1986 (when next-door Elmore County, then in his district, went against him). He started in tough times. The weather and years putting up fences and working land are etched into him. At times he almost looks and sounds as if he were running for office in 1884. That's appealing out here.

The Black Hole of Idaho

In its rural south and west, Ada County is all conservative, a few steps rightward of Canyon and Owyhee.

In the go-go seventies this fast-buck land — once a rich farm area - was subdivided and sold to urbanites who wanted both economic opportunity and a less stressful life where they could do as they pleased. A huge development south of Boise called the Southwest Community sprang up in the late seventies. Homeowners discovered they lacked some services they wanted, such as sewers. Cost-conscious Boise city officials had no intention of annexing and paying for them. In the mid-eighties Ada's population topped 200,000; at least 70,000 — more people than in any Idaho city but Boise — lived outside city limits. One day most will join Boise and create tax and budget chaos.

Boise has had annexation binges before. Until the early sixties, outskirts boomed while annexation was banned in Boise by an archaic city charter. When in 1962 Pocatello merged with Alameda and became Idaho's largest city, a humiliated Boise got its charter revoked and scarfed everything in sight. Gorged and feeling financial indigestion, it nibbled more selectively later.

There is some arrogance in Boise's sense of being the center of the state, ignorance of the fact that Boise is little like the rest of Idaho, insensitivity to the rawness felt when regional outposts are consolidated. (Elsewhere, Boise seems like the Black Hole of Idaho, absorbing light, heat, money, and people.) Surges of anti-Boiseitis periodically sweep Idaho, creating improbable alliances between the North and East like those that put four-year universities in those regions before Boise got one. In March 1977 a Republican complained to state GOP Chairman Vern Ravenscroft that the party's Boise office staff should be scaled back. "In spite of what some people in Boise think, the state of Idaho does not really rotate around that city, nor does civilization stop at the Ada County line," he wrote.

Ada, especially toward the west and south, is heavily Republican. For decades it elected all-GOP legislative delegations and courthouses. But it is changing, in increments.

That's reflected to some extent in its news media. The *Idaho Statesman*, the state's largest daily newspaper (with more than twice the circulation of any other), was for decades one of the arch-conservative papers of the West. Then in the sixties it was bought by the out of state Federated Newspapers group, which in turn was gobbled by the huge Gannett Co.; it has editorially been moderate or slightly liberal since in the mid-sixties. The change occurred in broadcast, too. Boise's radio once featured several extremely conservative talk shows; in the late eighties, an avowed liberal was given a microphone at station KIDO.

Boise is not monolithic. Its councils have had many Democratic refugees from partisan ballots. Non-partisan Mayor Wes Whillock ran unsuccessfully for the Democratic nomination for governor in 1966. Twelve-year councilman Ralph McAdams ran as a Democrat for Ada County commission in 1986 and lost. Boise State University professor Glenn Selander lost a race for state House as a Democrat before winning two council terms. Democratic attorney Mike Wetherell, a former staffer for Sen. Frank Church, lost for attorney general and legislature but resoundingly won a council seat in 1987. The councils were more liberal and pro-planning than many of Ada's commissions. In the mid-eighties two of six council members were former city planning staffers. Republicans run strongest to the west and south, especially outside Boise city limits.

Garden City, an independent municipality formed in defiance of Boise's refusal to legalize slot machines in the forties, has been an odd, contrary place ever since. Many people here are like those in the unincorporated areas, critics of any and all government who scoff at Boise's strict planning. Its main street, Chinden Boulevard, is an odd miracle mile of flashy and tacky businesses ranging from the area's premier convention center at one end to adult book stores a mile up the road. Garden City has had uproarious city hall politics, recalls, and sometimes extremist right-wing campaigns. And yet, on partisan ballots, Democrats running for state and federal offices often do well here, perhaps because of residents' relatively low income. A politically moderate takeover of city hall in the mid-eighties slowed Garden's political metabolism. A bit.[38]

Democrats' stronghold in the formerly Republican North End, north and west of the Capitol Mall area. It is the only large distinct in-city community in Idaho, complete with an outspoken and sometimes effective neighborhood association and a voting pattern more liberal than the rest of the city. It once was dominated by wealthy and retired Boiseans, but in the seventies more typical residents were young professionals, senior citizens, government workers, and students. Since the mid-seventies, when Boise began to elect a few Democratic legislators, the North End has voted for Democrats and moderate Republicans and moderate to liberal city council candidates.

Under the right phases of the moon, Democrats can win elsewhere: in Southeast Boise, a fast-growing residential area near corporate headquarters and Boise State University, and on the Bench above the Boise River, a working-class area. In the mid-eighties, Democrats in Boise organized more strongly than in years and mobilized for parity with the Republicans. They could succeed unless Republicans in turn mobilize to stop them.[39]

Jim Goller – *We used to be able to count on a good majority in Ada County. This used to be a well-organized county party-wise. It's less party-oriented [now]. A lot of people don't want to associate with the party; that's been, I think, one legacy that the hard right has left. People [here] don't like to have confrontations.*

---

[38] Garden City has gone through major changes. The older parts of Garden described here still exist, though they've been upscaled a bit. More significant is the large chunk of new territory near the Boise River annexed by the city, and turned mostly into high-end housing; that addition has changed the political mix of the city, and it has had much more stable and less emotional character since the early 90s. As a partisan place, Garden City remains mixed but increasingly seems to lean – no more than that – Democratic.

[39] Democrats in the 00s looking for good news anywhere in Idaho could look to the city of Boise, which by most reasonable measures now (as of the late 00s) leans gently Democratic. It has twice elected as mayor a former Democratic state legislators (David Bieter), in 2003 (against two strong Republicans) and 2007. In 2006 its legislative delegation, which had been split between the parties, was swept by Democrats; and Republicans who thought that was a fluke, were flummoxed in 2008 when all of those Democrats held those seats. A cautionary note: These comments apply only to the city of Boise, *not* to the rest of Ada County, which remains no less Republican than it ever was. In 2008 Ada County bounced the one Democratic county commissioner it had, and turned down another very strong candidacy.

4 | Use It And/Or ...

The passion in a land scramble rises with the land value. What fueled the debate over the use of federal and other lands was the fact that, after 1960, property in Idaho was becoming valuable.

Idaho's population and economy were stagnant for decades. In the fifties politicians ran for office against the dead economy, and Idaho might have lost population but for development of the atom-powered Idaho National Engineering Laboratory at Arco (most of the workers lived, and still do, around Idaho Falls), the Air Force base at Mountain Home, and the expansion of three or four corporations in Boise. The farm counties grew little or declined in population. Mining-based Shoshone dipped for a time. And only a few islands in the timber country – mainly Lewiston, Coeur d'Alene, and Grangeville – grew much. Not enough jobs were available for all the children born and put through schools.

Then came the late sixties, and with other changes came the fast growth that accelerated in the seventies. A third more people – 231,000 more – lived in Idaho in 1980 than in 1970.

But again the increases weren't spread evenly. All 44 counties grew during the seventies, but in most cases the extra people didn't change the scenery. More than half of the growth came in three counties. Close to a third of all those new people – more than 60,000 – came to Ada County. Another 25,000 of the new folks came to Kootenai County, and 22,500 to Canyon County. Those counties changed dramatically in the seventies.[40]

So the heavy battles over growth fastened on them, and especially on Ada and Kootenai.

The Boise Brakes

In the sixties and early seventies, Ada County was run by freewheeling pro-development types, conservative Republicans sympathetic to developers. That was almost as true of Boise, where lines between service in City Hall and speculation in land often blurred. Mayor Jay Amyx was by trade a homebuilder and developer (though it was during his eight years in office, from 1965 to 1973, that planning took hold in Boise).

---

[40] It has been so ever since. Idaho has grown in a big way since 1988, and the overwhelming majority of that growth has come in those three counties, while many of the rural counties have either declined in population, or remained at status quo (which generally has meant economic decline).

During the boom of the mid-seventies, though, Ada Countians sensed something amiss. Housing developments sprang up in odd places, often where water, sewer and other services would not easily reach. A sprawling unincorporated development a few miles south of Boise, called the Southwest Community, arose in just a few years in the seventies; soon it was so populous that if it were a city it would be the sixth largest in Idaho. Instead of building in Boise's southeast, where land was close to the center of town and mostly unsuitable for farming, developers built west, often atop rich farmland. (The boom in the southeast had to wait until the eighties.) The idea was that Boise, Meridian, Nampa, Caldwell, and Eagle – which grew 629 percent in the seventies – would become a metroplex, a la Los Angeles.

It didn't happen – or hasn't yet – because growth slowed before the land was filled, and because attitudes changed.[41]

When the move toward planning began in the late sixties it was accompanied by howls and screams. When the first hearing was held in July 1967 on a 195-page proposed Ada County zoning ordinance, more than 200 angry people showed up. One Ada Countian called planning "the closest thing to communism."

Jim Risch – *I was present on May 20, 1968 when they enacted the Ada County zoning ordinance. I thought there was going to be a revolution.*

[Reaction was] very adverse by the general public. Extremely adverse. Letters to the editor, calls coming in. Just a tremendous animosity toward the fact that government was going to tell anybody what they could or couldn't do with their land.

Interestingly enough, then, it wasn't the developers [complaining]. The big fight was over mobile homes. People would bring mobile homes and put them on their property out in the county. That's just what you did. If your children wanted to come live there, they'd bring in a mobile home and park it alongside your house. That's what the big fight was over.

In July 1971 county and other officials nervously formed the Ada Council of Governments (ACOG) to draft a master plan. It was detailed, and just what the officials had asked for. And it riled the masses, or at least the activists, who took ACOG to the hanging tree and kicked the horse loose. As on wilderness, Idahoans were torn. They wanted neither to lose control to faceless bureaucrats nor see their towns trashed.

Governor Andrus helped organize an "Idaho's Tomorrow" program, public meetings on what people wanted Idaho to be 20 years in the future. "People didn't want somebody telling them what to do with their property," Andrus recalled, "but they admitted we have to have some control so we don't have a dead-animal rendering plant located immediately next door to a golf course or residential area."

---

[41] As of 2000, though, it's happening. By then the Ada-Canyon area passed 400,000 in population, about 60% up from 1980; and by the mid00s was estimated to have cleared the half-million mark. The long-speculated solid infill from the east end of Boise (which has been extended ever further east) to Caldwell is coming within reach.

The 1975 Legislature, at Andrus' behest, passed a state Land Use Planning Act, requiring every city and county to come up with a land use plan and monitor it.

Not all did. More than a decade later, some local governments still hadn't complied. But the law greatly expanded the power of local governments. (Which made the fast-growing property taxes of those days all the more irritating.)[42]

Ada County politics bounced all over in the seventies. Moderate Republicans and, for a while, Democrats took over the county courthouse and started planning. Boise's city council grew more pro-planning; former newsman Dick Eardley, the mayor elected in 1973, 1977 and 1981, was a strong planning advocate. Only little Garden City, nearly surrounded by Boise, often run by ultra-conservatives and for years wracked with controversy and recall elections, stayed free and easy with developers.

Public sympathy for planning lasted as long as the economic boom did. When it subsided in the eighties, voters rejected pro-planning candidates. In 1984 the Ada County Commission swung around 180 degrees with election of new conservative Republicans determined to undo some of what had happened during the last 10 years. They fired the chief county planner and went to work easing restrictions on building in the Southwest Community.

But it was a slow process, and the most of the basic planning would stay in place. The county was hemmed in by the 1975 law.

The Boom in the North

In Ada, most land ranged from flat farmland to ugly desert. But Kootenai was gorgeous. What wasn't spectacular mountain was pure blue lake; what wasn't richly forested was pristine meadow. It was only 30 miles from a big city – Spokane, larger than any Idaho city - and it had a temperate climate. It was an attractive place for many people to move to.

In unincorporated areas, where building rules were few, land was carved into subdivisions, and here lay the heavy growth. From 1960 to 1984 Kootenai's largest city, Coeur d'Alene, grew from 14,291 people to 24,340, a solid 70 percent. Kootenai County rocketed from 29,556 to 67,500 - 128 percent.[43]

Mary Lou Reed, a state senator in the eighties and a planning activist in the seventies, said that "it was to some degree crazy, and I think we were scared. It was almost an anti-growth movement that was developing in reaction to the growth. That kind of anti-growth

---

[42] In January 2000, the *Idaho Public Affairs Digest* ran an article updating compliance with the act, and found that quite a number of Idaho entities either have not complied at all, or only minimally – this 25 years after the law's original passage. But planning and zoning decisions remain hot political topics all over the state.
[43] By the mid-00s, Kootenai had more than doubled in population again, to more than 130,000.

attitude has to some degree dissipated because, to some degree, the danger's dissipated."

Carol Stacey – *We were always accused of being against growth – we were, a little – but we didn't want all this cheapy, junky growth. All these developments were going on in muddy pathways and then later on, somebody has to go in and put in a proper drainage system, because people have 50-foot puddles in their front yards. That's what we had. Not in Coeur d'Alene, but all around the edge of Coeur d'Alene, we had disgusting situations where people would step out of their front door into a puddle ...*

[One upscale housing development] was going to look down on a trailer court. It is not a very successful development, but it likes to think it's hoity- toity. We have tons and tons of vacant lots. They were going to put in upscale houses for all of the hundreds of thousands of rich people who were going to move in here, and they subdivided accordingly. Each one was going to get the rich people; they didn't realize they were all going after the same tiny population.

Instead, a lot of the new people were retirees. Some were restless folk from Southern California looking for a more full-seasoned climate. These were not more-social-services retirees; these were Orange County individualists who despised government and taxes. A cadre of young anti-tax conservatives came too. Ron Rankin, the articulate conservative who led countless tax battles and helped organize the attempted recall of Sen. Frank Church, moved to Kootenai in 1965. Businessmen were attracted by the fast growth and a vision of Coeur d'Alene as a tourist mecca.

In 1978 the voters ousted a Democratic county commissioner and replaced him with Republican Chuck Harris, who vowed to abolish a county planning and zoning commission he said was too oriented toward environmentalists and too restrictive on development.

Harris and the other Republican on the three-man board, Douglas Frymire, tried to follow through by issuing an order eliminating the planning commission. The planners struck back with a court ruling saying the county commissioners lacked the authority to kill the planning commission until the planning commission itself held a hearing on it. The planning panel thumbed its nose at the county commissioners and kept on planning.

Harris' and Frymire's next target was the Panhandle Health District Board, which included members from Kootenai and the other four northern counties. In the early seventies the board passed an environmental health code and restrictions on development. In the mid-seventies it investigated the Rathdrum Aquifer, which runs southwest from Lake Pend Oreille about 50 miles to just west of Coeur d'Alene. Aquifer water generally was pure, but technicians found that near new developments where septic tanks were used, levels of nitrate – a contamination barometer – had risen. The health board slapped tough restrictions on new septic tanks, taking a bite out of new housing construction in Kootenai County. Developers were forced, to a greater degree, inside city limits. They screamed, and the county commissioners listened.

Harris and Frymire said the health board was too dominated by environmentalists. They targeted member Mary Lou Reed, who was also on the Coeur d'Alene planning commission and had just finished a term as the Idaho Conservation League state chairman. They voted to fire her from the board and sought support from the other 12 affected county commissioners.

"It was sort of like a basketball game," Reed recalled. "The Shoshone County vote came in for me, and Benewah County came in against me. I dashed up to testify in front of the Boundary County commissioners. It was really close."

The vote was eight to seven to oust her. It changed no policies: the board held to its regulations. But the fight showed how close-fought were these struggles.

In the mid-eighties the Kootenai commission turned moderate Republican, and toughened planning. Even activist Stacey described it as "the best commission we've had in 20 years."

As for Reed, "that really was my springboard into the Legislature, because I was a martyr." She became the catalyst for rebuilding the local Democratic Party, and Kootenai County sent her to the state Senate in 1984 and 1986.

Down to the Waterline

Lake Coeur d'Alene was the other battleground.

Folks in Coeur d'Alene loved sunning on their two beaches, City Beach and Sanders Beach. Then at the end of 1971 the Pack River Lumber Co., which held an extension of City Beach, announced plans to build condominiums out in the lake. An instructor at North Idaho College organized a committee which gathered 3,000 petition signatures against the construction.

"That made everybody very alert to waterfront problems in Coeur d'Alene," Stacey recalled. "We had a big petition drive. The city council politely accepted the petition and gave us that usual, What can we do? We said, well, you might deny them sewer privileges. There are things you can do. And they said, 'Oh, I don't know if we could do that. We're not exactly lie-down-in-front-of-the-bulldozer types'."

That same winter a seawall was built on Sanders Beach by nearby property owners. It blocked passage of swimmers for a time during the spring of 1972, and impinged on the sandy beach.

But when the fights were over, the swimmers kept on swimming.

Then came the Hagadone office.

It's the visible symbol of the shoreline fights, just off downtown and on the lake: an attractive, dark brown wood building connected to land by a pier and resting over a small boat dock. The boat below goes to the Casco Bay Lodge, businessman Duane Hagadone's family home on the lake. Hagadone is the big enchilada in Coeur d'Alene: he owns the local newspaper, the radio station, the big resort/hotel complex, the biggest apartment complex, and quite a bit else.

Once, what stuck out in the lake was a long pier with a railhead on it. The Red Collar rail line deeded it to the city and for years it was a center of Coeur d'Alene activities.

The Hagadone building site long had been privately owned, and a big warehouse had once been built there. But Coeur d'Alene's activists saw the new building as another intrusion on the lake. They speculated that a city committee on waterfront planning was basically geared toward helping Hagadone get his building built.

Stacey recalled asking, later, for the committee's lakeshore plan, but "I never could find where it had been passed at any public meeting. Everything was being done in the name of this plan, but there was no plan ... I interviewed members of the committee; one said, 'I had a broken leg and missed a few meetings.' But I found out later he had protested very strongly against moving the city dock (away from Hagadone's building site)."

In the end, Hagadone got his new main office and world headquarters.

Mary Lou Reed – *He is really insistent on getting his way. It's as simple as that; he likes his way. And his hobby is fixing up the town ...*

There's very much a mixed reaction. What's always been said about Hagadone is that whatever he does, he generally does first class. His architect, R.G. Nelson [who designed the Hagadone office building], is a great architect; he's a close personal friend of ours. There are lots and lots of mixed feelings.

Hagadone's ambitious building plans have remade central Coeur d'Alene. He usually has won, which isn't surprising, but often only after terrific fights. In 1988 he clashed for a time with Gov. Andrus over a plan to build a floating golf course out on Lake Coeur d'Alene. Hagadone made some concessions but got his floating green.

His biggest gamble, the object of fear and consternation while under construction, shushed the critics when it was completed. This was The Coeur d'Alene, a Resort On The Lake – the Coeur d'Alene Resort, to most people – a fine hotel, restaurant and convention center. It replaced the old North Shore Lodge, which by the eighties had become tatty, with an elegant and sophisticated state-of-the-art place to stay. It was heavily booked in its early years of operation. It did well enough that Hagadone promptly started work on a companion operation in Sandpoint.

And a companion struggle?

5 | Democrats: Booms & Busts

Utah was the land of the Saints, Nevada the land of the sort-of-cheerfully- wicked, Montana the land of the unvarnished West.

Idaho had no such easy image.[44]

In the Southeast the Mormon Church extolled hard work and decried something- for-nothing. The North, accustomed to bingo and stronger stuff, gambled with gusto. Therein lay conflict.

When Idaho's constitution was drafted, Mormons, then a tenth of the populace, were persecuted to the point of banishment from the voting booth. Intolerance extended to gambling; convention delegates said the legislature could not authorize a lottery.

But they didn't say what a lottery was. And as the Great Depression stamped its heavy boots, Idahoans looked south to Nevada. With the state's easy mineral wealth played out, Nevada's legislature in 1931 okayed legalized gambling. It revolutionized the state. From Idaho, it looked like easy money.

Illegal though they apparently were, slot machines popped up all over Idaho in the thirties in service stations, motels, and most every little cafe. Even remote Mormon towns had them. "Several in Tetonia," rancher Dick Egbert recalled. "The stores, the service stations, gasoline stations – they were everywhere."

A bill outlawing slots passed the Democratic Idaho House in 1935 but died in the Democratic Idaho Senate. In 1937, 1939, and 1941, as the House teetered from Democratic to Republican to Democratic control, outlawry bills became a skeet shoot.

In 1943 the Republican Legislature tried a new tack sponsored by Rep. Erwin Schwiebert from Caldwell, a stern anti-gambler.[45]

Erwin Schwiebert – *At the time the argument was that you can't get rid of them because the people want them, and since we have to have them, then we'd better tax them and get some revenue. Well, that offended my sense of good government from the ground up. I talked to people, said, this is not right. If you want to tax them and get the revenue from them you must first legalize them, and you can't do that until you change the constitution ...*

---

[44] All right, let's pause right here. Writing in 2009 a book about Idaho politics in general, would it make as much sense as it did in 1988 to devote more or less equal space to the Idaho Democratic Party? Idaho Democrats have had a decade and a half of being marginalized politically, with no indications that they were on their way back any time soon. Still: They were a bigger factor in Idaho political history than they have been recently. And: You never know what's coming around the bend. Idaho does after all now (2009) have a Democratic congressman.

[45] Erwin Schwiebert remained somewhat visible for many years after his withdrawal from electoral politics. I knew him as a Canyon County resident who wrote a column for the Nampa-Caldwell paper (now called the *Idaho Press-Tribune*); his was the relatively "liberal" voice, which may be an indicator of how times have changed. He loved to talk about the wars gone by, and remembered them quite clearly.

[I introduced a bill] to make possession of a federal tax stamp, which had to be affixed to a slot machine, prima facie evidence of a violation of the state's gambling code and the constitution. Some of the attorneys thought there might be something wrong with that, and I don't understand even now what their argument was against it. I did introduce the bill and we had a hard time getting it through the House. It finally passed the House, to my surprise and joy. So it went to the Senate, and we had trouble getting it through the Senate. But it passed and wound up on the desk of the governor [Republican C.A. Bottolfsen].

... I could appreciate the problem he was facing because of the tremendous pressure on him from a lot of people who should have known better but who had an economic interest in the continuance of the slot machines. That included the social clubs, who financed a lot of charitable things. They were opposed. And mostly in the North, but also areas like Sun Valley. Gambling was a popular thing ...

The governor called me up there and showed me the piles of telegrams and letters on his desk. Great Scott, a police dog couldn't jump over them. It was just tremendous. He said, "I know this bill is dear to your heart, but I just don't see how I can sign it with all this pressure coming from the public."

Bottolfsen's veto message said that attorneys advised him the bill may have been unconstitutional.

In 1945 a Republican legislature passed the Idaho Coin Operated Amusement Device Control Act. It upstaged the Supreme Court, which is supposed to interpret the Constitution, with the twisted explanation that slots were "gaming but not so lottery." It said slots would be allowed in non-profit or charitable "clubs," a provision guaranteed to generate smirks. The marriage of gambling and non-profit charities was headed for quickie divorce.

That came two years later, in the strangest legislative schizophrenia Idaho has ever seen. In February 1947 the Legislature, again Republican, wiped out most of the 1945 law and even gave refunds to private clubs whose licenses were revoked.

But they neglected – incredibly – to mention slots. So the legislators crafted a new bill. Passed in March 1947, it allowed cities and incorporated villages to license them. The incentive was powerful: each license would cost at least $500, and after the state/county cut of $250, the city got $250 or whatever it could squeeze out of the operators.

Slots even created cities. Island Park, a touristy stretch of 30 miles of road in eastern Idaho, was incorporated so it could license slots. So was Chubbuck, north of Pocatello. When prudish Boise turned up its nose at slots, little Garden City, which didn't exist in 1940 and had 764 people in 1950, was created as a haven for them. Don Chance, who was appointed to its first city council, recalled how almost everyone but him seemed to own a slot machine, and how as a result he resigned from the council within a few months. "Of course, there had to be some income, too, because there was no property out there that had much value to it. The ad valorem levy (property tax) wouldn't even support a police chief."

John Evans said that "Malad had their slot machines. They used all of the money – we always used to laugh about it – they used the money to renovate and improve the cemetery ... Now they've got one of the nicest cemeteries, well endowed."

Weiser got more than $100,000 a year from 64 machines; it built a hospital with the money.

Robert Smylie – *I think the reason for the place out there by Simplot's plant at Pocatello on Highway 30 – it was called the Highway 30 Club – is that it was just over the border in Power County. Power County had not made it illegal. I think Pocatello had, by a vote. You filed a petition for election and then the question was, "Shall they be allowed?", or something like that.*

As usual, according to form, Blackfoot and Idaho Falls were the centers of sin and splendor: they had slot machines. They didn't have them in Jefferson County, in Rigby and Rexburg. They had them in St. Anthony. They had them in Jerome, not in Gooding, and not in Twin Falls. They had slot machines in Burley and Rupert, in some of the little towns. They had them in Mountain Home, but not in Boise; that's how Garden City came to be. They didn't have them in Caldwell or Nampa. They had them in Weiser but not in Payette ... In Northern Idaho, it was pretty general.

It was a pretty good thing we got rid of them when we did, because they were getting so embedded in the local revenue requirement ... I can still find people down in Jerome that think I killed Jerome because I did the slot machines in.[46]

State legislative campaigns in 1952 often were dominated by gambling; Republicans like Perry Swisher and Democrats like John Evans won legislative seats their first time partly on anti-gambling planks. When the 1953 Senate convened, half its members were new, as were 23 of the 59 representatives. It was one of the heaviest turnovers the Legislature ever had, and it launched a generation of new politicians.

Governor Len Jordan declared war on slots, and the legislature outlawed them in February. That still didn't kill them; the law was tied up in court. Then the Idaho Supreme Court weighed in with a verdict on an old case that slots were after all lotteries and therefore unconstitutional.

Had enforcement been local, eradication of slots and punch boards would have been spotty. But state agents – "Goon Squads" – swept the countryside and uprooted almost all of them.

(Just as slots created cities in Idaho, so abolition created one: Jackpot, Nevada, the little casino town 45 miles south of Twin Falls, raised from the desert to handle the Idaho trade.)

---

[46] In his autobiography, Smylie wrote only a little about gambling, but made the intriguing comment that he suspected gambling had no more than 46% support in Idaho. The suspicion here is that it ebbed and flowed over time.

They Called Them Gambling Men

But gambling still wasn't dead.

For one thing, debate raged through the forties and fifties on parimutuel wagering. The horse industry, and investment in it, was powerful in Idaho, and betting on horse races became legal.

For another, there were the "Gambling Men."

In 1954 Bonner County elected Democratic attorney Al Derr from Clark Fork to the state Senate. In the next four years he became known as a skillful floor speaker and above-average legislator.[47]

But his impact on Idaho politics came after he announced on New Year's Eve 1957 that he was running for governor. A few weeks later he was talking with a friend, Boise attorney Vernon K. Smith who had been a defense lawyer in the infamous "Boys of Boise" scandal.[48]

The cases centered around charges filed in late 1955 against 16 men, one of them a bank vice president, accused of being involved in a homosexual ring. Smith was disgusted by the Boise power structure's approach to vice laws and was interested in allowing for Nevada-style gambling. Idaho was in an economic slump, he said, and the tourists gambling would bring in could help pull the state ahead. Some legislators and other prominent Idahoans had been urging a sales tax; the voters had kicked them out of office. The people did not want more taxes, and this might be an attractive option.

Derr was intrigued and spent two weeks talking to people on the streets of Boise, Sandpoint, Mountain Home, and other cities. The response was so positive he decided to campaign for local-option gambling. Smith, fairly conservative in other respects, ran as a Democrat for state senator on the same platform. The idea, Smith said, was not to promote gambling, but to recognize it existed, and then control and take advantage of it.

The Democratic party honchos balked, and other Democratic candidates struggled over how to deal with the "gambling men."

Joe Williams – *I talked to Al Derr before he spoke in Malad, and I said, "Al, the best thing you can do down here is not to mention it. We're not partly Mormon down here. We're 100 percent Mormon. In fact, I was about 12 years old before I knew there was anything but a Mormon, and that's not far from the truth. [Williams was raised in Samaria.] But the first thing, right off, he got right into it. It was murder down there."*

Oct. 8, 1958

---

[47] Oops – Derr was a teacher, not an attorney. His son, also named Al Derr, is in fact a Boise attorney, quite prominent in legal and press circles, and likewise a Democrat. He is married to a Republican, Judy Peavey-Derr, who has been a Republican Ada County Commissioner and a member of the Ada County Highway District Board.
[48] About which, little was said in *Paradox Politics*, the main reason being that the "Boys of Boise" scandal, while a good story (which became a highly readable book of that name), was really peripheral to the politics of the state. Although: It had some real impact in and around the 50s and 60s power structure of Boise and Ada County.

Gov. Robert Smylie
Dear Governor:
... It is unfortunate that these moral-destroying issues have to come into our political life but we have always dealt with them in the past and I guess we will have to battle them for the present and the future. It is difficult to approach voters lest they get the idea that you are telling them how to vote, which most everybody resents especially if they have an idea the Church is telling them. I did suggest, however, in our meeting last Sunday where about 1,600 people were present, that they consider carefully the moral issues in the coming election and allow their religion to govern their politics and not their politics to govern their religion. Yours sincerely, [LDS Stake President] Delbert G. Taylor Rexburg

Derr had three primary opponents: state Sen. Max Hanson of Fairfield; Democratic organizer John Glasby of Mountain Home, a key organizer of Frank Church's successful Senate race two years before; and political unknown Parma farmer Omar Maine. Hanson (who had labor support) and Glasby (who had party organization support) supposedly had the edge. John Martin, then Idaho GOP executive director, said in a memo to party leaders:

... the Democrat candidates for governor are dashing wildly about the state attempting to lambast our Gov. Smylie. However, as yet most of their barbs are falling on barren ground as they have come up with little or nothing in the way of constructive programs. Perhaps the only Democrat who has anything that is taking hold at all is state Sen. Derr who came out on the gambling issue, which is being favorably received in North Idaho and in some sections of Southeast Idaho. However, I am sure this type issue could not go far in the general election ... Derr's gambling issue will attract many voters but not enough to challenge frontrunners in the Democrat nomination for governor.

But Derr slipped past Hanson with 122 votes to spare, Glasby falling to third place. GOP strategist Evan Kackley of Wayan then quietly advised Smylie that:

... the Democratic Party is cut through with three factions: the Derr wide-open faction; the conservative Hanson, whose talks were distinctly more Republican than Demo; and third the [Frank] Church organization [including Glasby], which is much weaker than thought. Second, that the people are very tax-conscious or they would not go for gambling to sell themselves to the devil to avoid increases in taxes, or enactment of a sales tax. Third, that outside money to influence the election from gambling and labor organizations will flow into this state as never before, and it won't be into our coffers.

Some Democratic sourpusses said Derr won because Republicans voted in their primary for the candidate easiest to beat. Maybe.

But Derr got votes statewide, not only in the North but also from the southern anti-tax crowd. These groups taken together were a plurality in a split primary election but not the majority Derr needed to

77

win against incumbent Republican Gov. Robert Smylie. A whole slate of statewide Democrats won – and Democrats won both the Idaho House and Senate – but Derr didn't. Smylie held on with a slim 51 percent of the vote.

Still, his close shave inevitably prompted a rerun. In 1962 Smith announced against Smylie, who was seeking a third term. Again the primary was crowded, with six Democrats this time. And in June, Smith, proposing to allow local- option Nevada-type gambling, won the Democratic nomination with 43 percent. Soon after, Republican Schwiebert wrote Sen. Henry Dworshak that he was pessimistic about Smylie' chances. He said he often heard that Smith's Democratic primary votes probably would be all he would get against Smylie.

But, Schwiebert said, "it would probably be more realistic that he will be harder to beat than was Sen. Derr in the last gubernatorial election, when he lost by less than 5,000 votes. Smith is a superior campaigner, and he carefully baits his hook with a lot of talk about tax relief by building up a vigorous tourist and convention program in the state. Some people are inclined to swallow the bait without ever thinking about the gambling hook."

Others saw it as an issue in decline. When Frank Church sent a memo to Vice President Johnson ahead of his October 1962 visit to Twin Falls, he added a "special note of caution. Our Democratic candidate for governor, Mr. Vernon K. Smith, advocates legalized gambling for Idaho. In my opinion, this is a losing issue, although there is some sentiment for it in the Twin Falls area." Church was right. Smith barely won the North and lost most of Southern Idaho; Smylie got 54.6 percent of the vote. Smith got not quite as many votes (115,876) as Derr had (117,236) four years before. In 1966 a campaign aide to Derr and Smith, Lewiston businessman Phillip Jungert, ran for governor as an independent. Gambling still had enough backers to get Jungert on the ballot, but he finished fourth (23,139 votes).

And many Democrats said good riddance to gambling.[49]

Cowboy Ben

As they had to radicalism.

In 1892 high rail rates and low silver prices shut down some Silver Valley mines. Soon after, when management at the remaining mines refused to allow or listen to unions, a thousand men took a train to the Fresco Mill near Burke, planted dynamite and blew it up. Armies of guards, hired by often-ruthless mine owners, rushed in and began

---

[49] *Paradox* makes only a quick, glancing mention (later) of the Idaho lottery issue of the 80s – it did not clearly pass into law until November 1988. In shorthand, the voters twice (in 1986 and 1988) approved ballot measures to establish a state-run lottery similar to those in a number of other states, including Oregon (which had started drawing a lot of Idaho business). A number of leading Democrats, Cecil Andrus among them, opposed the ballot measures; but on passage, Andrus quickly named a governing commission. The Idaho Lottery has operated with only low levels of controversy ever since.

open warfare with the miners. Entire male populations of whole towns in the Valley were arrested; hundreds were confined and later denied work.

In that atmosphere, activists from the violence-prone Industrial Workers of the World, the "Wobblies," moved in. In 1899 Wardner erupted in rioting, people were killed, and Gov. Frank Steunenburg ordered in federal troops to impose martial law. Six years later Steunenberg, then out of office, was dynamited at his home in Caldwell. His assassin, Harry Orchard, implicated Wobbly national leaders such as George Pettibone and William "Big Bill" Haywood. Their trial was the most spectacular, and one of the most bitterly emotional, in Idaho history. It made the reputation not only of Clarence Darrow, the defense attorney who got them off, but of three Idaho attorneys: future governor James Hawley (a prosecutor) and future senators William Borah (another prosecutor) and John Nugent (on the defense, and – logically – the only Democrat of the three).[50]

Conditions were less violent on the farm, but turn-of-the-century Idaho farmers were hard hit as well. In May 1892 the Farmers Alliance and Knights of Labor formed the Idaho Populist Party. It denounced capitalism and pushed for government ownership of railroads and other utilities (as happened in Nebraska, North Dakota, and Minnesota). Republicans generally stayed dominant and the Populists never elected a statewide candidate. But in the first legislature elected by party in 1894, the 18-member Senate had five Populists and the 35-member House had eight – more Populists in each place than Democrats. By building coalitions the Populists, many from mining and timber country, controlled the Senate for four years.

With the new century Populism faded but didn't die. Deep in the forested recesses, in remote reaches of open prairie, paranoid radicalism survives. It can swing left or right. It needs only a leader.

Around World War I many Idaho farmers took radicalism where they could find it. A few became socialists; the party was popular for a time in Nampa, Coeur d'Alene, and Rupert. Earl W. Bowman of Council was elected as a Socialist to the Idaho Senate in 1914.

More joined the Non-Partisan League, a farmer group based in the upper plains states, calling for public ownership of utilities and banks. In 1918 League farmers took over the state Democratic Party and sent it racing to destruction. In the next few years Democrats lost every election in sight. The party fell into a coma when the Non-Partisans abandoned them and formed a new Populist Party, which won more elections than the Democrats did.

---

[50] No: Hawley as well as Nugent was a Democrat, so it was two out of three. If the Silver Valley conflict and Steunenberg trial interest you even slightly, by all means read *Big Trouble* by J. Anthony Lukas (Simon & Schuster, 1997), probably the finest work of history ever written that deals with Idaho – and it deals with this story both completely and thoughtfully. (It also deals with quite a bit else that was going on around the country at century's turn.) It's a long book, but an easy read; I've read it four times (so far). For anyone interested simply in Idaho, it's worth it just for the first chapter, on Caldwell.

After 1926 the Populists faded and farmers – the key voting bloc, since 40 percent of working Idahoans were employed in agriculture – were at a crossroads. Should they make the philosophical shift to the Republicans or join the comatose Democrats?

In Idaho, 1928 was a Republican year: every statewide and congressional office on the ballot went to the Republicans. By far the most successful losing Democrat was the gubernatorial sacrificial lamb, Pocatello Mayor C. Ben Ross (memorialized by the city's Ross Park). Pocatello then as later was a labor, factory, and railroad town, but Ross' roots were in farming; he grew up on a homestead near Parma and pioneered farming in the desolate Michaud Flats west of Pocatello.

Ross was an explosive man, a demagogue or popular leader – take your pick – in a class with Huey Long of Louisiana and Floyd Olson of Minnesota. He shared with them an anti-New York, pro-"common people" rhetoric. He called himself "Cowboy Ben" and handled crowds like a master entertainer; instead of pompous orations, he talked in a fast good-ole-boy style. He had a big head; "His ego was just absolutely out of sight," reporter John Corlett recalled. And he was a mystic; a spiritual adviser had convinced him that his destiny was to become president.

He was also the bridge between warring factions the Democrats so badly needed. As a Democratic county commissioner in Canyon County (before moving to Pocatello) he had made friends in the mainstream party, while his angry pro-farmer speeches encouraged Populists to back him. But though he sounded radical he didn't act like one. Ross was a founder of the Idaho Farm Bureau – later staunchly Republican – and toured Idaho on its behalf. His best votes came not in the North but in usually Republican Southern Idaho farm country. The defensive and skeptical Democrats who led the shell of a party in the twenties let him have the gubernatorial nomination in 1928 because it seemed worthless.

By 1930, they saw an upset in the making and wanted to deny the nomination to this outsider who sounded so radical. Democrats made only modest gains in 1930, but won the governorship because Ross' personal strength overcame party leaders to win both the nomination and the general election. The Republican candidate, John McMurray, didn't see the threat and got careless.

Joe Williams – *At that time I was working for either Goodyear or Goodrich Rubber Co. down on 12th and Main [in Boise]. We stored cars for the Owyhee Hotel across the street. We kept and serviced a good many state cars. Fred Lukens was secretary of state. He called the garage – I answered the phone – and he said he wanted me to prepare a car for John McMurray to go to North Idaho. I made every effort and serviced the car as much as I could, filled it full of gas, checked the oil and the tires, lubricated it. Then before noon [McMurray] came down and got in the car; I think the license number was 10. And he started off for Northern Idaho.*

When he was out of the garage and on his way I called Democratic headquarters and said, "Our opposition is now travelling north to campaign in a state car."
... That was the turning point in that election.

In the depths of a depression year, it was a killer issue. Ross won.

In the beginning, Ross did as Roosevelt would two years later: He brought together groups that had been at war for years. He also joined with the New Deal. Roosevelt was a powerful incentive for many hard-hit farmers to become Democrats. Dick Egbert, later elected to the Idaho Legislature as a Democrat over a span of 40 years, recalled that he entered the thirties as a Republican. "But I still remember the big depression of 1929 and the thirties. I was really hurting," he said. "I made the statement that the people with good money vote Republican, and the people who don't have much money are Democrats."

From 1932 through FDR's 13 years in office, Idaho Democrats held the upper hand, winning more than they lost. Partly because of Ross, Democrats won big in farm counties where they had been poison before and often have been since. In 1932 Idaho elected its first Democratic senator in 14 years – a liberal New Dealer. James Pope, a lawyer and Boise mayor who, like Ross, tried to weld Democrats and populists, challenged the tottering Republican machine directly. He ran against Sen. John Thomas, a former banker and organizer of the twenties' Idaho Republican Party. Pope sprayed shots at "the men who have worked our system for their own selfish advantage" and patterned his campaign after Roosevelt's nationally. Pope won easily.[51]

The Democratic sweep brought in Democrat Compton I. White as congressman in the first congressional district. He would hold the seat for 14 consecutive years and then be elected to one more in 1948. Still later his son would serve two terms.

Ross' success also encouraged the Clarks, who became the most powerful family in Idaho history: it produced two governors, two mayors, a U.S. representative and, counting an in-law, two U.S. senators. Brothers Chase and Barzilla Clark came to Idaho Falls from Indiana in 1885. Barzilla, the elder, studied civil engineering but made money in cattle and mining; he was elected to the Idaho Falls city council in 1908 and later mayor – five times. Chase got a law degree and put up a shingle in the mining and cattle town of Mackay, where he was elected to the state House when he was 27 years old. (Custer County was Democratic then.) After he moved to Idaho Falls in 1917, he became mayor when Barzilla left the job. Both were strongly

---

[51] Pope has become the subject of somewhat more interest in the years since this was originally written, as Idaho's only true major-office liberal of the New Deal years. He also set another long-standing mark. He was the last Boise mayor to rise to higher office for more than half a century, until his Mayor Dirk Kempthorne did it in 1992 when he too was elected to the U.S. Senate.

interested in public power and partly responsible for the city's public hydropower system.

Chase, the sheep-for-slaughter for the U.S. Senate in 1928, joined the 1932 Democratic landslide, unseating a Republican Bonneville County state senator. Barzilla was elected governor in 1936 and Chase in 1940. (Oddly, both were defeated for re-election by the same man: Republican C.A. Bottolfsen, an Arco newspaper publisher.) The Clarks' nephew, conservative Democrat D. Worth Clark of Pocatello, benefited even more. He became a two-term U.S. representative (elected in 1934 and 1936) and one-term U.S. Senator (in 1938).

Ross' personal popularity was such that he became the first Idaho governor elected three times, a feat not equaled for 30 years. But he could not sustain it. Roosevelt could forge broad alliances so strong they lasted half a century. Ross, less stable politically and personally, lacked that talent. He warred with Roosevelt's New Dealers and split his own liberal wing of the party. Ross was a forerunner of the successful post-war politicians: he was not a product of the party structure and did little to feed it once in office. When he outraged voters by jamming through a sales tax in 1935 – giving Republicans the wonderful campaign slogan, "A Penny for Benny" – no party safety net broke his fall.

Ross overreached in 1936 when he ran against legendary Republican Sen. William E. Borah. Borah won in a landslide, and Ross was personally crushed. He ran for governor again in 1938, but the old confidence and mystique were gone. And with him, after 1938, went much of the farm-labor alliance. Idaho Democrats did well in 1940 and 1944, when the state voted for Roosevelt, but as farmers pulled out of depression and no longer heard a Democratic agrarian voice, they turned Republican. Some conservative farmers, businessmen and professionals, such as legislators Egbert, Charles Gossett of Nampa and party organizer Tom Boise of Lewiston, stubbornly stayed Democratic. Conservative Democrats like them took over the party in the late thirties and forties. In 1938 conservative D. Worth Clark, with Republican crossover help, beat incumbent New Deal Senator Pope in the Democratic primary.

But the flame of Idaho liberalism was not yet extinguished.

It was passed unknowingly, one fall day in 1936, from C. Ben Ross to a young, dirt-poor vaudeville entertainer.

The Singing Cowboy

Ross was ill during much of his campaign against Borah but when he did campaign, he was intense. As Ross worked a crowd in Driggs, making constituents laugh and cry, a young actor and singer was struck by the idea that the skills he had honed on the stage over two decades could get him elected to office. Besides, Glen Taylor thought, he was a far better entertainer than Ross.

He was right.

Taylor was the most hotly-debated political property Idaho produced between the youth of William Borah and the anti-war years of Frank Church. Like them, Taylor was a senator and again like them, his best-known stands had to do with foreign policy. But Borah and Church projected an image of intellectual rectitude and a sense that they were born to be senators. But Taylor ...

Well, he was not the hick or boob his opponents made him out to be. He had a clear philosophy and worked through his ideas more than most politicians. But he was colorful and uninhibited, hardly the image of cool, reserved senatorial dignity.

He learned leftist thinking early on. Born in 1904 in a Portland boarding house to a nomadic minister, ranger and farmer, he roamed the West as his father "Pleasant John" visited mining and logging camps and preached a kind of early Christian socialism. When Glen left his home near Kooskia to lead vaudeville shows, he often faced hunger and destitution. In the late twenties and early thirties his shows were pushed out of larger towns by talking movies, and the small towns which welcomed him usually were as stricken by poverty and hunger as he was.

In 1932, Taylor chanced on a copy of *The People's Corporation*, a book by safety-razor magnate King C. Gillette that suggested socialism as a cure for Depression. Taylor was impressed and read more in the same vein. So he was ready when he walked into Ross' performance in the fall of 1936. He told his wife Dora that night, with no indecision at all, about his new career.

When Taylor stepped into Idaho's dull, pragmatic late-thirties politics he was unlike anything Idahoans had seen. Many Idaho politicians then were cut from the Borah mold – aloof, dry, pompous – without his stature. Taylor did things they would not have dreamed of. He cruised into town in his truck with the rest of the Glendora Ranch Gang, played and sang a few songs to attract a crowd, then eased into his message. Others were slow; he was fast. He would shake hands with whole downtowns, moving swiftly from person to person (while other politicians trapped themselves in philosophical discussions). He visited remote places that seldom saw major candidates. Perhaps because of his background, creative campaigning came naturally, and his genuine intensity welded an emotional bond. His message of near-socialism and world peace – in a state of free-enterprise isolationists – made him both loved and hated.

In his last 20 years he moved to California and became a rich toupee manufacturer, but in all his Idaho years he stayed poor.

Perry Swisher – *I remember going into his house in the '44 campaign, when he was running against Worth Clark. There was a table in the kitchen, a table in the dining room. One chair, maybe two. There were no chairs in the kitchen. There was a hot plate but no stove in the kitchen. And a refrigerator. I opened the* *refrigerator and there wasn't a hell of a lot there. Cheese, and maybe three or four eggs.*

Taylor's first race, for the House in 1938, got him fourth place in the Democratic primary. (The seat went to Republican Dworshak.) But years of travel through the back country gave him a base the Boise establishment little suspected. In 1940, in a three-way against two colorless conservatives, he won the Democratic nomination for the Senate seat opened by Borah's death. "Sure surprised the establishment Democrats," John Corlett recalled. "They just couldn't take it."

Taylor lost the general election, to a two-year term, to John Thomas. Taylor came back in 1942, again triumphant in the primary over four other Democrats who again split the party regulars.

This time, at the August party convention, Taylor lashed out at Democratic leaders who, he said, were trying to do him in. He tried to oust the party chairman, Robert Coulter of Cascade, and install his own choice, Asher Wilson of Twin Falls. Coulter had backing from the Clarks and Democratic leaders in Boise, Lewiston, Coeur d'Alene, and elsewhere, and he prevailed. Taylor took the podium, slashed at Coulter, and concluded, "You find the truth out there in the wide open spaces a lot more than you do here in Boise." The party organization was furious.

And again Taylor lost to Thomas.

After three losing races Taylor was supposedly finished. He was sheer trouble to the establishment. He was a popular candidate with long-term potential but who delivered a message alien to them, who approached politics with religious zeal. Taylor would cut no deals. He equated purity with honesty – and for him it was – but it made him self-righteous and limited his effectiveness in a system that depends on compromise.

And yet in 1944 the Democrats made the same mistake a third time. Worth Clark was running for re-election against two slightly less conservative mainstream Democrats when Taylor, seeing another split vote, jumped in. He now latched on to Roosevelt, complaining that Clark had not much supported the president (which was true) and that he had been weak in supporting the war effort (debatable, and in any event an odd point for Taylor to make). For a third time, he won the Democratic nomination.

Now Taylor refined his image. He became a more conventional candidate, smoothed the rougher edges of his platform. In all of his other races most other prominent Idaho Democrats steered clear of him, but his new image helped win him mainstream backing in 1944. Ross, who lost a governor's race in 1938 to C.A. Bottolfsen, Taylor's 1944 opponent, spent a couple of weeks with Taylor during the campaign. It helped give Taylor legitimacy.

In 1942 Taylor had lost almost every county in Eastern Idaho by overwhelming margins. In 1944 he won all the key counties of the

Upper Snake (Bonneville, Jefferson, Madison and Fremont) and nearly won others. He got 51.1 percent of the Idaho vote – the only time he won a general election in eight runs for office.

Taylor was a good constituent service senator. He brought home bacon; idealism didn't interfere with that. But the late forties were hard times for liberals, much less a peace-talker years ahead of his time on civil rights and other issues.

In 1948 his ego would not let him resist when former Vice President Henry Wallace, running for president on the Progressive Party ticket, asked him to run as vice president. Taylor was undoubtedly deeply concerned about foreign policy and other issues. During the 1948 campaign he went out of his way to get arrested in Birmingham, Alabama, when he tried to take a "Negroes only" door into a meeting house. In some ways the Progressives were a generation ahead of their time. But theirs was a hopeless crusade Taylor could have justified avoiding. (Taylor never made any excuses or apologies, though, and often said he would do it all over again.) The Progressives' timing, as the country moved into conservatism and as suspicion of liberalism flowered, was bad. The Progressive Party got few votes nationally. The best vote it got in any county in Idaho was 6.9 percent in Shoshone County, home of the once- radical miners.[52]

When Taylor ran for re-election in 1950 he was repeatedly accused of being a Communist dupe. Idaho newspapers cut him up unmercifully; Taylor said they were "nothing but propaganda organs. I am glad they are against me. When they are for me I will get worried." The *Idaho Statesman*, he said, was "a stooge of the Boise gang." He wrote an open letter published as an ad to its publisher, Margaret Cobb Ailshie. "I am no Communist, and you know it," he wrote. "Otherwise, you would not have been so careful to avoid making the direct charge. My patriotism is not the issue."

It became the issue anyway. First District Congressman Compton White Sr., who left that seat to run for the Senate, did not harp on it. But D. Worth Clark, the conservative Pocatello Democrat beaten by Taylor in 1944 (although some Republicans wanted Clark to run under their banner), had a grudge to settle. He called himself "an American Democrat," and ran his own "open letter" ads.

"Why have you continually followed the Communist line of propaganda in your Senate speeches which concern the foreign policy of our nation?" he wrote. "Why have you so consistently defended Soviet Russia?"

Taylor's backers shot back. Their ad, run days before the election, said: "They think we've forgotten his [Clark's] record of obstructionism before World War II, forgotten his vote against

---

[52] When I researched *Paradox Politics*, I asked a number of people what they thought might have happened had Taylor not gotten involved in the 1948 presidential race. Opinion was mixed, but tended toward the view that he would have survived 1950; had he managed that, he would have next faced re-election in 1956, a period trending toward Democrats in Idaho, and beyond the pale of McCarthyism. He might well have turned into a four- or five-term senator.

preparedness then, forgotten the use of his franking privilege by subversive and disloyal organizations, many of whose leaders were later jailed, forgotten his alliance with the forces of reaction and of the bitterness of his attacks on the leadership of Franklin D. Roosevelt."

Taylor lost that primary, which with Florida Sen. Claude Pepper's featured the most vicious red-baiting in the nation. (Clark lost to Republican Herman Welker.)

The respectability Taylor worked so hard to build evaporated, and he was left only with hard-core support. In 1954, when he again faced a Republican (after surprising two Democrats who split the moderate vote), he was again splattered with red paint.

The opposition, Taylor complained, was "the machine" – a shadowy, bipartisan group that ran Idaho politics, which fixed elections (or tried to) and despised him because he was too honest.

It sounds paranoid but it had a basis in reality. Idaho had no recount law, and elections were a loose and funny business. Perry Swisher maintains that he may have lost his first run for the Idaho House from Bannock County, in 1946, because of that.

Perry Swisher – *I lost by 20-odd votes. We had a precinct, Alameda No. 3, that had over a thousand votes in it in the 1944 election, in spite of the law that said that you divide precincts [that large]. So Kenny [Roebuck, Swisher's political mentor], warned me to get that precinct divided up, and he said if you don't - but I was younger and I had more important things to do, and I didn't get that precinct split. On election night I was 100-and-some votes ahead. And then ...*

People in that precinct were voting for legislators running at large; three would be elected out of the six. Even people who voted with a fountain pen, as they occasionally did, would - ah - cast a fourth vote in pencil, to invalidate total vote. There were over a hundred spoiled ballots and I lost the election by 23 votes ...

Of course, I wanted to sue and I wanted to jump up and down. But [Roebuck] said, "No, you're a Republican running in a Democratic county, and I told you what to do and you didn't listen. And you lost. Could have won. But if you turn into a crybaby your first trip out, there won't be much you can do. So just shut up."

The Organization

Will Rogers' famous line about Democrats was that "I'm not a member of any organized political party; I'm a Democrat." Glen Taylor missed the mark by not understanding how disorganized was Idaho's Democratic Party for most of its history.

After Ross's career was eclipsed and after Roosevelt died, the party was wracked by Taylorites battling anti-Taylor red-baiters. Then the party was torn by the gambling issue. (Republicans, who had fewer North Idaho votes to contend with, had less trouble with it.) Idaho Democrats seemed to be skidding toward oblivion.

But a few Democrats tediously put Humpty Dumpy together again.

Their leader was a Lewiston businessman never elected to public office and little known to the state. But for 30 years Tom Boise was a power in Idaho, as much as any governor or senator or – sometimes – the whole Legislature.

Tom Boise once was a Republican who made money in real estate. Impressed by Roosevelt, he became a Democrat in 1936. Boise was no campaign season pol; he worked at politics every day, year in and year out. He recruited party workers across northern Idaho, building a party structure where none had been. In the south he encouraged conservatives to run as Democrats and he helped elect many of them. Throughout the forties, fifties and sixties, most Democrats who rose to prominence in Idaho did so with his blessings and help. A few dared oppose him. But Tom Boise had to be reckoned with by every ambitious Democrat.

Carl Burke – *He saw that the Democrats who were elected, that all of them got money, all of them were financed. And he expected sometime in return, when they could, to return a favor. And they usually did ... A lot of people thought of him as sinister, but I never really did. He was an old-time politician who learned politics Daley-style.*

Through the fifties Democrats slowly regained strength, partly because of Boise's ceaseless building. The Idaho Senate went from 11 Democrats in 1953 to 27 – a majority – six years later.

"He was a strategist," Corlett recalled. "He knew how to take care of his power. He put together coalitions. He had a coalition of Democratic leaders in Eastern Idaho, all Mormons, and Northern Idaho. This way they controlled the state central committees and state conventions. It worked for quite a while."

A lobbyist too, Boise worked with Republicans as well as Democrats. He was so effective that, like Republican Lloyd Adams, then the other top lobbyist, he rarely came to the Statehouse. He lobbied from his Raymond Hotel in distant Lewiston, or from his two-room corner suite on the eighth floor of the old Boise Hotel, a block from the Capitol, working phones, pulling strings. "He wasn't there consistently," then-Democratic legislator Vern Ravenscroft recalled. "He wasn't a professional lobbyist day in and day out. But when Tom showed up you could expect certain things to happen."[53]

He was tight with Democratic leaders like Ray McNichols in Orofino, Jasper R. "Jap" Inscore in Moscow and key players in the Athletic Roundtable in Coeur d'Alene. He was close to Harry Wall,

---

[53] When I interviewed Cecil Andrus about Tom Boise, he was largely dismissive of him – not of his clout, but of his purpose and role: As just an influence peddler. In his autobiography, Andrus was a little more expansive. (Maybe the passage of another dozen years had an effect.) There he described him as "the closest there was to a Democratic Party boss in north Idaho. A small gentleman, nice dressed and soft spoken, he reminded me of the veteran senator played by Claude Rains in *Mr. Smith Goes to Washington.*

Idaho's Democratic national committeeman for 20 years. Their far-flung organization nourished and supported other Democrats.

John Greenfield – *[Jap Inscore] was a Moscow man; his wife Lillian is still there. He was a good friend of mine. They owned the [Hillcrest] Motel up there. When I was [Democratic] state chairman I'd be leaving to go somewhere else in the morning – I always stayed in the motel, she never charged me – driving to St. Maries or someplace and I'd look in my coat pocket for something and there would be a hundred dollar bill. That was the old style. That was Lillian; she'd always smile and say, "I don't know how it got there."*

Boise's alliances were so extensive that Republican governors asked him for and got help getting bills through Republican legislatures. Sometimes he even helped elect moderate Republicans, such as Gov. Robert Smylie.

He was a Democrat through support for the New Deal but his ideas – to the extent they showed, for he left no voting record – were often conservative and absolutely pragmatic. He looked at people like Glen Taylor with both alarm and distaste.

Tom Boise supported local-option gambling. He had slot machines in his Raymond Hotel in Lewiston. But he also knew the risks of running on a gambling platform, and he had no use for the new pro-gambling crowd. In 1962, Vernon K. Smith, who owed no allegiance to Boise, at one point seemed close to unseating Smylie. Boise had worked with Smylie, and he wheeled his campaign machinery on Smylie's side and helped him to re-election.

(Cecil Andrus has another sense of Boise's machinations. He agreed that Boise supported Smylie in 1962, "but I'll go back further. I suspect that he might have even had a hand in the primary process because of Smylie" – in other words, swinging the nomination to Smith thinking Smylie could more easily defeat him than an anti-gambling candidate.)

Unable to crack the Republican population centers of Boise city and Twin Falls, Tom Boise reached out from Lewiston, Pocatello, and Coeur d'Alene to snare rural votes. Some conservative agrarian Democrats baptized in the religion of New Deal were still around, and Boise put them to work.

They made a power base out of the first congressional district, which then consisted mostly of Northern Idaho. It included sparsely-populated Lemhi and Custer counties, and went south to Canyon County, but the Democratic north dominated. From 1932 through 1964 it elected Democrats to Congress 15 out of 17 times.

In 1952 it elected Democrat Gracie Pfost, a ferociously energetic campaigner. She had gotten her political experience getting elected as the Democratic treasurer of Republican Canyon County, and becoming unbeatable there. She worked the rodeo circuit as hard as any male candidate, riding every four-legged beast available, always making sure her cowboy boots were packed in the trunk when she drove around Idaho.

She had good staff, too, the best Democratic help, since she was the only Democratic employer around. She became almost unbeatable.

Democrats made inroads elsewhere.

In Elmore County organizers combined railroad workers at Glenns Ferry with federal workers at Mountain Home Air Force Base with the irritation of the farmers who gave Ross such big wins there in the thirties. Similar tactics turned Camas, Gem, and several Upper Snake River Valley counties Democratic at times in the fifties, electing conservative Democrats to legislative and local offices. Agrarian socialists they were not: their agenda was low taxes, small budgets, small government.

In the late fifties and early sixties Democrats, not Republicans, led the legislative "economy bloc." Liberal Democrats had no statewide winner since Taylor – who split the party more than unified it – in 1944, and no true leader since James Pope, the New Deal senator ousted in 1938.

They finally got one in the Senate race of 1956.

Church and the Liberals

It was Taylor's last shot.

In the fall of 1954, he was in a tight race with conservative Republican Sen. Henry Dworshak when McCarthyite Sen. Herman Welker trooped red-baiting witnesses across Idaho and opened the campaign to fear and innuendo – while Dworshak kept his hands clean. Taylor was blown out of the water. He carried five counties out of 44, and barely won three of those. But the day before the 1954 election, he would write later, he received solid evidence wiping out the witnesses' credibility, smashing Welker's case. Taylor itched to take on Welker personally, in 1956.

By then McCarthyism had run its course; the Wisconsin senator was discredited. Taylor's blast at Welker's informants had the desired effect. And Welker had serious personal problems. His memory slipped. He slurred words, became incoherent, and Republicans worried every time he stood to speak. The truth no one (apparently including Welker) knew was that he was suffering from a blood sugar disorder and a brain tumor, which killed him in 1958. But in 1956 people assumed that Welker was alcoholic.

Republican leader Rich Hendricks remembered a parade and rally he organized for Welker in Preston in 1956. "It was the first rally that had amounted to anything in our county for years and years, and I went and probably got a hundred people out," he said. Welker "talked for probably two hours. And he rambled. I thought he had been drinking. When he got through the common thought that even I expressed was, we'd have done better if he'd never shown up. He lost the votes of those hundred or so people. Everybody said, the man's drunk."

Taylor was ready, but the Democratic party wasn't ready for him. Tom Boise and others in the north, and the Clarks and others in the east, feared Taylor would split the party again. Welker had Republican primary opposition. But if he overcame it (as he barely did) this Senate seat, and the chance to develop a long-term Democratic leader, could be the opportunity of a decade. They settled on Frank Church, a young Boise lawyer married to Chase Clark's daughter Bethine. He was a good combination: ambitious, energetic, somewhat liberal, pragmatic. Two other more conservative candidates ran but lacked Taylor's deep support or Church's youthful vigor and ties.

Church was not new to politics. Since high school in Boise he had wanted to be a United States senator. Back home from World War II and practicing law in Boise, he wasted no time linking up with other young vets also interested in politics. One was Carl Burke, an attorney and his closest childhood friend. Another was George Greenfield, another attorney who went through law school in Washington on Glen Taylor's patronage (he was a Capitol elevator operator). They and others made their move in 1952.

John Greenfield — *It was the summer of the Young Turks. Every once in a while really good, progressive, dynamic people all show up at the same time and take over the Ada County Democratic Central Committee and throw the deadwood out. And that's what those guys did — Carl Burke and my dad and Frank Church. They handed these precinct maps out, color coded. My dad looked at them for a long time and finally said, "It sounds real good, but I don't know what you're doing. I'm color blind."*

Burke and Church ran unsuccessfully for the legislature in 1952, the year of the Republican Eisenhower landslide. But they took over the Ada County Democratic organization, and built on it. George Greenfield became state party chairman. And in 1956 Church announced for the Senate. Why not? It was what he always wanted. Anyone looking for deeper reasons need go back only a few years, when Church almost died of cancer. Life, he had learned, is short, and time is not for wasting.

Carl Burke — *To Frank's mind, Welker looked fairly vulnerable although to begin with [not to others]. We had debates about whether that was a wise thing to do, to jump right in the middle for such an important office so early on. He did that in a very modest way.*

It was not like any campaign we ran since. There used to be a paper called the Meridian Times, *and in the basement of the* Times *we sent off this announcement, to a list we had of Democrats, that Frank was running. Four or five of us did all the paperwork, did a very sloppy job of running things through a printer, stuffed the envelopes, put the stamps on and went down at three in the morning and mailed them at the Boise post office. That was the entry into the race. There was no press conference at all.*

We produced our own [TV spots] ... It was pretty crude. And one camera. We had one in a small business, one of the lumber mills out here. And out at a farm in Barber [east of Boise]. One in a building. One in a study. Six of them, as I recall. And we had to move those tapes from television station to station. We didn't have a whole bunch of copies, so we had to ship them about from one station to another. They were about five minutes long; we cut some excerpts from them for shorter ads.

Unlike more seasoned politicians, Church looked good on TV. He also worked the state hard. In Coeur d'Alene he got help from attorney William Hawkins, a leader in the Athletic Roundtable civic and political group; in Benewah County, Jap Inscore; in Orofino, attorney Ray McNichols.

Carl Burke — *In the spring we had a Democratic convention in Lewiston. We weren't delegates, but we had a booth out there. Frank had made friends with Ray McNichols, an attorney from Orofino who worked closely with Tom Boise. And McNichols, I'm sure with the blessing of Boise, talked about the need for Democrats to nominate somebody - he was giving the keynote speech - to nominate someone who was young, forceful, had some vision and ideas and so forth. There was only one guy running like that, Frank Church. Nobody else fit that ticket. So we had Tom's support in the primary. That was critical. And I got to know him pretty well.*

Church wound up the primary in a photo finish with Taylor.

What actually happened that August day has been hotly debated ever since. The official canvass gave Church 27,942 votes and Taylor 27,742. Results were slow coming in and for days mistakes cropped up. Convinced something was wrong, Taylor looked hard at precincts where his vote was less than what past trends suggested he should have had - especially Precinct 3 in Mountain Home. He and an aide spent five sweltering summer days, harassed by police who accused them of violating an anti-soliciting ordinance, personally canvassing 443 of the 488 voters in Precinct 3. He concluded he should have gotten at least 107 votes instead of the 71 allocated to him, and that Church should have lost 34 votes. If true, that would reverse a third of Church's winning margin.

Was the election fixed? It probably will remain Idaho's one of Idaho's most tantalizing political mysteries.

John Corlett — *I just couldn't see how it deliberately could have been done. The whole scheme of a statewide primary, how this one little precinct could have been the one that told the whole story - I couldn't see it. But you couldn't convince Taylor.*[54]

---

[54] It remains unresolved to this day, even in the generally thorough biography of Church, *Fighting the Odds*, by LeRoy Ashby and Rod Gramer. If *Paradox Politics* sounded

Others thought ballots in isolated precincts around the state easily could have been tampered with. Perry Swisher has speculated that the dead-heat 1942 governor's race was thrown to Republican C.A. Bottolfsen by friends of incumbent Democrat Chase Clark – so that Clark could be appointed to a federal judgeship which had just come open. (Bottolfsen offically won by 434 votes.) In fact, Clark was appointed soon after the election. About the 1956 Senate race, Swisher said later, "I think Glen Taylor's complaint about Mountain Home No. 3 is in the category of, it was stolen fair and square. Which is to say, you had to know your counties and know what was going on."

Taylor spent weeks twisting every which way. He got signed affidavits from Mountain Home voters, trying to force a recount. He asked Church to take a lie detector test. At the Democratic convention in Pocatello he confronted Church and asked for a federal investigation. Sen. Albert Gore of Tennessee, who chaired the Senate committee which oversaw questionable elections, was asked to investigate. Gore decided in Church's favor.

Idaho law then had no provision for a recount. It would, a few years later, mostly because of Taylor's experience.

Taylor wasn't quite done. He ran a write-in campaign that fall which, he said in his autobiography, was financed by $35,000 from Republicans who hoped he would take votes from Church.

But Welker was too weak for that to work. By early October, Church was headed for a decisive win. Then he got a bonus.

Carl Burke – *That was before any disclosure laws; all the information you were required to send to Washington, to the Senate, was confidential. It went to the committee [on campaign ethics] and the statute provided it was confidential, that they could not disclose it to anybody else, that only the committee would look at it and decide what should be done. But darn if Welker didn't file his statement with the secretary of the Senate instead of the committee. So it became public. And it showed an enormous number of contributions from the oil companies all over the country. It's front-page stuff. And that was disclosed about three weeks before the election.*

Church later figured Welker spent $120,000 in the 1956 campaign – an enormous sum then – to his own $40,000.

He beat the rap, this time, of being a leftist. One effective ad, headlined "Are You Sick of Smears?," ran Welker's railings (that Church was the "controlled candidate" of a "radical bunch of pinks and punks") on one side and those of Taylor (that Church was "front man" for a "corrupt corporate machine") on the other. Church, in turn, machine-gunned Welker's "disgraceful" record.

---

a little indecisive on the matter, that's a reflection of what people I interviewed had to say.

Church beat Welker by a huge 46,315-vote margin. That election opened a new era in Democratic organization in Idaho. It was the beginning of the Democratic organization that would defeat and supplant Tom Boise's machine, and would become the backbone of the Idaho Democratic Party.[55]

In 1960 John Kennedy was elected president, Pfost won big in the first district, and Kennedy Democrat Ralph Harding won in the second, a seat held 22 years by conservative Republicans.

In 1962 – the same day one Senate seat went to conservative former Republican Gov. Len Jordan – Idaho re-elected Church. Pfost lost to Jordan, after spurning pleas from Idaho Democrats and even President Kennedy to run for re- election to the House instead. But Harding and new Democratic Congressman Compton White, Jr., were elected. White was a businessman and rancher from Clark Fork, in the far north of Idaho, and son of the eight-term Democratic congressman. (Talk was that some voters thought they were voting for his father.) Despite some conservative instincts, he supported Kennedy and Johnson. Abruptly, liberalism had clout.

But it had limits.

"I have a friend down in Gooding County; we served on the Sawtooth National Advisory Board," Vern Ravenscroft recalled. "This friend was a Republican precinct committeeman and vice chairman of the Gooding County Republican Central Committee. Strong identity as a Republican. One morning, I think the day after the election [of 1962] as we got into the car, this friend said, 'Well, Vern, I voted for two winners in the Senate yesterday'."

Ravenscroft was incredulous.

"Oh," he says, "it's easy. Idaho needs the influence with President Kennedy and Frank Church has got a lot of influence with President Kennedy. So I voted to send Frank back there to continue to work on our behalf on these national issues and items where Idaho's welfare is at stake. And I sent Len back there to watch both of them."

---

[55] Although it should have been more clearly noted here that Church won in 1956 and 1962 with the strong support of Tom Boise's organization, which was a significant component of what Taylor called "The Machine." *Fighting the Odds*, the Church biography, makes a number of good points about the campaign. It notes how Church's chances were considered to be weak as the race began, and how many observers figured Welker for a winner even a few weeks before the election. It points out that Church was able to effectively use the point that, since he was attacked from the right by Welker and the left by Taylor, he must be a good solid centrist – or, at the least, either Taylor or Welker must be wrong in their assessment. Authors Ashby and Gramer also pointed out the key role of disclosures about Welker's campaign finances, from much-disliked national organizations including oil companies. Such disclosures were considered unusual then ...

6 | Republicans: Sorcerers Apprentices

If this story isn't true it should have been ...

One day in the thirties an Idaho farm boy went to Boise. When he returned home he told his family that he had seen the internationally-famous U.S. senator William E. Borah, shaking hands with people in the Owyhee Hotel.

His father scolded him. "Now what," he said, "would a man like Senator Borah be doing in a place like Boise?"

Whenever the Lion of Idaho roared, in the Senate or – less often – in Idaho, Republicans asked each other the same thing.

Borah, born in the farmland of southern Illinois, lived in Boise 17 years, about half as long as represented Idaho in the Senate. He returned only occasionally in his 33 Senate years to stay at the Owyhee Hotel in Boise and be driven around – Borah didn't drive a car – by a friend, Boise merchant C.C. Anderson.

When the only strong Democratic opponent he ever had, Democrat Ben Ross, challenged Borah to say what he had done for Idaho in 30 years, Borah's list was embarrassingly skimpy.

But Ross was demolished. Ousting Borah was inconceivable.

When he arrived in the Boise of 2,000 souls in 1890, just as Idaho became a state, Borah was fleeing a dried-up practice in Lyons, Kansas. He started practice in Boise even before becoming a full-fledged lawyer, he said later, only "one licensed to prey on the public." But Borah became a renowned courtroom lawyer.

He was a Republican by affiliation and, some said, a Democrat by inclination. He resisted joining the Silver Republicans or the Progressive Party, whose founder, Teddy Roosevelt, was an idol and mentor of Borah's. (These Progressives – a personality cult built around T.R. – were different from the Progressive Party founded by the LaFollettes of Wisconsin in the twenties, and from the Progressives of the forties, led by Henry Wallace and Glen Taylor.) But in 1940, convinced FDR wouldn't run again, he planned to support a liberal Democrat, Montana Sen. Burton Wheeler, for president; Borah died before the campaign started. The party system, he said, was "the vice of democracy."

He rose to international fame on the Senate Foreign Relations Committee. During the Hoover Administration, it was said, a European news organization once cabled its Washington reporter: "Never mind Hoover statement, rush comment from Borah." With some exceptions (he fought for diplomatic ties with the Soviet Union in 1933) he was the Senate's premier isolationist. "I want no alliances, no leagues, no entanglements," he said less than two months before the United States entered World War I. "What this passion-torn world needs and will need are not more leagues and alliances but a great, untrammeled, courageous neutral power ..."

Not all this was popular in Idaho, though isolationism was. But Borah was a special case. So legendary had he become that Idahoans could not conceive of unseating him. Years would pass between visits to Idaho; his reputation was so strong he got away with it. Borah was a creation of not his party but of himself.

Mainstream Republicans

He did not remake Idaho politics as like-minded liberal Republicans elsewhere (such as Wisconsin's LaFollettes) did. He left no political legacy when he died in 1940; his Senate seat was taken over by a conservative Republican. (Borah's indirect legacy was Frank Church.) He could have led Idaho Republicans but never did. After his early career he stayed away from the Republican Party organization.

The founder of the modern Idaho Republican Party was less well known but more intriguing. Frank Gooding was a deeply conservative governor and a senator, a shaper of Idaho's banking and sheep industries; both a county and a city (in the Magic Valley) were named for him. Frank Gooding's was a fierce and abrasive, sometimes off-putting, personality. Ripley's Believe-It-Or-Not, take note: Born in England, he was elected state senator in 1898, state GOP chairman for four years and governor in 1904 and 1906, all before he became a United States citizen. He did correct that oversight by the time he was elected to the U.S. Senate in 1920.

Gooding had a keen mind for organization and developed a strong campaign structure while he was governor. When he chose not to run again in 1908 he was able to hand over state government to a close ally, fellow Republican James Brady. His grip on the party was so strong he could have blocked Borah's first Senate win in 1907. (Senators were elected by state legislatures then.) And for a time he was of a mind to.

Just how strained was Borah's and Gooding's relationship was hinted at in a nasty little battle between them in 1906, apparently overlooked by Borah's biographers. The Boise *Capital News* was a Republican paper but anti-Gooding, and Gooding sued it for libel. According to trial testimony, Borah had bankrolled the paper's manager, R.S. Sheridan, allowing him to keep control of the News and continue attacking Gooding. The weekly *Boise Citizen*, gleefully reporting this in December 1906, remarked that "to bring the Brady-Gooding machine into disrepute was the political salvation of Borah. It rallied to his standard all those who desired to free the Republican Party from the domination of the two men who use it for their own purposes."

Cooler middlemen, including Magic Valley businessman John Thomas, mediated the war. Gooding relented in his opposition to Borah and let him go off to the U.S. Senate. It was a wise move: it got Borah off Gooding's back in Idaho.[56]

In January 1918, Republican Brady died. He was then a U.S. senator, having inherited the machine Gooding built when he was governor. Democrat Moses Alexander was governor at the time, and he frustrated the Republicans by appointing popular Democrat John Nugent to the Senate. Gooding regrouped his old forces and ran for the seat in 1918 but, drawing on support from progressives, the radical Non- Partisan League, and others, Nugent beat him.

Gooding declared war on Nugent and the League, which had also supported Borah. The shrewd former governor first kept the foreign affairs-minded senator off his back. Then he sought out help from an old aide, Rexburg businessman and then-state Sen. Lloyd Adams from Rexburg.

The Machine

Adams, like Democrat Tom Boise, was a classic backroom politico, a power player for more than 50 years, perhaps the most influential individual in Idaho's political history.

In 1918 he won a single term as state senator from Madison County. But his clout didn't come from that. Born in Nephi, Utah, in 1885, he grew up working on weekly newspapers and came to Idaho as a printer for the *Fremont County News* in St. Anthony. He edited the *Sugar City Times* and later owned the *Rexburg Standard*. Often identified in later years as a Rexburg attorney, he did not become one until 1933. His was one of the strangest applications the Idaho State Bar Association ever saw, for Adams never attended high school or college.

Many knew him as a lobbyist – the best in Idaho – for First Security Bank, Union Pacific, Utah Power and Light and other moneyed interests. He seldom visited the Statehouse, but worked out of suites in the Boise Hotel and Owyhee Plaza. Some thought him sinister, a spider who spun an iron-clad web around Idaho.

He was not taken lightly. Rexburg newspaperman John Porter recalled his father's advice at a time when John negotiated with Adams about buying Adams' newspaper. Adams and the Porters were close

---

[56] In his superb book *Big Trouble*, about the Haywood trial, author J. Anthony Lukas threw some new light on Gooding's role in Borah's election. He writes on page 292, "Even a loner like Borah had to make some political accommodations. In 1904 he and Frank Gooding, though they never got along either personally or politically, struck a deal: he'd support Gooding for the governorship that year and Gooding would back him for the Senate two years later. But at the Republican convention in August 1906, Gooding tried to welch on the deal, hoping to put the Republican state chairman, James H. Brady – or even Judge James H. Beatty of the federal bench – in the job instead. After two days of 'battle ax and tomahawk,' Borah rallied his forces, beat back the challenge, and received the convention's nomination for senator ...".

friends and often worked together. But the elder Porter warned, "Listen, I want you to know this (about Adams). You're talking to the shrewdest man that there is in the state of Idaho. He can convince you of anything. So you be careful."

Richard Egbert – *He wrote the governors' State of the State messages for them. He was very articulate for them, you know.*

He just sits there with that smile ... A perfect fixer. He did a little real estate. And he was a defense attorney; he would get you out of any kind of problem. He did it the smooth way.

Then, he had money for entertaining. Or if you needed housing, he'd say – he'd say this to freshman legislators – "Do you know where you're going to stay when you get to Boise? How are you fixed for housing?" This sort of thing. He would go over there and get you nice apartments or whatever. We used to get five cents a mile and $5 a day, and that's all you got. It was costly to go over there.

"He was good once a governor was in office and the governor had a legislative agenda," Perry Swisher said. "His agenda couldn't work without Adams. Adams was the guy who, when the chips were down, could chip together the roll call consensus."[57]

At 21 Adams was into regional Republican politics; at 27, a key strategist behind the razor-thin primary win (by 17 votes) of Gov. John Haines in 1912. He engineered creation of what became Madison County and Highway 20, from Idaho Falls to West Yellowstone. He was a secretary for James Brady and signed on with Gooding after Brady died. By 1918, when he beat a popular local Mormon leader for election to the state Senate, Adams was steeped in Idaho politics.

He built what was admiringly or fearfully called the "Gooding Machine"; in the twenties, he was called the chief personnel officer of the Idaho Republican Party. Adams was a pragmatist – he dealt with Democrats, too, and was friendly with them in Rexburg.

John Corlett – *After I got over to the* Statesman *I found out about him and called him up and we got together. And I finally found out that he knew a hell*

---

[57] A story about Adams – reflecting his understanding of human nature – I heard some years after *Paradox* was published, from a relative of his who was pleased to note he had gotten some attention after all these days. The female relation of his, who also lived in the Rexburg area, told me that she was shy as a girl and Adams apparently had made up his mind to do something about it. One day he invited her to accompany him to Boise on one of his political trips. Shortly before lunch, he told her they would be dining with the governor. She was flustered, but agreed to go along. Just after the three sat down to eat, Adams rushed off – a sudden appointment had arisen, he said – leaving her alone with the governor at the restaurant. Whereupon the governor proceeded to display terrible table manners, to the point that clientele in the restaurant took notice. After lunch, Adams picked her up and asked her what she thought of the governor. She told him about the governor's performance at the restaurant, and Adams replied: Remember this. You had lunch with the governor and while he made a fool of himself, *you* did just fine.

of a lot. He really gave me things – gave me columns I'd never get from anyone else. He was just a very astute politician, had people in his pockets.

When Gooding ran for the Senate a second time in 1920, again facing Nugent, he won but ran behind other Republicans in a very Republican year. He took the warning.

In office Gooding, unlike Borah, paid attention to the Idaho Republican Party. For the next decade he, Adams, and a few others ran it and, by extension, Idaho government. In the twenties Idaho elected only Republicans to congressional and statewide offices. Candidates for major office were carefully chosen. Borah aside, the Idaho Republican Party was one shade of conservative.

Splits

Gooding and Adams were not universally loved; no one who attains power ever is. They *were* powerful, and their opponents wondered how long their stranglehold on the Republican Party and on Idaho would last. Adams would retain influence in Idaho for decades, but as the bustling twenties gave way to Great Depression, he faced what would be the first of many reversals.

Gooding died in June 1928 while still in the Senate. Adams got Republican Gov. H.C. Baldridge to fill the vacancy by appointing John Thomas, a Gooding protege involved in the Borah-Gooding deals. Thomas long had been part of the inner circle; when Gooding had left for Washington, he had turned over his banks in the towns of Gooding and Shoshone to Thomas. Later in 1928, Thomas won election to the Senate, campaigning as an incumbent, to the remaining four years of Gooding's term.

During that time the Depression hit and Idaho was turning Democratic. In 1932, battalions of conservative Idaho Republicans, including both veteran U.S. House members from Idaho, were mowed down. Thomas was beaten by Boise Mayor James P. Pope, a New Dealer. (Thomas then moved to California, but his Idaho political career was revived when he was re-appointed – again to the tune of Adams' fast footwork – to replace Senator Borah when he died in 1940. Re- elected to the Senate in 1942, Thomas died in November 1945. This man who had been twice appointed to succeed senators who died in office, also died in office.)

Idaho Republicans had to struggle during the Depression. Some moderated. Others stayed conservative, biding time until the right moment. The party developed an open split that would not heal for decades.

The signs of disarray were easy to read.

In 1944 Bill Detweiler, a Hazelton farmer and legislator outraged at Lloyd Adams' manipulations, ran for the Republican nomination for governor. Detweiler was a budget conservative but favored expanding

Idaho's higher education, and – in contrast to many conservatives – supported school district consolidation. Adams did his best to beat him and failed; Detweiler got the nomination. Rather than support the GOP nominee, Adams then backed conservative Democrat Charles Gossett, who won the election.

A year later, in 1945, John Thomas' death opened a U.S. Senate seat again. Following Adams' advice, Gossett resigned as governor and had his Democratic lieutenant governor, Arnold Williams, appoint him to the Senate. It was a carefully orchestrated move.

John Corlett – *Gossett was waiting for all the letters and telephone calls to come in and add them up about whether he should be the one or [Weiser attorney George] Donart. After he got them all added – I was in there at the time, adding them up – that was enough for him. Lloyd Adams was pushing him on the thing. I don't know if Lloyd was looking ahead to think, well, we can get rid of him somehow. Lloyd was a Republican but he was quite friendly with Democrats.*

Adams was used to working with those who should have been his political rivals; Ross once said he got 60 percent of his ideas from Adams. Adams was even closer to the conservative Gossett, who once hid Adams in a closet in his office when a couple of reporters dropped in, to avoid the scandal of their seeing his Republican advisor. Adams probably was even closer to Williams, who like Adams was from Rexburg and who would become the first Mormon governor in Idaho's history on Gossett's resignation. The prime builder of Idaho's Republican organization carefully built ties to Democratic governors, giving them sound advice on how to stay out of trouble. "And as a result," Porter recalled, "he would get a lot of help."

But Adams was capable of great subtlety, and his motives for pushing Gossett into the Senate were never clear. Porter figured Adams was a genuine Gossett enthusiast; others suspected Adams intentionally engineered Gossett's political suicide. Gossett was one of the most conservative of Democrats; in the thirties he led the legislature's "economy bloc" which often squabbled with Ross. He was a popular governor and might have won another term. But voters rebelled at his self-appointment to the Senate and ousted him in the Democratic primary. Williams, the new governor, was not only the perpetrator of the Gossett appointment but a Mormon and an ally of Glen Taylor, who campaigned against Gossett in the Democratic Senate primary. (Gossett lost that primary.)

So 1946 was a banner year for Republicans. For governor, voters elected moderate St. Maries physician Dr. C.A. Robins, who easily beat Williams. Republicans took back the long-Democratic first congressional district seat and overwhelmed Democrats in the Legislature. Henry Dworshak, a newspaper publisher from Burley originally backed by a strong little local machine led by businessman Roscoe Rich and propelled into the U.S. House by Adams, was elected to the Senate to replace Gossett. (Once very conservative, Dworshak moderated with the years.)

But a closer look showed how weak the Republicans still were.

First, 1946 was a strong Republican year nationally, a year of reaction to 14 Democratic years of depression and war. In Idaho during the forties, presidential election years were Democratic and off-years were Republican. In 1948, the Democrats rose again.

Second, Dworshak's tenure was short. In 1948 he was beaten for re-election by Democrat Bert Miller, a former attorney general and state Supreme Court justice who was then so aged and infirm – and incapable of hard campaigning – that he lived less than a year after his 1948 election to the Senate. (Dworshak then was appointed by Robins to replace Miller.)

Third, Robins was not the choice of the Republican party organization. He had been drafted into the race by a batch of Republican and some Democratic legislators. As he had with Detweiler in 1944, Adams now opposed Robins. And when Robins became governor Adams was on the outs with his party's leader.

Robins and the lively 1947 Legislature brought Idaho government into the mid- twentieth century. They did much more substantial work than Ross and the Democrats had: Robins made lasting changes in the structure of state government. It was a far cry from the old-line conservative agenda.

Robert Smylie – *I would rank [Robins] as certainly in the top three governors in the state's history by what was accomplished in those four years – much more productive in four years than Ross was in six, in terms of actual accomplishment. The whole school reorganization thing – we started the Robins Administration with 1,291 school districts and ended with 119. That by itself is monumental. The first effective liquor law enforcement, the first appropriation to the public school fund. Almost a complete rewrite of the workman's compensation act. They reorganized education so that Lewiston and Albion became colleges of education. Pocatello had a substantial increase: the Southern branch of the University [of Idaho] became Idaho State College ... So I give him pretty good marks, confessing to being a little partisan in my viewpoint, as they say. It was he who set my feet upon the rainbow.*

Adams and the old guard were by now far afield from many of the Republicans who were winning office. He moved still further away when, along with most of the banking community, he supported Thomas Dewey for president in 1948, and Dwight Eisenhower in 1952. Most Idaho Republicans were solid for conservative Ohio Sen. Robert Taft in those years.

So 1946 was not a watershed.

But as the forties drew to a close Idaho turned increasingly conservative. Democrats resurged in 1948; they regained the Idaho Senate, and Compton I. White, Sr., recaptured the first congressional district seat he had held six terms until 1946. And they still had Glen Taylor in the U.S. Senate.

But times were against them. Taylor and, to a degree, White were liberals in an increasingly conservative era.

It showed in reaction to the most important Idaho reform of the forties: the 1947 Legislature's consolidation of nine-tenths of Idaho's school districts. Erwin Schwiebert, a moderate Republican and a Canyon County legislator, recalled "a huge delegation came over (to the Capitol) from Canyon County to fight it. They were concerned about losing control of their schools. And there was an element at that time fed by some of the stuff they were getting on the radio – right wing stuff about how the communists were trying to take over their schools."

Cold War Republicans

In the middle of 1950 President Truman ordered troops into combat in Korea, spy trials dominated Washington, and Wisconsin Sen. Joe McCarthy (up for re-election in 1952 and worried he might lose) had delivered the "205 communists in the State Department" speech that launched his career as the nation's chief red-baiter. What worked in Wisconsin worked even better in Idaho.

One of McCarthy's most ardent Idaho admirers was Republican Payette County state Sen. Herman Welker, who was roused to an energetic U.S. Senate campaign and early on presented himself as a moderate. Welker could be personable and jovial; he was singer Bing Crosby's bird-hunting companion. (He had practiced law in Hollywood and was a friend of actor Wallace Beery and other Hollywood types.) Crosby, who had a vacation home north of Coeur d'Alene, visited Boise to put on an exhibition golf game, pass out Welker brochures, and say that "a vote for Welker and there'll be a pheasant in every pot." Idahoans were dazzled.

But Welker also was inclined – at the slightest provocation – to rip and tear with absolute moral outrage. In 1950 he called Taylor "a vicious desperate weakling who would stop at nothing in order to further the Communist-line path he has been travelling." (Never mind the inherent conflicts of character that would have meant if it were true.) Taylor, so brilliant running against the establishment, seemed at a loss playing defense. He wanted to ignore Welker; when he tried to rebut, his responses were weak and off-base. Taylor was defeated in the Democratic primary; Welker in turn easily beat the Democratic nominee, D. Worth Clark.

Welker became a harsh critic not only of Truman but of Eisenhower; he was close to McCarthy and became his spokesman on key committees. Dworshak, newly- appointed to the Senate, had similar ideas for a while, but he was less flamboyant, uneasy with red-baiting, and less easily led. During his reluctant participation in the

Army-McCarthy hearings he put some sharp questions to a couple of McCarthy's investigators. Louise Shadduck, then a staffer for Dworshak, recalled "he got to probing a little bit too much for Sen. McCarthy, who made some comment about how, had he known he was going to be this way, he would not have appointed him to the committee. Whereupon the senator (Dworshak) jumped right out of his seat and said, 'You had nothing to do with my being on this committee and I want everybody in America to know it.' I don't know the exact wording but it was marvelous, it was worth the whole thing."

When Taylor threatened to overtake Dworshak in 1954, it was Welker who rushed to the rescue with later-discredited McCarthyites who said Taylor was a Communist dupe. But even then gears ground in Washington to censure McCarthy for bullying tactics and for bringing the Senate "into disrepute." A week after the election Welker took to the Senate floor to call McCarthy the greatest living supporter of liberty and charge that censure was unconstitutional. He and Dworshak voted against the Senate censure of McCarthy, but they lost. McCarthy became a recluse and his movement dispersed.

More than that troubled Welker by 1956. He had a blood sugar disorder and was slowly dying – though probably unaware of it then – of a brain tumor which made hash of his mind, speech, and even physical balance. But word spread that he was alcoholic.

John Corlett – *His eyes would get glazed and he would really take off. Just a crazy thing. I don't know if I told you about this water meeting in Idaho Falls. It was in '53 ...*

The Legislature was here [in Boise] and they just let everybody loose to go over to the state water meeting in Idaho Falls with the Army Corps of Engineers and the Bureau of Reclamation discussing water in the Snake. Dworshak and Welker were there. Welker, at the hearing, did very well; he talked about water and so forth. Then they had a luncheon out at the place where INEL is now, and they'd all gone down to lunch. I remember Earl Wright, who was in the Legislature, telling Welker, "Talk about the pioneers, don't talk about Communism, just talk about the water and the Snake River."

We sat down and went through lunch. Dworshak let Welker [give the speech] and Welker got up there and he just – his eyes were just like he was drunker than a skunk. He talked about the Communists in China, about the Communists everywhere, talked just Communists, Communists in the State Department. I never heard anything like it. It was just strange.

When it was all over with I went to Henry and said, "Did Welker have anything to drink?"

He said, "I don't think he could have. He wasn't out of my sight 15 minutes. He went up to his room for something and came right back down."

Welker lost to Frank Church in 1956. The tumor killed him less than a year later, in October 1957.

Welker was the best-known of Idaho's fifties far-rightists, but he was not alone. Dr. John T. Wood, a 72-year-old physician and former mayor of Coeur d'Alene, was also elected in 1950, to the first congressional district seat. Incumbent Compton I. White had left it to run for the Senate.

If Welker played prosecutor, Wood was a prophet of doom. In 1950 he warned that America was "a financial wreck" about to become a "foul fascist state." He predicted the nation would be split into seven districts governed by three-man boards holding dictatorial powers. He said at a rally that "if we do not have a Republican Congress it will probably be the last election of a two-party system." He devoted much of his brief congressional career to getting the United States out of the United Nations.

(Wood was a great example of how extreme converts can be. In 1912, when he was elected mayor of Coeur d'Alene, he led a Socialist city ticket to victory, and flipped sides years later.)

Welker was a powerful speaker; critics hesitated to mix it up with him. That was not true of Wood, whose opponents swung at him as Welker did at Democrats. Wood was "Doc Quack" to Ed Emerine of the *Boise Bench Journal,* who said that "if the people of the First District knew how Doc Wood ran his Washington office, how he wasted money, how he welcomed questionable forces and organizations and let them use his franking privilege, and how he let his prejudices and passions influence his voting, we believe he wouldn't receive a handful of votes in Idaho this fall (1952)."

First district candidates then ran in a vacuum. The district went south to Canyon County but not to Boise. In those days, before the Spokane news media realized Idaho existed, no big city paid attention to Idaho's first congressional district.

Wood won in 1950 over Democrat Gracie Pfost by 783 votes. He lost to her two years later by 591 votes. On the way he survived an energetic primary contest by Caldwell legislator Erwin Schwiebert, the gambling critic and school consolidation backer.

Wood died in Coeur d'Alene on Election Day, 1954. Though he and Welker did not survive the fifties, their conservatism did. It gained power when its adherents went beyond thundering ideas and discovered how to make the political structure work for them.

Jordan Conservatism

In 1950 the Republicans nominated conservatives to all their important races: the two Senate seats, both House seats, and governor. It was a sweeping victory perhaps best symbolized by the man who was the most unlikely big winner of the year.

He was Len Jordan, a Grangeville rancher and businessman. His political experience until then was unimpressive. Jordan was elected to the Idaho House in Republican 1946 and promptly lost his seat two years later. By the time he considered running for governor in 1950, the Republican primary was jam-packed with a lieutenant governor

(Don Whitehead), secretary of state (Cy Price), state safety commissioner (George Vaughn), state liquor dispensary director (Seth Harper) and a wealthy former state GOP chairman (Reilly Atkinson). Jordan had attracted a crowd of conservative friends during his short stay in the Idaho House, but he was unknown by comparison, except among party leaders who knew him as the man who lost a legislative seat in his home county. Lloyd Adams and his crowd backed other people; Adams and Jordan didn't like each other.

Jordan did have rough campaign charm. Many Idaho politicians try to come across as though they have lived a rough life close to the land. Glen Taylor didn't have to fake it, and neither did Len Jordan: he had lived on remote farms and ranches most of his life and spent eight years in the rugged, awe-inspiring isolation of Hell's Canyon, far from civilization.

He also had Boise insurance salesman Bill Campbell, then 30 years old. Campbell recalled meeting Jordan one day in the spring of 1950, in the Owyhee Hotel in Boise. "I'd never met the man before," he said, "but I can tell you I took an immediate liking to him. He looked me right in the eye and he gave me a good, firm, honest handshake. I felt that here was a real man, the kind of man you can look up to, the kind of man you can follow."

Campbell did. Years later he would be renowned as a master campaign tactician and strategist, one of the best in Idaho; Jordan's 1950 campaign was the genesis of that reputation. Campbell was endlessly creative, devising on the fly campaign gimmicks commonplace decades later but unheard of in 1950. Idahoans first saw new-style bumper stickers and store-front displays courtesy that campaign. Even Jordan's inexperience was used well; he was called "the only new face in the race."

In a sense, they took a leaf from Glen Taylor: attract people's attention first, then deliver the message. The combination of that insight and Jordan's sturdy, intelligent and yet homespun nature was a winner. He flew over second- placed Atkinson in the primary and beat Democrat Calvin Wright in the fall.

Jordan proved himself a staunch conservative, starting by slashing the state budgets Robins had expanded.

Robert Smylie — *I don't know who convinced Jordan at the beginning that he didn't have any money and the only thing to do was to hunker down and act as though you were poor. That was a classic budget misjudgement. The money was there.*

He called the elected cabinet — the state treasurer, the auditor, attorney general, superintendent of public instruction, secretary of state - to listen to his budget before he sent it upstairs [to the Legislature]. He told us what it was he was going to do and why he had to do it. What he was obviously inviting, I think, was a vote of confidence. And everybody said, "Well, thank you governor," and left. Didn't get his vote of confidence even from his own elected cabinet. But most of us who had been around knew his revenue figures were about 25 or 30 percent off. And it turns out we were right. He faced the Legislature two years later with a whopping surplus, having killed two colleges.

His budget cut the public school appropriation by a third. At State Hospital North, Jordan's budget paid for one physician for more than 400 mental patients.

But his biggest row came when he proposed closing North Idaho College of Education at Lewiston and the South Idaho College of Education at Albion (NICE and SICE). Aside from being an economy measure, he said, teachers should be educated amidst many disciplines, not just education. The Legislature went along.

SICE was founded in 1892 as Albion State Normal School. It gave teachers a two-year program until 1947, when it expanded to four years. The 40-acre college was Albion's sole claim to distinction and the one beauty spot in town. Albion was and is remote; the college drew in the outside. The college, staff and students, accounted for half of Albion. Jordan's decision did more than take away payroll; it shattered Albion's identity.

Malad rancher and Democrat John Evans was first elected to the Senate in 1952 as an opponent of the closure.

John Evans – *We had a very strong contingent of teachers that had gone from Malad to Albion to school. They came to me on a personal basis, as a group, saying the incumbent state senator [Republican D.P. Jones of Malad] had voted against our school, closed it down, and we want to send somebody over there that will represent us. If you agree to run we'll make sure you're elected. And they did.*

SICE's closure did make economic sense. In 1957 the Church of Christ leased the campus from the state and re-opened it as Magic Christian College, but after 10 years it closed. The land was sold to Albion city for $10. It sits now as a ghost campus.

NICE was located in more populous Lewiston. Early in Idaho's history, nearby Moscow got the state's premier institution, the University of Idaho (part of a deal on locating the capital, the penitentiary, and other goodies). Lewiston, Idaho's first capital, got little, and word of the NICE shutdown was too much. Lewistonians were more outraged than the Albionites. Jordan was hanged in effigy from a tree on the NICE campus. He was pointedly not asked to dedicate a new bridge across the Clearwater River. For months state police advised him to stay away from Lewiston.

In his latter two years, Jordan so opposed tax increases that the state had a $50 million budget and $40 million of tax revenues – leaving the next governor to raise taxes by 25 percent, or about $10 million.

Jordan did some popular things. He led the last lap of the fight against gambling and for private power – Idaho Power – dam construction in Hells Canyon. But he also attracted criticism (which drew his friends closer) and got into squabbles with his attorney general, Robert Smylie. If the political axiom holds that friends come and go but enemies accumulate, Jordan would have had serious trouble winning re-election in 1954.

That point wasn't tested because Idaho law then did not allow a governor to succeed himself. Idaho had two-year governors with no limit on re-election until 1946, when Robins became the first four-year governor. For the previous decade Democrats won in presidential election years and Republicans in off- years. So the Republicans pushed through a change providing four-year terms for state officials, their elections falling on off-years. The trade-off was that governors could serve only a single term.

So who would follow Jordan?

The Smylie Era

Idaho Republicans could vote for Hagerman attorney John Sanborn, an extremely conservative former second district congressman (elected in 1946 and 1948). An intellectual and a friend and neighbor of novelist Vardis Fisher, and in the fifties a supporter of McCarthy, his hard-right ideas would have been more popular in 1950. Sanborn started the race with – apparently – strong backing from Lloyd Adams and other old-liners. (Smylie said later he never figured out who Adams supported in that race.)

They could try for an unknown quantity, conservative Coeur d'Alene Mayor Larry Gardner.

Or they could support moderate Attorney General Smylie.

Smylie was on a fast track. He lived in Idaho while attending the College of Idaho at Caldwell – he had relatives in Caldwell – but left to take his law degree at George Washington University. He returned to Idaho in 1947 as deputy attorney general for AG Robert Ailshie. Ailshie was asthmatic and on the edge of death almost from the day he took office in 1947. He turned over his sensitive work to Smylie, who worked closely with Robins. When Ailshie died in November 1947, Robins appointed Smylie to replace him. Smylie became enamored of Robins' plans for state government, and clashed with a Jordan Administration determined to reverse them.

Smylie won election in his own right in 1950. He was a good campaigner; George Hansen, one of the finest Idaho campaigners ever, said that "Bob Smylie had the best knack of meeting people I ever saw." Smylie also showed a knack for handling touchy issues and finding centrist positions. The closed colleges, for example, was a hard issue. Sanborn said they should not be reopened. Smylie suggested putting their future on the ballot. That put the colleges on hold at least two years, but it got him into less hot water. Smylie did propose spending $5 million more – big money then – on public schools.

Robert Smylie – *That was foolhardy, according to John [Sanborn]. Well, John didn't catch on.*

Then the establishment people switched horses in midstream. I think he [Sanborn] didn't have the energy left. This was a campaign that started in March. I was only 39 years old. I had lots of stuff to burn and I kept busy; the primary was in August. Poor Sanborn was trying to drive his own car around the state, calling people, the old fashioned type of campaign that was real fast going out of style. The primary campaign was the first time television was ever used [in Idaho]. And I used it, in little five-minute ad-lib, straight-on shots. It was enough of an oddity that you could get people to watch whatever it was. They wouldn't turn the program off because it bored them, which they would now.

Then they [party leaders] switched to Gardner.

... They pulled out most of the stops. They tried to shut off the money and did everything in the book.

We're now talking about stupendous sums, like $25,000 [for a campaign]. It mostly came in $100 bundles from a lot of people. We ended up just about $4,000 short at the end of the primary campaign. When you win a primary election that's contested, the money you get in the morning after the election is amazing. It's all postmarked the day before, of course, people rushing around trying to account for their bets - like [Idaho Power President] Tom Roach came around headquarters and left $500 three days before the primary. Well, you could not possibly have profitably spent it then.

Smylie got 41 percent in that primary; the conservatives' eyes were glued to Democrat Glen Taylor, not to the governorship.

If Smylie was to become a strong force in the party, he had to put his own people in charge and bring others into his camp. This he did, with breathtaking skill. The GOP convention followed the August primary by about a couple of weeks. In that time the Idaho Republican Party was radically changed, its leadership turned from conservative ideologues to moderate pragmatists. Dworshak, the other big primary winner, accepted Smylie's state chairman choice: an old ally, Wallace Burns of Idaho Falls. Votes to install him were rounded up fast enough to pre-empt the field.

So began the Smylie network and domination of the party that would last 10 years. Political patronage was eroded during that time, but Smylie used it skillfully where it existed. He kept close watch on party machinery, and unlike Jordan and Robins got along with the old guard, including Lloyd Adams.

Smylie's only problem was the constitutional ban on governor's re-election. The story of how he overcame it is one of the most complex bits of behind-the-scenes politics in Idaho history, and a masterwork of maneuvering by Lloyd Adams and Tom Boise.

The basic deal was that Democratic votes for the constitutional succession amendment were the payoff for reopening the Lewiston college. Beyond that, stories differ. Bill Hall recalled Adams once telling him how Smylie complained to Adams that the one-term rule would kill his career, and Adams taking it on as a challenge. In this version, Adams collected $10,000 from Boise high rollers and gave it to Tom Boise, who passed it through his machine, which in turn got enough Democrats to switch sides.[58]

John Porter of Rexburg, a former Senate secretary, was at the capital when Boise grabbed him and asked him to talk with a Democratic legislator and make sure of his vote. Then - enough votes secured - Adams and Boise brought it to a floor vote before anyone could react. Porter was dispatched to the print shop where he slipped a $20 bill to a printer to get the legislation out early. That afternoon, Democrats were surprised to find it on their desks and up for a vote – where it passed.

"Everybody that was in on that deal thinks they did it all," Porter said. "I think the whole deal was planned and organized by Lloyd Adams and Tom Boise."

Smylie's resulting re-election didn't come from wildly massive popularity. Elected four times to statewide office, he never got as much as 55 percent of the vote in a general election.

But Smylie was a skillful administrator and politician; he was so good that when he had to raise taxes $10 million in his first year, he was able to pass it off as a conservative measure. He had a knack, as Lloyd Adams did, for reading human nature.

"I've seen him when he was walking up the wall and across the top of the ceiling mad about something," Don Loveland recalled. But "when everybody had their say, before you opened the door you all shook hands and it was over. I've always appreciated that about Smylie. If he lost, he'd shed it; it wasn't personal."

The LDS District

Hamer Budge, like the two second district congressmen before him – John Sanborn and Henry Dworshak – was a conservative intellectual, low-key, dignified, more shy than a politician ought to be. He did not like to campaign.

Budge was a state senator from Ada County when it was all in the second district; that plus his Mormon heritage and family ties to Southeast Idaho put him in good stead for a congressional race. He was swept into Congress in 1950 with other conservatives; the district's Republicanism kept him there five terms.

By 1960 a little-known Blackfoot Democrat named Ralph Harding got the nomination without opposition. Harding's credential was winning in 1954 a term in the Idaho House from Oneida County. (He learned campaigning from then- freshman Sen. John Evans.) Harding turned out to be energetic and capable, the strongest opponent Budge had faced. He went on overdrive against an entrenched incumbent who didn't take him seriously.

---

[58] There are many stories told about the maneuvering involved. Smylie himself told a rather different one in his autobiography, *Governor Smylie Remembers.*

Power in Washington cuts both ways back home, as Frank Church among others knew. Budge was a rock-solid conservative who butted heads with the House Democratic majority. Church advised Harding that the powerful Rules Committee, on which Budge served, "has been the bottle neck which has prevented such major legislation as federal aid for school contruction, the housing bill and the wage and hour bill from being enacted." He pointed out that the *Washington Post* had described Budge as one of "six willful House members" blocking the bill.

Richard Hendricks – *[Budge] was a short man, brilliant and really warm and enjoyable to be around. But when it came to campaigning?*

He said, "Richard, I need a hair cut." I said okay, so we went down to the barber shop. That was in the days when you had 10 or 12 barbers in a town like Preston, where now you've got one or two. This barber shop had three barbers in it and they all had people in their chairs, and there were four or five people waiting, and he and I walked in. He just walked in and sat down. Now of all the places in the world to meet people and shake hands and say who you are, where could have been better? They were all sitting there quietly, really wanting to say something to him but not knowing how. All he had to do was say, "Gentlemen, I'm Hamer Budge," and everybody would have yelled, "Hi, Hamer," because everybody liked him. He was a marvelous man, really qualified, probably the best congressman I have known in my 40 years in politics ...

That night he got a phone call about a news story that would kill his career. Washington columnist Drew Pearson tossed into his October 16 column a two-sentence item saying that "Budge ordered the ward teachers, who are supposed to visit every Mormon family once a month, to stay away from his home."

Hendricks was stunned. "To kick them out is akin to - death. I mean, no matter whether you like them or not, you've got to let them come. You're their responsibility." He was convinced the report wasn't true, that Budge "was too much of a gentleman – he wouldn't have kicked them out if they had been any religion ... But those two things went through Southeast Idaho like brushfire through grass."

While Budge tried to rebut, copies of the column mysteriously flooded the district (carried, it was said, by AFL-CIO organizers). In the 24 hours after word of the column came to Idaho, its substance was spread on the telephone trees of the Mormon Relief Society and ward-level LDS Church structure. Budge was wiped out overnight and Harding, a Mormon with no spots on him, won. It was still close; Harding got 51 percent.

Church and Birch

The Budge race could be taken as evidence that the Church of Jesus Christ of Latter-Day Saints is neither Republican nor

Democratic. Its distant Idaho history is bipartisan, even tending
Democratic, since the early Mormon-baiters were Republican. But
increasingly through the latter half of this century, the Republican
Party has been powerful where the Mormon Church is.

Founder Joseph Smith proclaimed "we will be influenced by no
party considerations ... But we shall go for our tried friends, and the
cause of human liberty, which is the cause of God."

Mormons are taught that people have the right of "ree agency," the
duty to make independent decisions, but also adherence to the
authorities of the church.

That is why Ezra Taft Benson, long before he became president of
the Mormon church, threw such a curve into Idaho politics.

Church President David O. MacKay, called "the missionary
president" because of the church's growth during his years, was a
political moderate who tried to steer the church from political battles.
That became harder after 1961 when Benson, a native of the Idaho
farm town of Whitney, ended eight years as secretary of agriculture for
Eisenhower. Benson had been, for about 19 years, a member of the
Council of Twelve, the highest governing body of the church, just
below the president in authority.

After his return to Salt Lake in 1961, Benson drifted into alliance
with the John Birch Society; his son Reed was a regional coordinator
for it. The JBS was founded in 1958 by Robert Welch, a candy
manufacturer who said American government was overrun by
communists. His peak of publicity came with publication of his book
The Politician, which said Eisenhower was "a dedicated, conscious agent
of the Communist conspiracy."

By the early sixties the Society had pockets of support in Eastern
Idaho, Canyon and Ada Counties, in large swatches of Northern
Idaho. F.G. "Bill" Barlow and his son Rusty, both of Pocatello and
active in local politics in the seventies and eighties, became local
leaders. Leaders described the JBS as an educational organization, but
it left an imprint on politics. In fact, although it was most visible group
on the right, it was too small to have great impact by itself. George
Hansen, later a congressman, recalled that the Farm Bureau then was
also busy promoting anti-communist films and literature, and Cleon
Skousen, who founded the conservative Freedom Institute in Utah,
was active and winning adherents. Together, they helped create a very
conservative voting community in Idaho. It was the beginning of the
fabled "Hansen hard core."

But the JBS got most of the attention.

In September 1963 Benson spoke at a Los Angeles dinner for
Welch, whom he called "one of the greatest patriots in American
history." He said the JBS was "the most effective non-church
organization in our fight against creeping socialism and godless
communism." Asked if he agreed with Welch that Eisenhower worked
for the Communist conspiracy, Benson replied: "He supported me in
matters of agriculture. In other areas we had differences." When

Harding picked up his morning paper and read that, he exploded. He marched to the House floor and fired all cannons. He said he loved the church and respected Benson, whom he had known from childhood. But he said Benson was wrong not to defend Eisenhower. "More than the Benson family is involved," he said. "A wrong impression of the Latter-Day Saints Church policy is being given to millions of citizens of this nation and of the world by this lack of judgement and restraint." After all, he said, Benson was often described in news articles as a Mormon leader.

Harding was in line with McKay, who had said in January that "we deplore the presumption of some politicians, especially officers, coordinators and members of the John Birch Society, who undertake to align the church or its leadership with their partisan views. We encourage our members to exercise the right of citizenship, to vote according to their own convictions, but no one should seek or pretend to have our approval of their adherence to any extremist ideologies." Benson was dispatched to Frankfurt, Germany, to head the LDS European mission. During the sixties, JBS membership in many areas of the Rocky Mountains slumped.

But Harding's speech gave him immediate trouble among the LDS faithful who could not handle an attack on a church leader.

In April 1964 Sen. Len Jordan wrote Benson, then in Europe. "Perhaps you are unaware of it," he said, "but it seems to me the controversy emanating from Ralph's intitial speech has resulted in a quasi-church-state free-for-all involving the John Birch Society, the Latter-Day-Saints Church and the two political parties. Wherever it may end, I believe that no good can come of it and that it is a great dissservice to your church. The effect on political affairs is difficult to assess at this time."

Harding's speech split Mormon voters, and Republicans lined up to take him on in 1964. Harding was energetic, did solid constituent service and worked hard. He was a Kennedy loyalist, and that was appreciated by the White House.

But the Right did not forget.

Enter George Hansen

In the fall of 1987, George Hansen spoke of the need to tackle AIDS and to reform prison and justice systems. The poor and unconnected were not getting justice, he said. The Reagan Administration came in for stinging barbs. Once, the press was a gang of liberals out to get him on orders of big-money eastern bosses; now, it was an essential bulwark against too-powerful forces.

This Hansen seemed less attuned to flat-out anti-government ideas and more opposed to authoritarian government of any kind than the one who served in the U.S. House for 14 years. Who set up residence in the right wing of the Republican Party. Who was often deeply in debt and cut deals with twilight fatcats. Who kept some of the biggest deals out of public view – for a while. Who went to prison when they came unraveled.

And yet there was another Hansen, renowned as the progressive young mayor of Alameda, improver of city services, raiser of pay for employees, successful mediator of disputes. He was tall and handsome, the youngest mayor in Idaho and one of the most respected, and he worked painfully hard to wipe out his own job for the good of his city. He was one of a group of creative thinkers around Pocatello in the early sixties who realized the idiocy of having three abutting cities: Pocatello, Alameda – then the ninth largest in Idaho – and Chubbuck. Hansen was the key. Largely because of him Alameda voted, barely, to fold into Pocatello. Chubbuck, lacking such a leader, stayed independent.

In the impossibly complex tale of George Hansen, the most fascinating Idaho politician of the last quarter-century, two threads of consistency run through.

First: However many twists or turns in his story, he was loved or despised. More than anyone since Glen Taylor, Hansen reached to the gut – no compromise, no quarter, no prisoners taken.

Second: However different his tune, Hansen's rhythm stayed on beat. Midway in his congressional career, he would say, "some journalists in Idaho thought I was very moderate and acceptable, and then later they thought I shifted, and they didn't understand." Perhaps not. Hansen has described himself as a "conservative populist," and there's something to that in the way he has identified himself with individual struggles and random causes. But the point stretches only so far: his individual stands – not all "conservative" – cannot be woven into a coherent fabric.

He was born in September 1930 in Tetonia, remote farm country a long way over bad roads from Idaho Falls. Glen Taylor often played here; Driggs, where Taylor heard the Ross speech that started him in politics, was 10 miles south. The Teton Valley had a different effect on Hansen, because he lived there. In 1930 Teton County was three-fourths Mormon – one of the first places in Idaho with so high a percentage – and Hansen grew up in the church. (For a time his bishop was Dick Egbert, a conservative Democrat.) If someone had a problem, folks from the tight-knit church would help. Government was a last resort.

His parents ran a service station-cafe-store-motel and a grain elevator. Hansen was hard at work from an early age; his father died while he was young. Out of the Air Force, he ran a grain elevator in Soda Springs but left for Ricks College in Rexburg where he took degrees in history and Russian. He was a mathematics teacher in Pocatello (his mother and stepfather were teachers), and then drifted into insurance and the Copycat, a print shop in Pocatello. He talked with other businessmen about the future of Alameda and Pocatello, ran for mayor in Alameda and became absorbed. He had found his calling.

He had more ambition, energy, and guts than wherewithal. He may, in 1962, have set an Idaho record running for the most offices in one year. He won a seat on the reorganized – post-merger – Pocatello city commission. Next he ran for the Senate seat held by Democrat Frank Church. Hansen was whupped in the primary by Boise attorney Jack Hawley, who was backed by state Republican organizers and had more money. In July Dworshak died and a Republican convention had to choose a Republican to appear on the ballot in November. Hansen scrambled for convention votes but wound up in fourth place. Finally, Hansen ran for one of Bannock County's three Idaho House seats; Democrats swept past him.

Every time he had run as a Republican, Hansen had lost. In 1964 he wanted to run against Harding, but so did two other Republicans, former state Sen. Dick Smith of Rexburg and Deputy Attorney General Keith Scofield. Both had wider webs of support.

Hansen did the sensible thing. He drove to Soda Springs and walked into the insurance office run by Richard Hendricks.

Hendricks had been around Republican politics a long time. His father, a Franklin County commissioner, suggested Rich run for precinct chairman. Hendricks became a Republican worker for 35 years, holding almost every available job in the party, and by 1960 was a chief strategist on legislative races. That was the year Republicans took the legislature from Democratic control.

Hansen was going to link Benson's backers with his own Mormon ties in Tetonia, Soda Springs, Rexburg, and Pocatello to unite the LDS vote against Harding. But getting on the ballot wouldn't be easy. He needed enough votes from delegates to the state party convention, and Hansen had little support from the Republican organization. (He did get support from John Sanborn, the conservative forties congressman.) Hansen needed Hendricks' help.

Richard Hendricks – *I had originally promised Scofield I would give him my first vote [at the convention]. Then George came to my office in Soda Springs and he sat down and started going through his program. And I perceived in George a stronger winner than in Scofield.*

Scofield was of the Hamer Budge personality: a brilliant boy, excellent thoughts, small of stature, like Hamer Budge. He had been back east in government service, and he was outstanding intellectually. But he didn't have George's salesmanship ...

And with Hendricks' help, Hansen got on the ballot.

They started with little money. But Hansen's opposition had other disabilities. Scofield, Hendricks would recall, was a "three-piece suit. Didn't cut it with the farmers."

Smith, a moderate, had other problems, such as the Hamer Budge ailment of shyness on the stump. Perry Swisher remembered "going to the bank in Twin Falls with (Smith). We walked through the bank on a Friday. There may have been 50 people plus the employees. He walked straight back through the bank to the office, and then walked out. George would have met everybody."

As it was, George Hansen met a lot of Idaho's second district.

Richard Hendricks – *What we did was string and glue ...*
I'd line up breakfast in the morning, and a dinner and supper and an evening meal, and when we got through there we'd go through the bowling alleys and pool halls and wherever we had to go. Just shake hands and move on, shake hands and move on. Because of his imposing size and the fact that he was a salesman - and he likes it - if there are two people there [in a room] he's going to meet them both. He's going to give them a bear hug and the phenomenal thing is that when he comes back, he'll remember. He can remember those people. He's a natural.

If Hansen had any ties to the John Birch Society before 1963, he kept them under wraps. But he and the Idaho JBS became cozy in the winter of 1963-64. Hansen said the Birch cause was honorable and worth a look. At a couple of Birch meetings in Pocatello in March 1964, Hansen and his bother Dean passed out JBS literature.

Hansen said "efforts to link me with controversial organizations, financially or otherwise, are completely unfounded."

Nevertheless, an alliance was there.

In the Wake of Henry Dworshak

No one suspected unpheaval in Idaho politics one Washington afternoon in July 1962 when the four Idahoans in Congress – Senators Dworshak and Church and Representatives Pfost and Harding – sat down for their last lunch together. Dworshak seemed fit, hearty and cheerful. But at home that night, he had a heart attack and died.

His death turned Idaho politics upside down.

It put heat on Smylie, who would appoint a senator to serve until January 1963, and state Republican and Democratic central committees, which would fill the Senate party slots on the November ballot. Smylie so badly wanted to go to the Senate that he had considered running against Church in 1962. Now what?

July 26, 1962
Dear Governor:
Let me put on paper what prompted Monday night's call.
When you announced for governor [rather than Senate] you said you could better serve there. But this emergency did not then exist. If the party through its central committee decided now you could better serve by running for the unexpired Dworshak term, what would you do? The party could well insist. Should.
In respect to your own future, any other choice of candidate will be unsatisfactory. Pick a winner and you preclude your own chances four years hence.

Pick a loser and you "planned it that way" and the party will blame you, not the central committee. Inevitably. This is why you should consider letting the state central committee choose, not the Senate candidate who would thereupon become your liability under any circumstances, but a governor candidate.

Without some solution, two Senate races [in 1962] at the top of the ballot would feature (1) a Republican candidate of less than proven statewide popularity if you are not that candidate; (2) a major campaign invasion on the part of the Kennedy Administration which no one short of a governor could counteract.

You never had a tougher one to call ...
Perry Swisher
Pocatello

And Smylie did struggle with it.

Robert Smylie — *Vernon Smith was running just a shade ahead of me in the last poll we had. I'd have probably figured out some way to appoint myself to the Senate, which would have been relatively easy, if I hadn't thought I'd be handing the Statehouse to Vernon K., which I regarded as an unmitigated disaster. I could have had the judgeship [federal appellate court] if it hadn't been for that.*

Dearly beloved Bill Drevlow [the Democratic lieutenant governor]. How funny that is. Bill asked me not to go to Henry Dworshak's funeral in Washington, which I should have done as a matter of courtesy, simply because, he said, "I do not think I could withstand the pressure to appoint a senator." So I stayed home ...

What I could have done was appoint someone for the interim, taken the nomination for the Senate, and had them nominate a governor. But we were within about nine weeks of the general election ... [Hamer] Budge was the logical choice. Hamer had been chairman of the Rules Committee in Washington, was on the district bench here in Ada County at the time. He didn't decide that he wanted it until it was too late. I think he thought it was inconceivable that I would say I didn't want it.

In the end, Smylie decided to wait until the Republican convention chose a Senate nominee, and then appoint that person.

Smylie's favorite was former state Sen. Raymond White of Boise. George Hansen, who also announced for the Senate nomination, was campaigning against the influence of big business, which was there. Before the convention, a cadre of Boise-Cascade Corp. execs flew to Pocatello to help organize for the main attraction: former Gov. Len Jordan. Jordan, who announced for the nomination a week after Dworshak's death, was back in Boise after serving on an international trade commission. He sent letters declaring for the Senate and promising to run "a vigorous fight." His old friends, especially from the cattle industry and some of the big Boise corporations, swarmed around him. So did some of Budge's.

Jim Goller — *There was a little group that got together and they invited me to the meeting; by then I was getting a little stature, was a good leg man and interested. They talked to Hamer. Would he run? He wouldn't make up his mind*

... By that time there was a group of people lined up behind Len Jordan. But that got to be a bitter convention. Bill Eberle was the chairman of that convention, and it was such a tight vote that he did not announce it [immediately]. They recessed until the roll call was announced, and there were some people changing votes out there on the floor. You had a lot of bitter hollering and confusion. That was a rough one.

Jordan's troops outworked everyone, pulling in helpers like state Sen. Don Samuelson, who turned over votes from the north. Jordan got the convention's nomination; Smylie then appointed him to the Senate.

But the Smylie-Jordan clashes of old resurfaced. In September 1963 Smylie wrote Jordan, "It is now being told around the State that you are leading a faction designed for the purpose of embarrassing me, and of driving me out of public office. In fact it has been said by some of these people that the first real objective is to deny me membership on the delegation to the next National Convention ... Only by disavowing these activities can you prevent a very destructive and debilitating fight."

Jordan shot back that he had heard Smylie was trying to embarrass him, too. But he said he gave the rumors no credence and suggested both of them ignore the whole thing.

To which Smylie replied that he knew of nothing he had done to embarrass Jordan. Friction between them grew. And the conflict grew into a party conflict as well, as Jordan's conservative friends began taking on Smylie more openly.

Their leader was state National Committeewoman (since 1960) Gwen Barnett, a tactician with years of experience and endless contacts. She became the true leader of Idaho's conservative Republicans, working diligently to build their strength around the state, visiting every little hamlet, creating a new organization. Soon Barnett's creation would overtake Smylie's and become the foundation of the conservative Republican organization that would dominate the party in the seventies and eighties.

The test battle was Barry Goldwater's 1964 presidential candidacy. Conservatives wanted to declare for him early; Smylie wanted Idaho uncommitted. Barnett's strength grew as Goldwater got closer to the nomination. That summer National Chairman Dean Burch appointed her to a national GOP post, increasing her Idaho clout. By the time Idaho Republicans held their Pocatello convention in June 1964, she matched Smylie's influence in the party.

During his frequent flights around the country Smylie became a national figure – early in 1966 he was talked up as a possible presidential contender in 1968 – and a friend of Nelson Rockefeller. "I would have preferred Rockefeller," Smylie said, "simply because I could not conceive of Barry Goldwater being president of the United States." He doubted Goldwater could win and to that, he said, even Len Jordan had agreed.

But the convention committed the Idaho delegation to Goldwater and exploded into a Goldwater rally. Morrison-Knudsen Executive Vice President James McClary, the state Goldwater chairman, was elected party treasurer. The Goldwater fight song played on the public address system while supporters marched up and down convention hall. Smylie was left with only shards of the machinery he had run since 1954. His friend Harley Markham was re-elected national committeeman only after a close call. Conservatives rushed in and used their new-found power in the primary election.

As Smylie's control weakened, the new conservative organizers helped George Hansen. He got 38 percent of the Republican primary vote and the nomination for the House. It might not have happened if Smylie had been in charge. But Hansen had the confidence of the people who had seized the moment. He won the general election, ousting Harding with 52 percent of the vote.

Goldwater went down hard nationally. He lost in Idaho by one percent – a better showing than anywhere outside the Deep South or his home state of Arizona.

In Idaho, it foreshadowed what would happen next.

7 | Painful Realignment

Monday morning in Boise[59] after Christmas 1965 was dismal: cloudy, windy, freezing. Snow had fallen hard and drivers slipped their way to work. They bundled up and tuned their radios to KATN-AM for their daily dose of talk show controversy.[60]

"Good morning," said Bob Salter. "Coffee time."

"Good morning, Bob. Say, reading what Smylie has to say and hearing what he has to say, what philosophy do you think he follows? Do you think he is a 'middle of the roader,' 'liberal' or what? Have you had any idea from his utterances?"

Salter's fluid baritone eased into it. "As far as anything, as the term liberal, moderate or conservative or what is concerned, the only thing I have seen in reference to that is, it occurs to me that I have seen a newspaper article which says – I think I have a copy of it somewhere – that Gov. Smylie would like to see the Republican Party get a more liberal image. So that's the only way I know."

The caller tried again. "I always thought he had been talking, oh, during the last campaign, about the 'middle of the road' all the time, the middle of the stream, and was talking about so many of the Republicans are out of the main stream. And now here he comes out with an article in the paper and on the evening news where he thinks that anyone who voted for this resolution before the committee, against extremism, anybody who voted for that apparently has to be a liberal Republican."

Salter bit. "Well, I quite agree with you," he said. "I think that there certainly has been a jelling of the political thinking in the U.S. in the last few years, and certainly since the last presidential election ..."

Another caller. "I was wondering – did you read the full-page article in the paper yesterday about the John Birch Society?"

---

[59] The focus of this chapter, as you'll see, is the 1966 campaign – by far the most tumultuous, uproarious, and long-term decisive in Idaho history. I felt in 1988 that all Idaho politics in the 22 years since that time had flowed from that election; and now, 34 years on, I still think so. Not all but many of the roots of Idaho's one-party status in the 90s can be found in the election of 1966. That year even had all kinds of drama attached to it: Two plane crashes, the rise of a new generation of Idaho political leaders, the last hurrah for the old guard, the fundamental wrenching of Idaho's political parties from where they were, to where they have been ever since. This election years merits a book all by itself. And that's why it's the longest chapter in this one.
[60] Salter is long gone, and when this section was originally written, talk radio seemed an antiquity as a serious driver of politics. Now, of course, things have changed back: not only Rush Limbaugh but also a number of local radio talk show hosts have had political impact in recent years.

It was an ad on page 5-D of the Idaho Statesman under the headline "What is the John Birch Society? The truth may surprise you," a lengthy essay written by group leaders giving their side.

Salter told her he saw it. "I wonder if Gov. Smylie read it?"

Conservatives and JBS members had been on Smylie's case since 1964, and Smylie hit back. In mid-December he asked the Republican Coordinating Committee – which wrestled with policy issues – to condemn the Society. The panel, including Smylie and future President Gerald Ford, urged Republicans not to join extremist groups. That prompted a JBS spokesman to say the committee hadn't specifically meant the Society. Smylie said it most certainly had. Then boxcars of mail, some threatening, some calling Smylie a fool or worse, flooded the governor's office.

The first letter had come from Ezra Taft Benson, who delivered a ringing defense of the JBS. "In my humble judgment," he wrote, "any attempt to ride these fine Americans out of the Republican Party could lead toward political suicide while plumbing the depths of demagoguery. It is estimated that 40 percent of the membership of the John Birch Society are Democrats. We should be trying to convert this 40 percent to our side, rather than ejecting the 60 percent who are already with us."

The letter didn't go public. It didn't have to. People knew where Benson and Smylie stood and what had happened to the last Idaho politician – Ralph Harding – who shot so hard at the JBS. The extremely conservative Salter knew, and so did his listeners.

"I think this was very true, that many people probably do join the John Birch Society because they are so concerned. And really, what else can we join?" the woman told Salter.

"Well, there you go," Salter replied. "You asked a question that I can't answer."

On the Run

Smylie was then starting his twelfth year as governor – twice as long as anyone had governed Idaho before – as the dean of governors, a national political figure. There was, critics said, an arrogance about Smylie; he had lost touch, thought the governorship was his by divine right. The critics were not conservatives only. Some were from isolated rural places. Their unrest was vague, real but hard to quantify.

A few saw it. Allan Shepard, then attorney general, was one. "I don't recall that I saw a great change in (party) personnel," he said. "But it's my impression there was a change in the thinking." It had to do with party leadership, and some disenchantment with Smylie, he felt.

Don Samuelson saw it too.

In years ahead people would savage him. He was playing with a deck of fifty-one, they said. But Samuelson was one of the first to see

Smylie's troubles clearly. And he had a hard time – in retrospect, an incredibly hard time – getting others to see it.

Samuelson had spent two years of World War II at the Lake Farragut Navy training installation near Coeur d'Alene. He so loved it that in 1946 he quit the Davenport, Iowa fire department to return and start the Pend D'Oreille Sport Shop in Sandpoint and become a gunsmith. "I knew probably every family in Bonner County because not just dad had the rifle, it was mom and dad and all the kids had rifles and pistols and shotguns – practically every family in the county. So I knew a lot of people and they knew me, and I ran a good, successful business." He led hunter safety classes and the local Idaho Wildlife Federation district.

Samuelson ran for the Idaho House in a Democratic year, 1958. Friends said he could win as a Democrat; Samuelson said no, he wouldn't run under that banner, that he didn't believe in their ideas. He lost. But people liked his earnest, stolid nature and in 1960 he beat an incumbent Democratic senator.

He joined a new GOP Senate majority as one of only two Republican senators – the other was Watt Prather of Bonners Ferry, later a district judge – from the north. GOP leaders needed them all, since the Senate had 23 Republicans and 21 Democrats.

Don Samuelson – *That's how I got on the Finance Committee right off the bat. I said hey, I came down here to really get involved in something, and I want on the Finance Committee. These old guys from South Idaho, Tom Heath [of Preston] and K.C. Barlow [of Burley], said, "No way are we going to put a freshman on the Finance Committee."*

I said, "Hey, look, I came down here this year and if I'm going to come back I've got to be on some kind of meaningful committee, something besides the Aviation Committee or some crappy little committee. If you don't put me on that [Finance] I'm going to raise hell with you guys from here on."

The day before the committee appointments were made, I think it was Barlow that came over to me and he said, "Don, we're going to put you on there but by God you do what we tell you to do." And I just said, "Thanks." They never told me anything after that. I did what I thought was honest and right.

Samuelson would not have been branded most likely to succeed. Fellow senator Dick Egbert recalled "he never learned how to stand on the floor and properly word a motion. He'd stand up and you never knew what was going to come out."

He had some advantages. In 1960 he sold his sport and rock shop – Samuelson was a dedicated rockhound; his house in Sandpoint was made of rock – to start selling and leasing mining and logging equipment. In the next six years traveling around Idaho, he made an impressive number of contacts and heard thousands of people talk politics. What established politicians and newsmen little suspected came through: Smylie could not be re-elected.

The end of 1965 was an ideal time to reach that conclusion. Smylie was in a hissing match with the John Birch Society then. But heavier than that was the sales tax.

Smylie long opposed the sales tax. But in January 1965 he changed his mind, the Legislature passed it, and he signed it. A referendum to give the voters their say went on the November 1966 ballot. To Sen. Perry Swisher, the bill's guide and guardian on the Senate floor, if no gubernatorial candidate defended the tax it might die, though no one knew if it would help Smylie or eat him alive. But the sales tax issue increased the decibel level of debate over whether Smylie should get 16 years in office.

Don Samuelson – *I had nothing against Bob Smylie. I've worked with him and I like to say I've probably got half a dozen letters [from him] here in my file commending me for things I'd done while I was in the Senate. [But] if somebody doesn't run in the primary and give people a chance, he's going to get beat in the general.*

Samuelson personally asked Shepard, House Speaker (later Secretary of State) Pete Cenarrusa, and Senate President pro tem (later Lieutenant Governor) Jack Murphy to run, figuring someone better known than he would run better. They all said no, for various reasons. Shepard didn't want to run against Smylie, who had given him his first job as a lawyer in 1951 in the Idaho attorney general's office, and felt the timing was bad for him personally. In hindsight, any of them probably could have become governor that year simply by saying yes.

As Samuelson finally did.

On January 10 Smylie received a letter from him. "Dear Gov. Smylie: During the past two years I have been asked many times to consider running for the position of Congressman from the first district, or Governor of the state. I have given a lot of thought to this, and what part my past experience could offer to Idaho's future. I believe very strongly in our free enterprise system and would like to have a part in trying to preserve some of the freedoms that you and I have enjoyed for our children and grandchildren." He was running for governor, he said, and closed with the ironic question: "Will you help me?"

When Samuelson announced for governor he proposed a constitutional amendment to let voters set a tax ceiling. He said both Smylie and Democrat Cecil Andrus "want to do our thinking for us" on the sales tax. His was undiluted conservatism, and GOP conservative Gwen Barnett, the national committeewoman who had become a power in the party, helped focus his campaign and bring to it the Goldwater forces. Samuelson didn't need to build an organization, although he did; the organization came to him.

Samuelson, not a gifted orator, met mainly in small groups, where he came across better. He set up county organizations along the lines of (and overlapping) Barnett's. He used Smylie's overconfidence and kept a low profile: Samuelson had one billboard, on Capitol Boulevard in Boise, that primary campaign.

And Smylie didn't take him seriously. His readings showed the sales tax would pass on the ballot. He had beaten opponents more formidable than Samuelson. And he was nationally recognized; in 1964, he had been talked up as a running mate for Nelson Rockefeller, and now the national press was listing him as a presidential possibility for 1968. Why worry about Samuelson?

But there were signs in the months ahead he might have heeded.

A Crash and a Phoenix

February 2 dawned cool and sunny at the Boise airport. John Mattmiller walked to his Piper Comanche and guided his friend William Lloyd, a Boise realtor, aboard. Lloyd was hitching a ride to Northern Idaho. Mattmiller, a realtor, was headed home, to Kellogg, from Washington, a place he planned to make home.

He was returning from a Republican candidate training session, prepping for another run for Congress. In 1964 he had gotten what everyone thought was a worthless Republican nomination against the incumbent Democrat, Compton White, Jr. But Mattmiller almost beat him. Since then the district had been reapportioned to include the biggest county in the state, Republican Ada, and if Mattmiller did as well in the old district in 1966, which was shaping up as a Republican year, the seat was his.

Mattmiller was a controversial businessman – a quick, sharp operator – and conservative enough to block challenges from state Sen. Jim McClure of Payette, who had thought of running, and Boise attorney Jack Hawley, who had lost the 1962 Senate race to Frank Church. Moderate Erwin Schwiebert of Caldwell, who ran in 1952, 1954, and 1962 to no avail, was lukewarm about a fourth try. Mattmiller had money and fine operatives, like campaign coordinator and Boise businessman Jim Goller. Goller had been around Idaho politics since the mid-forties, working with state Republicans. He had helped with Republican Dick Smith's losing campaign for the second district congressional seat in 1962, learned from it, and wanted to run a campaign himself.

Jim Goller – *Mattmiller was a crazy man. And you probably have to define that term. Mattmiller was an absolute honest to God war hero. He became a frog man, worked over in China, swam underwater and planted explosives on Japanese ships ... When I say "crazy" I've got to put it in quotes, but a guy that's willing to put on a wet suit and swim underwater up to Japanese ships and put explosives on it – well, he liked the excitement of the race.*

... He went over to Arco one time; it wasn't in his district but they had a big rally and wanted him over there. The lights were out at the airport. A bunch of

people with cars dropped by the airport, turned their car lights on so he could see the runway and set the plane down. He was that kind of guy.

Now in February, Mattmiller barreled into overcast Northern Idaho, trying to land in the tricky Shoshone County Airport at Smelterville, a narrow sliver of Silver Valley east of Kellogg. He dipped below the clouds and flew barely above U.S. 10, a twisting road with one straight stretch. Just outside Smelterville a truck rolled into view. Mattmiller pulled up and snagged the plane in power lines, swung it around and smashed it against the bank of the Coeur d'Alene River. He and Lloyd died on impact.

People who saw it said it was a spectacular crash.

So, too, was its effect on Idaho politics.

Schwiebert now wanted in. So did Robert Purcell, a manager of the Caldwell and Lewiston chambers of commerce. McClure announced March 10. (His announcement press release made him sound like a moderate. He complained about spending for Job Corps programs and a centennial celebration in Alaska but added, "While money is being spent in this manner, Mountain Home Air Force Base schools face closure because of withdrawal of funds.") There was talk too of Bill Campbell, Len Jordan's campaign manager, and Hawley.

Jim Goller – *McClure said, "If any of those people want to run they could do better than I, and if they don't run I'm very serious about running." And I said, we ought to go around and see them. [State Sen. and future federal Judge] Hal Ryan was with him and I said, "You guys go around – but I'd be positive, Jim, and say, 'it's time for one of us to announce. If you'll announce, I'm not going to'."*

He came back and said one of them hedged.

I said, they'll hedge the next time you go around [too].

He said, well, let me think about it.

And I said, meantime, I'll type up an announcement. I typed up the announcement, had it all ready to go. And he said, let's do it, and I dumped them in the mail.

Later, Schwiebert would recall the day he knew running would be futile. He had flown from Idaho Falls and was taxiing up to the Boise air terminal when he looked out the window and saw McClure strolling with party leaders to a plane bound for a Republican dinner in the north. It was over, Schwiebert thought. And it was.

That left Purcell, and conservatives aimed their guns at him.

After Purcell decided to run but before he announced, he visited Smylie to let him know: a normal courtesy. But Purcell stepped out of the office into a nest of reporters, mysteriously tipped that he was meeting with the governor. Purcell was tagged as Smylie's candidate. For Smylie, the incident – suggesting a disadvantage in being "Smylie's candidate" – and the support McClure got should have alerted him to the storm ahead.

On March 21 Smylie wrote McClure, Purcell, Hawley, and Schwiebert pleading for peace. He complained about "factional practices which have slowly eroded our party strength over the past two years." He said he played no favorites and "who paid a courtesy call on whom is unimportant." The first district could be had, he said. "It would be grievous indeed if that last clear chance (to win) is lost simply because the factionalists refuse to take advantage of the opportunity to win."

It boiled down to McClure against Purcell. McClure sewed up the race early on – another warning flare for Smylie.

Finally Smylie and his backers saw the Samuelson threat. The last week before the primary election they saturated the state with newspaper and television ads. It was too little, too late.

The Democratic Split

Many Democrats were convinced they could have beaten Smylie in 1958 and 1962 had they not nominated pro-gambling candidates. Now that the gambling forces seemed routed, should they run a conservative, as Tom Boise urged, a harvester of moderate Republicans, or a liberal closer to the party's future?

The opening moves were played out in the 1965 state Senate when Andrus, a star of the liberal wing, tried to wrest the Democratic floor leadership from Bill Dee, who led the conservatives.

Dee outshined him. He was a Grangeville attorney, a former lobbyist who had known the legislature well before Andrus had even considered running for it. He was an effective speaker and skillful floor leader, with an air of reserve and dignity, and a resonant voice. He was a tough caucus leader – good enough to also lead the bipartisan "economy bloc" of low-ball spenders.

"Where they got the conservative image was, in 1963, in order to balance the budget, Bill Dee got the idea we'll just cut every budget in state government five percent," Andrus recalled. "And the budget committee would give their budget recommendation and Bill Dee would stand up and say, 'Mr. President, I move we amend Senate bill such and such,' and it was always that you subtract five percent ... A bunch of them would stand up and vote, and they would be voted down. That's where this – if they were the conservative wing, it was a single issue, single session deal."

But many of the 19 Senate Democrats in 1965, such as Cy Chase of St. Maries, Don Fredericksen of Gooding, Joe Ausich of Mackay, Wayne Tibbitts of Lorenzo (later elected to the House as a Republican), and Dick Egbert of Tetonia were conservative and had conservative constituents to satisfy. Few wanted the sales tax, the big issue that year. The sales tax drew together moderate/liberals of both parties and conservatives of both parties.

But beyond that Andrus was alienated from the power structure led by Tom Boise.

Cecil Andrus – *Tom Boise was considered to be the patriarch of the Democratic Party from the North. He was an influence peddler, is all he was. He used to take money from the S&H Green Stamps Co. and tried to deliver all the votes [to allow Green Stamps in Idaho]. I voted against S&H Green Stamps. I was saying, don't give green stamps, but lower the price of all the goods four percent, and we'll all be better off. Tom tried to influence me on my vote. I told him I wouldn't vote that way, and he made some rather unkind comments. We kind of drifted apart, you might say. I was a young man and he was an old man, and I was respectful to him in public, but I had him figured for what he was.*

Ed Williams [a Democratic legislator from Lewiston] and I used to talk about it. He used to say, "Well, he beats us, but then we'll outlive him." And we did.

So Andrus developed his own base, sometimes where Democrats seldom reached, including the Boise business community. It would serve him well years later.

When the emotion-soaked 1965 session ended Andrus, then 34, announced for governor. Taking a note from his losing bid for minority leader, Andrus announced early. He toured the state and drafted a detailed program for running state government. He ran such a carefully-planned campaign that it carried him through events that might have killed other politicians.

His campaign was paralleled by Dee's, also running for governor. It was a fine matchup: in an Andrus-Dee faceoff, the party could get a clean settlement.

Tom Boise wouldn't let it happen that way.

Old and ailing now, Boise was dissatisfied. Democrats had a shot at the governorship but they could blow it by squabbling over the sales tax. There was no telling what the public might do. The party would be foolish to take a stand, he thought, and run someone for governor who made an issue of it as Andrus and Dee were doing. Besides, he still wanted local option gambling – not as an up-front issue, but by doing away with the state "goon squad" enforcers. Neither Andrus nor Dee would play ball.

In the summer of 1965 Andrus and Dee clashed over the sales tax at a Young Democrats meeting in Coeur d'Alene. En route north to watch, Twin Falls attorney Lloyd Walker, the party chairman since 1962, stopped in Lewiston to pay a courtesy call on Boise. "Mr. Boise said to me, 'Walker, I think you ought to consider getting into this governor's race. If these two guys (Andrus and Dee) keep on going the way they're going, we're just going to tear the party up and elect another Republican.' So I went on up (to Coeur d'Alene), and he'd sent emissaries to tell Bill and Cecil to cool it, cut out the fighting."

Walker's withering blasts at the Republicans stole the show at Coeur d'Alene. He was one of Frank Church's original backers, a Kennedy enthusiast, a powerful speaker, a man of Andrus' philosophical stripe who also got along with Tom Boise's crowd. So when he drove south after the meeting and stopped in Lewiston to see Boise again, the old pol told him, "Well, Walker, there just isn't any question about it. You've got to get into this race." And Walker announced for governor.

As sometimes happened with Tom Boise, there was a little catch. "Tom was one that never really committed himself," Walker recalled. "He never really said, I think you should run and you'll get my full support. He just encouraged me."

Soon afterward, Walker was in Boise city for a meeting; Tom Boise was there too, and Walker was summoned to his hotel room. Walker recalled Boise saying, in his soft and gentle manner, "out of the clear blue sky – 'You're going to be our next governor. What are we going to do about the goon squads?'" Walker was stunned; the floor seemed to fall out beneath him. He told Boise that he supported the state "squads," that he didn't want locally-enforced, semi- unregulated gambling.

Walker stayed in the race, but his candidacy died that day.

Boise seldom got mad. "I can't believe Tom Boise ever politically threatened anybody," Walker said.

But Tom Boise often got even.

Days after the meeting with Walker, Boise called Salmon attorney Charles Herndon, who had run for governor in 1962 with Boise's blessings but lost to Vernon K. Smith. As 1966 approached Herndon thought of running for Congress. But Boise persuaded him to try for governor again; whatever deal they cut, they carried to their graves. Boise mapped out a strategy of grazing on the middle, leaving the left to Andrus and the right to Dee.

In Herndon, Tom Boise saw a winner.

What he did not foresee was the splintering of his venerable and, till then, solid organization. Harry Wall, Boise's Lewiston ally and Democratic national committeeman, stayed out of the governor's race and neutral on Andrus. Jap Inscore, the old-line Moscow Democratic chieftain who for decades had deferred to Boise on state matters, broke with Boise and became an early Andrus supporter. It was a serious breach in Boise's ranks.

Five Democratic candidates – the fifth was former Boise Mayor Westerman Whillock – ran that summer, but not all could get on the ballot. In 1966 candidates had to receive a certain level of support at their party's convention before the voters could get a crack at them in the primary. Walker withdrew at the convention, and Whillock had little support outside Ada County. Herndon, Andrus and Dee made the ballot. Herndon's campaign was beautifully handled by Boise, and pundits predicted a fall Smylie-Herndon contest Herndon would win.

Wrong on all counts. It was not a good year for the pundits.

Another Crash, Another Phoenix

On primary election day in August 1966 Herndon benefited from the support Tom Boise mustered – considerable, even as he lay in a hospital bed in Spokane – and won the primary. Herndon finished 1,277 primary votes ahead of Andrus, who got almost twice as many votes as Dee. It crushed Dee's political career; he returned home to Grangeville to practice law. That did put on fast-forward the career of his campaign manager, state Rep. Vern Ravenscroft of Tuttle, who became heir to the Dee forces and would run for governor in 1970. But it showed, too, that conservative dominance of the Democratic Party was ending.

On the Republican side that August day, Samuelson beat Smylie with 61 percent of the vote – a landslide. McClure beat Purcell with 55 percent. Moderate Republicans and conservative Democrats were crushed. Smylie would not run for office again until 1972, and then finished last in a four-way Republican Senate primary.

Robert Smylie – *It was partly the Goldwater thing, partially the sales tax, partially [having been governor] 12 years. But in retrospect, I think that probably the people were smarter than I was.*

I have told the story a couple of times about the morning Samuelson was going to make the speech on the state of the state. I was shaving upstairs in the house and got to thinking, God, I was glad I didn't have to do that, because I didn't know one more thing I could tell them. They had done every damn thing I had ever asked them to.

You know, the system has a sort of a patient wisdom all its own. They knew they had to have the sales tax but they had to kill somebody. And I was convenient.

In August, writing in the *Idaho Observer*, Dwight Jensen said of Herndon: "The attorney from Salmon has shown himself to be a tough campaigner, not at all averse to hard political infighting and quite willing to deal in half-truths. He can stick to facts and cut his new opponent into dog food."

Then three things happened with breathtaking speed.

First. Perry Swisher, the Republican senator from Pocatello, filed for governor as an independent. His sales tax baby was hanging from the ledge: Herndon was neutral on it and Samuelson had voted against it in 1965. Swisher had figured either Andrus or Smylie would win. When they didn't, he announced in mid-August he would run as an independent. "Someone," he said, "must go into the campaign and defend the good things the sales tax is paying for and speak up for the new faith in Idaho's resources."[61]

---

[61] This race for governor was, really, the centerpiece of Swisher's autobiographical *The Day Before Idaho*. He has a good deal to say about that period in the book.

It was a fluke. The law disqualified anyone who voted in the 1966 primary election from appearing on the ballot that fall as an independent. Swisher hadn't voted. He had planned to get out of politics with a flourish, running as an independent in the second congressional district against George Hansen, as a bluff to throw the fear of moderates and liberals into him. But now Pocatello labor leaders and Boise businessmen who knew he hadn't voted asked him to run for governor. "And without telling you any more than that," Swisher said later, "I will tell you I did talk to Andrus on the phone."

Swisher threatened to filch liberals from Herndon. He got labor's support, costing Herndon an important ally. And when Andrus displayed a brisk coolness toward Herndon after the primary, his organizers and workers took the hint and joined Swisher. Swisher even maintained that the Republican state platform, crafted mostly by Smylie people, had been repudiated by Samuelson – so he was the real Republican. His entry threw the election into doubt.

Second. Philip Jungert of Lewiston, the campaign manager for Vernon Smith in 1962, announced as an independent pro-gambling candidate. (Jungert declared in July but got little attention until fall; starting with scant support, he picked up steam at the end.) Conservative financially – he proposed dropping the sales tax and auctioning off most state lands – he was liberal on gambling and liquor law. He never had a chance to win. But no one knew where his votes would come from, or how many there would be.

Third. Wednesday, September 14.

That morning found Herndon in Pocatello, needing to be in Coeur d'Alene at 3 p.m. Nearby airports were fogged in. He drove to Twin Falls to catch a plane to fly over Idaho's most jagged and, for pilots, treacherous mountains. The plane hit severe stormy weather and smashed into Elk Mountain, southwest of Stanley. Herndon died as the rescue team carried him down the mountain. A Herndon brochure lay in the mud, bearing the slogan, "It Can be Done."

But what would be done now?

A Lewiston Andrus backer said after the crash that "things would be entirely different now if Cece had come out in full support of Herndon the day after the primary. He'd have the nomination by acclamation." Instead, the fight turned ferocious at the meeting of the Democratic state central committee, which would choose a replacement nominee for governor.

Tom Boise and Herndon's other friends were mad. Boise, bedridden in a Spokane hospital, used the last of his strength working the telephone while campaign workers met with committee members all over the Hotel Boise in downtown Boise. Tom Boise threw his support to conservative Democrat Max Hanson, who had considered but declined to run for governor that spring. (Boise had supported John Glasby rather than Hanson in the 1958 governor's race, but Hanson said that he and Boise got along well.) Hanson quit his job at the Farmers Home Administration, and Boise pulled all his strings to help.

On Saturday, three days before the committee meeting, the Andrus people surveyed the 167 central committee members. They were stunned that Hanson - who had quit the FmHA but would not even announce his candidacy until Monday – seemed likely to get 117 votes. Andrus and his backers pushed the clock that weekend, working as hard as Boise.

Dee stayed out, averting a conservative split. On the liberal side, Lloyd Walker considered re-entry. His years as state chairman of the central committee could have gotten him enough votes to deadlock the proceedings. Boise attorney Byron Johnson (an Andrus appointee, 21 years later, to the Idaho Supreme Court) helped plug the dike. "They importuned and cried and whined, and Byron sat on my lap (figuratively) all night long," Walker recalled. "I agreed, because I had been a loyal member of the Church organization, to stay out."

Frank Church turned out to be the key. He, Compton White and Senate candidate Ralph Harding were all from the liberal side of the party, in line more with Andrus more than with Hanson. White already had fallen out with Tom Boise, who had been a key supporter for years, that spring. For Church, siding with Andrus meant a dangerous break with the powerful party leader.

"It wasn't necessarily the wisest political move," Carl Burke recalled, "because you usually do make some political enemies any time you take sides in a primary you're not involved in yourself. But Frank felt strongly that his future was tied to a strong gubernatorial candidate. Besides, he and Cece were friends."

Lt. Gov. Bill Drevlow, the elderly man from Craigmont who had held the number two job for eight years, joined Church, Harding and White. "We would be remiss in our responsibilities to the party and to the people if we were to remain silent at this time," the four said in words bearing the tone of Church's writing. "We hope the committee will give due weight to the special entitlement of Cecil Andrus. He was the first choice of the Democratic state convention and the second choice of the voters ..."

It threw the fight into relief, liberal against conservative, and on Tuesday morning the core of the Democratic Party had to choose sides. Early on, former Sen. Glen Bandelin of Sandpoint, seconding Hanson's nomination, shot at Church. "I've been warned that I could lose my job as a legislative district chairman for what I'm about to do. But I don't like pressure. I don't like pressure no matter from how high it comes." He was loudly cheered; the Andrus-Church wing seemed about to take a bashing.

But Church won more votes for Andrus than he pushed away. Verda Barnes, Church's brilliant political analyst and aide, flew to Boise, where she, Burke, and others pulled vote after vote into Andrus' camp Monday night and Tuesday morning. "It was very hard," Burke recalled. "Wee hours in the morning. That was old-time politics."

Tom Boise pulled the other way and made his efforts uncharacteristically public; pages were sent through the Hotel Boise, yelling that Tom Boise was paging this person or that. But Boise wasn't there personally. And he had an Achilles heel: legislative districts. Boise's strength lay in county organizations which had been around back to creation. But reapportionment in 1966 created legislative districts not based strictly on county lines. New party structures were created for the 35 districts, and they voted too. But for them, Andrus would have lost.

When the Democrats met in the ballroom of the Boise Elks Temple, no one knew who would win. Church aide Myrna Sasser, trying to keep track of the tally, recalled that "I sat there with my sheet shaking so hard. It was such a tough night, my hands were shaking so hard I could not write it down." Rumors flew so freely that at one point Herndon's widow supposedly had the nomination. (She didn't run.) Hanson won the county delegations, 69 votes to 63. But Andrus took 21 of the 35 legislative districts, including most in Eastern Idaho and a few in Tom Boise's Northern Idaho back yard. The result was an Andrus win with no votes to spare: 84-82, one abstention.

He had finally beaten the conservatives.

Sept. 22, 1966
Sen. Frank Church
Dear Frank:
Just a note to commend you and the other candidates and other office holders for uniting the Democratic Party behind Andrus ... Had Andrus been defeated in this effort, in my opinion, we would have had the most disintegrated, factionalized party in the history of Idaho.

Tom Boise was disgusted with Andrus because he didn't think Andrus came out and gave Herndon enough support after the primary. His reasoning there is understandable, but to reverse it now would compel him to endorse the convention nominee and those who have an entre to Mr. Boise should emphasize that fact, although I think his power has been weakened by this convention vote, and I am sorry that his health is not what we all desire ...
William S. Hawkins [attorney]
Coeur d'Alene

Boise, then 81, would be dead a month later.

The liberals had top leaders and fresh organization. Many conservative leaders were dead (Herndon), dying (Boise), defeated (Hanson) or trying to figure their next move (Ravenscroft).

Church had reshaped the Idaho Democratic party into something closer to his own image - which terrified many Democrats. Gilbert Larsen, a Rexburg merchant and veteran of 30 years of Democratic politics, sent Church a ferocious, angry letter. "Frank, yourself and Verda came to Idaho and engineered a political disaster for the Idaho

Democratic Party and for Ralph and Comp," he wrote. "Why did you do this to us? Why didn't you endorse Andrus alone? As of today, we're going to lose the governor, both congressmen and the senator. The dam[n] endorsement has already cost Ralph thousands of campaign dollars. His campaign was really rolling. Now, thanks to you, he's in trouble and the Republicans are gleeful."

Years later, Compton White Jr. cited the open support of Andrus as one reason for his loss that year. "That effectively killed the past arrangements that had been made," he said. "And it made some enemies for me in the party."[62]

Some disgruntled Herndon/Hanson backers sat on their hands the next six weeks and did little for Andrus. It hurt. Six weeks isn' much time to put on a statewide campaign. Andrus' people had no time to plan; critical television commercials were written and designed in the backs of cars one stop ahead of the shoot. Conservatives felt less at home in the Idaho Democratic Party as, from the day of Smylie's defeat, liberals and moderates felt left out of the Idaho Republican Party. The party swapping to come would not happen at once, but it had become inevitable.

And Swisher's world turned upside down the second time that year.

He was in Rexburg speaking when he got the call from his press aide Don Watkins, who told him Herndon had been killed. "Watkins started crying on the phone," Swisher recalled. "He said, 'what are you going to do?' I said, 'Well, you can't hang it up'."

Before the central committee meeting was over, Swisher flew to Boise. Hours after the vote for Andrus, Swisher sat down at a table at his campaign headquarters and told a clutch of reporters that Andrus had compromised on the sales tax. (Andrus said he had not, that he flatly supported it.) Then a reporter said, "The question is, are you going to cop out?"

Swisher delivered an uncommonly short reply. He said, "No."

Andrus met with him to talk him out of the race. "We got nowhere," Andrus said. "We had mutual friends who got us together and the ego of the two men involved – well, you know both men today, you know we both have our share of ego – and in 1966 it was, well, let the chips fall where they may. And that's what happened."

Perry Swisher – *And my problem was, a lot of Republicans had gone out in the street for me. I couldn't leave. More importantly, I couldn't leave the issue. I mean, everybody can say, why don't you get out? But he [Andrus] had to live with the long traditional Democratic opposition to the sales tax, which in the precincts is a tough thing to deal with. With me out of the race, that was quite a consideration: not only could Andrus lose, and probably would, but ...*

---

[62] The 1st District seat White lost that year would remain in Republican hands for 24 years.

If both the sales tax and Andrus lost, to me that was cutting out about 10 years of my life. I just couldn't do something like that. So I stayed put.

The campaign would cost Swisher his newspaper at Pocatello, his finances, his health, and any future he might have had as a Republican. Within days of Andrus' re-entry, Swisher's corporate and labor backers melted away.

Andrus attracted some moderate Republicans, even a few conservatives, such as Twin Falls attorney Ed Benoit. He "helped me in '66 because he was a head alum from the University of Idaho and he couldn't stomach what had taken place," Andrus said. (Years later, Andrus appointed Benoit to the state Board of Education.)

On September 29 Tom Heath, a former Republican state chairman and a seven-term senator from Preston, wrote Samuelson a personal letter packed with advice. "I am getting very concerned about this coming election," he wrote, "particularly the outcome of the governor race with our candidates. Frankly, I don't believe you yourself are making any headway." Heath pointed out that as a state senator he, too, had voted against the sales tax. "But now things have changed," he said. The public wanted better education, he said, and if the sales tax failed, "the question is, what in hell are we going to do? ... Don, you must get off your dime and assert yourself." He urged Samuelson to say that if the voters rejected the three percent sales tax, that he would urge the Legislature to pass a two percent sales tax.

Samuelson didn't.

The next day Heath wrote Smylie that he was afraid the tax would be rejected and that Jungert was doing so well he might be elected. "If he should win and the sales tax loses then the state is in a mess," he wrote, "and those damn Ada County burghers who worked against you should feel very proud of themselves."

Anger

But the angriest race may have been the other one, between Republican Sen. Len Jordan and Democratic former Congressman Ralph Harding. It too was not what they had expected it to be.

Jordan was transformed in the sixties. He was the lodestar for many years for Idaho conservatives. In 1964 he was a staunch Goldwater man. And yet he was an iceberg: more lay beneath the surface. In 1964 he broke with many conservatives and supported the Civil Rights Act. In rhetoric, too, he subtly changed. That would be more obvious later in his questioning of the war in Vietnam and refusal to support Nixon Supreme Court nominee Clement Haynesworth. With the Haynesworth vote, some conservatives would accuse Jordan of selling out to liberals. Even in 1966 Jordan left Harding in a spot. The Democrat went into the race smarting from

George Hansen, determined to beat the top conservative. But Len Jordan already was a far cry from George Hansen.

Harding long had disagreed with Jordan on water policy. Jordan had suggested a study of diverting excess Columbia River water to the Southwest to diminish flood water and yield $30 million or more in income to the Northwest. In April 1964 Harding wrote Jordan he would "oppose it as vigorously as I can. I believe that such a study represents a great threat to the water and water rights of all of the Columbia River Basin including Idaho."

Jordan shot back: "It is apparent that either you have not read my statement carefully or that you do not understand it, which hardly seems likely." He had referred to water near the mouth of the Columbia River, not in Southern Idaho.

The debate blew up in the fall of 1966, when Harding ran full-page newspaper ads implying Jordan was trying to divert precious Idaho water to the Southwest. Jordan got the best of it, tagging Harding as a mud-slinger.

(A former Jordan aide issued a caustic reply to Harding, and Harding responded likewise. Time would demonstrate just how small a state Idaho is. In 1978 Harding again would run in the second congressional district in the Democratic primary, while that aide would be running against George Hansen on the Republican side. Both lost their respective primary races, so they never bumped heads. But the aide, a Jerome attorney named Jim Jones, later became attorney general of Idaho.)

In one piece of campaign literature the Republican state central committee (which, to keep Jordan "senatorial," took the tough shots at Harding) complained about Harding's "sorry record of spend, spend, spend," his job as a special assistant to the secretary of the Air Force, and "Mr. Harding's shabby campaign tactics, so obvious every time he runs for public office." It did not specify what those tactics were.

And the Winner Is ...

It was the wildest political year in Idaho history, maybe the most important, and yet 5,000 fewer people voted in the 1966 general election than two or four years before.

The results were still dramatic.

Reapportionment – adding Ada County to the first congressional district – meant what the sharp heads thought it would. The district went Republican, Ada County giving McClure the edge while elsewhere he got votes comparable to Mattmiller's in 1964.

Jordan, whose Senate record had been more conservative than the rest of it would be, won 55.4 percent of the vote against Harding.

Samuelson won 10,842 votes more than Andrus (only 41 percent of the total). Swisher got 12.2 percent; Jungert, 9.1 percent.

Veteran Lt. Gov. Bill Drevlow was unseated by Republican Jack Murphy, a veteran state senator.

But it wasn't an utter conservative sweep. The people approved the three percent sales tax by almost 64,000 votes – the biggest margin any candidate or ballot issue had ever received in Idaho.

Republicans lost seats in the state legislature.

Samuelson received only 41 percent of the total vote for governor. No one will ever know what would have happened if Swisher and Jungert had stayed out, but many of their votes were Democratic. A line of thought cropped up that Andrus would have won a two-man race. He and Church thought Swisher cost Andrus the election; Swisher felt that was not so. Andrus lost the election but remained a leader of his party.

The Trendline

The balance of power in Idaho stayed remarkably constant in the years ahead. Republicans held the upper hand, but a Democratic presence in major offices never was eradicated.

The trendline suggested that should have happened in 1968. Only one top Democrat was left: Sen. Frank Church, mired in Vietnam and up for re-election.

Nov. 15, 1966
Frank Church
United States Senator
Dear F.C.:
This may be a rather incoherent letter. The campaign wounds are still bleeding and the Democratic workers are looking for solace. Be that as it may, I have a few thoughts I thought I would ship along because several things worry me.

I am inclined to believe that the resurrection must come with some new blood. The problem with politics is that politics and money are so closely entwined. Andrus' campaign ended in a deficit ... The state of the party is such that there is not much chance to raise more local money ...

We do need some new faces, too. Both Verda and I have lots of scars now. In the last decade I have butted heads with county heads and party workers and my effectiveness is diminished. A lot of these people are highly suspicious and refuse to work with the old guard. I am told young Democrats feel this way, too, because they want part of the action. I don't know what to do except talk about it. Yet, it is a serious problem ...

This is a pretty gloomy estimate of our situation. Yet, I think that a close association with the President would be more harmful than helpful. You already have an image of honest dissent, although most people felt your appointment to the U.N. was LBJ's way of bringing you back in the fold. They don't know facts but only what facts appear to be.

We have a lot of things to do about the political situation in the state and how it should be run. Suffice it to say we have to get some money in here soon from somewhere or this thing is going to wither on the vine.

Aside from all this, the squirrels are still happy.

Carl [Burke]
Boise

The next day Burke changed his mind. "Today, I am in Mood B," he wrote. "Things aren't as gloomy as they seem."

And by 1968 Church was solid.

The 1967 recall attempt against him had prompted him to campaign hard all over the state. Idahoans were irritated at the out of staters who had started it and rallied around Church. So did all factions of Democrats, who had no other major officeholder left. Congressman George Hansen, who ran against Church, discovered that he could not be perceived to be attacking Church, that he was "walking on eggshells" that campaign. "I walked onto a stage where any opposition wasn't to be tolerated," he recalled. "I had to tread a careful line between exposing his voting record and not attacking him personally."

Six years before, Democrats pleaded with Gracie Pfost not to run for the Senate. Now key Republicans pleaded with Hansen not to run, not to throw away his House seat. So did his own aides.

Richard Hendricks – *I advised against it. I said, "You're the boss. Whatever you say. You're signing the checks. But there is no way you can make it. Absolutely no way." I said I'd give it my all and I did. After that campaign I collapsed from physical exhaustion ...*

Church hadn't done enough wrong. There were too many Republicans who felt - maybe not just Republicans, too many independents, that's where you win or lose elections - there just weren't enough anti-Churches. All you had to do was go around. Church was taking good votes out of Franklin County. He wouldn't win two to one. But against anyone else George won three to one [there] ...

George. You have to understand the ego of the man. There is nothing he can't do if he wants to; all he's got to do is work hard enough. Dan Adamson [a 1984 and 1986 congressional candidate for whom Hendricks worked] is the same. There is nothing Dan can't do if he works hard enough.

George and I were debating the thing; he hadn't formally announced. We were campaigning ... driving home from Idaho Falls, and we got talking about it.

I said, "George, there's no way. You pay me to tell you what's happening in the district, and I've been over the district, and there is no way you can win Northern Idaho. The best you can do is hold even in Southern Idaho." That turned out to be right.

He said, "Richard, I have the burning of the bosom."

It's a religious term. Mormons believe in it devoutly. If you have a problem for the Lord, you pray and can talk to the Lord about it. And then after you've gone through this religious mental exercise, you leave it up to the Lord. And if it's true, you'll receive a warm burning within your bosom. If it's not, you'll have a stupor and it's gone.

And he said, "Richard, I prayed to the Lord, Connie and I both, and we had a burning of the bosom that we should do this."

And I said to George, "Are you sure the burning of the bosom isn't green onions for supper?"

But Hansen later said that "the only burning I felt was the fact that not only did we need the Senate seat, but we needed to change the philosophy."

Theoretically, Church's opposition to American involvement in Vietnam should have hurt him in 1968. But the events of late that year helped him. "I got caught in the switches of the Vietnam War," Hansen recalled. That fall was a time of optimism for the new Paris peace talks; the talks collapsed later, but Church's campaign surely benefited from them.

The 1968 election went to Church. It reinforced his role as the leading Idaho Democrat, and that of liberals as the leaders of the Idaho Democratic Party.[63]

George Hansen was replaced by moderate Orval Hansen. But the party hierarchy stayed with Gwen Barnett conservatives, some plotting the ouster of Orval and his replacement with a conservative. That would happen, but not for six years. No matter. These were determined people.

Samuelson's administration

People sort of chose up sides when they talked about Don Samuelson. Or when he talked about them.

Jan. 22, 1967
The Honorable Don Samuelson
Governor of Idaho
Sir:
In reference to your "Kick a Beatnik in the Seatnik" week:
(1) The communist countries do not tolerate freedom of speech or dissent. If the United States does not tolerate those freedoms then we are merely lowering ourselves to the level of a communist country.
(2) Many of the "beatniks" have been called communists or unpatriotic simply because they are for peace. If a man is for peace then he cannot be a communist, because being for peace is completely contradictory to communist doctrine.
(3) To be frank, sir, you are generalizing about "beatniks." And generalizations rarely, if ever, apply.
Yours truly ...

Dear [Sir]:

---

[63] George Hansen turned out to be a long way from finished in Idaho politics – he would be on the ballot until 1984 – but in hindsight, that 1968 campaign turned out to be pivotal, sending him down a rocky path. But that would take years to play out. George and Connie Hansen still live in Pocatello

Because we live in a free country, people have a perfect right to be anything they wish, even a beatnik.

For the same reason, I have the right to express my opinion of the beatnik set, just as you have the right to disagree.

Thank you for writing.

Sincerely

Don Samuelson

In 1967 George Hansen sent Samuelson a letter on a lands issue and scrawled on the bottom, "You seem to be coming on strong in your new job, Don – keep up the good work!"

Samuelson did work on issues as remote as poverty on Duck Valley Indian Reservation. He wasn't as smooth an administrator as Smylie but he did uncover and solve some problems. He rearranged auditing and some state financing procedures. "That first month we caught that one guy out at the Highway Department that stole a million and a half dollars," Samuelson recalled. "He was taking $17,000 a month. What he put in a bill for was to move telephone lines or power poles. He had set up a dummy company and then he'd send in the bill, and he'd approve the bill, and then it would go through ... We caught him." The man did time in prison.

Samuelson could come across friendly and down to earth and bluntly honest. But he was not at his best in formal events; at these, even some Republicans cringed. Dwight Jensen of the Observer, one of Samuelson's roughest critics, recounted in the summer of 1969 how Samuelson was smooth and precise at a meeting of the National Governors Conference in Colorado Springs and at a Western Governors Conference meeting at Seattle – yet flubbed Boise press conferences. "It could be," he speculated, "that the problem of facing a roomful of reporters, most of them hostile and a few of them unfair in their hostility, unnerves Samuelson."

Much of the press was hostile.

Sam Day, the editor of the *Intermountain Observer*, said this about Samuelson in 1970: "After three and a half years of non-governing, he has reduced government in Idaho to a shambles. It is perhaps no gross exaggeration to say that since January 1967 Idaho has functioned without a governor. The agencies of government have simply gone their own way, each at its own pace and according to its own mood, and each trying, with varying success, to keep out of the way of that aimless hurricane on the second floor of the Statehouse."

In the fifties Idaho's news media was almost exclusively conservative, aside from the *Lewiston Morning Tribune* and the Observer and its predecessors (such as Swisher's *Alameda Intermountain*, and the *Idaho Observer*). In the late sixties papers moved to the center and reporters got as involved in politics as they were outspoken about it. Swisher was in and out of the legislature while he ran a paper. (He scorned purist "Cistercian monks" in the press who wouldn't dirty their hands with practical politics.) Don Watkins, an *Observer* columnist and *Idaho State Journal* reporter, was a press secretary for Smylie, Swisher, and White, later for three superintendents of public instruction, and for Gov. John Evans. Van Wolverton of the *Journal* took leave in 1966 to be one of Andrus' campaign press secretaries.[64]

When the *Idaho Statesman* was sold in October 1963 from family ownership to Federated Publications, its editorial page went almost overnight from arch-conservatism to near-liberalism.[65] Smylie dealt closely and smoothly with the *Statesman* and political editor John Corlett. Samuelson on the other hand ...

John Corlett – *I don't think I was in his office more than once or twice, as I recall, outside of a press conference. I didn't talk to him at all. I started to. Lloyd Adams was pretty close to Samuelson. I've got some letters in which he wrote Samuelson, telling him to talk to me, "Don't make an enemy out of Corlett, the guy has ideas," and so forth. I told Lloyd I don't want to be put in this position to be one of his advisers.*

But anyway, I got in once to see him. We started talking and the first thing you know he was just lecturing me, just giving me hell about things I wrote and so on. I said, let's forget that, I just want to sit down and talk to you about your agenda and so forth. He just kept it up. And I said, "Well, governor, this isn't getting anywhere and I'm afraid I'm just going to have to go." That's about the only time I got in there. It was unfortunate.

Smylie wrote columns for the *Observer* and often slashed at Samuelson – a public display of the Republican rift. It became official when the Smylie faction found a leader in Dick Smith.

Smith was a former state senator and a Smylie-appointed member of the state Board of Education. He clashed with Samuelson in 1966 on the sales tax, and as board president in 1967-68 he fought Samuelson's budget and other edicts.

In 1968 Samuelson heard that educational television was producing a report on Sen. Frank Church. "Since Sen. Church is running for re-election, and a political campaign is in progress, this activity by a state institution has raised considerable question and criticism," he wrote Smith. "Is the board aware that this activity is going on? Is this board

---

[64] A quick note about Wolverton, press secretary on Andrus' first run for governor, who's had as remarkable a life since 1966 as any of the other players in this story. After the campaign he left daily journalism and politics entirely; within a few years he was settled down in the San Jose area of California. This was the area poised to become Silicon Valley, and Wolverton got involved in computer writing. He was for years on the leading edge of that area, and wound up writing the definitive and bestselling how-to guide on an "operating system" (whatever that was) called DOS, for this scrappy little company called Microsoft. Wolverton now lives on a ranch a half-hour from Missoula, Montana, still interested in high tech – and still interested too in Idaho politics.

[65] In 1975 Federated, in turn, was sold to Gannett newspaper, which held it until the mid-00s, when it briefly went to Knight-Ridder and then to the McClatchy newspapers. Through those years, its editorial page (on which I pulled a couple of years worth of work) has seemed to me to be centrist, to the point of often almost making a fetish of carefully splitting endorsements between the parties. Of course, that said, it also has typically run to the left of the overall readership point of point.

policy?" Samuelson scuffled with Idaho State University President William "Bud" Davis and University of Idaho President Ernest Hartung, both recent hires. The governor pushed for tight budgets to the point that even legislative Republicans rebelled.

Samuelson was not alone. In February 1969 Eugene Halstrom of the American Legion, Department of Idaho, wrote to gripe. "Why is it that a nationally- known draft resister is given a platform at taxpayer expense at our state university to expound his motives for not supporting our commitment in Vietnam? Must we distinguish his viewpoint by arranging his appearance?"

Don Loveland – *We said [in 1967 after the sales tax passed] we have a little money, we have some needs in higher education, why don't we make an honest effort to put them in the shape they ought to be in ... But we'd no more voted on them than Samuelson comes out the next morning with an article criticizing, and that he's going to veto them. They [the bills] hadn't even been to the House.*

I went down there and I said, "Now, governor, your prerogative is to do what you want ... But for heaven's sake keep your mouth shut until those bills lay on your desk ..."

Don Samuelson had one problem. He had - and he was very honest about it, and it was a part of him and I don't know why - a fear of professional people. He called me one afternoon and said, "Would you step in when you're done for the day?" So I went down there. We had just passed the drug bill on marijuana and all these things. It was a pretty hefty bill. And there the governor sat, and he's reading it. Hell, he couldn't pronounce half the words in it. And I said, "Don, why don't you call a doctor or druggist or somebody, some professional person, have them take this bill, read it and have laying on your desk by 10 o'clock in the morning one paragraph telling you what it says."

"Oh," he said, "I can't do that. The people elected me to read these things."

He was a work horse, that man. No question about it. He put in a lot of time. His heart was in the right place. He just had a fear of asking for help.

In March 1970 Samuelson bumped Smith from the Board of Education when his term was up. Articulate and experienced, Smith was an obvious choice to run against Samuelson. On March 30 he wrote the governor: "You have been most unsuccessful in uniting the people of this state toward common goals. It is probable that you have driven more people away from the party than you have attracted."

(Smith's campaign slogan was that "Idaho needs a governor who can both think and speak clearly.")

From Samuelson's perspective, "I had as many Democrats come down (to the office) to talk to me as I had Republicans. And I had Republicans who were so damn liberal down there that, you know, they did everything in the world to cut my throat."

Only an incident was needed to split the party open. That came in May with Vice President Spiro Agnew's visit to Boise for a fundraising dinner. The money was to go to the gubernatorial nominee. But the guest of honor was Samuelson, and when the dinner was announced, it was tabbed as a Samuelson benefit. Smith's backers were outraged, and in-party sniping grew more frequent.

Long-time Republican strategist Evan "Doc" Kackley of Wayan was concerned enough to write a personal letter to Jordan asking him to do something. "In a lifetime in active Republican politics, I have never witnessed such a disastrous course than we are now on within the state and nationally in this dinner," he wrote in April. "That dinner as now set up will blow the Republican Party to pieces in Idaho this election, and no one can put it together now or in the election two years from now."

In June, Smith saw the results of a survey of 589 Idaho residents by Central Surveys Inc., of Shenandoah, Iowa. It said that Andrus would be the Democratic nominee and Smith would do better than Samuelson against him. But it also said Smith was far behind Samuelson. "Samuelson's advantage is his political experience and his image of being honest and sincere," it said. "He is most vulnerable on the issues associated with education."

Samuelson won the primary with 58.3 percent of the vote, and not just because he was governor. Samuelson campaigned hard and in the summer of 1969 he had held a carefully orchestrated series of courthouse meetings around the state. One-on-one campaigning was his forte, and he had enough time to make it work.

Conservatives controlled the Republican party. But what did that say about the general election?

Rematch

The Democrats, in contrast, had quit bashing each other over the head.

Rep. Vern Ravenscroft of Tuttle, who had the conservative rural Democrats, was Dee's heir apparent, and ran. Lloyd Walker, who couldn't give up the idea after his try in 1966, was in. And so was Andrus, although it took some convincing.

Cecil Andrus – *It was probably better that I did not win [in 1966] when I was 35. I was a better governor when I was 39 because I had been defeated and had some of that kicked out of me ... I learned a lot of things. I learned to say, "No, I won't be a candidate again." But remember that same girl, that I told Orofino was just outside of Spokane? I told her, "Babe, don't worry about me -"*

I was in debt, which I had to pay off. I had no help. The phone doesn't ring when you're a loser. But I paid all those bills. I went to a banker, and I said I need to borrow $8,100. This was 1966, immediately after the campaign. I had used up what money I had and what I could beg and borrow, and I said there are some campaign bills owing out there. I didn't charge them. Ed Williams, the chairman of my campaign, had strict orders not to spend any money he didn't have, but at the end of the campaign he got carried away and bought radio and newspaper ads and anyway, I owe $8,100, or the campaign does.

The banker said to me, "How are you going to pay it back?"
I looked him in the eye and said, "I don't know."
But I said I will pay it back. He loaned it to me, and I paid it back in about three years ... I promised my wife. I said, "I put you through this and I'm not going to do that again ..."
Herman McDevitt and Eddy Williams and Darrell Manning and myself and a few others were supposed to find our candidate. We tried to get Ernie Hartung, who was president of the University of Idaho, to run. He said no, you're out of your mind. We went to [William] "Bud" Davis, who was president of Idaho State University, and he said, no way. Then met with him a second time, in a hotel room in Lewiston. And he was almost ready. The interest was there but he said, "I don't see how a Democrat's going to win."
We thrashed about, got nothing done and Eddy and them started turning to me and said, "well, you've got to do it again."
And I said, "No way. I'm not going to. I told Carol I wouldn't do that."
"Well, you've got to, you owe us" — all the rationale. They knew I was susceptible, I guess.
I said, "Look, you've got to put together $25,000, put it in the bank, to prove you're serious. They came up with $21,000 or $22,000. I went to Carol and said, "Guess what? We're still on the outskirts of Spokane, babe."

At first it looked like another 1966 debacle. It wasn't. In February Andrus, Ravenscroft, state Sen. John Evans, and spokesmen for Walker and Sen. Ray Rigby of Rexburg met in a Boise hotel room for three hours. They set ground rules to keep from killing each other, and stuck to them.

The primary showed where the Democrats were headed. In 1966 Andrus lost to a more conservative candidate though the conservative vote was split. In 1970 he and Walker ran as relative liberals and Ravenscroft — backed by the Dee people and the shattered Tom Boise crowd — had the conservatives. Andrus won. One reason was the absence of Tom Boise. "His lieutenants were nowhere as good as he was," Ravenscroft recalled. Ravenscroft and Walker were from the Magic Valley, splitting its vote. Andrus' campaign skills improved. But the party changed, too. Ravenscroft, like many other conservatives, would leave it soon.

Andrus also got help again from Church's troops, fresh from their superb 1968 campaign organization. Their people and voting lists were intact, and Andrus was the beneficiary. (Walker said that some of them encouraged party workers to vote against giving Walker a spot on the 1970 Democratic primary ballot, and that he barely made it with help from then-state Sen. John Evans.)

Having won the nomination, Andrus showed he had learned a great deal, bringing Walker and Ravenscroft aides into his own campaign. Headed into the 1970 election the Idaho Democratic Party was more united than it had been since the twenties.

One Andrus appointment kept Ravenscroft in office as a Democrat two more years before he switched parties. Andrus pushed

Joe McCarter, Ravenscroft's campaign manager, for state chairman. McCarter had sought the state House seat Ravenscroft was vacating to run for governor. Appointed chairman, McCarter resigned as a candidate for the legislature, and Ravenscroft replaced him.

Mythology

Myth has it that Samuelson was a pushover in 1970 for the new-model Andrus. Not so. Many Democrats, perhaps spooked by their 24-year jinx on the governorship, thought Samuelson would be too tough to beat. On his talk show Bob Salter took a poll of the first 100 people to call in, and Samuelson got 69 votes to Andrus' 31. (Admittedly, Salter's was a conservative audience.)

Andrus used what became known as "quality of life" concepts in his speeches.

Jack Peterson – *I came to Idaho in September 1970 as the first chief of environmental quality for the water resource board. I was the first person formally charged with taking a hard look at the quality of Idaho's rivers and streams, in Don's last few months.*

As I traveled around the state – I had responsibilities statewide and I would travel a lot on the old Air West – I would often times see Cece on the plane campaigning for governor, travelling alone, no entourage. And then a few months after I got here, he was my boss. He was one who understood quality environment, quality of water - quality of life was a phrase that I am led to believe he coined. The concept, I think, was valid. He was one of the first governors to emerge with those concepts.

Polls released before election day showed Andrus and Samuelson in a dead heat. "I worked my tail off," Samuelson recalled. "A lot of people, time and time again, would say 'Don, quit running around and go back to your office and attend to business. You've got it made.' I heard this all over the state. My wife and I worked 18 hours a day."

And labor was well-organized.

Don Samuelson – *About 10 days before the election one letter came out and went to every union member. They were pointing out the unemployment and some problems that were happening at the national level, and it said, if you don't want these to happen in Idaho, vote Democratic. About three or four days later, another one came out and it went to every household in the state of Idaho. It said about the same thing, just reworded a little bit, and it said the same things: if you don't want these things to happen, vote Democratic, vote for Andrus. And then just three days before election another one came out, and that was a bulk mailing statewide. It said the same things: if you don't want these things to happen, vote for Andrus. That's what happened.*

Andrus won by 10,896 votes, about 52 percent – but he carried only 15 of 44 counties. He made few inroads into southern Idaho; Samuelson won south of the Salmon River. In Custer, where the White Clouds debate hit white heat, Samuelson got 89 percent.

Republicans, stunned at losing the governorship after 24 years, went through reappraisal. One line of thought pinned blame on the conservatives, easy since their guiding force was leaving. In 1971 Gwen Barnett resigned and moved to Oregon.

In June 1971 Robert Robson, a Republican Silver Valley attorney appointed attorney general by Samuelson – and who also lost in 1970 – wrote Jordan that the party was in trouble.

"If the 1970 campaign taught any lesson it is that for a majority of the candidates for public office on the Republican ticket, Idaho is a swing state and that if Republican candidates are to be mostly successful, it is necessary that we bring together within the party structure all the various factions and ideologies," he wrote. "It appears to me that it is quite necessary that no further wedge of any kind be driven into the Republican structure."

Some Republicans were so upset with conservative leadership, he said, that they quit donating to campaigns.

Reconciliation would not be easy.

Tour | East in Zion

Eastern Idaho, land of empty plains, wooded mountains, nuclear scientists and hardscrabble farmers, is a place apart from the rest of Idaho - for one fairly obvious reason.

This is Zion North. Northern Extension of Utah. Second Home of the Church of Jesus Christ of Latter Day Saints. The Mormons.

The notion is that Eastern Idaho – the counties from Oneida, Power, Bingham, Butte, Clark, east to Wyoming and south to Utah – immigrated en masse from Utah. In fact the first settlers, 1860s farmers, were Mormons who sank deep roots in Bear Lake and Franklin Counties. But then came the rush of Gentiles who dominated government and politics in early statehood, and elected anti- Mormon politicians like Democrat Fred T. Dubois of Blackfoot. In time the Mormons rebelled, voted heavily, and assumed power as they outpopulated everyone else.

In 1920 five Idaho counties – Bear Lake, Franklin, Oneida, Madison and Teton – were at least half Mormon. By 1970 11 of 14 counties in the East were half Mormon, and the other three hit at least a third. Only one elsewhere - nearby Cassia - hit one-third. Mormon dominance was regional.

And dominance it was. Being an active Mormon is no mere matter of attending church an hour on Sunday. No alcohol, tobacco or caffeine are permitted. No gambling. And the church is a comprehensive organization. Wards (led by lay bishops) are organized into stakes (led by lay stake presidents), stakes into regions (led by lay regional representatives). Church leaders are community leaders; to ask which comes first is to ask a chicken-and-egg question. Church leaders are well-known already if they run for office. More important, the church's expression of confidence in them is an enormous political advantage. But doing it all isn't easy. The LDS church has no professional clergy; lay members are "called" to serve, and the work load isn't light.

In 1976 Mark Ricks, a Rexburg farmer, was pressured to run for the state Senate. He was interested. But he was a stake president who helped with Deseret Industries and social services in 23 stakes from Shelley to Salmon, and he had no time. Two years later he ran and won, and Ricks was pushed to the limit. He was by then a regional representative, and in the busiest month of his first session he also presided at four LDS stake conferences, which took him back to Rexburg each Saturday and Sunday.

Richard Hendricks – *If you're a member of the bishopric, the priesthood leadership or relief society leadership, those kind of people will put in close to 18 hours, 20 hours a week. It really doesn't leave time - that's why we're not good* *golfers, good bowlers. You go out on our golf course right now [on Sunday], I'll bet you wouldn't see six couples on it all day ...*

[But] we're encouraged to be conscious that the leadership of our community things don't get in the hands of the wrong people.

I'll give you a prime example. Our golf course [in Preston] was built out here. Everybody on the committee to do this, except two or three people, were LDS. Two or three people on the committee were non-LDS, and they got the leadership. LDSers are so busy with church jobs that we don't have time to get involved with the leadership of other jobs. That's not a divine calling, and we think that church positions are divine calling.

So all of a sudden we faced the fact that they were voting whether we should have liquor by the drink on the golf course; of course, to the LDS, that's taboo. I was bishop of the ward at the time and they were having a vote that night at the golf course to see if they should [allow liquor]. And it all of a sudden dawned on us that the [non-LDS] leadership wanted it and we had been sitting around on our butts, not watching who was in charge of it, and we were going to get liquor by the drink. Tuesday was the night it was, and Tuesday night was bishop's meeting for all the wards. All the priesthood leaders were in church Tuesday nights. At the golf course there was nobody out there but those guys that wanted liquor by the drink.

The word went like wildfire. Our stake presidents got on the phone. We had two stake presidents who were over 10 or 12 wards. They immediately called us all, dismissed us. All of us who were on the committee or active in golf went out. We had a big hullabaloo and a big vote, and we don't have liquor by the drink. Now we're careful to see that the people who are on that committee are acceptable.

Non-Mormons can be "acceptable." Republican Tom Heath, Senate pro tem in 1939, was elected seven times from Franklin County. "Tom Heath smoked. Tom Heath drank. But he was totally acceptable," Hendricks said.
"The Democrats here put a stake president against him. He was beloved, had been a stake president for 25 or 30 years. Yet Tom Heath beat a stake president."

Hendricks recalled how, as a state Senate employee, he kept a bottle available for certain senators, including Heath. "I'd keep little cups in there and he'd pour himself a drink, and turn to one of those people who was having a drink with him, and he'd say, 'Well, come on. We've got to go out and cast another anti-whiskey vote for the Mormon folks.' Always voted right."

Democratic identification with gambling in the fifties, or with the drinking North, may have mattered. And Republican rhetoric sounds much like Mormon church doctrine. The ascension of Republican super-conservative Ezra Taft Benson to the church presidency couldn't have hurt. Whatever the reason, as the Mormon population boomed it also became more heavily Republican.

Hues of a Color

Power County, over low mountains east of Burley, is less Mormon than most of the East.

Power is agricultural, but the parties are competitive. One reason is the presence of the federal American Falls Dam in the county seat, American Falls, where most of the people live. Another is the Fort Fall Indian Reservation in the northeast quadrant of the county; native Americans farm the Arbon Valley. There's also spillover from FMC and Simplot phosphate plants on the east border; the plants are identified with Pocatello but sit in Power County because of the lower taxes there, and some of the workers live in Power County subdivisions. Power grew from 4,000 people in 1960 to 6,900 in the mid-eighties.

To the south are tiny farm towns, Rockland and Roy. This is remote, hilly, rocky land; farming comes in isolated spots.

In Oneida County the land is also like this except for the valley along the Little Malad River, where small farm communities like Samaria and Daniels sprang up.

Malad, its center, is one of the oldest towns in Idaho and one of the most isolated, set in a deep valley just north of the Utah line. Its 1,800 people, inside the Mormon sphere, depend on farming and ranching. But it was founded as a stage-rail stop, forcing Mormons, apostates, and Gentiles to work together. (Malad lacks the orderly grid road pattern of many Mormon towns.) A handful of families ran Malad. David Evans, its most prominent businessman at the turn of the century, was Democratic speaker of the Idaho House in 1899. Almost a century later his grandson, John Evans, became governor. Malad is Republican in national races but elects some Democrats locally. (The Jones family also elected many politicians. John Evans beat Republican Sen. D.P. Jones to win his Senate seat in 1952. Myron Jones served four terms in the Idaho House in the seventies and early eighties.)

East, past jagged mountains, are the flat plains of Franklin County, upward of 95 percent LDS. Preston's 4,000 people – the number has grown steadily but slowly – are almost all Mormon. At civic and many other meetings, guests are introduced as "Elder Johnson from the Sixth Ward." It is an ingrown society, but a successful one; Preston hasn't boomed, but neither has it busted. It is in many ways a Norman Rockwell town, pretty and neat.

And it is Republican, more than anywhere in Idaho except, maybe, Payette.

John Evans – *In Franklin County I have a dear friend that's a businessman, a cousin of mine. He came to me one time, in all seriousness, and asked me, "Why are you a Democrat? I can't imagine you continuing to be a Democrat. You know, in Franklin County, Democrats are always the losers, always the ones who haven't accomplished anything in life. They're just nobodies out here. Why would you be a Democrat?"*

I said, "Well, I guess it's a result of my grandfather — and your grandfather — being a good Democrat, and a result of my father and the family and interests and philosophies, and this is all ingrained in us."

But he continued, "Well, of course, you'd never get anywhere over here."

Bear Lake County, across the Cache National Forest mountains, has more variety. Mormons did settle it and make it farm country, and it was three- fourths LDS before that was true anywhere else in Idaho. But Bear Lake never was as agricultural as Franklin; it is more forested and has a tourist trade.

Montpelier, once a farm burg, got its boost in the 1880s when the Oregon Short Line (later added to Union Pacific) began at Granger, Wyo., in 1881. The line ran northwest through the Bear Lake Valley toward Soda Springs and Montpelier; the lay of the land made the railroad bypass Paris, the county seat. While Soda Springs 30 miles north became a cattle shipping center, Montpelier shipped horses, hay, and grain to miners in Western Wyoming. The rail boom did not always please the Mormons who feared the influence of rough rail workers - who, in turn, didn't much care for the stuffy Mormons. For decades Montpelier, like Berlin, was a divided city, with a Mormon "uptown" cut off by a north-south fence from a saloon-packed, fun-loving "downtown." Montpelier even had two commercial centers, one Mormon, one Gentile.

With time, the Washington Street gate swung open more often. The rail gave commercial advantage to the Gentile "downtown." Mormon merchants moved there and the town integrated. The railroad phased down in the mid-twentieth century, but Montpelier retains a Gentile influence and a sense of compromise. While the rest of Bear Lake is resolutely Republican, Democratic candidates can break even, or win, in Montpelier. (Richard Stallings did in 1986, while his Republican opponent won Bear Lake with 55 percent.) Bear Lake could become more Democratic if the enormous phosphate deposits there attract industry and new union workers.

Some of that happened in Soda Springs, also once a key rail stop.

Richard Hendricks — *Soda Springs in my day growing up was tough, tough, tough. It was once the major shipping point of sheep and wool in the United States. It's been a tough town. More bars per square inch than any other town in this area. They had murder for breakfast ... It was a place where people who didn't want to be seen, go get drunk.*

But Soda's founders were a different breed of cat. Though it was even older than Montpelier (Soda is the second-oldest town in the state) and also had a strong Mormon founding element, the stable down-home folks were calmly convinced they would outlast the rougher elements. And they did. They outlasted the railroad, in decline by mid-century. Soda turned sedate; ranching has been the linchpin for the county through the decades.

The key politician in Bear Lake Valley - which runs north of Soda Springs - for years was Republican cattleman Reed Budge, a Caribou County commissioner and 20 years a state senator, blunt and stubborn. Many tried and many failed to beat him.

But though farm, ranch, and LDS elements made Caribou Republican, Democrats have a niche in the phosphate mines north of Soda. The mines go back to 1906; the industry became politically significant in the fifties and sixties when big plants, operated for years by Monsanto Co. and Beker Industries, Inc., expanded. Soda boomed from 2,400 people in 1960 to 4,000 in 1980. Then the phosphate industry slipped in the eighties and the Beker plant shut down for a time. It reopened under new ownership in 1987, and Soda may yet become politically competitive.

Soda Springs and Montpelier are the aberrations; the more rural places are solidly Republican. That is also true of southern Bannock County towns like McCammon, Downey, Arimo, and the quaint resort town of Lava Hot Springs (although the large state-run spa has moderated it). All that changes in the north of Bannock , where five-sixths of its people live, around Pocatello .

"Sin City"

For the Mormon farmers, Pocatello was the height of exotica.

Richard Hendricks – *When I was a kid, Pocatello was Sin City, U.S.A. It was the place to go to get your first drink of whiskey, because they'd let you in a bar when they weren't supposed to. It was a tough area for a Mormon Caucasian. That was the only place we could go where there were blacks. And there were prostitutes in Pocatello . For a kid 18 or 20, that's what Pocatello was. You'd never send one of your children from Franklin County to Pocatello , to ISU, unless you were really sure they were founded on straight living and the gospel ...*

It's dying out. A few of our kids are going there. [Once] the only kids who went to Pocatello were those who wanted to be pharmacists; we sent our kids to Moscow [University of Idaho].

Pocatello, Idaho's second city (at 45,000 people, less than half of Boise), is a true aberration, the one Southern Idaho city with a Democratic tradition that delivers big Democratic votes. The reason is the labor unions which hustle when need be. But leaving it at that ignores the key word about Pocatello politics:

Chaos.

The Gate City may be Democratic but not the way Preston or Burley or Idaho Falls are Republican. Politics in those places is steady and solid (sometimes too much so). Politics in Pocatello is politics in upheaval. No one runs Pocatello . No one could.

Charles Moss – *Pocatello is not only diverse in people but in issues, and in the intensity in which they support those issues. They've got three senior citizen groups. They won't hardly talk to each other and they won't hardly get together. And you know the Democrats have got about six factions over there ...*

It's a hard town to accept success and remember it. The biggest example I think of: When [ISU] won the national championship in football and flew back - I was down there, and it was a great game - we came back and the terminal was full of people. I walked in there and I wondered if we'd designed it so the damn balcony wouldn't fall down and kill half of them.

This lady came up to me and says, "Oh, Mr. Moss, I know we won the national championship, and that's so great. We'll probably lose our coach."

If a city – as opposed to a town – is a collection of communities, then Pocatello is Idaho's only real city. The Fort Hall Indian Reservation faces it on three sides. Migrant Hispanics show up. The city has a significant Greek population and Idaho's only black community. (It had the state's first black mayor and city councilman, Les Purce, who later headed the state Democratic Party and state Department of Health and Welfare.) Half of Pocatello is Mormon – a smaller portion than any other major town in Eastern Idaho – and other faiths are well represented.

Pocatello has been willing to experiment. It was one of the first to try city manager government (in 1951). For years it didn't work, and the city almost ended the system in 1969. Then the council, which included former legislator and gubernatorial candidate Perry Swisher and future state Democratic chairman Mel Morgan, hired Kansan Charles Moss. For the next 15 years he displayed uncommon expertise in running city hall and an uncanny knack for handling councils, even council members elected on anti-Moss platforms.

Pocatello is not a farm town; it is hemmed in by mountains on two sides and mostly desert on the others. It is a manufacturing, merchant, shipping town, the only Idaho city at two interstates.

And a university town. Idaho State University has less impact here than the U of I does on Moscow, but that's a matter of relative sizes. It adds to the local Democratic organization (though it has left the lead role in the party to union organizers). Its biggest impact is psychological. ISU puts Pocatello in direct competition with Boise and Moscow, and in the eighties many Pocatellans felt it was slighted by state budgeters. That contributed to the city's slightly surly view of the rest of Idaho.

Pocatello and Ogden, Utah, long were the key intermountain stations for Union Pacific, and Pocatello politics grew from that. In World War II a naval ordnance plant was built here, later bought by firms including the Bucyrus- Erie mine equipment builders. After the war phosphate deposits nearby were mined by the J.R. Simplot Co. and FMC Corp., which built big plants west of town. All this brought in thousands of union workers. A central labor council was set up and in the fifties and sixties had a series of sharp leaders who cut their teeth fighting the Right to Work initiative in 1958 and electing a Democratic legislature. In the eighties the unions still could manage two-to- one wins in Bannock for certain Democratic candidates.

But Pocatello also has Mormon business leaders, students and some farm interests. These groups form ever-changing coalitions. Anyone who wins in Pocatello has to appeal to more than one.

So it's no surprise Republicans have a strong, often competitive organization in Bannock . If the Democrats have unions as a conduit, Republicans have the LDS church. Bannock Republicans once were a moderate bunch, including people like Swisher (later a Democrat) who appealed to the center. With the rise of conservative Congressman George Hansen, a Pocatello councilman, conservatives took heart. In the seventies they won over the local Republican party, ran very conservative candidates and won when they outworked and out-organized the Democrats, as they proved they could do. And Pocatello's Democrats were not all liberal. Pocatello is a great party-switching town.

In the late seventies it elected, alongside Democrats, some of the most conservative Republicans in the legislature and a city council dominated by John Birch members and their allies. Moderate Republicans couldn't get the hard core support the conservatives could. (One exception was Ed Brown, an LDS Institute instructor who became a mayor and state legislator; he started as a conservative leader but moderated once in office.) Then Pocatellans tired of shrill voices and turned back toward quieter Democrats, and in the mid-eighties moderate Republican began to regain some of their old strength.

In the eighties Union Pacific trimmed its Pocatello operations, Bucyrus-Erie closed its Pocatello plant, and Simplot and FMC had rough patches. Pocatello entered a slump from which in the late eighties it had not recovered. Declining union membership did not end the Democratic dominance, but a well-organized GOP resurgence easily could change that.[66]

Charles Moss – *I guess you could almost write some kind of a dissertation on the lost opportunities of the seventies ... In the seventies the Chubbuck consolidation, although that had been voted on in the sixties, could have been pushed for. That would have pushed the town over 50,000 [population], and in those days federal funds were about 14 times as high for cities over 50,000. That's a lost opportunity of the seventies. That's a lost opportunity now ...*

I bet we had 14 runs at almost getting the downtown producing neat things. Like on a lot of Center and Main Streets, tying the second floor buildings together with arcades and using the second floors and making a mall out of the existing buildings. That was in the mid-seventies. I think the price of it was somewhere in the neighborhood of $700,000 total.

---

[66] In the 00s, Pocatello has leaned Democratic in local and legislative races, and its mayor in the decade has been Roger Chase, a former Democratic legislator. However, Bannock County often votes for Republicans these days for top-line offices.

Most bruising was loss of the old Bannock Hotel, for decades Pocatello 's meeting place. In the seventies it fell into disrepair and by mid-decade faced destruction. A Bozeman businessman conceived of a new 145-room hotel downtown on a vacant lot and of the Bannock as a convention center. The owner of the empty lot wouldn't sell. Moss recalled standing in an alley with the owner, yelling he was "a short-sighted son of a bitch," the owner yelling back, "You never speak to me again. I'll get you."

Moss's enemies did, using a typically odd Pocatellan combine. In 1985 property tax protesters and union leaders critical of city management uprooted manager government and elected a full-time mayor. (Moss later became the state's budget director.)

Pocatello's old base seems to have little growth potential. But if nuclear operations to the north link with the city's idled manufacturing capacity and with ISU, Pocatello could bloom. Civic leaders have founded a research park. And Pocatello has hidden assets. "Ninety-five percent of it has got sewers and water," Moss said. "Somewhere down the road the towns that have got water are the places where you got to go, and there are a whole bunch that ain't got it. That's been protected. The last I looked, there was somewhere in the neighborhood of 850 building sites you could get a building permit on."[67]

Between Two Cities

On Pocatello's north is the growing, mostly Mormon suburb of Chubbuck, conservative and Republican. Its resistance to merging with Pocatello may come partly from the difference in world view.

The world changes again on the Fort Hall Indian Reservation, largest and most populous in Idaho. Thanks to the American Falls Dam, this is good farm land. But no thanks to federal land inheritance laws, tribal land is chopped into ever-smaller chunks with the passage of generations, limiting tribal members' economic opportunity. The Sho-Bans are more concerned with tribal elections (often extremely heated) than with other politics. Few vote in state or federal elections. Most who do, vote Democratic.

North of the reservoir is the irrigated farmland of Bingham County, the center of Idaho's potato crop. Western Bingham lies on the eastern edge of the Craters of the Moon National Monument's huge lava fields that draw visitors but block settlement in parts of Blaine, Minidoka, and Lincoln counties. In Bingham, farming was tough, soil light, rocks close to the surface. The farmers, mostly

---

[67] Pocatello has fared better than many people from outside would suspect, though it has not been one of the Idaho boom communites. It attracted some high-tech development in the 90s, replacing diminished railroad activity. Pocatello seems to rebound reliably when it gets bad news, but hasn't yet burst through to major growth.

Mormon, who survived were proud of it. They mostly became staunch Republicans.

Blackfoot, a city of 11,000 – a third of Bingham – is the site of State Hospital South for the mentally ill, and of food processing plants, where state workers and unions give Democrats a base. Bingham politics amount to whatever Democrats can get from Blackfoot (which is variable) and the Sho-Ban reservation (small but solidly Democratic) against Republican farmers. Usually, Bingham stays Republican.

It has been pulled between Pocatello to the south and Idaho Falls to the north. At times it has benefited: it was the compromise choice, early in the century, for the Eastern Idaho State Fair. At other times, it has an identity crisis.

Nuke Land

Northwest of Blackfoot lies a breeding ground for jackrabbits and little else.

Irrigation and cattle ranching return at the Big Lost River, which runs through Lost River Valley north to Challis. On its southern end is the town of Arco, founded as a cattle transfer point, still dependant on farming.

In 1955 it was the first city ever lit by atomic power.

That came from what was then called the National Reactor Testing Station of the Atomic Energy Commission (now the Idaho National Engineering Laboratory, INEL), founded in 1949. Dozens of nuclear reactors were built in the desert east of Arco.

More than 10,000 people, a fifth of Eastern Idaho's employed work force, work for INEL, Idaho's biggest federal installation. Contractors like EG&G (employing 3,500 people here) and Westinghouse Idaho Nuclear Co. - the two largest - employ thousands, and there are spinoff businesses. In the mid- eighties INEL's budget was $850 million, more than state government's.

Ironically, INEL had little effect on Arco, which had 961 people in 1950 and fewer than 1,200 in 1984. Most INELers preferred bigger towns. INEL commuter buses run to Pocatello and Blackfoot. But most of the INEL 10,000 live in Idaho Falls , where headquarters and main computer operations are located. The well-paid technocrats tend to be Republican; the majority of the employees are a more mixed bunch who split tickets.

Jack Peterson – *Many times when you visit INEL and visit particular test reactors, if you have a seasoned contractor or DOE official with you, they will point out that Frank Church built this, this was funded by Frank Church. That was all through a 20-year period. And now the newer facilities that are located there, the R and D facilities, Jim McClure built these, or Jim McClure funded this or got a* *line-item. Between Frank Church and Jim McClure, Idaho Falls, INEL and DOE and the nuclear energy establishment have a lot of IOUs.*

Originally most INEL operations and residences once seemed destined to go to Blackfoot, where the Arco road led, and to Pocatello, home of ISU. But the Idaho Falls Chamber of Commerce and other groups raised money for a new road that became part of Highway 20, linking Idaho Falls directly with INEL.

The investment paid off big. In the city once called Eagle Rock, it meant fast population growth and a huge influx of money. Some of it shows up in ritzy Falls suburbs where the technocrats live. Along the Snake Riverside in Idaho Falls the government contractors – "go-cos" – have built the sharpest new office buildings in Idaho. That's still only scratching the surface.

When the millennium turns, Idaho Falls kids may be taught that the pivot in their recent history was no governor or senator but a federal bureaucrat. His name is Troy Wade, and he was for several years the top fed at INEL. What he did was to break down the walls between Idaho and INEL, just as Marco Polo brought a vision of China to backward Europe.

Jack Peterson – *Under the old rules of the Atomic Energy Commission, the predecessor to DOE, all these [INEL] activities were done in post-wartime secrecy. There couldn't be any cross-fertilization because there were security clearances in just about everything that was done. The national labs, wherever they were located in the United States - Los Alamos, Lawrence Livermore - tend to operate behind a security veil. As DOE has become more an agency dealing with public needs, it has begun to find its role and mission. The management has developed a recognition that there are valuable things going on here, and let's transfer some of this stuff out. Let's share what we know ...*

Troy Wade pioneered that. The doors at INEL were opened by Troy Wade and he did it with a modest DOE mandate which he took and ran with. He took the rusty chains and cut them open and said, We're open for business. It was a major shift. Now Don Ofte, who has succeeded Troy Wade, has continued that ...

Idaho Falls could be Idaho's next 100,000-population city, not just the gateway to Yellowstone and Jackson. It could be the emerging western city that has a 21st century technology base. I don't know of any other Rocky Mountain city that has the potential of Idaho Falls .

It was a rail center a hundred years ago, until Pocatello took that away. Farming became the mainstay, and Idaho Falls - the small "falls" were man- made - anchored the Upper Snake River Valley, rich farm country extending another 60 miles northeast. Idaho Falls remains a farm center, and the Farm Bureau and the irrigators' Committee of

Nine retain influence even beyond their economic impact. In time, INEL could reduce it.[68]

Idaho Falls long was an odd place. Once in the forties a Bingham senator thundered that "hellish practices" existed there. In 1958 Perry Swisher described it as "a curiously mixed city. Home of the first LDS temple north of Salt Lake City, it is also the only Idaho city in which strippers work the year around in night clubs, and is more nearly wide open than any other Idaho city of the first class. Pocatello, home of Idaho State College, is under much tighter wraps ..." X-rated businesses and a red light district flourished in the sixties. (Parts of Idaho Falls still look like Las Vegas with casinos stripped out.)[69]

For decades Idaho Falls was a close-split city politically; it was home base for a couple of decades to the powerful Democratic Clark family. But during that time, Idaho Falls Democrats were a conservative group. As INEL grew and many of its workers joined and took over the local Democratic organization, it turned more liberal. Many Mormons joined the Republicans, who developed a powerful organization in the seventies. (Many of the top LDS and Republican leaders have been the same people.) In the eighties Idaho Falls was Republican even in otherwise close races.[70]

John Evans – *I probably lost that [1986 Senate] election in the Upper Snake River Valley. We needed reasonable support out of the Idaho Falls - Bonneville County area to offset losses we expected to suffer in the outlying agricultural areas. But we weren't able to muster that. There was a lot of politics involved but it was a convincing story that, "you support Ronald Reagan because Ronald Reagan is going to take care of INEL and Steve Symms is going to support Ronald Reagan, and you don't know what John Evans is going to do." ... As I was going around I visited one of the technicians, an engineer, who I was hoping would give support. He said, "I have a question. Will you support INEL if you become a United States senator?"*

Still, if INEL continues to grow, so may the Democratic vote in Idaho Falls. If Bonneville Democrats regain the energy they had several decades ago, they could become competitive again.

---

[68] INEL later was renamed (at the urging of then-Senator Dirk Kempthorne) the Idaho National Engineering & Environmental Laboratory (INEEL), but more recently changed again to the simpler Idaho National Laboratory (INL).
[69] About Swisher's reference to "city of the first class": Nowadays under Idaho law, all cities are treated the same, from big Boise down to tiny Warm River. All are considered to be the same as far as Idaho state law is concerned. That was not true back in the 50s and earlier, when Idaho had a more complicated system (akin to a classification system some other states still have) splitting localities into various classes of cities, and allowing other local designations (towns and villages) as well. That system has been swept away in the Gem State.
[70] It has remained Republican, from top to bottom of the ticket, though the center of town has moderated and actually elected a Democratic legislator in 2006 (though he lost his re-election bid in 2008).

The Upper Valley

The Upper Valley has been firmly Republican; Democrats do well to get much more than a third of the vote. It is monolithic from little Clark County to more thickly populated Madison County.

John Porter, veteran Rexburg mayor and newspaperman, said "I think it has a lot to do with the LDS church ... What happens is that if a stake president is a highly partisan Republican and gets in there, he doesn't hesitate to let people know to vote."

The one big non-farm influence is Ricks College in Rexburg.

Certain popular conservative Democrats have been elected here. As key Republicans like Lloyd Adams worked here, so did top Democrats like Gilbert Larsen and John Porter. For years Adams and the Porter family ran competing newspapers located next to each other. Their friendly competition ended when the Porters bought out Adams. That experience was typical. Democrats and Republicans get along in Rexburg. Leaders in both parties often urge someone in the other party to run, and then support them; church and other ties bind people together here more than political differences separate them. That background allowed Adams to work easily with Democrats when they ran state government, and Democrats often sought out Adams for advice. When Republican Mark Ricks considered running for the state Senate, Democratic former Sen. Ray Rigby was one of the first people urging him on.

Rexburg, prim and dry (a rarity for a college town), has been dominated by pioneer families like the Ricks, Porters, and Rigbys. It was co-founded by Thomas Ricks in 1883 and named for him. Descendant Mark Ricks was state Senate majority leader in the eighties. Generation after generation, members of key families are called to top church positions and elected to office. Democrats as such stand little chance, but the right one – a Ray Rigby, for example – can be unbeatable.

They get no help from Ricks College. Unlike Moscow's University of Idaho or Pocatello 's Idaho State University, Ricks is as conservative as its town. The teachers – Democratic Congressman Richard Stallings, a former professor here, notwithstanding – are deeply conservative. Ricks is owned and operated by the Mormon Church, showing again how strong are the LDS ties here.

But beneath a cooperative and obedient veneer lies much more. Rexburg may be the only Mormon town ever to rebel – and successfully – against an order from the high councils of the church.

In the spring of 1957 Ricks' president and Rexburg's stake presidents met with church leaders in Salt Lake at a meeting conducted by LDS President David McKay. The top LDS school administrator, Ernest Wilkinson, said Ricks should be moved to Idaho Falls . The Rexburgers felt ambushed and shocked. In July, word from Salt Lake was: it stays in Rexburg. But then rumors filtered through Idaho Falls that the city might get a state-run junior college – which would compete with Ricks. Mormon versus Gentile sensitivity in Eastern Idaho reached a high pitch then.

In 1958 Madison County Republican state Sen. Kenneth Thatcher, an administrator at Ricks, was running for re-election. Because of his job he had to get, and got, routine written permission from Wilkinson to run. That letter leaked, and Democrats hinted it meant Thatcher was a Wilkinson pawn. "Friends of Sen. Thatcher urged that he vehemently and publicly deny the charges," Lloyd Adams wrote in his memoirs. "Sen. Thatcher came to my office seeking advice, and I told him I thought it would be extremely unwise even to mention the letter from Dr. Wilkinson. I pointed out that it not only would be damaging to the church and Ricks College to make Dr. Wilkinson a campaign issue, but also that it was bound to antagonize Dr. Wilkinson to be brought into a brawl in county politics ..."

Adams was, as usual, on target.

Thatcher rebutted the charges on a radio program. Word hit newspapers statewide – and in Utah. "Dr. Wilkinson was understandably indignant, if unreasonably retaliatory, over being exploited in this manner," Adams wrote. "And on the day before the election [in November 1958] the announcement was made publicly that Ricks College definitely would be moved to Idaho Falls." Thatcher lost the election.

But the move also probably was ordered to quash the plan to build a competing public Idaho Falls junior college. The church even bought land in Idaho Falls to try to cut off state planners.

"There's no question that [prospective move] caused quite a stir," Mark Ricks recalled. "Some felt the institution was synonymous with Rexburg." During the Great Depression the LDS church closed all of its schools and academies except Brigham Young University in Utah and Ricks in Idaho. Ricks survived through local donations and assistance.

Rexburgers' response to the move was not the meek submission church leaders might have expected. The *Rexburg Standard* ran hard-hitting front page editorials against the move. One complained that "We could cite figures and statistics until black in the face but we realize that no matter what we say will be of little avail." A "Committee of 1,000" printed a booklet tearing up Wilkinson. Cards and letters on the evils of big-city Idaho Falls poured into McKay's office. Moving plans ground down.

A turning point came with a bit of Salt Lake foolishness. One day when the Idaho Falls move seemed certain, a man walked into Porter's newspaper office saying he was a businessman from Oregon thinking of setting up shop in Rexburg – but not if Ricks moved. By then, Porter said, "I got a little suspicious of everything. Wilkinson had spies everywhere. So I was a little cautious."

When he left, Porter's brother walked in and asked about the visitor. Porter told him. His brother said that was odd: the man's car had Utah license plates. Porter dashed outside, wrote down the license number and checked it out. The visitor was a private detective from Salt Lake, as Porter swiftly wrote in his paper. Rexburg was in uproar. Mayor Gilbert Larson wrote church officials that he doubted they would hire a private detective to spy on Rexburg, but he wanted to know just what was going on. "And I think that blew the whole thing," Porter said.

By April 1961 moving plans were dropped, the result of a stunning display of independence, perhaps the only time a town ever got top LDS leaders to change course on something important.[71]

The church is also important to the isolated ranch and tourism communities of Driggs and Victor in Teton County, in the valley past the Big Hole mountains to the east, places once split between Republicans and conservative Democrats but staunchly Republican in the seventies and eighties.

St. Anthony is less Mormon; its national forest headquarters, state offices, and other employers bringing in outsiders. It registers in politicians' minds most because of its annual early-summer Fishermen's Breakfast, which draws huge crowds of Eastern Idahoans and as many politicians as want to meet them. Byron Johnson, a 1972 Democratic U.S. Senate candidate, recalled how he and fellow Senate candidate George Hansen, a Republican, stood together and met 10,000 people at the breakfast. "I shook hands with all of them," he said. "I learned that day what sidewalk campaigning was all about, because I watched George."[72]

In the logging and tourist hill country beyond, Mormon impact declines further except in Ashton, a prim farm town. Fremont County turned more Republican in the seventies and eighties. Ashton has been much more Republican than St. Anthony.

The most distinctive community is Island Park, 160 people spread 30 miles on Highway 20 near Yellowstone. When cities were allowed in 1947 to license slot machines, local businessmen incorporated and for six years had tourist- grabbing slots and $5,000 annual income from them. The village didn't have to keep up streets – Main Street was a state highway – or much else. In 1953 slots were outlawed but the city remains, its freewheeling spirit keeping it Democratic in Republican Fremont.

---

[71] So, this point of high irony: In 2001, Ricks College lost not its location but its name, redesignated by church officials as Brigham Young University-Idaho. There was some grumbling in town about the name change, but that was mitigated by an accompanying transition to four-year status, and a removal on what had been a strict limit on growth. The city of Rexburg (and Madison County) have been growing in the 00s at a high clip, owing considerably to the change.
[72] The partisan description of St. Anthony is relative, of course: It was and is a reliably Republican city, but by lessermargins than some of the communities around it. The same applies to descriptions here of most eastern Idaho communities that are maybe "a little less" Republican: Democrats should not count on winning very many of these places even under excellent conditions.

8 | Out of Control

The seventies were the harvest of seeds sewn in the sixties, the battles more grown-up. The conservative-liberal-moderate intra-party clashes were largely gone, as were Lloyd Adams (who died in 1969), Tom Boise (1966), and Jap Inscore (1971.) Their loss weakened both major parties in the seventies. Candidates became not faction symbols but merely themselves.

Len Jordan, for example.

Mr. Conservative was in an odd position. In November 1969 the Senate rejected Nixon's Supreme Court appointee Judge Clement Haynesworth. Jordan, convinced Haynesworth had lied on a conflict of interest question, opposed him. Jordan's friends accused him of selling out to the liberals. Jordan broke with Nixon elsewhere too. Though never a Frank Church dove, after 1968 Jordan became increasingly critical of Nixon's Vietnam policy. Church, after hearing of his retirement, wrote, "Our relationship as colleagues has been so satisfactory – indeed the better word might be ideal – that I hardly need say how much I will miss you."

Jordan could have been re-elected overwhelmingly in 1972. But the criticism wore on him. After a decade in the Senate and no prospect of serving in the majority - with the chairmanships that would entail - he decided to retire in Idaho.

That announcement in August 1971 set off a wild scramble. So rare are open Senate seats in Idaho that Jordan became the first (and, as yet, only) Idaho senator ever to retire rather than die in office or be defeated for re- election.

The players in this race would take central roles in Idaho politics for years.

Andrus would stay where he was; for one thing, his wife Carol didn't want to go to Washington. But Democratic Attorney General Anthony Park was raring to go, and by October he was the favorite for the nomination. Three others also surfaced. Idaho State University President William "Bud" Davis, who had declined to run for governor in 1970, filed. So did teacher and Lloyd Walker supporter Rose Bowman. They were joined by Boise attorney Byron Johnson, a college Republican (he wrote a paper at Harvard on why the federal government shouldn't dam Hells Canyon) who got into Democratic politics in 1963 after going to work in Carl Burke's law firm, and working with Park in the Young Democrats.

At first Park dominated the field: he was the only one of the four who had won public office. Besides attorney general, he had run for the legislature and Ada County prosecutor (and lost) in the sixties. But he had the disadvantage of running against two other Boiseans also perceived as liberals, while Davis was seen as more conservative and older (and more senatorial). Park's other problem was having become AG only a few months before.

Anthony Park – *Yeah, that was too soon. You don't pick your time in this business. Successful politicians are the ones who have impeccable timing ...*

Davis was perceived to be the most moderate of the four of us. His support pretty much reflected that; he had people from the more conservative end of the party. Byron had labor. That's how Byron got in the race, and that's what killed me. I'd have won the race without Byron in it ... The problem was that Byron just wasn't a good candidate. He was a good speaker and bright as hell but he was missing something: the Andrus warmth. He was kind of stern and didn't exude personal charisma.

To ease that sternness, Johnson developed his trademark: abandoning neckties, even on formal occasions.

The advantage went to Davis, the ISU president who so enraged Samuelson. Davis personally was moderate and worked well with business, farm, and other Republican constituencies; low-key and amiable, he had a keen wit and consuming interest in Idaho politics. (He wrote the only serious study of the life and times of Lloyd Adams.) Andrus had such respect for Davis' potential that he tried to talk him into running for governor in 1970. Davis declined, wisely; a Samuelson-Davis race would have been a referendum on campus radicalism that Davis would have lost.

Days after Jordan's announcement, at an Andrus birthday party, Davis' name popped up again, and now he decided to run. One of his organizers was Pocatello city councilman Mel Morgan, who ran Perry Swisher's independent campaign for governor in 1966, later a state Democratic treasurer and chairman. Another was Jay Shelledy, one-time high school basketball coach and deputy sheriff, formerly of the Associated Press and the (Pocatello) *Idaho State Journal*; later, at the *Lewiston Morning Tribune*, he would be one of the most feared and respected reporters in the state.

"You had a campaign that was run by a bunch of amateurs, me included," Morgan said. But they were shrewd amateurs.

Davis won the primary, pitting him in the general election against Republican Congressman Jim McClure. For a time it was a close call. But this was the year of George McGovern, when young McGovernites swept the state Democratic convention, shocking party old-timers. (As elsewhere, the McGovernites were outnumbered but learned the rules and applied them more effectively than anyone else.)

It was also a year of shaky Democratic campaigns in both congressional districts. The first district candidate, Ed Williams, was a solid veteran legislator and an old friend of Andrus', but he never caught the district's imagination. The second district candidate, Willis Ludlow, was a campus minister at ISU. Unlike Davis, Ludlow was a genuine liberal activist, even organizing an anti-Agnew rally in 1970. In December 1970 the Intermountain Observer asked him to cover a

Republican Governors Association meeting in Sun Valley. Ludlow was denied accreditation; when he persisted trying to cover the meeting, state troopers arrested him on a charge of disturbing the peace. The charge was later dropped. Both Democrats lost in 1972.

McClure's campaign was well-financed; he outspent any previous Idaho candidate for any office up to that time. But Davis was respectably financed too, and as late as Oct. 2 Evan Kackley, the old Republican strategist from Wayan – now disgruntled with Republican leadership – wrote Frank Church that "Dr. Davis is in command of sufficient votes that if he bring(s) on a compelling issue the last three weeks he can win, perhaps by a large majority." He suggested pointing up links between McClure and the utilities. "A few days ago, I dropped Dr. Davis a letter relative to the issue. On the same day I tried it out on 10 people as a random sample when I was in Soda Springs and Wayan – no pressure – just friendly talk. These were Republicans. Eight of the 10, I feel, shifted then to Davis. All had been wavering."

McClure's manager, Jim Goller, recalled the race as "fairly close. Bud Davis was a very credible candidate. [In the East] they didn't know Jim that well and Bud Davis was a likeable university president."

Morgan figured one Davis-killer was the McClure-Davis debate. Davis slipped and stumbled through the debate. Morgan recalled, "McClure is not exactly a TV star, but he was that night."

Even worse was the lettuce boycott.

Davis had signed a pledge sheet supporting Cesar Chavez' California lettuce boycott at the state Democratic convention, amid McGovernite ferment. Other top-level Democrats, including other 1972 Senate candidates and Frank Church, also signed. (The petition with Church's signature vanished, sparking another controversy in 1974. Witnesses clearly recall that he signed.)

When Shelledy found out Davis had signed, he met with Chavez' representatives, told them Davis' signature could badly hurt his chances, and asked them if they would be willing to quietly lose the Davis signature; after some debate, they agreed. Then Shelledy put the idea to Davis. But Davis said no: he had once lived among migrant workers and knew their poor standard of living, supported the lettuce boycott, and his signature would stand.

On the Friday before the election, newspaper ads appeared saying, "Davis signed in spite of his knowledge that this same Chavez had announced a nationwide boycott of the Idaho potato in April. A potato boycott which, as Chavez has stated, is designed to do away with the farm labor legislation passed by the 1972 state legislature, and bring all Idaho agriculture under the Chavez United Farm Workers thumb ... We believe Bud Davis would be a disaster for Idaho." (At that time Chavez had threatened but not called for a boycott of Idaho poatoes.)

On the following Monday Davis shot back: "Once and for all ... Bud Davis is totally opposed to any form of a potato boycott. A vicious and unethical advertisement was released last week in which

Bud Davis was linked with Cesar Chavez and some insidious plot to do in the Idaho farmer ... Idaho voters have a time-honored tradition for rejecting smear tactics of any nature."

Actually, Idahoans' record on smears isn't so hot.

Reflecting the Nixon landslide, Republicans swept Idaho in 1972. Davis did well to get his 45.5 percent.

He left Idaho a few years later for New Mexico and Oregon. "I still feel the farmers are more threatened by the takeover of agribusiness by big business, the spiraling interest rates, the smelly wheat scandal and the potato futures manipulation than they were by my signing the Chavez pledge," he was quoted as saying. "I was never approached by Chavez, only a group of Chicano youngsters asking for my help. And then when I saw them later they were all wearing Byron Johnson for Senate buttons."

Park's Narcs

As Tony Park looked ahead, his political future was fuzzy. Park started his term in 1971 well; that gave him confidence to run for the Senate. Then his plans blew up in an explosion that threatened to sink the Andrus Administration as well.

Park's consumer protection effort was popular, and later Republican AGs would battle with legislators to get money for it. He also tried some effective environmental initiatives. His problems started when he took over the Bureau of Narcotics and Organized Crime (BNOC).

Narcotics enforcement then was handled by the state board of pharmacy, which "didn't have the clout, didn't have the law enforcement expertise," as Andrus recalled. The question was where to move it. Memories differ on how and why exactly it got to the attorney general's office. But that is where, in 1971, it went.

"I have only myself to blame," Park said later. "I should have seen it would be a terribly difficult thing, even without all the scandals that ensued. I should have just said no ...

"My own predisposition is that I'm not a cop. I'm a defense attorney, and by Idaho lights a pretty liberal guy. It shouldn't have been something I should have taken. But I saw at that time, too – with the benefit of hindsight I can look back on it – I saw that as a way maybe to offset the liberality I was perceived as having. And it came back and bit me hard."

It got good publicity at first. Reporter Shelledy, by then with the *Lewiston Morning Tribune*, was in a cheerful mood when he dubbed them "Park's Narcs," a nickname that made the attorney general uneasy even before disaster hit.

By mid-1973, BNOC was out of control. Idahoans like to elect zealots to public office but have little tolerance for overzealous government agencies, even overeager narcotics officers. But BNOC was rudderless. Some of its officers were professional but others had less experience than ambition and naivete. Park said later that background checks on many of them were inadequate. Some of their informants had little credibility but mile-long rap sheets.

Many of BNOC's most publicized activities were in Pocatello. Once, a pack of agents spent hours on Scout Mountain outside Pocatello waiting for a regional drug money rendezvous predicted by an informer. It never happened.

Their balloon popped in September 1973 while investigating a supposed "Mr. Big": Mel Morgan, Democratic state treasurer, former Davis and Swisher campaign manager, and then a contender for state chairman. The investigation became elaborate even though, Park would say in court later, all the narcs ever had to go on was the word of one paid informant, whom he described as an unreliable drug user.

Anthony Park – *I told Bob King, my chief of bureau, "Bob, we've got to be absolutely sure of our facts. We cannot make any mistake." I couldn't tell him to whitewash it. It was hard for me to believe and I was tempted to say, "Bob, come on, go find something better to do." But I was afraid to do that. If I had done that, I could legitimately have been accused of whitewashing, and the narcs would have seen to it that the other side got it. They didn't trust me at all. They thought I was a lily-livered liberal ...*

We still might have gotten out of that okay except that we couldn't keep the lid on it ... What we were trying to do was persuade him (Morgan) to let us conclude the investigation, give him a clean bill of health and close the book on the whole matter.

When Morgan found out, he set out to clear his name. He passed a lie detector test and was cleared; no charges ever were filed, and Park apologized to Morgan. But the businessman had received threatening phone calls and was otherwise harassed, and finally he talked with reporters. The story broke in the *Idaho Statesman* on September 14. Morgan held a press conference that day to complain about the narcs' implicit attack on not only his character but that of other Pocatellans. (An informant said that a doctor, three attorneys, half a dozen Pocatello police officers and other people also were supposedly involved in the drug ring. They too were cleared. Apparently no organized drug ring existed at all in Pocatello.) The day before the story came out, the Pocatello city council blasted the narcs, saying they had acted "with complete disregard for individual rights."

The Morgan incident was a turning point. It put the narcs on front pages across Idaho and dramatized their tactics while several narcs faced criminal charges ranging from arson (of a station wagon in Pocatello) to perjury. "The moral corruption was just ghastly," Park recalled.

Park fired most of BNOC. Shelledy bit into the issue and held on like a Gila monster. He reported that the fouled Pocatello drug investigation had cost $30,000 (a figure disputed by the BNOC chief) and wrote about a 1972 shooting of a drug suspect in a Coeur d'Alene parking lot by BNOC agent Michael Caldero.

(Caldero sued Shelledy and the *Tribune* for libel, launching the key libel suit of the decade. Legal action centered around an anonymous assessment in the story of Caldero's actions. Shelledy was ordered by a judge to reveal the source or go to jail; he refused to reveal it, showed up at the Latah County jail, and was denied admittance. The source was Gene Lee, a former assistant chief of BNOC who died in a 1975 traffic accident; his widow released Shelledy from his pledge of confidentiality. At trial, a jury sided with Shelledy and the *Tribune*.)

So Park was vulnerable by 1974 when a Boise Republican, former state Sen. Wayne Kidwell of Boise, ran against him.

Anthony Park – *The ex-narcs were vicious. They followed me around the state, and informers, and drug addicts, and every time I debated Kidwell they'd be out there ... They would stand up and accuse me of being soft on drugs and kind of implying I was part of the conspiracy. And it distracted attention from everything else I had done. Kidwell was a very skillful campaigner and very good at honing in on the negative things. He did a good job of exploiting it ... It cost me my traditional areas of support. A lot of liberals, the young, campus-type people, were very angry, saw me as a Nazi. I lost [Democratic] Bannock County; that was an 8,000-vote swing. And it hurt me in the North, in Latah County.*

The narcs were not the only law enforcement squabble of the early seventies that tarred Park. Other news reports splattered on him too.

The state law enforcement chief then was former Kootenai County Sheriff John Bender, a man widely suspected of various under-the-counter activities while he was sheriff. Kootenai – like Shoshone next door – was reputedly a place where liquor was run across state lines and prostitution and gambling flourished.

Park recalled, "I used to hob nob with a lot of these cops around law enforcement planning, and they thought Bender was the crookedest son of a bitch that ever drew a breath. There was a lot of feeling that way, that we better not put narcotics under Bender. That didn't come from Andrus, and that didn't bother me either. I'd known John Bender for years, and I admired his competence; I thought he was a very bright man and a very good cop. My office investigated him at least three times and never found anything." With Andrus' approval, Park ordered an investigation that lasted six months. The results never were publicly released; when Park left office the file was given to Andrus, who gave it to Bender.

Stanley Crow, a Boise attorney who had worked for the Human Rights Commission in the Samuelson Administration and was helping Pocatello Republicans trying to recall Democratic state Rep. Patricia McDermott, had kept in touch with the narcs. He picked up enough bits and pieces to launch a series of accusatory articles aimed at Andrus. He found out about the Bender investigation and charged that

Park cut it off before damaging information was uncovered. Park bitterly denied it, and said that some of Crow's key facts were wrong.

Then Crow said Andrus had issued an order "not to put too much pressure on Northern Idaho." His articles, which ran rewritten in the Statesman, were full of colorful detail - but nearly all of it came from anonymous sources.

This could have meant trouble for Andrus; it kept re-surfacing years later, when Andrus became interior secretary. But no proof of any wrongdoing emerged. "I don't know that anything factual came out even in all the investigations later," Andrus recalled. "But there was so much ink spilled that it became an issue simply because the media couldn't prove it, they couldn't disprove it, and there was so much written that where there was smoke there must be fire."

A batch of Idaho law enforcement officials converged on Andrus' office one day (at Andrus' request) to pronounce the governor not soft on crime. By then Park had been so closely identified with law enforcement that he probably was more damaged by the reports, even though Bender reported to Andrus.

Andrus won a smashing victory in 1974. Park lost to Kidwell.

Park quit politics. He says that someday he might run for office again, but "I'd never run for attorney general again. Ever."[73]

The Arrangers

To fill the chasm left by Len Jordan's retirement Democrats fielded one big vote-getter (Park) and three little-knowns in their primary. The Republicans flipped that around. The GOP names took time to jell, but soon after the August announcement a long line formed to the right and a short one in the middle of the road. For former Gov. Robert Smylie, "that was mostly, I had to find out," he said later. "I knew I was a gone goose before it came to the wire, but much of that was party organization, people who said I didn't support Samuelson. Which I didn't. I rather thought that was a great deal to require of me."

He was joined by McClure, former Second District Congressman George Hansen, and F.W. "Bill" Bergeson of Pocatello.

McClure was in Alaska on a House Interior Committee trip when aide Jim Goller tracked him down and told him about Jordan. "Nothing I can do up here. Wait till I get back," McClure said. His announcement didn't have long to wait after that.

These were the post-Lloyd Adams days. The makings of a primary war were in the wind. Some worried that with conservatives split so deeply, Smylie might slip through and take the nomination.

---

[73] To date, Park never has run again for public office, though he did serve as chair of the state Democratic Party for a stretch in the mid-90s. He has been a successful Boise attorney and a behind the scenes figure in state Democratic politics.

So money men from Idaho's biggest corporations stepped in. They accurately judged McClure the Republican best able to win. Bergeson, whose credential was having been a two-term Bingham County state senator in the fifties, had a pleasing campaign manner but was unknown and untested. Hansen had fared badly in Northern Idaho against Church. Smylie would turn off conservatives. But McClure had done well in the first district and seemed likely to match that in the second.

One day in October, lobbyists from the J.R. Simplot Co., Idaho Power Co., Boise Cascade Corp., and Morrison-Knudsen Co. met with McClure (and Goller), Hansen (and campaign managers Rich Hendricks of Preston and Joe Preston of Burley), and Bergeson (who showed up stag) all met in a hotel room in Boise.

Everyone seemed to see that meeting differently.

Industry spokesmen said they discussed only the goal of keeping a low number of contenders in the Republican primary.

Smylie, who wasn't there, said he thought nothing shady happened because Hansen invited him (Smylie declined). "The powers that be wanted McClure to win," he said. "They did, and they said it with money." But he also said he had no problem backing McClure for the Senate after he won the nomination.

Jim Goller – *George was really trying to promote himself, and he talked to [Second District Rep.] Orval Hansen and Jim. He said, you guys ought to stay in the House and we'll all lock arms and sweep this race. Well, a lot of people had doubts about George Hansen, partly because of '68. Everybody told George [then] not to run and to stay in the House, and he didn't listen to anybody.*

But Jim McClure said, "I'll tell you what I'll do, George." This was a result of a couple of meetings, one in Pocatello where we met George. Jim McClure said, "George, let's take a survey. And if it shows you've got as good a chance to win this race as I have, I will not run, I will stay in the House."

"Well," George says, "how are you going to finance it?"

He said, "I can get some people together and we'll finance it. We'll all put up a share."

George said, "Well, you'll get these guys over here, and they're prejudiced against me and we won't have a fair survey."

... So we set up this meeting, and the sole purpose of the meeting was to see if George Hansen, not Jim McClure, was the best candidate, if it was a good, clear shot ... We put some money in from our campaign, and George was going to put up some, and these other [corporate] people were going to put up the rest ... And these people weren't even going to see the poll. They just helped finance it.

The poll, Goller said, showed McClure had a clear advantage.

Hansen said it went further. He said he and Bergeson were told McClure was the man and were offered both carrot and stick: if they didn't get out of the race, their campaign funding would dry up – but if they did, the corporate leaders would back Hansen for governor and Bergeson for state chairman in 1974.

That meeting, and another in Washington where Hansen said he again was urged out of the race, left a bad aftertaste. He said nothing of it in the primary campaign. But in the fall of 1972, as the McClure-Davis campaign heated, Hansen let loose. For the rest of the campaign, McClure had to beat back insinuations that his candidacy was bought by big money interests.

McClure, his treasury stuffed, still won the primary election. Hansen was second. Little-known doctor-lawyer Glen Wegner, a White House fellow formerly of Kendrick, who had entered the race after Bergeson died in an auto accident early in 1972, was third. Former Governor Smylie came in forth.

The arrangers incident chilled relations between McClure and Hansen (although Hansen said that he was able to get along well with McClure later). But Hansen's claims made him something more than merely damaged goods. Now he was a martyr, a fighter beaten once by the big-moneyites but eager to swing at them again for the little guy. He was ready – but for what?

The Battle of the Hansens

Two years before George Hansen was elected to Congress in 1964, Idaho Falls attorney Orval Hansen was the Republican congressional nominee who lost to Democrat Ralph Harding. He was uncommonly bright, first in a class of more than 1,000 at the University of Idaho (the third student in its history with a straight-A average). He had served in the Navy and in the Air Force reserve, had worked for former Senator Dworshak, and was a solid state senator, where he was majority leader. But he could not excite the conservative Republican troops, and he lost.

In 1968, with George Hansen vacating his seat, Orval's chances were better. He had returned to the state Senate, continued to build, collected support, and bided his time. In the Republican primary he ran against Idaho Falls probate judge Mary Adams and a three-term state senator from Burley, Don Loveland. Adams, backed by the conservatives, came close to winning. Loveland was from a political family: he and his father both had been Cassia County assessors. His contacts were intricate and helpful. When K.C. Barlow, a veteran Cassia Republican senator, retired, he asked Loveland to replace him. In days when party organization meant more, Loveland could have been a congressman.

Don Loveland – *I just didn't put together as good an organization as I should have done. You know, it was ironic. At that time you had to have 20 percent of the delegates [at the state convention] to get on the ballot. Mary Adams needed one vote. And Jack Murphy and [state Sen.] George Blick and myself went into the back room. And I argued, "Let's keep her off" ... Murphy argued, "Let's* *put her on." His argument was that you had Orval Hansen and Mary Adams from Idaho Falls [splitting that vote].*

She got the vote and wound up second, with Loveland third. But Orval Hansen's strength was fragile. He beat Darrell Manning, a Pocatello Democrat, with just 52.6 percent of the vote.

Hansen did much better in 1970 and 1972, and Democrats began to write off the district. Other Republicans did not oppose him those years, but that didn't mean conservative leaders like Gwen Barnett were happy. Even in 1969 some spoke of Orval as a one-term congressman, of running someone like Bergeson – who later said he was approached by fellow Republicans – against him.

George Hansen saw all this and moved on it. The Hansen name was still hot: in 1973 George's wife Connie ran for the Pocatello City Council and won. (It was an odd election. The other winners were Mel Morgan, who would clash with the Hansens, and Les Purce, who soon would become the first black mayor in Idaho. They barely edged out Perry Swisher, an incumbent councilman and former legislator who had worked hard for Purce.)

George Hansen still had the goods. He rebuilt his campaign network and cranked it up in February 1974. As he had 10 years before, he ran for Congress against an incumbent. Beating an incumbent Republican was trickier than an incumbent Democrat, but the key was the same in both cases: the LDS Church.

A Washington newspaper ran a feature story on Orval Hansen's wife June, a stage actress. It quoted her as saying she enjoyed occasional "candlelight and wine" dinners with her husband – a quote harmless anywhere but in the heart of Zion. The piece was reprinted in Idaho and word was passed through LDS wards that George was the Hansen who didn't drink.[74]

Orval also had a voting record that outraged conservatives. He was closer to Andrus than Samuelson in the White Clouds debate. He backed new aid to education programs, child development centers, poverty programs, and – maybe most odious – the Occupational Safety and Health Administration bill, something George Hansen would rail against for the next decade.

Orval Hansen himself would attribute his 1974 loss largely to Watergate. As everyone else chose up sides, he wanted to wait and see all the evidence; both sides lashed into him for that.

He could win a general election but never had a solid Republican base. George, who did, got 52 percent in the primary.

---

[74] A comment relating this to more recent politics. In 1998 Republican Mike Simpson ran for the same second district congressional seat, and the open secret of the day was that Simpson drank (lightly) and had been a smoker until fairly recently. (As a state legislator, he was a frequent puffer off the House floor.) Would this damage him, either in the primary or general, in both of which he was facing Mormons who neither smoked nor drank? Evidently not, since he won both races convincingly. Hence this curio: Even as the second district has become more strongly Mormon in its population, such issues may be losing their effectiveness.

George Hansen *(office photo)*

In the Republican second district, that was enough for the general election. When Ralph Harding won in 1960 and 1962 he got votes from conservative Democrats; now they were Republicans. Too, the Mormon share of the population was growing faster than any other, and it tended conservative. The Democrat that year was Max Hanson – 1974 was called "the battle of the Hansens" – who had run for governor in 1958 and 1966. In November George Hansen got 56 percent of the vote.

Yet even then George Hansen's career was coming apart, though no one knew it at the time. It would unravel through 1986 when, beaten for re-election, reprimanded by the House, he entered a federal penitentiary in Petersburg, Va. It was the longest and strangest political dying act in Idaho history.

Creative Financing

Perhaps not even the Hansens know where it all started.

It may have begun in 1971 when the "arrangers" told George they would not underwrite his Senate campaign and – he said – undercut other fundraising. Hansen, a gutsy man, bucked them. His campaign went into debt; he said later he personally paid $9,431 of the deficit. Hansen was trying to re-establish an insurance business; the campaign interrupted that. Some political types saw Hansen's lack of money as his initial liability for a 1974 race.

The coolness of key Republican contributors didn't help his race against an incumbent. Richard Hendricks, who had managed campaigns for him before, was back. But Hansen's attorneys said in a court memorandum the next year:

Mr. Hansen started his primary campaign in March or April of 1974, acting as his own manager and using his wife and children as the principal campaign work force. The availability of Mr. Hendricks as manager kept being postponed because of business commitments arising in large part from the sudden and unexpected illness of a key employee in Hendricks' company. Through the spring and summer of 1974, as weeks turned into months, George Hansen kept expecting Mr. Hendricks to be able to step in as manager; Mr. Hendricks kept having to delay assuming these duties; and George Hansen was experiencing great difficulty in attracting other experienced personnel to his staff, mainly because his primary bid was in opposition to an incumbent.

Interest in his finances grew when his first federal campaign report wasn't filed by the June 10 deadline. Hansen said his campaign organization wasn't in place until well into June, and had been unable to write the report on time.

When Hansen filed July 19, he ended his list of contributors with a notation that he had loaned the committee $10,551 during March, April, and May. By primary election day he had loaned his campaign $21,995. He was personally making up the gap between contributions – $27,360 by then – and what he wanted to spend – $49,354. (He reported a cash balance of less than $2 a few days before the primary election.) Hansen certainly is not the only candidate ever to personally underwrite a campaign, but he was one of the few to do it without independent wealth.

Where had he gotten the money to loan his campaign? A week after the primary Hansen said he got it from a bank loan. In September, the *Lewiston Morning Tribune* and *Idaho State Journal* said it was a personal loan from First Security Bank and that in May, as his campaign coffers ran dry, Hansen had approached a Pocatello Democrat, a friend of years' standing, for help. The Democrat backed a $25,000 line of credit for Hansen, who drew on it for his campaign. Hansen's attorneys said the line of credit and loan didn't have to be reported since it was made out to Hansen personally, not to his campaign.

The money picture took another turn in August when Hansen filed a lawsuit against Mel Morgan, the Pocatello Democrat and businessman, charging Morgan had obtained Hansen's private credit rating for political purposes. Morgan said he did get a copy but only for his own use, that "no one else has the credit rating of Mr. Hansen and no one will get it from me." Later, Orval Hansen said under oath that he had a copy and turned it over to a House committee. The case was finally settled out of court in May 1980. Hansen claimed a "victory of principle"; Morgan's attorney said they settled "to get rid of the expense."

After the primary election, Hansen's outside contributions picked up, but problems dogged him. In the fall he was handed an $8,273 telephone bill from his 1968 Senate race. By year's end he had collected $63,123 and spent $78,264.

Democrats wanted to know more (and to keep stirring the pot) and asked Congress to investigate. In late August, at a meeting committee member Orval Hansen did not attend, the House Administration Committee ordered an inquiry. Chairman Wayne Hays, an Ohio Democrat, was especially eager. Hays was very public about the inquiry, predicting Hansen would not be seated if elected.

A push was on in Congress to expand campaign reporting laws. Hays opposed it. Reporters speculated he was interested in Hansen's case as proof the law was tough enough as is.

The day after Gannett News Service broke the story about the committee investigation, Hansen said the report was "vicious and unfounded." But in late August allegations of criminal violations went to the Justice Department amd were kicked around for months, while Hays threatened Hansen would not be seated. (He was.) On February 19, 1975, two criminal charges – of not having filed his June 10 report on time and not reporting properly $2,150 during the next period – were filed against Hansen by the Department of Justice's fraud section. These were misdemeanors, but punishment could be up to $1,000 or a year in prison.

Two days later Hansen pleaded guilty, figuring to get it over with and pay the fine. But Federal District Judge George Hart ordered Hansen to report to the Federal Prison Camp at Allenwood, Pa., on May 2, and stay there for two months. "If the people who make the laws can't obey them, who can we expect to?" he said.

Hansen, his attorneys, and his supporters were stunned. "I am not a criminal," the congressman said, and immediately protested the sentence. Aides researched whether the constitution allowed a judge to jail a congressman. Idaho Republicans asked the faithful to deluge Washington with telegrams urging clemency.

April 21, 1975
Dear Gov. Andrus:
... George V. Hansen is an honest man and certainly not a criminal worthy of a jail sentence. I object to the Idaho representative being made a political example to the country. This is "cruel and unusual punishment" for such a minor mistake. Our Bill of Rights gaurantees us protection from this type of oppression.
Gov. Andrus, as the governor of our state you are a spokesman for the people. You are in a position to lead the people of Idaho in the quest for justice. Your appeal to the president would carry great weight. We don't have time to let the voters of Idaho decide in the next election. If Rep. Hansen is allowed to go to jail not only will justice become a mockery, but he will be greatly damaged personally. Is this what the citizens of Idaho want? They elected him knowing he had these charges against him. Is this what you want? Is he that much of a threat to the Democratic Party? ...

But in an April 25 letter to Willis Ludlow, who ran for Congress in 1972, Andrus said "it makes me sick at heart to know that this is the type of representation we have."

On that same day Hansen went back before Hart. The hearing opened with a powerful plea for leniency by attorney Robert Bennett. Hart relented, swapping two months in prison for a $2,000 fine. "While Mr. Hansen handled these funds negligently, he didn't handle them in a fashion that could be called evil or felonious," Hart said. "Congressman Hansen was stupid in the way he handled his campaign finances but committed no willful violations." (Democrats loved and often repeated Hart's description.)

Events turned sweet for Hansen in 1976. A woman Hays paid for secretarial work, Elizabeth Ray, told the world that her real duties were decidedly non-clerical. A scandalized Hays went into eclipse and left Congress. So much for Hansen's chief nemesis.

Southern Idaho became polarized as Hansen's opposition sniffed a wounded candidate. An Idaho Falls woman circulated petitions calling for his ouster, and sent them to the House Ethics committee. His supporters became aggressively defensive, pointing out that Hansen was not the only candidate who had bookkeeping problems. In May 1975 Hendricks rebutted an *Idaho Statesman* editorial critical of Hansen with a list of glitches in campaign reports of other candidates. He said Orval Hansen's campaign treasurer in 1973 wrote the clerk of the U.S. House that "some of us treasurers are neither public accountants nor attorneys and that we are honestly attempting to follow instructions. However, the complexities of the law, coupled with your requests for these type of corrections, may drive the little people with the little organizations collecting small sums from large groups of ordinary people right out of existence."

Hansen went further, weaving into his speeches a picture of Eastern Liberals and news media out to get him. No such conspiracy existed. Some of the Idaho press did see Hansen as someone who didn't belong in public office, and some of it saw in his troubles a great news story. But some papers stayed friendly, and he had friends among conservative reporters in Washington.

And he still had a campaign debt. In September 1975 he reported $51,000 in debts, and the 1976 race was around the bend. Hansen needed more than Southern Idaho pass-the-hat fundraising.

So he grew closer to national conservative mail-order fundraisers and other moneymen. In 1975 he got help from the conservative Committee for the Survival of a Free Congress and from Richard Viguerie, a top national mail fundraiser. South Carolina Republican Sen. Strom Thurmond signed a mass-mailed Hansen fundraising letter which brought in tens of thousands of dollars, enough to clear Hansen's campaign debts by March 1976. He raised more than $120,000 for the 1976 race.

Republican opponents, wailing that Hansen was unelectable, got little support. An unelectable Hansen beat them easily.

The truth was that Hansen was neither a pushover nor invulnerable. He was a fine political tactician who knew his district intimately: he had campaigned across it more often than not since 1962. He was a natural politician, bombastic in speeches, low-key, upbeat and self-effacing in conversation. The combination was faultless for southern Idaho. Though his attendance on committees and the House floor was weak, Hansen worked hard, 10 to 12 hours a day in his office. He loved Washington but led little social life; his life was being a congressman.

Even disasters helped him. In June 1976 the big new Teton Dam near St. Anthony broke, unleashing tons of water on the upper Snake River Valley. Sugar City was nearly wiped out, Rexburg devastated and 30 miles downstream Idaho Falls suffered great damage. Idaho politicians flew there in force and emergency government aid flowed. But much of the best aid came from the LDS Church, which organized a huge volunteer effort. As the Mormon in the congressional delegation, Hansen was in a unique position to coordinate. His staffers talked proudly for years about their flood work. In later elections when Hansen's support faltered in the Magic Valley and elsewhere, his support in the Upper Snake River Valley stayed intact, greater than anywhere else.

The Democrats who faced him in 1976 were more formidable than the Republicans. Freshman state Sen. Stan Kress of Firth, former Congressman Ralph Harding, and former Pocatello-area magistrate Kelly Pearce thought of running; Kress and Pearce did. Kress won the tough primary and charged hard up Hansen Hill.

The campaign was a barnburner. Kress, a young educator, hit Hansen hard on finances. The campaign was spiced when Shelledy – who had trailed Hansen for two years - reported that the congressman had been not filed income tax returns, while a sitting congressman, for 1966 and 1967, but that he filed and made payment two years later during a security check for appointment to the Nixon Administration. Hansen pointed out that, as a salaried federal employee, tax money had routinely been withheld from his paychecks, and that he was up to date on all his tax payments. But the news raised eyebrows.

The result was a lightning-close finish: Hansen won by 1,938 votes out of more than 166,000 cast.

Logic suggested that Hansen's worst troubles were over. His campaign was debt- free, his legal battles behind him.

And yet in March 1977, he asked the Federal Election Commission if he could solicit money, either in person or by mail, for personal, not campaign, use. He said he would not solicit from constituents or large groups and would report what he received and where he got it. Hansen even came up with a form: "I, the undersigned, hereby affirm that the purpose of this gift in the amount of $(amount) is donated to (the office holder) for his personal use only, and that this gift is not given to influence any nomination or election or as a campaign contribution or for the purpose of promoting or maintaining the official activities of (the office holder)." He gave the FEC a sample fundraising letter, it, too, signed by Strom Thurmond.

He said he had huge debts connected with serving in office. He would not say what he owed the money for - other than legal fees - or to whom. If the law allowed unlimited gifts to congressmen by anyone who might want to influence legislation, every ethics law on the books might as well be repealed. But the FEC copped out, saying non-campaign finances were outside its jurisdiction.

Hansen promptly said, "the FEC ... found no objection to my request to solicit funds to fend off vicious politically-based personal attacks launched against me during my past election." With that creative analysis in hand, he said he probably would forge ahead – but he must have sensed a need for more grounding. He asked the House Select Committee on Ethics if a congressman could solicit personal gifts through mass mail and whether an independent committee could do so on a congressman's behalf. In May the committee said no to both. A non-member of Congress could raise money but House rules restricted what a congressman could accept. Hansen said he accepted the ruling. And that was that ...

For two weeks. In late May the Twin Falls *Times News* reported that Hansen flew to Idaho for quiet meetings in Boise, Pocatello, and Twin Falls with key contributors. He outlined a desperate financial quandary, debts of $400,000 or more, and pleaded for loans. He also mentioned a new possibility: dividing the Hansens' assets and debts, so Connie could fund-raise and pay off her half. Hansen later said the column reporting the meetings was flawed, and he did not confirm $400,000 as the right figure (that number did keep cropping up through the years).

But within days the Connie part, at least, came true. She wrote the House Ethics Committee that she and George were "legally and properly dividing our property ... Let me inform you that I don't intend to stand by and let a committee of Congress or anyone else deprive me of the basic rights of a citizen of this nation to pay my bills and protect my home." The agreement was executed in September 1977, but Congressional investigators later would point out that no document dividing the property was ever put on record in a government office.

Soon her letter was out. "My husband has beaten the attacks by the liberals now for three years," it said. "However, they have wounded us badly financially, and now have succeeded stopping him personally from any financial repair, short of resigning from Congress. This is what the liberals want, of course. If they can't defeat you at the polls, it seems they won't quit until they ruin you financially."

Money poured in.

Again Democrats were gleeful and Republicans skeptical: how were they going to explain this? State Senate President pro tem Phil Batt said he might not support Hansen for re-election in 1978. Several top Republicans, including Vern Ravenscroft, considered running against Hansen, convinced he was unelectable. (But Ravenscroft ran for governor in 1978.) Instead, Hansen drew a little-known attorney from Eden, Jim Jones.

Jones was not new to politics. He had worked for Sen. Len Jordan, and was then Jerome County prosecutor.

Jim Jones – *I gave it a little thought in February [1978], when there was a big expose about George's financing problems. I think it was a story Dave*

Morrissey did in the Times-News, saying that George had not reported Connie's financial affairs, and there was an investigation going on. I thought, "Oh, geeze, that's the last straw. We're going to lose this seat." And it might be a good opportunity to get in. So I called Jordan and said I was concerned about this deal, and it looks like it might be a time to run. He said, "Nah, other people have been polling" - I think Vern Ravenscroft had been polling - and it showed George had a hard core of support. He said, "I wouldn't try it." So I said okay, fine. I was satisfied with that.

Then another story hit ... And I thought, well, criminy, you know? Here we go again. I decided to follow my own counsel, so I jumped in not knowing anything about the deal, about two and a half months till the primary. Probably not the most reasonable thing to do ...

I made my announcement about five days before the Republican convention in Pocatello. I hadn't done any campaigning. On my way over there, I remember stopping in Carey, and it was the first time I had ever walked up to anybody anywhere and said, "Hi, I'm running for Congress." I went into the Merc at Carey and introduced myself to the store clerk. It was a traumatic experience.

He did get good help. He sought out Hendricks, who had just been fired from the Hansen staff after a series of conflicts with the Hansens. Hendricks helped Jones. But as a campaigner Jones - small, thin, soft-spoken, a shadow of Hansen - was outclassed. He ran into hostility from Hansen's troops and much of the Republican organization. And as the Mormon population in the second district grew, so did the importance of being Mormon. (Hansen was, Jones wasn't.) Hansen won the 1978 primary, though his vote among Republicans – 56 percent – fell far short of two years before. Jones himself was surprised he did so well. "I think I caught them by surprise," he said later. "They didn't think anybody would be able to come that close."

Hansen looked vulnerable enough that two Democrats, Kress and Harding – in his first race since 1966 – launched into a knock-down drag-out over it. Both badly wanted a rematch; Kress, with his burnished organization from 1976 intact, prevailed. It was an empty win. Kress ran a fine campaign but Hansen's financial problems were too old. Hansen's fundraising machine had been perfected, and he outspent Kress nearly two to one. He won a solid 57 percent of the vote.[75]

---

[75] Kress, one of the Democratic leading lights as a campaigner in the 70s, hasn't sought office again since. He did run the gubernatorial campaign of Democrat Larry EchoHawk in 1994, and currently is superintendent of the Cottonwood School District.
His races did go some distance toward paving the way for Hansen's eventual defeat in 1984, by building organization and bringing key people into the picture. An especially notably example: Kress' key campaign organizer was a veteran Pocatello Democratic worker, Angie Neitzel, who went on to work on the campaign organization that helped Democrat Richard Stallings to win the seat four times, from 1984 to 1990. (Perhaps significantly, she wasn't his campaign manager in the 1992 Senate and 1998 House races that Stallings lost.)

After that, thinking about Hansen changed. Southern Idahoans quit perceiving him as being forever on the ledge of a political bottomless pit. While in trouble he had run three consecutive primary and general elections against respectable opponents and won every time. Word spread that Hansen was unbeatable.

He wasn't, of course. Any politician can be beaten, given the right circumstances. In his case, those took time to evolve.

After 1978, Hansen stayed flamboyant. He took on the IRS and OSHA and the Panama Canal treaties. He crashed the world stage in 1979 when, during the American hostage crisis in Iran, he flew to Teheran and met with the prisoners and top Iranian officials. (Hansen said the trip may have done some good, and that at least the prisoners' morale was raised for a while. Critics said it undermined the U.S. negotiating position.) His issues were sometimes off center stage, but Idahoans accepted that, and the issues he did choose tended to be popular back home.

In 1980, Jones opposed him again. He was a much improved campaigner now and had prepared powerful and detailed analyses of Hansen's record. Hansen stomped him, and did even better against the underfinanced Democrat, former state Sen. Diane Bilyeu of Pocatello. Once again came the word: Hansen is unbeatable.

By 1982 he seemed to have settled in for the long term. He jumped onto the financial turmoil at the Washington Public Power Supply System with vigor and imagination. Hansen in 1982 had no Republican primary opponent, and Democrats settled for pitting an unknown against him. Competition for the Democratic nomination was between Ricks College history professor Richard Stallings of Rexburg and Buhl businessman/Filer resident George Anthony; their chief political credentials at that time were having previously lost races for the legislature. Stallings won the primary.

But Hansen's financial problems had not gone away; they were merely in cocoon stage, developing, waiting to spring forth. Constituents and Idaho reporters paid less attention. So it should be no surprise that people far from Idaho picked up the string that unraveled Hansen's political career.

In March 1981, according to a congressional report, Texas billionaire Nelson Bunker Hunt received an anonymous letter detailing financial activities between he and Hansen "to secure Rep. Hansen's support in your bid for a large silver mine in Idaho." Hunt contacted Hansen, who urged the letter be turned over to the Justice Department, as it was a few days later. As Hansen later would tell the House, he "demanded an immediate and vigorous investigation." But, after tracking down the blackmailer, the investigators took turns Hansen may not have expected.

That inquiry crossed paths with two *Wall Street Journal* reporters. Political reporter Brooks Jackson had been following congressional ethics; he was convinced the House Ethics Committee was asleep at the switch. Edward Pound was following Herbert and Nelson Bunker

Hunt. In the spring of 1982 they hit the mother lode – the blackmail letter – and verified the details.

In 1979, for example, Hunt had helped Mrs. Hansen turn a quick $87,475 profit in silver futures. The Journal detailed how the transaction worked and said that Mrs. Hansen never had risked any money, that a series of concessions by money people let her pay for the futures the same day the profit was realized. None of this showed up on Hansen's personal finance reports. Hansen said he didn't have to report it because the deal was Connie's and the profit wasn't his. But Congressman Louis Stokes of Ohio said later that Hansen had "arranged for the delivery and spent all of the $87,000," and that he and Connie routinely commingled their finances, filed joint tax returns and had a joint bank account.

Other deals surfaced. One of the most intriguing, in Stokes' words: "In 1981 Mr. Hansen, this time in his own name, without his wife being involved, arranged for three separate loans totaling $135,000 from three Virginia businessmen. At the same time that he asked for and received unsecured loans from these men, the men were involved in a plan to develop a hydrogen-powered automobile. During this same period, they asked Mr. Hansen to help them in their effort by arranging and attending meetings with Defense Department officials to discuss the automobile. In fact, the day the first loan funds were deposited in Mr. Hansen's account, he took these men to a meeting he had arranged with the secretary of the army at the Pentagon." Hansen said that money was being raised not for personal purposes, but for a tax policy committee he was working with.

The *Journal's* article outlined the complex financial dealings with Hunt, and other transactions besides. Its thrust was that the Ethics Committee wasn't paying attention to its job.

Hansen attacked the *Journal* in the *Congressional Record.* But the *Journal* article, appearing as it did in a national paper, had started a ball rolling.

Stallings waffled for months between advisors who urged him to slice Hansen apart and those who urged him to take a high road. Hansen beat him in November 1982. But it was the closest shave for Hansen in years: he got only 52 percent of the vote.

The Ethics Committee had been stirred by the Journal's reporting. A grand jury already looking into Hunt indicted Hansen in April 1983 on charges of making false statements on 1978, 1979, 1980, and 1981 financial disclosure reports (his 1982 report was not yet due). Hansen, the first public official indicted under the 1978 ethics law, declared it an outrage. He was arraigned a few days later and, in contrast to 1975, pleaded not guilty.

He tried to go on being a congressman, but that became difficult. Hansen was facing felonies now, and because he contested the charges the prosecution would show in open court mountains of information about his finances, reviving the issue in Idaho. Stallings announced again in 1984. So did Dan Adamson, a Republican Jerome attorney and Jim Jones' former campaign manager.

Early in 1984, speculation was that Hansen had escaped so many tight squeezes before that he surely would again. But the trial testimony took the case into new realms. The jury convicted Hansen of four felonies - which was, Hansen said, "a gross miscarriage of justice." He never gave up and seldom admitted legal reversals were reversals: usually, he said, they cleared the way for a new attack on the government's case. But the verdict stuck. He was sentenced to five to 15 months in federal prison.

And he launched his eighth campaign for the House.

Days after the conviction, he flew home to Pocatello where state Republican Chairman Dennis Olson organized a mass meeting at the Quality Inn. More than 300 Republicans led by top party leaders listened to Hansen and his attorneys explain the case, while Adamson fumed outside the room. Hansen distributed a ballot to the faithful, asking them: Should he run? A few days later he said the results were good, and he filed.

The party hierarchy, which so opposed him in his early days, stuck by him. Adamson, an inexperienced campaigner, could raise little support or money. Despite that Hansen prevailed in the primary by a single percentage point. Conviction of felonies had badly shaken people in the outlands. A key to a successful major campaign is knowing who will and won't support you. There were signs in 1984 that while some of the old Hansen supporters publicly stuck with George, they privately shook their heads.

On the last day of July the House voted, 354-52, to reprimand Hansen. It was the lightest punishment the House could administer, but it hurt Hansen. In August a report in the *Idaho Statesman* startled even the jaded: In one month in 1979, $840,000 had passed through Hansen's Glenns Ferry bank account, one of many accounts he had. The numbers were a shock, and Stallings exploited them. "At my present earning power I would have to work 28 years to equal the amount of income that George and Connie Hansen put through one checking account in one month," he said. "People are frustrated and angered to learn their congressman was able to write checks for $840,000 in a one month period while going around the nation claiming poverty and persecution."

Then wheels turned and Hansen's fabled luck seemed to return.

His trial over, legal work in the hands of attorneys, Hansen spent time in Idaho mending fences. And he got an incredibly lucky break. Geraldine Ferraro, the Democratic vice-presidential nominee, filed financial reports for six years without describing her husband's income and assets. Hansen was exultant: she had done what he was accused of, he said, yet he was prosecuted and she wasn't. The cases were different but the point hit home in Idaho, especially since Mondale and Ferraro were the least popular major party presidential ticket in Idaho in the twentieth century. Against a backdrop of Reagan

Landslide '84, Stallings got undecided votes but Hansen won back many old supporters.

The result was yet another photo finish, almost as close as a congressional race could be. Stallings won by 170 votes – a statistically insignificant margin. Hansen got a recount of a few precincts; the few discrepancies were to Stallings' benefit. Hansen's supporters still contested the election, and Stallings was seated in the House only after a debate on the House floor. (It was tangled in a squabble over an unrelated Indiana case.)

Hansen ran out of legal appeals, and pleas for intervention by the White House went nowhere. In the summer of 1986, he entered federal prison at Petersburg, Va.

After six months he was released on a form of probation. Hansen said he would not agree to some of the terms limiting his travel around the country – his work as a speaker and consultant kept him moving around – but corrections officials let him out anyway. Months later – perhaps not coincidentally on April 15, Income Tax Day - he was arrested in Omaha and as secretly as possible, to throw off the press, hustled back to Washington, charged with violating probation, and returned to Petersburg.

He was harshly treated compared to many non-violent prisoners: roughly handled and shackled more than necessary, housed with heavy-duty offenders. When he was released in October 1987, sympathy blossomed. Conservative friends in Washington threw a coming out bash for him. A week later he returned to Idaho, to another party in a Chubbuck motel. The crowd was a smaller than in the old days, but many of the faithful were there.

Thinner and younger-looking than before prison, Hansen seemed neither sullen nor depressed. He was as outgoing as ever; he smiled, shook hands, and speechified as of old. He even got along with the press which, he said, had by its interest in his case spared him further torments. Hansen, who years before had collaborated on a book on IRS abuses, said he planned two more, on the nation's legal and prison systems.

And politics? Hansen had been nominated by the Populist Party, a right-wing fringe group, for president. Hansen had addressed a Populist meeting months before, during his time out of prison. Hansen initially waffled on allowing the group to use his name, and later rejected it. But that was the minor question.

In Chubbuck, loyalists talked up another Hansen run for the House in 1988. Hansen splashed cold water on it. He had a consulting business to run and it was based in Washington, he said.[76]

And yet you couldn't miss the gleam in his eye ...

---

[76] Unmentioned here, but should have been: Hansen's wife Connie ran for theHouse seat in 1986 (she lost the primary, but was herself a skillful campaigner). Hansen has never run for office again. We should note here too that some of the charges against Hansen were eventually thrown out.

9 | Sunnyslope & the Supply Side

When Steve Symms told his neighbors early in 1972 he was going to run for "representative," they thought he was talking about the Idaho legislature. When they realized he meant Congress, they shook their heads. One of his best friends, Caldwell businessman Ralph Smeed, tried to talk him out of it. Symms was setting himself up for a fall, he warned. The semi-libertarian philosophy they treasured could be discredited if Symms were shellacked.

Outside the Sunny Slope hillside, where the Symms family orchards overlook the small farm town of Marsing, he was unknown. Inexperienced unknowns often run for Congress and get nowhere because they lack the skills, contacts, supporters, and money. Even Frank Church, who never held public office before being elected to the Senate in 1956, had first run for the legislature and had spent years as a top state Democratic Party organizer.

Symms's campaign experience was managing a Sigma Nu fraternity brother's campaign for University of Idaho student body president. (The candidate, who lost, was future state Sen. Laird Noh.)[77]

His party experience was volunteer work for Barry Goldwater in 1964 and leading a local Republican booster club. He attended the 1966 state GOP convention and chatted with then-Gov. Smylie. "I certainly appreciated hearing your views on the sales tax," he said in a hand-written note, "and was most happy to help keep our delegation from wanting to fight the issue." In February 1970 Symms wrote Frank Church, asking him to support a farm labor bill favored by the produce industry. And that was about all.

Biting Apples

Even Symms took for granted that he would lose in 1972.

Which didn't stop him. He did call a few friends, including former and future state Sen. Phil Batt, to make sure they weren't running for Congress. (Batt instead ran the campaign of Wayne Kidwell, whom Symms would oppose.) He didn't bother to inform Republican powers or to line up money. His disdain for political hierarchy was clear from his choice for president. While almost every other Idaho Republican backed Nixon, Symms favored conservative Ohio Congressman John Ashbrook.

Symms just sat down at his kitchen table one night, scribbled his announcement message and mailed it to newspapers and radio and television stations. He held no press conference. He had never held one and probably wouldn't have known what to do.

---

[77] Correction here: It was the other way around. Noh served as *Symms'* campaign manager in the unsuccessful campaign.

The pros who declared Symms DOA when they got those announcements – which have become collectors' items – can't be faulted. Symms' win in 1972 was Idaho's political upset of the century.

Anthony Park – *I had known Steve for years, from the University of Idaho; he played football up there with my brother Lonnie ... He was a fine football player and a nice guy. Lonnie liked him. I liked him. I lost touch, and the next thing I know he's running for Congress.*

We all kind of laughed. There was this – kind of buffoon, running up and down the street. There'd be parades and he'd be out on the street, not sitting in any car. He was running up and down and throwing his stuff around and shaking hands. He was a dynamo. We laughed because we figured Kidwell had it locked. And he surprised everybody. He was a hell of campaigner. He worked his butt off, running around, talking this Libertarian stuff.

Symms did not have to learn how to campaign. He was a natural, like Glen Taylor or George Hansen, relentlessly cheery and gregarious. His lack of polish – he acquired some of that later – was no disability. It pointed up his status as an outrider, happily plotting a shakeup in Washington. The underlying appeal was similar to Hansen's, but Symms was no bombast and he did not preach doom. He was a happy warrior, like Church (or Hubert Humphrey), a Mr. Feelgood. His ads featured, and his trademark became, an apple with a bite taken out of it. The sight of Symms crunching into a bright red Symms Fruit Ranch apple, talking of taking a bite out of government, became a familiar sight. It was a brilliant bit of instantly memorable advertising.

His other advantage lay in his message – less in its popularity than in Symms' devotion to it and the way it set him apart from other Republicans.

In 1972, Symms was not just another conservative Republican.

He could have been; his background suggested he would be. For years after the Symmses sank roots at Sunnyslope in 1912 they faced hard times. They were largely over by the time Steve was born in 1938, but they imprinted the family with a tough free enterprise ethic, shared by much of western Canyon County. And his service in the Marines gave him a hawkish world view.

One of his best friends was Ralph Smeed, a businessman whose family once owned a big chunk of Caldwell. Wheeling and dealing was the norm to the Smeeds, and Ralph loved the free enterprise system. He didn't run for office himself but was often in the background when like-minded Republicans hit the trail, a local guru in the coffee shops when folks tried meshing libertarianism – cutting back government on all fronts, economic, social and military – with old-line conservatism.

Smeed and Symms attended a Presbyterian Church in the Caldwell area and, in the mid-sixties, became upset with it. Its leaders got involved with the more liberal National Council of Churches. Symms and Smeed were ringleaders of a group that tried to turn the church rightward, even printing an opinion sheet called *The Layman*. When they made no headway, they left the church. (Symms then joined a Methodist Church.)

With Robert Smith, a Nampa attorney of similar persuasion, they published *The Idaho Compass*, "A Journal of Fact and Opinion with Emphasis on Idaho Affairs." The first of only a few editions came out in June 1969, paid for by contributions and sent to contributors and colleges. (These, too, are collectors' items.) The four-page first edition had a statement of purpose, a critique of Idaho higher education – which didn't teach enough capitalism, the authors said – and a reprint of an Earl Nightingale column.[78]

Steve Symms *(office photo)*

In 1969 Symms became president of the University of Idaho alumni association; the *Compass* so riled the faculty that he was forced out. Idaho's campuses were not nearly so unruly as others nationally, but conservatives in Idaho, from Symms and Smeed to Samuelson, were deeply suspicious of them.

By 1972, Symms was restless. The *Compass* defunct, the booster club quiet, fired as alumni president, he had no platform. He wanted to push his message and decided to run for Congress, for the seat McClure was vacating, to talk up and down the district.

He broke all the rules. He got into the campaign late, after two others had entered. Robert Purcell, who opposed McClure in 1966 and picked up the moderate organization and votes, was trying again. The favorite was Wayne Kidwell, the smooth, articulate state senate majority leader and former Ada County prosecutor. Symms was an afterthought.

But Purcell had been out of Idaho nearly six years, working for a group promoting blood research. Kidwell was stuck in a long Senate session. Both made the mistake of ignoring Symms.

Unfamiliar with the dos and don'ts of campaigning, Symms made mistakes. But he showed sparks of creativity. Campaigning in the Silver Valley, he had a hard time winning over skeptical Democratic miners. He promised that if he won the primary he would work a week in a mine. (And he did.) Symms was good at campaigning, enjoyed it, and outworked Kidwell and Purcell, who were watching each other rather than him.

---

[78] Their significance lay in focusing the thoughts of this group. As so often happens, political philosophies often stay rather hazy until they're written down. Which this group, unlike many others in Idaho politics, did, and did independent of standard-issue party platforms.

Two weeks before the primary election, six political reporters were asked who would win. Five predicted Kidwell, the sixth Purcell. Not until days before the election did the pros sense something else. Bill Hall wrote in the *Lewiston Morning Tribune* that earlier, Symms was "expected to use the forum to make a few ultra-conservative points and then be laughed out of the race ... Today, no one is laughing. The secret of Symms' ongoing success is as simple as the candidate: he stands out in the crowd."

Symms got 28,422 votes, Kidwell 22,445 and Purcell 11,926. That and Smylie's devastating loss in the Senate race the same day showed the impotence of moderates in the Republican Party. It also showed how conservative the first district had become.

Symms had the perfect Democratic opponent: legislator and close Andrus friend Ed Williams of Lewiston. Williams was a respected House minority leader, but Mr. Excitement he wasn't. Symms took to the race with relish, biting apples all over the first district and even in a televised debate with Williams.

He was taken very seriously that fall. A McGovern for President worker climbed all over Symms when Symms declared that McGovern's proposed $1,000 payback tomany citizens would mean an average $1,000 increase in many people's income taxes. Symms was reported to have proposed turning the U of I's College of Mines over to the Anaconda Copper Co. and its School of Forestry over to the Boise Cascade Corp. He denied it. Then, speaking in Moscow a month before the election, he said, "I'm not sure we can't run a school at a profit ... We might try leasing the schools."

Symms eclipsed Williams for attention value (Idaho voters love to be entertained) and won with 55.6 percent of the vote.

"Who is Bob Smith?"

Symms's early House years reflected his first campaign: carefree, cocky, and as close to libertarian purity as anyone in Congress. On his first day in office, January 3, 1973, he proposed two bills, one allowing Americans to own gold and the other allowing private companies to deliver the mail. Both were ahead of their time and both vanished into the black hole of House subcommittees. Symms did not compromise or play games to move them. And so it went. Symms proposed repealing the Occupational Safety and Health Act and engaged in guerrilla warfare on the budget process. The gregarious Symms was personally popular with other congressmen, but few cared for his ideas.

He also stayed popular back home, a point noted by Bob Smith, the Nampa attorney, former Methodist minister, and old friend who went with Symms to Washington. Smith kept close watch on Idaho politics and saw reason for encouragement.

There was McClure, close philosophically, if not in temperament, to Symms, winning his Senate race in 1972.

There was a batch of new state legislators who thought much as Symms did. Several – notably C.L. "Butch" Otter of Caldwell, son-in-law of spud king J.R. Simplot – came from Canyon.

A new wing of the Republican Party was taking form, as conservative as the Hansen-Mormon wing but grounded in libertarianism. It did not incorporate church doctrine into its politics, as so often happened in Eastern Idaho. Until Symms's election it had a vague, vaporous presence because it lacked a spokesman. Powers that be – money men and leading politicians – had not had a reason to think it had widespread appeal in Idaho. But it did.

Smith watched these changes and began laying the groundwork for 1974, when Frank Church would be up for re-election. He had some experience: Smith had managed Symms' 1972 race. And he had a reputation: Symms once said he had thought early in 1972 that Smith, not he, ought to run for Congress. That was understandable. Smith had the easy, cool demeanor politicians like to think they have. He was a natural political animal, at home in the world of give and take (while not giving in on ideas). That is why Symms was the better Idaho candidate: he had natural effervescence and conveyed a sense of not being a politician. Smith's polish made him seem vaguely slick. Californians or Utahans like slick; Idahoans don't.

Smith started early: after six months on Capitol Hill, he made his intentions clear and in November 1973 made it official. Smith won his contested primary election and set after Frank Church.

In 1973 pundits declared Church unbeatable. He had survived a recall attempt and challenge from a sitting congressman in 1968, at the peak of emotion over Vietnam. If it could be argued that year was a turning point in public attitude on Vietnam, then by 1973 the war of ideas was over - and Church had won. By late 1973 disillusionment had set in with the Nixon Administration, and the forecast called for a Republican bashing in 1974. But Church hadn't worked the state as he had in 1967 and 1968, and he underrated the first-time campaigner.

Smith, however, didn't content himself with Symms's happy warrior style of generally ignoring the opposition (as Lloyd Adams usually advised young campaigners to do). Smith was trying to unseat an incumbent, and Church was such a big fact of life in Idaho that he could not be ignored.

So Smith hit hard, often on traditional subjects such as criticizing Church as a big spender. Sometimes he misfired. In July 1974 he pointed out that Church's wife Bethine had an option to buy a piece of her family's Robinson Bar Ranch near Clayton. It meant a possible conflict of interest, since Congress was considering a national recreation area bill affecting nearby areas. He said the option to buy hadn't been disclosed by Church. Church replied that the option was his wife's, not his. (George and Connie Hansen would use a similar argument later for different purposes; by then, disclosure laws were toughened.) Mrs. Church's acre was sold to avoid conflicts. It was a minor squall, but most Idahoans who took an interest in it probably sympathized with the Churches, who were made to sell off ancestral holdings.

Symms also inadvertently gave Smith a big obstacle: the John Birch Society. Church denounced it often; it had become involved in the 1968 Senate race, weighing in where it could for George Hansen. George Wallace's American Independent Party, which had a strong Birch element, endorsed Hansen. In 1974 the JBS went all out against Church, running in its American Opinion magazine one article slamming Church and another praising Smith. The first came out in June, a 14-page piece called "Chameleon in the Senate," by Alan Stang, a contributing editor who also delivered radio commentaries in Idaho. Between 50,000 and 100,000 copies were distributed statewide. It alleged that Church was "pro-Communist" and with gleeful abandon made charge after charge. But far from hurting Church, "Chameleon" was so extreme that Church again won sympathy.

It was up to Smith to say something, and many Republicans as well as Democrats asked him to disown the article.

He didn't. He couldn't.

A week after the 1972 election, Symms was interviewed in the *Intermountain Observer* about his philosophy. "I'm sure there are a lot of people," the interviewer said, "who think you're –"

"A John Birch conservative?" Symms said. "They're wrong."

"How do you differ from extreme right wingers?"

"I don't see the big communist conspiracy," he said. "I don't think communists are that smart."

Birchism hadn't been big in Canyon County libertarianism. Smeed said later that "I just don't relate to Birchers."

But once in Congress the gregarious Symms edged toward other conservatives, and one of his closest allies was John Rousselot, a California Republican and a national JBS leader. Symms's Marine background came to the fore, and he got tight with national Birch leaders. In 1972 and 1974 he received contributions from top JBS leaders; one year the Society named him its "Number One Congressman." In mid-June 1974 he flew to Chicago and delivered the keynote address of the JBS annual convention. It was not his first address to a Birch group, nor his last. Symms's opponent in 1974, Coeur d'Alene attorney J. Ray Cox, brought it up, to no avail. Symms easily won re-election.

It was a bigger migraine for Smith. How could he, one of Symms' closest friends and a leader of his staff, take on the John Birch Society when Symms was so close to it? "I was in a very difficult spot on that article," he would say years later.

He kept quiet and absorbed attack after attack.

In all it was a bitter campaign. Church and Smith never did debate; each accused the other of breaking off talks. Smith made some inroads but Church roared back when he started seriously campaigning. Church got 55 percent of the vote.

Smith then spent four more years on Symms' staff. After 1978 he left Symms, and Idaho – and politics – as well.

Purists

Symms kept winning. He cruised in 1976 over Democratic Boise attorney Ken Pursley, who worked hard but didn't catch on. In 1978 Roy Truby, the popular Democratic superintendent of public instruction, was backed by the Frank Church forces in hopes he would eliminate Symms as a contender for 1980. Truby was expected by political prophets to give Symms big trouble. He didn't.

All this time, Symms was drifting away from the Smeed crowd back home. His conservatism now matched that of McClure, who had managed the trick of appealing across conservative factions. Symms often fell into harmony with George Hansen, although the two had wildly different work habits and styles. (Symms' were probably more conventional.)[79]

But like Hansen and Church, Symms was a polarizing figure.

Jim Goller – *One reason Steve Symms has tough campaigns is because he has a high negative rating; he evokes strong likes and dislikes. It's partly his style. In some ways, he has a stronger support base than Jim McClure. But I've always thought that people feel comfortable with Jim McClure. It's a little like the bad kid and the good kid. Nobody pays too much attention to the good kid; he's always expected to do good. All the attention is paid to the bad kid.*

So Symms did not answer the question: could a Canyon County near-purist libertarian succeed in statewide Idaho politics?

A more precise case study was C.L. "Butch" Otter.

Otter was even more of a natural than Symms. He was the most gifted Idaho campaigner in the second half of this century, a great salesman, full of charm, perpetually bubbling over, almost impossible to dislike. Canyon Countian that he was, he was big on free enterprise and entrepreneurship, although he personally climbed the rungs of an established business, the J.R. Simplot Co., from field hand to executive suite. (Marrying J.R. Simplot's daughter couldn't have hurt.)

He loved politics, and had been a legislative staffer for a few years. In 1972, while in Caldwell, he won a seat in the Idaho House and became one of its most outspoken members. Usually, he voted with other conservatives and helped found the Conservative Caucus, a group that became more powerful and influential in the House through the seventies. But sometimes he broke ranks. He refused to support an anti-pornography bill, for example, announcing that "I don't vote no, I vote hell no." (He pointed out a decade later,

---

[79] Although: Only up to a point, as the coming years would show.

accurately, that the law did not end or curb pornography in Idaho.) Much more than Symms, he stayed close – while never calling himself a libertarian – to libertarian ideas.

Symms assiduously built bridges; Otter didn't.

But after two terms Otter retired in 1976 to do as a crowd of other Republicans did: plot a campaign for the governorship.

Easy Pickings

In 1976 the expectation was that Cecil Andrus would run for a third term as governor in 1978. (Rumors had arisen that Andrus considered running against McClure. Andrus quashed them. Andrus-McClure was the perpetually envisioned big matchup that never was.) Andrus' defenses were well nigh impregnable. In 1974 Andrus had beaten Jack Murphy, who spent 12 years in the state senate and eight as lieutenant governor, with 71 percent of the vote, the second best win ever by an Idaho gubernatorial candidate.

He helped carry Democratic state Sen. John Evans with him as lieutenant governor. Evans ran against Vern Ravenscroft, who had switched parties and become a Republican, and who had an excellent shot at winning. The irony was that Andrus and Evans weren't close. (Evans had backed other Democrats for governor in the 1966 and 1970 Democratic primaries.) They came from different traditions and were starkly different personalities. Evans had competition: two former state senators, Nels Solberg of Grangeville and Ray Rigby of Rexburg. Rigby was assisted by young Rick College professor – later congressman – Richard Stallings. Evans locked in the labor vote and won.

Andrus had skillfully built bridges to factions all over Idaho and had become a superb campaigner. He had charisma and fit the image of governor beautifully. In Boise, in suit and tie, he looked every bit the executive; visiting small towns, in jeans and a plaid shirt, he radiated down-home warmth. By late 1973 few Republicans thought he could be beaten. Murphy's campaign seemed half-hearted. Andrus won more than 70 percent of the vote, and in 1976 he seemed headed for a rerun in 1978.

Then Jimmy Carter was elected president. Andrus backed Frank Church as long as he was in the race, but Andrus and Carter were friends from their days together as governors. They kept in touch in presidential politics even before Church got into the race.

Personal and Confidential
The Honorable Jimmy Carter
Atlanta, Ga.
Dear Jimmy:
I had the opportunity to visit with Gov. Harriman last week about Democratic politics. He finds himself in the position of most Democrats - not really knowing

which candidate will be our strong man in '76. He has reason for not supporting some candidates but is very ready to support any of the rest. I mentioned you and my feelings about your ability, integrity, and concern to Gov. Harriman; and, although he is not about to endorse any candidate, he expressed to me a desire to get to know you better ...

My involvement in presidential politics must still remain upon the shelf until we see what Sen. Church is going to do at the conclusion of his CIA investigation. Until then, I will remain somewhat apart and aloof from the actual campaign. We've discussed this, and I know you understand ...
Cecil D. Andrus
Governor

Then Carter won and tapped Andrus as secretary of interior, and John Evans became a governor far different from Andrus.

Evans did not project the easy confidence Andrus had; his staff wasn't of the same caliber. (Many of Andrus' top people went to Washington with him.) A garrulous small-town politician in private, Evans seemed stiff and pompous in public.

March 17, 1977
The Honorable Cecil D. Andrus
The Secretary of the Interior
Dear Cece:
How would you like to trade me jobs? Just kidding. It seems we are both getting our share of the lumps right now. Hope we both come out on top ...
John V. Evans
Governor of Idaho

Republicans looked at Evans and lined up for easy pickings.

But Evans was underrated. He loved shaking hands and chatting with people; aides despaired of getting him out of a crowd and to the next appointment. And he became governor better prepared - or at least, had a better resume - than any before him. The Evans family of Malad, where he grew up, had interests in ranching, farming, retail, and banking. (After he left office he became president of an Evans bank in Burley.) He was a six-term state senator and both majority leader (in the brief Democratic dominance of the late fifties) and minority leader, lieutenant governor two years, and executive of a local unit of government (mayor of Malad). He had never lost an election.

Many Republicans didn't see all that in 1977. They saw a man who sneaked into the lieutenant governorship on Andrus' coattails, the unelected governor. (Neither of the two Idaho lieutenants governor who had moved up prior to Evans had held the governorship beyond the following election.) Even Evans delighted in telling Rodney Dangerfield stories about himself, like the day, shortly before he was sworn in as governor, when he stopped for gas at a service station en route to a meeting at the Statehouse and realized he'd left his wallet at home. "I'm the lieutenant governor of Idaho," he said. "I'm good for it." The attendant would have none of it. Evans had to leave his watch as security.

He was the governor who couldn't get no respect.

Vern Ravenscroft, who had considered running against George Hansen, was convinced he could beat Evans this time. He had not been idle. Ravenscroft spent a lot of time chairing the state Republican Party, rebuilding it after its 1974 debacle. He won over doubters about his party fealty and assembled his allies. From the moment he announced, he was front runner.

But every faction of the Republican Party was also represented in this crowded primary. From Blackfoot came Allan Larsen, the House speaker and a top LDS leader. From Boise came Larry Jackson, co-chairman of the budget-setting Joint Finance-Appropriations Committee, leading the remains of the moderate wing. Disaffected Northern Idaho had Coeur d'Alene businessman Jim Crowe, a political neophyte who came across with ease and confidence, a before-the-fact Donald Trump. Boise businessman Jay Amyx, a former mayor, filed. And from Caldwell came Butch Otter, backed by libertarian conservatives (and J.R. Simplot). It was the most crowded primary in Idaho in either party for the next decade, and it taught Idaho Republicans a slew of lessons.

Leading Democrats considered Ravenscroft the most likely nominee and privately thought Evans would lose to him. (In spite of that, no primary opposition to the governor emerged. The Democrats had no demonstrably better candidate.) Ravenscroft was conservative but centrist; nominated, he probably could have pulled together the conservatives as McClure had and as Symms was beginning to. Ravenscroft had pleased all factions as state GOP chairman.

Instead, each faction backed a champion. They sliced the Republican vote so thoroughly as to make the race unpredictable.

It became an angry race.

Vern Ravenscroft — *There was one poll and some observers that indicated to me that the bitterness of the fight between the Libertarian Otter group and the LDS Larsen group had gotten emotional to the point that - that type of thing, usually in a primary, tends to have people fall away from both and go to the third candidate. My advisers felt this was happening [and I would benefit].*

One of these private polls here in Boise picked it up just a week before the election. The weekend prior to that, and then the weekend following, they had done some telephoning. They had indicated to me that the battle between Otter and Larsen had potential. Larsen had become so bitter that the Eastern Idaho vote was emotional, and that they were picking up steam for Larsen that normally would not have been there. It was locking in behind Larsen not on a political basis whatsoever but on a personal or religious affiliation. Their man was under attack and they had to defend him. That's actually what happened.

I have sensed it [acrimony]. I think that is still there, because it did get personal, and it did get bitter.

Many of Larsen's key supporters in Eastern Idaho were fellow LDS leaders. That was normal. He knew them, they knew him, and many – like Mark Ricks in Rexburg – already were prominent and respected in their communities. This was dutifully noted and muttered about elsewhere. "We felt it was unfortunate that some of his opponents were dragging church into the campaign too much," Ricks recalled. "And we people who belonged to the same religious organization as Allan Larsen, we resented that."

Vern Ravenscroft – *My advisers said, go home Friday night, catch up on your sleep and rest Saturday and Sunday, and Monday start writing your acceptance speech. I didn't have that good a feeling. I went home and Saturday, Sunday afternoon, all day Monday and Tuesday until four o'clock I campaigned on the Main Streets of the Magic Valley, or city park picnics on Sunday afternoon ... It was more darned fun than I had had the whole election because it was not that structured. No speeches to make. No interviews to give. No television. Just working the streets, introducing myself, asking for their help.*

It wasn't enough.

On primary election night 1978, Jackson was a distant fourth, showing again the weakness of Republican moderates. Otter was third, taking Canyon County and some of the north (softened for him through Symms' campaigning). Ravenscroft was second, taking various counties. The surprise winner was Larsen, who won solidly in the Mormon East. In such a fractured primary, that was enough.

But not enough to win the general election. Larsen's financial conservatism appealed to Idahoans, but he turned them off when he made explicit every Gentile fear of a strongly Mormon governor. He spoke of "legislating morality," stepping over the line people like Symms, McClure, and Samuelson did not cross; they emphasized leaving Idahoans alone, mostly. Evans was Mormon, too. He enjoyed morning coffee and wasn't a teetotaler; but he came from Mormon Malad and knew how not to offend. Running against Larsen, he lost most of the Mormon vote, but did not rile it, while forging links elsewhere. In conservative Republican Ada County, for example, Evans was perceived as a practical businessman who, like they, didn't want Idaho turned into a Utah-style theocracy.[80]

In 1978, Evans won a strong 57 percent victory over Larsen. The Republican split ran deep. Otter's libertarians had no more use for Larsen and his Mormon backers than did Democrats.

In Idaho's early days senators and governors built careers on harassing Mormons. The founders even put a clause into the constitution barring Mormons from voting or holding public office. (It disqualified anyone who believed in "celestial marriage," as practicing

---

[80] One wonders in hindsight if Larsen was a decade or two ahead of his time. In the 90's, the objections that arose in the 1978 campaign might have carried less weight with a revised Idaho. electorate

Mormons do.) The religious bigotry of that day watered down with time, as the Mormon population grew and dispersed.

But the bigotry never vanished. In 1982, as Evans, the incumbent Mormon governor, was re-elected, voters repealed a constitutional provision banning Mormons from voting. (For years that provision had simply been ignored.) Yet 100,113 Idahoans voted to keep it: in 1982 a tenth of the state, a third of the electorate, thought Mormons should not be allowed to vote. While the vote against repeal was strongest in the north, it showed up even in Mormon counties. It was a shock to some, but not unpredictable. As late as 1988 an Idaho Human Rights Commission survey showed that Mormon had much "warmer" feelings about non-Mormons than non-Mormons did about Mormons.

The lesson was clear. A conservative attracting only one faction - semi- Libertarian, Mormon, or older-fashioned Main Street businessman - had trouble. A McClure, fusing them, could win big. (He got 68 percent of the vote in 1978, against former television and Intermountain Observer reporter Dwight Jensen.) Exploiting the rift didn't work - although doing it in a Republican primary would remain a temptation.

In 1986 Otter was on the statewide ballot again, running for lieutenant governor. At first he was a shoo-in for the Republican nomination: he had money and support, and the broken party fences of 1978 had been mostly mended. Then came opposition: Post Falls attorney Chuck Lempesis, a former Kootenai County Republican chairman. Lempesis was proof of how far you could go in Idaho politics on sheer panache and imagination. He didn't win, but he came closer than anyone had thought he would.

There was a spark of political brilliance in him. When unknown Bob Smith ran for the Senate, he made "Who is Bob Smith?" his campaign slogan. It didn't work. When Lempesis ran as an unknown, he met the underlying question – of whether he was a serious contender – with buttons saying, "Chuck Lempesis is serious." It was a superb tactical choice.

But he set the tone when he said, "My priority in this world is to serve God. I wouldn't be in this race if I didn't believe that God had called me to enter this race." Although Southern Baptist rather than Mormon, his campaign intentionally or not was aimed directly at the Mormon voters so skeptical of Otter eight years before. Lempesis seized on "moral issues" that cost Otter so many eastern votes – on drug and pornography laws, and a bill Lempesis said was pro-abortion – and pounded them mercilessly month after month. He was good at it, too. Lempesis was a powerful and skillful debater. Although Otter was a decade older and had far more political experience, Lempesis was capable of outmaneuvering him; his reputation in Kootenai County as a terrific courtroom attorney was proven out.

Otter seemed shaken, stunned and about to lose. Toward the end, this normally cheerful and upbeat candidate started counter-punching.

Lempesis' tactics were costly; Otter won 58 percent. Lempesis did best in Kootenai County and the Mormon East.[81]

The split in tone and emphasis was real and lasting. It showed up again in February 1987, after Otter took office.

The Legislature passed a bill raising the drinking age from 19 to 21, partly because Congress planned to cut highway funding to states that didn't. It hit the governor's desk when Andrus was out of state and Otter was acting governor. As a shot at the feds, Otter vetoed it. (Andrus signed a followup bill.) Rep. Mack Neibaur of Paul, a conservative Mormon Republican, said when he heard of the veto, "That just about shot him in the butt."

Time will tell.

---

[81] That Lempesis did so well in Kootenai County, even bearing in mind that he was from there, should in hindsight have been a more potent indicator to political observers about the direction that county was taking. His big win there, on the platform he used, would make perfect sense in the context of the late 90s.

10 | Showdown in 1980

On a cool, overcast Saturday in Preston in mid-October 1980, the leaves fell like oversized, multicolored snowflakes. But few saw the spectacle. Utah State and Brigham Young were engaged in serious football that drew more interest in Preston than most Idaho games would, and far more than the scenery.

A big blue car pulled slowly into town, its passengers observing more the absence of people than the presence of colors.

Sen. Frank Church and his wife Bethine were in the back seat. The driver, J.D. Williams, Franklin County prosecutor and water rights attorney, one of the few local Democrats who could win office, was a little concerned. Not only was the game running late – he hadn't counted on that – but he had heard that protesters might show up.[82]

Williams pulled to a side street and stopped in front of the Robinson Fair Building. While Congressman Steve Symms, Church's opponent, toured Idaho in a bus, Church covered it by car – many cars, owned and driven by supporters.

Church stepped out and surveyed the streetscape. "I think we should postpone all activities until the end of the football game," he said. Williams pulled a small radio from his coat pocket and tuned in. The game had long minutes to go. The Churches still had to hit Montpelier – 50 miles of twisted mountain road away – for a dinner, and then Lava Hot Springs for late-night handshaking. They had to get cracking.

Bethine Church sensed a chill in the air. "Frank, do you want to put on your other coat?" she said.

"This one's okay," he said.

"Frank, put on your other coat."

He did. Presidents could chew him out, as Lyndon Johnson did, and he would be nonplused. When Bethine spoke, he listened. She grew up in the political Clark family, whose members had been governors, senators, mayors, and federal judges. Politics was in her blood even more than in his – and he had loved it since high school. She was widely considered the better campaigner. If the Churches were in an Idaho restaurant and someone sat down across the room, she would make Frank walk over and break the ice. When they worked crowds – as they often did together – she often greeted people first, so

---

[82] Williams was not a major state figure at the time *Paradox* was originally written, in 1988 (he had at that time run one losing race for attorney general, in 1982). But he became a statewide elective official in 1989 with appoi9ntment by Governor Cecil Andrus as state auditor (the job title later changed, at Williams' suggestion, to controller), and was elected to the job three times – on two of those occasions, in the face of huge Republican landslides. From 1994 to 2002 he was the top elected Democrat in Idaho. As this little 1980 vignette shows, his political preparation for it goes back quite a few years, and helps explain his political longevity

she could speak the person's name for the senator to pick up. Her memory seemed better than his.[83]

After a few minutes people trickled into the Robinson building. They walked up to the Churches and shook hands.

They were followed by four or five protesters with big signs: "Hey Frankie! No ERA" and "Independence 1776 Not Interdependence 1980." The protesters milled around, talked among themselves, and sat in the back of the room. Church took little notice. A few of them tried to talk with Church supporters, but they got nowhere. "I read it," one supporter snorted, glancing at a sign. "I'm smarter than that. You're barking up the wrong tree."

Church stood up to applause and delivered a cautious speech. Preston was conservative Republican and he took no chances. Politicians necessarily use boilerplate speeches repeated endlessly – it's less work and less risky – but Church usually kept reinventing his, recycling from a long list of topics. In Preston he hit on agriculture, pointing out what his water rights and other efforts had done for farmers. He skipped his Sagebrush Rebellion stuff, which got applause most places. Church's instincts were dead on: remarks that drew applause or laughter earlier in Malad or later in Montpelier got dead air in Preston.

Then he noted, wryly, "It's easy to distinguish between my friends and opponents here." Part of the audience clapped loudly. Part stayed silent.

Church the Winner

Just as Church wasn't a stereotype – he was conservative on gun control and abortion, for example – so were both his supporters and critics eclectic. His friends especially came from all over, and his opponents often underestimated them.

Church was always supposed to lose. In 1956 the pundits said he was too young and inexperienced to beat Glen Taylor and Republican Sen. Herman Welker. He won anyway.

In 1958 a key Church organizer, former Mountain Home Mayor John Glasby, ran for governor and finished back in the pack. Republican strategist Evan Kackley privately concluded

it is apparent that the vote that elected Church two years ago was a vote against Welker, not for Church. In the primary, he [Church] had to win by precincts in Mountain Home. Now his organization in the state has come out a very poor third. Four years hence, we can take strong heart from this.

---

[83] The Church biography *Fighting the Odds* is full of stories about the Frank-Bethine relationship; a lot of them have a feel similar to what you just read here.

Actually, it meant Church's was a personal organization and that its loyalty could not easily be transferred (although, at times, that would happen).

In 1960 a Lewiston supporter warned Church he could lose North Idaho because Republican senator Henry Dworshak was perceived as the one who rolled the pork barrel home. "You are quite right about the publicity, or lack of it," Church replied. He said that he alone, as a member of the public works committee, had pushed through the final Orofino-to-Missoula highway bill. "Sen. Dworshak was not even present at the meeting when the committee took this action," he said. "But Dworshak and Smylie keep working and getting the credit through repetitive press releases and occasional trips along the road. This is just good political press, for which I give them credit, and I agree with you that I will have to work harder at it during the next two years."

He did, and he got a break when Democrats won the White House in 1960 - and therefore got to announce federal spending plans.

In 1962 even his father-in-law Chase Clark fretted that Church's stands on wilderness and mining would cost him re-election. When he won that year Republicans were not surprised. In January a Republican scout wrote an internal memo that "Republicans in the state regard him (Church) as a heavyweight and some feel he could carry the rest of the ticket in with him if we do not have a good well-known candidate to oppose him." Lloyd Adams confided to Smylie that "unless something unforeseen eventuates, it is going to be next to impossible to beat Church." Church's Republican opposition, Boise attorney Jack Hawley, was a competent candidate but never caught fire.

In 1968 Church was challenged by George Hansen, an incumbent congressman - and yet Church won, big.

In 1974, when his strategists warned that he could lose, they must have sounded like Chicken Littles.

It was the year of Watergate. Democrats hadn't been stronger in Idaho since the early sixties. They had a popular governor in Cecil Andrus – an advantage new to Church – who owed his office partly to the senator. Republicans were deeply divided in the second district, and they were less organized than usual. None of the Republican Senate contenders had ever been tested in a major race. Church also had 18 years of seniority in the Senate with chairmanships just around the bend.

Such was the atmosphere at the state Democratic convention. During the proceedings a former Church aide, Martin Peterson, and state Democratic leader Joe McCarter sat down for a talk with Bethine Church. They ran through their concerns and by the time they were done, her senses said they were right: Church was headed for defeat in 1974.

Later John Corlett, who had spent weeks traveling around the state, told his son Cleve, then Church's press secretary, that "Your man is going to lose."

The message was received. Church got serious and he won again.

Part of the problem had been letting the basics slip.

Anyone looking for a secret to Church's success can find it in the boxes of letters which are the bulk of his official papers. Church put Idaho under a microscope. His constituent service may have outdone any Idaho politician's. Like all members of Congress, his staff helped constituents handle problems with federal agencies. His office was reputedly more effective than most. But that was only the beginning.

Consider the letters policy.

A Boise newspaper clipping service was hired to do nothing but clip weddings, anniversaries, graduations, and other notable events across Idaho. The clips went to Church's office, where congratulatory letters would be written, signed and mailed en masse. On election days Church, like other politicians, sent congratulatory letters to major winners. But he also sent them to every minor party functionary his people could find. Church's staff had standing orders that absolutely every letter from Idaho had to be answered - immediately.

Much of this was the doing of Verda White Barnes, the most influential woman in Idaho politics.

Myrna Sasser, who worked with her in Church's office for two decades, described her as "a brilliant woman. I never saw her keep a list in all the years I worked with her; her desk just looked like chaos. She'd have stacks and stacks of things and she knew where everything was. She never dropped the ball; it was all in her head ... Her mind was so active she had difficulty sleeping, especially in her later years. She would come home just exhausted but be awake by four o'clock in the morning, ready to go, because she had so many things on her mind to be taken care of ..."[84]

Verda Barnes grew up in Fremont County in a political family. She was a young mother when she got a letter from Democratic National Chairman Jim Farley asking her to get involved in politics. She took it as a command and organized a Democratic dinner-dance to which many Depression-struck farmers contributed food rather than money. From that success she never looked back.

She worked for the Idaho Democratic Party in the thirties, for the national CIO – before it joined the AFL – and ran the Idaho state liquor office after prohibition.

And helped run the Young Democrats of Idaho with people like future state auditor Joe Williams. (Williams was an experienced political worker even then: Ada County Democratic chairman since the late twenties, he first campaigned helping his father stump for Woodrow Wilson in 1916; as a reward, the elder Williams became

---

[84] Talk to Democrats who've been around more than a few years, and you'll find Verda Barnes remains as legendary as she remains little-known to most of the Idaho public. Her lessons could do Idaho Democrats some good, though, even now.

Idaho's first income tax collector.) YD was a substantial organization. "We had 1,800 members," Williams recalled. "We had a candlelight parade that took up three blocks in Boise." Barnes later was national YD vice chairman. When Glen Taylor was elected senator in 1944 she became one of his key staffers.[85]

When Church hired her in 1957 she became his constituent worker and in-house Idaho analyst. She had a political equivalent of a musician's perfect pitch: with a dozen phone calls she knew precisely what was happening in Idaho and how to deal with it.

Martin Peterson — *I still remember the first lesson I learned from Verda in letter drafting, and I can remember the phrase she rejected.*

Somebody had been out from Idaho and in Washington, had dropped in to see the senator, and the senator wasn't around: he was in the state. I had drafted a letter over the senator's signature saying he was sorry he missed them. I had a phrase in the letter, "sorry I missed you while you were in Washington, D.C. Unfortunately, I was in Idaho at the time."

It came back with a big red X and this note from Verda saying, "It is NEVER unfortunate that the senator is out in Idaho." After a few of those, you become very sensitive.

George Hansen, Church's opponent in 1968, recalled Church's office handled constituent service "exceptionally well." Good service can do wonders for an officeholder; Hansen said it "almost saved Church in 1980. It almost saved me [in 1984] when I had the whole federal government on my back."

When a recall attempt started against him in 1967, Church's review of the law and Barnes' reading of the political temperature convinced them it couldn't succeed. But even by 1966 Hansen had been mentioned as a candidate against Church, and Church's forces wanted to be prepared. They exploited the recall to develop the most elaborate campaign Idaho had ever seen. Barnes and Sasser pushed their gifts for detail to the limits, expanding the possibilities of Idaho campaigning. Until then no one had compiled a thorough voter list. The Church people did, noting who in every precinct was for Church, for Hansen, or undecided, and acted accordingly. They used billboards with messages that changed every couple of weeks.

They pioneered in Idaho vinyl bumper strips; since vinyl peels off while paper has to be scraped off, more people accepted vinyl. Church had strips printed in Spanish. And just before Halloween the campaign bought tens of thousands of chocolate kisses and wrapped them in tiny imitation bumper stickers. The campaign budget was not extraordinary, but the uses it was put to were.

---

[85] You'll search in vain, though, for a reference to her in Taylor's autobiography, *The Way It Was With Me.* Her defection to Church was neither forgiven nor forgotten, and he apparently wrote her out of his life. Which did not lessen at all her contribution to him.

After 1968 the emergency dissipated and sharpness dulled. Barnes retired in the early seventies, though she stayed active until she died in May 1980.

In 1974 Republican Bob Smith pulled close to Church, and Church suddenly had to hustle to win. Finally the campaign shaped up, and Church barnstormed the state. Andrus won 71 percent of the vote. Church got 56 percent.

The Gathering Storm

Oct. 25, 1979
Peter Fenn
Office of Sen. Frank Church
Dear Peter:
... The most encouraging news to us from this poll is the amount and nature of the negative baggage Steve Symms brings to the race. His problems are essentially those of competence and character, both problems difficult to deal with, we've found. There is, as you know, ample evidence that Symms may be too small for the job. His negative job rating, reservations about his maturity, the feeling that he talks a lot but doesn't get results - all of this adds up to a big problem for him. In addition, a larger percentage of his support, as opposed to Church's support, is weak and the dominant quality used to describe him, "conservative," is based on ideology rather than ability.

This is not to say that Church doesn't carry substantial baggage of his own. His issue positions are out of sync with many of his constituents. Foreign affairs is not perceived to be nearly as important as other issues and Church's position as chairman of the Foreign Relations Committee is not a terribly persuasive reason for voting for him ...
Jill B. Buckley
Rothstein/Buckley

Idaho was changing. By 1980 growth and prosperity were dampened. Idahoans looked for scapegoats, and the easy ones were Washington and a president – Jimmy Carter – they didn't like anyway. In 1974 Church's Washington was led by Republicans in a time of scandal. In 1980 Carter, whom Church could not repudiate outright, had both economic and foreign policy trouble.

And Church was becoming too well known.

In the thirties, a William Borah could be revered as Idaho's link to the world of nations. In the seventies Church became that, too. But the world was smaller; the White House, Iran, and South Africa were in the living room every night. Having an important senator no longer meant as much emotionally. Church benefited little from celebrity – but he did draw the attention of multitudes nationally who liked or despised his politics.

Church started as a protege of Democratic leaders. His extended Idaho political family, the Clarks and the Tom Boise organization, were essential to winning in 1956, prying loose critical campaign money from Florida Democratic Sen. George Smathers, who chaired the Senate Democratic Senatorial Committee. In 1960, when Church pleaded with Smathers for money for a long-shot Idaho Senate candidate against Henry Dworshak, Smathers reminded him: "I went way out on a limb in the distribution of un-earmarked funds during your election, but at that time we had more money to distribute and I had confidence in your ability to win."

In the Senate, he was Majority Leader Lyndon Johnson's protege. Johnson put him on the Foreign Relations Committee and on Interior, to Church's delight. Church, in turn, carried water for Johnson on civil rights and other legislation. He also got attention as one of the best speakers in the Senate.

Church's rise from anonymity began with his keynote address at

Frank Church *(office photo)*

the 1960 Democratic convention; it wasn't a great speech but it hit the New Frontier-ish note organizers wanted. Yet here, too, sponsors were key: the campaign for the keynote began months before the convention.

In 1958 LBJ picked Church, rather than a senior senator, to deliver Washington's Farewell Address in the Senate; Church was loudly praised. In October 1959 Lewiston businessman Harry Wall, the veteran Democratic national committeeman, used that speech. He sent National Committee Chairman Paul Butler "the most serious letter I have ever written to you," pushing Church as keynoter. He noted Church's skill as a speaker and effectiveness on television (one reason, he said, for his 1956 win). "He has youth, vigor and the aura of success. Frank is not identified with any single candidate for the presidency, nor with any regional or divisive issue. Although he is a Westerner and a liberal, his orientation is consistent with the national mandate which our party holds ..." He noted that no Idaho Democrat had ever been elected twice to the Senate. But "Idahoans remember the Borah tradition, and national recognition accorded to Frank represents his best chance for breaking the jinx and winning in 1962."

Church got the job, although in retrospect it probably had little to do with his 1962 win.

Later the nation became aware of him as he called for an "agonizing reappraisal" of Vietnam. He caught the eye of conservatives, too, and if a California conservative was moved to start a recall drive against him, that's hardly surprising.

His profile ratcheted upward in his fourth term. He led an inquiry into presidential war powers and then another into multinational corporations, a favorite target of his in the seventies. Next he chaired a Senate committee investigating the CIA and other intelligence agencies, uncovering an endless and embarrassing stream of lawbreaking. Security in the committee was tight – unusual for Capitol Hill – but the released findings made headlines. In the CIA, and in conservative circles, "Frank Church" became a swear word.

Then he assumed the ultimate high profile: like Borah 40 years before, he ran for president in 1976. He spent too much time on the CIA to organize properly. He started too late and with too few resources to have a real crack at winning. (Like Borah's too, it wasn't an all-out serious race.) His grand strategy for the campaign – which hinged on a strong early showing by Washington Sen. Henry Jackson – had collapsed even before he announced, and Church wavered on entering. Church's own aides split on the race; Verda Barnes strongly advised him not to run, fearing a bad showing could hurt him in Idaho. He still didn't do badly. Church's old-timey announcement on the steps of the Boise County Courthouse, above the muddy streets of Idaho City, home of his ancestors, lent a Western flavor duly noted by a jaded national press (much of which had, by the time he spoke, become thoroughly acquainted with the saloons across the street). In Idaho, Church's supporters beamed. He interrupted Jimmy Carter's roll by winning four primaries (admittedly, one was Idaho's), and some wishful thinkers thought that if California Gov. Jerry Brown had not also entered the race and split the anti-Carter vote, Church might have won. That's doubtful; Carter had almost locked up the nomination by then.

For Church, the race mainly meant more national exposure.

After 1978 Church became in title what he had been in practice for four years: chairman of the Senate Foreign Relations Committee. Running for president was a lark; from boyhood he wanted to chair Foreign Relations as Borah had. The bitter pill was that it had become a headache. The big foreign policy issues of Church's lifetime were past. The elections of 1978 turned the Senate more conservative, and the once-liberal panel was closely split between Church's doves and new Republican hawks. The Republicans demanded and got minority staff, which they hadn't had before. When Church tried to bring the committee more directly under his control by weakening the subcommittees, fellow Democrats rebelled. The committee produced plenty of legislation, but it wasn't the powerhouse of yore. Church forged no major new initiatives. And as he began to make headway over the hawks and the subcommittees, he had to return to Idaho. It was election time.[86]

One issue Church did push through, just before he took over the chairmanship, gave focus to his problems.

In 1978 he was floor leader for the Panama Canal treaties; they passed the Senate 68-32, with one vote to spare. Church saw the agreements, which meant eventually turning over Canal Zone operations to Panama, as necessary for keeping peace in Central America. The other three-quarters of Idaho's delegation saw them as a craven giveaway. Rep. George Hansen, who wasn't in the chamber that handles treaties, used court cases and other maneuvers to try to kill or cripple them. Their provisions, he said, not only gave away the Canal Zone but, because they would turn over American assets to Panama, amounted to a "payaway."

The treaties never could have been expected to be popular in Idaho, but the criticism was overwhelming. In some places the Vietnam experience led to a willingness to seek cooperation rather than military action as a primary policy. In Idaho, where support for the war lasted longer, people felt that a failure of defense meant retreat and defeat elsewhere. It was not so much "anti-Communism" – though that was part of it – as unease about America's security and place in the world. That attitude could summed up on an easy bumper sticker: "Stop the Panama Giveaway."

Even so Panama might have died down by 1980 but for revolution in Iran and the humiliating imprisonment of 52 Americans there. The 444 days of Iran crisis, ending in January 1981, set the scene. Iran made Americans mad. Church's talk about the normality of revolution, of rolling with the punches rather than punching back on reflex, didn't mesh with how Idahoans felt in 1980.

Battle is Joined

From the beginning, the campaign was about Church. Symms had served as many terms in the House as Church had in the Senate – four – but only a third as many years, and he was barely known nationally. Partly because he was a minority Republican (and so had trouble passing legislation) and partly because he was more inclined to flamboyant guerrilla warfare than detail work, Symms had a slender legislative record. Church pointed that out. But getting an effective handle on Symms was tough.

---

[86] While I researched Church's background for a series of articles on the 1980 election, I spent some time in Washington and interviewed the Forest Relations committee staff chief, Bill Bader. One of his comments stuck with me. He pointed to a small room off to the side of the meeting chamber where we were talking, and said that was where Church was keeping his records – keeping them in preparation of writing either his memoirs or a book on foreign relations. Church, unlike quite a few legislators, was both an avid reader and a skillful writer, and it's always seemed sad that what might have been an excellent book never got done. It was one more bit of psychic encouragement that prompted this one …

The battle didn't even start with Symms.

In 1979 Anybody But Church was founded by Don Todd, a former aide to Attorney General Wayne Kidwell and the canny manager who steered Allan Larsen to the Republican gubernatorial nomination in 1978. He opened an office in downtown Boise, collected information on Church, published flyers and ran broadcast and print ads against him. ABC affiliated with the National Conservative Political Action Committee (NCPAC), which targeted Church and four other Democrats for defeat in 1980. (Four of them lost that year. NCPAC called Church "the radical chairman of the Senate Foreign Relations Committee who single-handedly has presided over the destruction of the FBI and the CIA.") Todd also tied in with the New Right money machine.

These were free-swinging folks, to say the least.

NCPAC/Church 60 sec. spot
(Rep. [Jim] Golder standing in front of missile site)
GOLDER: I'm standing in front of these missile silos to dramatize one of the effects of Sen. Church's power in Washington. These silos aren't filled with missiles anymore. They are empty. Because of that they won't be of much help in defense of your family or mine.
(Different shots of missile silos)
GOLDER: You see, Sen. Church has almost always opposed a strong national defense. He led the fight to give away our Panama Canal and he voted to slash national defense procurement. Now Sen. Church is one of those who wants to push through the SALT II treaty through the Senate which I believe would seriously weaken America. We in Idaho are going to have to do our part to keep America strong. First we need to defeat the SALT treaty. And then work to replace Church with an advocate of an America second to none in military strength.
If you agree write to us, ABC Project, Boise, Idaho.
(Dissolve to Logo: If Church Wins, You Lose)

The Titan silos were abandoned, however, not because of Church but as part of a Defense Department upgrade to new missiles like the Minuteman. Precision was not a hallmark of politics in 1980.

Church traditionally responded to attacks hardly at all until the end of the campaign, when he would turn them around, rebut them, and decry mudslinging. But the times and the shrillness of ABC prompted Church to lash back early on. Again and again Todd goaded Church into it, months before either Church or Symms announced. Conventional wisdom then said that Todd hurt Symms more than he helped. All that purely negative campaigning just built up sympathy for Church, the pundits said.

It did build some sympathy, but it seemed to do more damage. Todd successfully kept attention focused on the controversial parts of Church's record, giving Church no respite even after Symms announced in February 1980. And he probably goaded Church into making the biggest mistake of his career.

In August 1979 Church called a surprise evening press conference at his Boise home. He told reporters he had just learned Soviet troops had been spotted in Cuba. He was asked what that might do to the SALT arms treaty. Not much, he replied. Days later, he said the treaty probably was on hold until the Cuba problem was settled. The incident seemed to show Church as an opportunistic flip flopper. For years Idahoans who disagreed with him returned him to Washington on grounds that he wouldn't do the kind of thing he had just done.

(He was even savaged in the comic strip Doonesbury, which spent a week depicting a Senate hearing on Cuba. Cartoonist Garry Trudeau showed a general testifying before the committee, telling Church, "By refusing to fan the flames of moderation, a calm, negotiated solution has been narrowly averted ... Thank you Senator, and good luck with your re-election.")

Conservatives sensed a wounded liberal and pounced.

The audience he got one day in the Ricks College auditorium – mainly students – was not just hostile but virulent and surreal. Church delivered a mild speech and then was stung with a string of questions inspired by right wing speculation about the Communist conspiracy, questions Symms and Todd would have been embarrassed to ask. Many were influenced by the newly-published novel *The Spike*, which portrayed a world of betrayal to communism. One character was a senator who investigated the CIA and weakened it in the process. One woman held up a copy of the book and asked Church, "Does this remind you of anyone you know?"

Church lost his cool and let it show. "It reminds me of the kind of political fiction that sells very well these days to people who believe that kind of thing," he said.

He was not at his best.

In Bonners Ferry a girl carrying a John Birch Society pamphlet wanted to know why he "repeatedly voted against increasing military defense." A student asked Church why he had "given away the Panama Canal." Another asked whether he belonged to the Tri-Lateral Commission and Council on Foreign Relations that wanted to take over the world through a "shadow government."

Church said later the questions "were obviously planted." No doubt they were, but that made them no less unnerving.

Late in the campaign Symms said ABC-NCPAC's efforts were "inconsequential" and he even defended Church. Symms' attacks in 1980 were mild compared with ABC's in 1979. If the election was held in January 1980 the results probably would have been about the same as they were in November. But in those ten months Idaho politics changed forever.

The Great (?) Debates

In the fall of 1980 the Symms campaign asked Idaho Attorney General David Leroy, a skillful public speaker, to help with debate strategy. He was a logical choice. Leroy had done well in his 1978 debate with Democrat Mike Wetherell in their statewide race for attorney general. Wetherell was a former Church chief of staff and had picked up some of Church's speaking patterns.

Many campaign managers would not have actively sought such outside assistance; some would have let pride get in the way. Symms was fortunate. His manager was a complete professional.

Phil Reberger had known Symms since they both grew up in Canyon County. Reberger helped Virginia Republican Sen. John Warner get elected, then in 1978 returned to Idaho to run McClure's re-election. McClure was a shoo-in. Reberger's job was not to work a miracle, just keep McClure's train on track. McClure got two-thirds of the vote, but Reberger had never tried for a grandiloquent gesture that might have backfired. Asked once how many votes he hoped McClure would get, Reberger gave not an idealistic but the practical reply: "50 percent plus one." He was so good at this that he became a brand name. In the eighties, political types in both parties, in picking over a faltering campaign, would say the contender "needs a Reberger."

In the fall of 1980 Reberger asked Leroy what Symms should do in the debates October 23 and 26.

"Basic rule: Attack, attack, attack," Leroy wrote on his 13 legal-sized pages. "The key in this type of encounter is to seize the initiative and put the opponent on the defensive ... Appropriate attack themes may be concepts such as Church's voting record of fiscal irresponsibility or his weakness on national defense ..." He advised Symms to forget the diehards and focus on undecideds; to emphasize his own themes and avoid seeming to respond to Church; and to show a grasp of the issues. When Symms debated Democrat Roy Truby in 1978, Leroy said, "in the seated format, Steve tended to slouch in his chair. At one point, the candidate did not appear to be familiar with what the format required next. Steve's remarks were too conversational in structure and tone, and should be more formal as little speeches. Some answers tended to lack structure, specifics and enthusiasm."

A debate was potentially most useful to Symms. Church was a renowned Senate orator. He had not debated Bob Smith in 1974, but against George Hansen in 1968 he clearly won. Symms could not let that happen. But he didn't need a knockout punch either. Symms was an easy conversationalist, less skilled at formal speaking; Idahoans knew that or sensed it. Symms had merely to go all rounds and see the contest called a draw. Church absolutely could not be seen as the loser. Church the risk-taker, who lived each day as if it were his last, had to fight cautiously.

They took rabbit punches instead of wild swings. They disagreed on defense spending, inflation, Panama. Both started reserved, cool, nervous. Church warmed to it more quickly but suffered from the format: he was used to taking more time to explain positions than response times allowed. Symms, though stiff and with his natural charm muzzled, looked dignified and senatorial. In all, anyone confused when the debates started probably was as confused when they ended. Back to the car for Church and the bus for Symms.

On the Road Again

Symms's campaign was more flamboyant than Church's. Since 1972 he had turned stops in small towns into big events. He had started then with his parents driving their RV van plastered with Symms for Congress signs. It was a cheerful little family affair.

But this was big-money 1980. By springtime Church and Symms raised more than $1 million apiece. By election day their campaigns and those of the many committees which injected themselves into the race raised spent about $5 million - more than $5 for every man, woman, and child in Idaho. Polls consistently showed that few Idaho voters were undecided even early in 1980, so all that money was spent to influence maybe 50,000 of the 450,000 voters. The money became a debate topic too: Symms was the candidate financed by oil (he did get a lot of contributions from Texas) and Church the favorite of the New York money men (he did get heavy old-line liberal and Jewish support).

ABC's Todd once suggested that a kind of Parkinson's Law applied to campaigns: after a point, the more money you have, the more is wasted. These bloated campaigns mainly established that both Church and Symms were serious candidates – which no one doubted – and that each had enough cash to profoundly irritate television viewers and radio listeners.

Idaho was invaded by outsiders. The press came first, this being the classic liberal-conservative matchup of 1980. Then came a parade of interest groups on abortion, wilderness and sundry, proclaiming their membership was wild about – or despised – Church or Symms. Some of these groups were created to endorse candidates, but they still got plenty of attention.

Symms was at least a moving target.

He was on a three-week, exhaustive trip blitzing little burgs. His parents still accompanied him in their RV, but the featured attraction now was a bus plastered over with campaign signs. The bus would pull into town center and Symms, who sat in a front seat, would swing off and hunt down prospective voters. He would slip a brochure, shake a hand – "Hi, how are you, Steve Symms, running for the U.S. Senate, I need your vote" – and move on. It was the old Glen Taylor approach, one Church, caught now in his need to explain complicated issues, was less able to use. (Church never seemed arrogant or aloof, but he did seem more distant.)

Some towns were so small they weren't mapped. "Where's West Jefferson?" someone called from the back of the bus. Symms had no answer and scavenged for a map. Between stops he would open maps and study them, fixing them in his mind.

The bus turned a bend in the desert and rolled into little Howe, halfway between Mud Lake and Arco. "Music," Symms said. And it played, as the country singer sang, "Yes I was born to be, Idaho at heart." "Idaho at Heart," the theme from "Rocky" and Willie Nelson's "On the Road Again" played everywhere.

A dozen adults and 30 grade school kids gathered at the Little Lost River store. In front was strung a sign: "Vote for Symms and Norm Allen." Allen was a Republican candidate for Butte County commissioner popular in Howe (though he didn't win in November). The back of the sign said, "Vote for Norm Allen."

Since this was pretty much all of Howe, Symms didn't blitz; he just passed out brochures and balloons and fielded questions. The toughest was, "Who do you support for the World Series?"

Symms replied with ease. "Half of my friends are for the Phillies," he said, "and half of my friends are for Kansas City, and I'm for my friends." Symms, the ex-college football player and ardent sports fan, avoided talking about the Series.

He had enough controversy to deal with.

For one thing, there was ideology. Symms shed many of his libertarian ideas the longer he stayed in Washington. He had what amounted to a "pro-choice" position when he was first elected, but by 1980 anti-abortion groups proclaimed him more "pro-life" than Church. (Actually, their positions then were similar).

In the mid-seventies Idaho libertarians formed their own party, in 1976 gathering enough momentum and organization to get their presidential candidate on the Idaho general election ballot. In 1980, they ran a candidate for the Senate against Church and Symms: Larry Fullmer of Pocatello, an across-the-board purist. His campaign was bug-sized compared to the Church and Symms beasts, but he got a percent of the vote – enough that the question of whether it bled Church or Symms became pertinent.

Affiliations were important, too. Church took heat for owning New York City municipal bonds and voting for financial aid to that city. Symms's silver investments attracted notice. He was tight with the Texas Hunt brothers, and reporters spent months dissecting Symms, the Hunts, and silver legislation. Symms said he properly disclosed his interests and besides, silver was important to Idaho. Few voters seemed to care.

The silver stories fueled another campaign, one against the news media. Symms personally stayed friendly with journalists, but supporters took to blaming the messenger often and vehemently. Bumper stickers and billboards screeched, "I'm voting for Steve Symms – The *Statesman* made me do it."

But the press was split. The *Idaho Statesman* endorsed Church but also Reagan (and Symms, in 1978). The Twin Falls *Times-News* endorsed Symms. Most Idaho dailies endorsed neither, though editorials in Idaho Falls and Lewiston favored Church while those in Nampa, Caldwell, Burley, and Wallace generally backed Symms.

The journalist most open in support of a candidate was Rick Coffman, managing editor of the Nampa-Caldwell *Idaho Press-Tribune* – an enthusiastic Symms backer. In 1980 Coffman himself became news. He and some friends "were sitting around the pool one night making up some funny stuff on Church and Symms and the *Statesman* and our newspaper. And it was recorded," he said. Later he was asked to help cut a professional version; it aired on Boise and Caldwell radio stations. Coffman said he had thought it would be recut by professionals, but didn't seem to mind. "What's the difference between writing editorials and going on television or radio?" he said. But his paper's campaign reporting was even-handed.

The below-the-belt stuff didn't start with the press anyway. Personal issues that would not have hurt Symms in his old district could kill in Mormon eastern Idaho. Symms' family owned the Ste. Chapelle Winery at Sunnyslope, word of which spread through the wards. Rumors made the circuit, too, most notably one that Symms, who was married, was a womanizer. That would dog Symms for years and pick up force again seven years later, when he separated from his wife Fran. It went public in the summer of 1980. New bumper stickers – "Wine, Women, Oil and Symms" – appeared. So did letters to the editor in weekly newspapers. State GOP Chairman Dennis Olson decried the "smear" and quieted it.

In the End

In 1980 the whole world passed before the eyes of Idaho. Everything was brought up, hacked apart, debated – Church and Symms managed to disagree on almost everything – and considered by the electorate. The mass media was flooded with ads, some of the most sophisticated Idaho had ever seen. To avoid droning repetition they covered a lot of ground. Some issues came and went. Some returned. A few bloomed late in the campaign.

Church tried to argue that, when it came to protecting Idaho water and other rights, he could better help Ronald Reagan than freshman Symms. Long before anyone foresaw a Reagan landslide nationally, any obtuse observer could predict a big Reagan win in Idaho. Church's argument never sold. It was shattered one Tuesday afternoon in October when Reagan flew to Idaho Falls. He was on the ground less than two hours. He delivered a well-tailored speech to about 3,000 people at the Bonneville High School gymnasium, never referring directly to Church but endorsing Symms. And then he left. That may have turned around the election.

Carl Burke – *I suppose if I wanted to list things in priority of what happened negative toward Frank's campaign, I think the Reagan sweep has to be very important. They did a good job: you vote for Reagan, you've got to have a Reagan team. In spite of that, they almost didn't get the job done in Idaho.*

But there were a host of other things, from the Panama Canal to the charge that Frank had forgotten Idaho. And I think Frank was a little defensive in his campaign. He defended himself more than he should; he should have been on the attack. I think the year and a half of eroding comments about him, and Symms' sympathizer committees, sort of hurt his spirit ... It really hurt him inside, so he was more defensive, not as sure of himself. He almost felt like Idaho itself was changing and the people in it were changing, and somehow lost sight of their great work together. And all the money that was spent - good Lord ...

The worst thing that happened: I was on the way to Frank's house downtown. On the car radio, about 6:30, they predicted Symms' election. The polls weren't even closed in Boise.

Jim Goller – *Frank was one senator who for a long time did good constituent work. He paid a lot of attention. I think Frank would have survived the election against Symms if he hadn't run for president. He had lost people from his staff - he lost Verda Barnes - and they weren't paying attention to some cases. I've got a quite a few examples where Democrat friends came to me and said, "Jim, can you help us on this? I can't get any attention in Frank's office."*

Perry Swisher – *I think Frank Church was defeated by two things: Frank Church and Jimmy Carter. Not by Symms. When Carter at 5:30 our time, 4:30 [in Northern Idaho], conceded -*

But if I had to put my finger on just a second guess - and I've known him [Church] since high school days - I'd say it was what he went through with that intelligence thing [in 1975]. He thought it would come out so much different. I think he thought there would be sufficient information that people [would be outraged]. But Frank was too close to the picture. We had just come through the Watergate thing, and he had seen the level of indignation. You would have expected a repeat because what that committee disclosed was even more horrendous than Watergate. People probably were jaded. And not only that, because the public was jaded, he didn't have its attention, and it was possible for the White House regulars and the defense department conservatives to make the allegation that it did some harm. I suspect that 90 percent of the National Guard voted against Frank Church.

Reagan made for big changes in Idaho on election day. Republicans ousted the Democratic senior senator by a single percentage point. When Symms moved to the Senate he was replaced in the House with another Republican, state Sen. Larry Craig, who would prove to be as conservative as Symms. In elections to come Craig would develop a tight lock on that seat. In the second district George Hansen won his best victory since 1966. Republicans picked off six Democrats in the

Idaho House and three in the Senate - enough to come within one vote of a two-thirds majority.

1980 did not wipe out the Idaho Democrats, although many Democrats suspected on election night it had. They had mounted their most sophisticated effort ever to keep an incumbent in the Senate and they had failed. They had tried to take over the state Senate and failed. The number of Democrats in courthouses declined.

And yet the decline was incremental.

While Jimmy Carter lost Idaho by nearly two to one, Church and Symms fought it out to a dead heat, and Symms won by just 4,262 votes, less than one percent. It was a win but no mandate. Nearly 60,000 more people voted for Church in 1980 than in 1974.

Idaho's 44 counties have 396 elected officials. After 1980 the Republicans gained 16, a fairly normal shift. (In 18 of the 44 counties, the Republican- Democratic balance stayed the same.) Most Democrats who lost legislative seats ran in basically Republican country and had had close races for years.

The election didn't destroy the Democrats. It did shatter the structure of their politics in Idaho.

The job of organization had become Church and Andrus. Church left politics and became a Washington lawyer and lobbyist. The cancer Church beat back so many years finally killed him in April 1984. After 1980 Andrus moved back to Boise and into consulting. He had been in the most unpopular (in Idaho) administration in this century, and in 1981 was without political portfolio. Democrats still had Gov. John Evans, but he looked to Republicans like a gnat to be swatted. He no longer was protected by the Andrus and Church machines, which scattered to the four winds.

The Democrats were a low-voltage battery, unconnected to any useful machinery.

The Republicans had leaders and unity. It would be easy to rerun the formula in 1982 and watch Democrats go into decline ... right?

Tour | Middle Mountains

Forty miles through the mountains northeast of Boise is Idaho City, seat of Boise County and the most visible remnant of an Idaho that once was.

Idaho City had more than 6,200 people in its mining boom days a century ago. Now it has a tenth as many and depends on the tourists who visit its saloons and frontier streetscape. They were great grist for TV cameras when Frank Church announced for president here. Mining towns not lucky enough to be on a highway – Placerville, Pioneerville, New Centerville – were mostly abandoned. Only Horseshoe Bend, a lumber-ranching town across the mountains, kept pace. Horseshoe is strongly Republican.

Boise County's population doubled in the seventies and eighties (to 3,100 people). Growth in Boise city pushed lovers of peace, quiet, and beauty out to the mountains. Here, unlike in rural Ada County, they often were liberal environmentalists.

Boise County for decades was staunchly Republican. The new settlers, some of whom still want the services they had in Ada County, are changing that. Idaho City voted one-third for George Wallace in 1968 but only 50 percent for Ronald Reagan in 1980, unusually high and low numbers for Idaho. In the seventies Idaho City and Lowman, further up Highway 21, turned Democratic in statewide elections, while off-highway settlements stayed Republican. Boise County overall stayed Republican in the mid-eighties, but it may be up for grabs.[87]

Small and Far Away

Further in the mountains the population thins out. The few towns are an hour or more, by car, apart. Each is distinctive. Each votes differently. As a whole, the mountains are strongly Republican, but as in Boise County do have Democratic pockets.

Up a twisting mountain road is the resort town Stanley, home of Casanova Jack and the Stanley Stomp. Stanley joined the world in 1969 when Highway 21 from Boise was completed. About 100 people lived here in 1980, 150 in the mid- eighties. Republican in the sixties and early seventies, it changed as new people came and voted, especially in the mid-seventies when Nevada gambling magnate William Harrah bought chunks of town. Republican Congressman George Hansen won re-election big in the second district in 1980 but lost badly in Stanley. Democratic Gov. John Evans barely got re-elected in 1982 but won big in Stanley.

---

[87] Well, no, it hasn't. Rapid growth has resulted in only marginal changes in Boise county politics, which continues to lean strongly Republican at all levels.

Stanley is notable because the two bigger towns in Custer County – seat Challis (population 1,500) and Mackay (750) – are strictly Republican. Challis is the center of mining boom and bust cycles running so fast that unions never got a foothold. "Environmentalist" is a swear word; in 1970 Cecil Andrus got eight percent of the vote here while winning statewide. But Challis is mainly a cattle town; this is one of the most concentrated ranching spots in Idaho. Mackay also is a ranching and farming community, and has been a small rail shipping outpost.

To the northeast is Salmon, home to 3,500 people. It is the largest town for more than 100 miles, the most remote Idaho city of its size; it supports a newspaper, radio station and a full range of businesses. Known as a jump-off to the Idaho wilderness, its economy turns more on ranching and agriculture. Few outsiders have moved in, and Salmon is deeply conservative. But for a few scattered precincts, all of Lemhi is the same; it ordinarily goes Republican two to one.

At times Salmon has elected conservative Democrats. Local politicking is highly personal.

When Boise lawyer and future Supreme Court Justice Byron Johnson ran for the Democratic Senate nomination in 1972, he won three big counties – Ada, Canyon, and Bonneville – and little Lemhi. "I know exactly how I did it," Johnson recalled. He was a friend of Salmon attorney Jim Herndon, whose father had run for governor in 1966. "What Jim told me in '72 was, I'm going to support you but I've got to do it my own way. All I ask you to do is to give me one Saturday." So one summer Saturday Herndon brought Johnson to Salmon. That night, "what we did was, we started at one end of Main Street, and we hit every single bar that Saturday night. It took us a long time, until just about closing time, to get to the other end of the street. I mean, he personally introduced me and bought a beer for everybody. He knew everybody. That's why I carried Lemhi County. There was no other reason."[88]

Schizophrenia

Blaine County is the most deeply split Idaho county.

Most occupied land – less than a fourth of it is privately owned – is dominated by ranchers and farmers who make Southern Blaine towns like Carey, Picabo and Bellevue Republican.

But north of Bellevue the mountains rise, ranch land diminishes and people turn Democratic. Hailey, the county seat, has a tourist trade and an extensive mining history. It was founded as a trade center

---

[88] Generally, these tendencies seem as true now as then. But that hasn't changed the area's politics; although occasional unusual local circumstances might allow for the occasional courthouse Democrat, Lemhi and Custer remain among Idaho's most Republican counties. Which is to say, *very* Republican.

for once-extensive mining in the Wood River region; the miners were organized by the same Butte (Montana) Miners Union that organized miners in Shoshone County. Mining declined but northern Blaine kept a Democratic base.

One reason is the resort trade, which generated support for gambling in the forties and fifties. More recently the small neighbor towns of Ketchum (3,000 people) and Sun Valley (600, more a resort with post office than a true town) attract well-heeled tourists, the artists and craftsmen who sell to them, and the restaurateurs who feed them. Ketchum is a lively town, more fun and funky than Sun Valley. Its people, too, are mainly not ranchers but from other more politically liberal places, geographically and mentally. Northern Blaine Democrats are in perpetual combat with down-county Republicans. It's a close match.[89]

South and west is tiny Camas County – tied with Clark as least populous in Idaho, at 700 people each – and its seat, Fairfield. Like southern Blaine this is farm and ranch land and it veers Republican. But it has a Democratic rancher tradition, and in the eighties a Democratic organization grew, led by Gene Sullivan, who runs a restaurant and motel in Fairfield.

Local boosters have pushed hard on a ski resort and associated business at Soldier Mountain north of Fairfield. If they succeed, and it becomes a spinoff of the Sun Valley economy, Camas' usually stable Republican politics could become less predictable.[90]

A Bit of All of Idaho

To the west and south, across more mountains, is Elmore County, the most varied county in Idaho. It has every kind of environment and people found elsewhere in Idaho, and some found nowhere else.

To its north are old, barely populated mountain mining towns, like Idaho City but smaller: Atlanta Rocky Bar, Featherville. They vote like Idaho City, sometimes but not always Democratic.

To its south are most of the people. A few are Republican ranchers on plains or in small towns like Hammett. More live in Mountain Home (8,500 people) and Glenns Ferry (1,400). Although surrounded by ranching country, their people are an eclectic mix.

---

[89] Or it used to be, but not any more: Owing to the population growth in the Ketchum-Hailey area, and its overwhelmingly Democratic base, Blaine is now solidly Democratic. Republican Senator Larry Craig even joked about the idea that Blaine (geographically near the center of the state) wasn't really a part of Idaho. If you consider the factors of culture, philosophy and partisan politics, he had a point. Blaine is the only Idaho county to vote Democratic for president in 2000 and 2004 and one of only three in 2008, and as of 2009 he has had a Democratic legislative delegation which isn't much seriously challenged.
[90] Nope, it's stayed predictable, even with some growth around the Soldier Mountain ski area. That development, backed by actor Bruce Willis, was thrown into some question in 2009 when the main ski lodge building burned.

Mountain Home's mainstay since World War II has been Mountain Home Air Force Base, the only big military installation in Idaho. It is why Elmore grew three times faster than any other county in Idaho in the fifties. (The next largest houses the Air National Guard at Gowen Field in Boise, which has less impact in that city than Mountain Home's base does there.) The base brings more varied people than most Idaho farm communities ever see; their voting ranges all over the map. Mountain Home's railroad background – it was founded as a stage and rail stop – a large Hispanic population, and extensive New Deal projects based there in the thirties also help give Democrats a slight edge.

And one other thing. The hazardous material dump near Mountain Home, called Envirosafe, generated terrific controversy in the eighties. The debate wasn't partisan: Republicans too pushed for cleanup. But in 1986 the issue turned Elmore a bit more Democratic, enough to oust veteran Republican state senator Walter Yarbrough of nearby Grand View. The winner was Democrat Claire Wetherell, an experienced Mountain Home politician whose son Michael (a Boise city councilman) and late husband Robert (a veteran Elmore senator) had long political records.

Glenns Ferry's railroad background long made it a Democratic stronghold. It was a crew transfer point, so railroaders lived in town and were an important base. But Union Pacific shut down the transfer point in 1973. Glenns Ferry probably will become more Republican with time.

That would make it more like the places to its east.[91]

---

[91] And exactly this has happened. Elmore County was a "swing county" when this was originally written. Now it should be placed firmly in the Republican camp. The case of Sher Sellman in the late 90s was instructive. A popular and well-regarded Mountain Home city council member, Sellman ran as a Democrat in 1996 against a poor Republican opponent, and lost. Two years later, she ran as a Republican for the same seat, and won, comfortably.

11 | Back to the Future?

Gov. John Evans, Idaho's only major Democratic office holder in 1982, was almost blown out of the water one January night that year at the Democrats' Jefferson-Jackson Dinner.

The keynoter, Colorado Sen. Gary Hart, a presidential prospect, was a dry speaker that night and didn't turn on the 900 Democrats. (He won the 1984 Idaho Democratic caucuses anyway.) Meanwhile, mere mention of Ronald Reagan's name sent Republicans into spasms of ecstasy. The Democrats had no one comparable.

The location didn't help. The usual place for these dinners was the Red Lion Motor Inn-Riverside, which had meeting rooms and a classy feel. In 1982, the Democrats met down the road in the inelegant decor of the Western Idaho Fairgrounds Expo Building. It was fine for displays of cattle and homebuilding supplies, less appropriate for the premier annual gathering of the party faithful.

Evans was talking about the need for Democrats to rebound. Perhaps because Democratic times were lean, perhaps because of his years as state Senate floor leader, Evans could be stoutly partisan. Former Governor Smylie said that "his way of handing a Republican an olive branch is to hand them an olive branch and say, "Here's an olive branch, you son of a bitch'."

Then a leader of the electrical workers' union in Pocatello walked to the head table carrying a bag.

A bag full of checks. About $6,000 worth.

They were collected in two days from individual workers at the INEL site west of Idaho Falls. Each check was properly marked for campaign reporting. Nothing improper.

"We had met in the afternoon," Evans recalled. "He said, I've been out collecting dollars here and there from the membership. I said, why don't you make a presentation this evening? So he did."

Evans was all that stood between them and a Right to Work law (although he would win and they would get the law anyway three years later). "Right to Work" was the odd moniker for banning employer-union contracts that required employees to join a union to work at the place (or, that did not allow employees to work at a unionized shop without joining.) Since Idaho had small unions Right to Work would send only small ripples through the economy. But to unions freeloading – weakening unions in the process – was outrageous.

As of that night Evans had not vetoed a Right to Work bill, but no one doubted he would. Evans was a key Senate vote for killing Right to Work in 1957. He did not seek re-election the next year; word was, he would have lost because of that vote.

In the seventies Right to Work came back to the Legislature. It didn't get far; the House would pass and the Senate would kill the bills.

Many Republicans, including Jim McClure, remembered with alarm what happened in 1958, when Right to Work was on the ballot and they had lost the Legislature partly as a result. But proponents like Gooding Republican Rep. John Brooks said Idaho had changed. And it had.

At the 1982 banquet Evans said, "I truly believe it's the wrong thing for Idaho and it will be vetoed." Weeks later the Legislature passed a Right to Work bill and Evans vetoed it.

The Incredible Shrinking Unions

In the post-war forties, as labor organization grew, merchants and others who benefited from higher wages backed unions. In the late fifties union membership peaked at about a quarter of the non-agricultural work force; unions killed Right to Work and turned the Statehouse mostly Democratic. But their vote margins, ever slim, vanished as unions' share of Idaho's work force fell. By 1982 it was down to 16 percent. Right to Workers who suspected they no longer would lose were probably right.

Too, Idaho Mormons were fruitful and multiplied, and church leaders supported Right to Work. President David McKay, for example, said, "Any person is free to join a union, when to do so favors his best interests; but no one should be compelled to join."

In 1984 a pamphlet distributed in Eastern Idaho quoted church leaders as supporting Right to Work. It was hooted at by labor leaders, and word from Salt Lake was that the church had no official stand on the law. But the LDS leaders' feelings were clear. When the public vote came in 1986, support for Right to Work was strongest in the Mormon counties of eastern Idaho. In Franklin, about 95 percent Mormon, Right to Work won almost five to one.

The late-seventies recession had cut employment deeply. When timber demand picked up in the mid-eighties, managers turned to automation rather than new employees to increase production. Idaho's timber mill worker population fell from 8,400 in 1977 to 6,100 in 1986 – a loss of at least 3,000 Democratic votes.

The biggest union crash was in the Silver Valley. For decades it was spared most of the jarring boom-bust that devastated so many western cities. In 1979, due partly to a federal bill – co-sponsored by Congressman Symms – requiring the government to buy $513 million of silver, Texas fatcats Herbert and Nelson Bunker Hunt drove up silver's price while collecting huge blocks of it. But they went too far. The market crashed in March 1980 and with it the reliability of silver prices. As low-paid Mexican and Peruvian miners poured silver into the world market, prices fell again. Prices for zinc and lead – the valley's other big metals – weakened with slumps in the housing and auto industries.

All this happened as easy ores played out and silver got more expensive to produce. In 1950 mining employed about 2.6 percent of working Idahoans; by 1980, 1.1 percent.[92]

In the first half of 1981 the Bunker Hill Co., the largest employer (of about 2,400 people) in the Silver Valley and the second-largest industrial employer in Idaho, lost $7.7 million. Analysts figured losses could hit $20 million or more for the year. Bunker Hill managers proposed freezing wages, and most workers agreed. But organized electrical workers balked, the freeze request was withdrawn, and Bunker Hill's future went to Gulf Resources & Chemical Inc., of Houston. "We could all go to church and pray for higher metals prices," Bunker Hill Vice President Jerry Turnbow was quoted as he waited for the decision.

The idea of closing Bunker Hill seemed incredible. The plant had 94 years of history. It was the biggest silver-lead-zinc mining complex in the United States, producing 15 percent of the nation's zinc, 16 percent of its lead. Union contracts didn't even have provisions for closure. Bunker Hill was Kellogg; its enormous smelter tower was the town's landmark.

But on August 25 – Black Tuesday – Houston said Bunker Hill would close by year's end and 2,100 employees would be laid off. It meant devastation to Kellogg, shock to the Northwest. It led to closure of the mining equipment manufacturing Bucyrus-Erie plant in Pocatello, which employed hundreds of people.

Jack Peterson – *[The closure] changed Idaho's status with regard to being a producer of refined lead and zinc. We produce no refined lead or zinc now, only lead or zinc concentrate, and we produce very little refined silver ... That [closure] had a major impact not only from the loss of jobs but from the loss of income to that area through processing. When Bunker Hill closed, what a lot of people weren't aware of is that approximately 75 percent of all the raw materials that were processed at Bunker Hill in the last few years of its operation came from South America ... The largest mining, manufacturing and chemical processing region of the state became Southeast Idaho and its elemental phosphorus and phosphate industry with five operating mines, two elemental phosphorus plants, two major phosphate fertilizer plants. Southeast Idaho became the leading employer and producer of minerals for the state of Idaho, and still is by far.*

In Silver Valley bars and cafes the mood turned surly as miners awaited pink slips. Their fathers and grandfathers were miners; nowhere else in Idaho did roots run so deep. Many had cut short their schooling to take high-paying mine jobs. Now Gulf had wiped out the jobs and the miners had no other marketable skills.

---

[92] And has steadily continued to decline in the years since. In 2000, the only large mining employment base remaining in Idaho was in the phosphate industry in southeast Idaho. The Silver Valley is not yet quite finished with silver mining, but it is coming close.

Like Pocatello, the Valley had a worse-than-deserved reputation as a bad place to live. It became a public issue that fall in a $20 million lead poisoning trial in U.S. District Court. A Kellogg delegation took to the Statehouse a petition bearing 4,337 signatures – more people than lived in Kellogg – protesting news stories of the trial. "Descriptions of the city of Kellogg as 'a very unhappy place' and 'a small, backward community' where 'plants won't grow, pets die and there is never a clear day' are without any substantiating basis in fact," it said.

The locals worried about scaring off a potential Bunker Hill buyer. None came – at least, not in time to stop the closure.

Harry Magnuson – *The first thing, you're in utter shock. The damn thing can't happen ... So then you wait a while and you say, well, somebody will do something about it. Who was somebody? The obvious thing is that maybe the government will do something. We went through that. John Evans appointed a task force and they worked for several months. Nothing was forthcoming.*

That's how I got involved. I figured, well, the damn thing had gotten so ridiculous. I mean, hell, you had this big Bunker Hill, a billion dollars of facilities, somebody ought to do something.

So I got hold of Duane Hagadone. I said, "Goddammit, Duane, we ought to do something. You've got the [news]papers, you've got Coeur d'Alene, I've got Wallace. Let's put some pressure on some people. Let's put some pressure on our congressional people. We're not going to let Bunker Hill go down." So we got involved.

I got a call from Jack Simplot. "Harry," he says, "dammit, if there's anything I can do, let me know." He says, "I'm for America, I'm for Idaho." So we got going.

What I didn't know, what we didn't know, and what wasn't generally perceived, were the fundamental structural changes going on in our economy and especially in basic industries like mining. That change was just starting. The change is that you just can't compete with the foreign deposits and foreign operations and the cheap labor.

Then one morning in mid-December the Valley heard on its radio station, Osburn's KWAL, about a miracle. Magnuson, Hagadone, and La Jolla, Calif., investor J. William Pfeiffer had an option to buy Bunker Hill from Gulf. The J.R. Simplot Co. in Boise got involved. And they all made their pitch, keeping budgets and payrolls pared down, to Bunker's union leaders.

But local Steelworkers leaders, backed by regional spokesmen flown to Kellogg, held tough against the Magnuson-Hagadone deal. It meant, they felt, too deeply cutting into union contracts.

It was a Battle for hearts and minds. On option deadline weekend, KWAL generously opened its mikes to both sides. Friday afternoon Hagadone went on the air, explaining his plan and calmly answering questions. Hours later Ken Flatt, the Steelworkers local president, did likewise. Speeches, rallies, and pleas went on all weekend.

On Sunday came "The Vote": accept and cripple the union, or reject and risk their jobs? On that bitterly cold day – indoors as well as outdoors – they voted 695-506 to accept. That night the local leaders resigned, saying it was a vote of no confidence. Regional leaders took over.

They said they could not sign. A contract scheduled to run until August 1983 was in place, and the law said it had to stay even if management changed. If the union took Hagadone's deal, they said, it would be open to lawsuit. Hagadone went on the air again and warned the deal would not be offered much longer.

The next 48 hours were a peak of emotion in the history of Kellogg. On Monday night steelworkers gathered at the union hall, denouncing the nationals, electing new leaders. On Tuesday morning they signed an agreement and gave it to Hagadone, who gave it to his attorneys, who questioned its legality. The national Steelworker representatives said it wasn't legal.

The next day Hagadone called a press conference and said, "It's over with." The investors disbanded. The deal fell through.[93]

Republicans swiftly jumped the union for not going along with the workers' vote. "The union bosses in Pittsburg (Steelworkers headquarters) seem to hold the upper hand," Steve Symms said.

Ten days later, at the Democratic Jefferson-Jackson Day dinner, John Evans was handed a bag of money by a union official.

The 1982 gubernatorial race was on.

Actually, that wasn't the end of the Bunker Hill investors' story. Just before election day, 1982, Hagadone, Magnuson, Simplot, and Bunker Hill President Jack Kendrick bought Bunker Hill. By then no union members were employed there and the operation would stay closed until the market picked up. Bunker Limited Partnership kept the mines dry – without pumping they would flood immediately. Finally, Bunker Hill did celebrate a limited reopening in the summer of 1988. But Kellogg was forever changed.

Harry Magnuson – *We didn't know it at the time but I think the union did us a good favor [in 1981]. I think the union saved us a hell of a lot of money. It was high emotions, but I often wondered what the hell would have happened if we had kept that thing going when the bottom dropped out of that [silver] market in '82, '83, and '84. You'd have lost your shirts.*

---

[93] That was surely one turning point for the mining economy of the Silver Valley, and for its cultural life too. But another occurred after *Paradox* was published that was at least as significant, in the way the Valley views the world. That came in June 1991, when federal agents swept through the communities in search of illicit gambling activities which were effectively condoned by local law enforcement. There were shutdowns and charges files – all of it much generating powerful intense anger among Silver Valley residents who saw outsiders disrupting, once again, their way of life. The decline of the mining economy, and unions, might have been expected to lead to a Republican surge here, but as of 2000 it has not. The reasons may have in part to do with a local sense that people there are under siege – and that which is local, and of long standing, is best

New mines are forever dug, and some succeed. Gold was hardly important in Idaho for 50 years, but it stormed back in the eighties. Idaho Mining Association President Jack Peterson points out that after strict government control of gold ended in 1973, gold prices rose. "It began to respond in the late seventies and the price of gold today, about $480 to $500 an ounce, is high enough that complex bodies of gold ore and low-grade bodies of gold ore can be recovered, as the price will sustain the capital costs. As a result of that, we've had Stibnite gold mine come on, and Thunder Mountain come on, and Noranda announced a major new mine south of Burley. We have many gold exploration companies exploring in Idaho right now that have never been here before."

Phil Batt and the Thin Line

But that was in the future in 1982. Point one, then, was that unions were in decline. Point two was that recession had cut deep into the timber industry. Point three was that the Bunker Hill shutdown had given the Republicans a campaign issue.

The obvious Republican for governor was Lt. Gov. Phil Batt, who had considered running against Evans in 1978. Batt was one of the most respected people in state government. In 1968, in his second term in the Senate, he became Senate majority leader. It was a fast rise – mirrored by Risch in the next decade – that made sense. Batt was a born legislator. His quick wit and shrewd, agile mind showed up best in small groups like Senate caucuses or committees. (He was also an amateur jazz musician and sometimes played clarinet with the Gene Harris combo in Boise.) He led work on a farm workers bill and other human rights issues, so moderates felt kinship with him. But conservatives liked him too, and in 1976 he became Senate president pro tem. Then, feeling he'd reached "up or out" time, Batt ran for lieutenant governor.

He had a sure grasp of issues, processes, and people, a fine knack for negotiation. His judgment was good enough that years later Democratic Gov. Cecil Andrus tapped him to unravel a snarled state computer foulup. In a few weeks he came up with a solution which Andrus used. And it worked.

Batt never had trouble winning re-election in Canyon County, where so many people knew either him or some other Batt. But running statewide he looked and felt uncomfortable. He was not as gregarious as Symms or Evans. His short stature and high, fast voice didn't make for the preferred Marlboro Man image.

He made his intentions clear in 1980, picking up support early so a 1978-style snafu wouldn't happen again. Yet the rise of a Republican more conservative than Batt may have been inevitable. After Symms' 1980 win, after so many Republican primary wins by conservatives (like Larsen in 1978, though that was fueled by the Mormon vote), surely someone would challenge Batt. Someone did.

House Speaker Ralph Olmstead of Twin Falls seemed to neatly bridge the gap between libertarian-conservatives – he had been an ally of Butch Otter- and Mormon-conservatives. His reserved personal style helped; so did living in Twin Falls, on the cusp of the philosophical constituencies. He had a reputation as a tax and budget hardliner, and in 1978 was elected House speaker with help from the growing conservative crowd. The prediction was that he would give no quarter to moderates or Democrats. But though his votes and views stayed the same, he did not use the speaker's office that way: even Democrats considered him scrupulously fair. In 1980 Boise Rep. Dan Emery, a former Lewiston Democrat turned very conservative Boise Republican, challenged Olmstead's speakership; Olmstead beat him and swatted down conservatives who had supported Emery, taking away their top committee spots. He did not forget where loyalties lay. Neither did the conservatives.

So his race for governor as a conservative alternative to Batt had built-in problems. But it also nettled Batt. Knowing the fate of moderates in Republican primaries, Batt emphasized his conservatism to push back the Olmstead threat – even as Olmstead, too, had to veer right. "Of course, that probably cost me some moderate support later, because I was obligated to demonstrate my conservative credentials to come back at Olmstead," Batt recalled.

Batt rolled over Olmstead in the primary with 63.9 percent of the vote. But Batt and campaign manager Dirk Kempthorne had to be concerned. What about all those conservative votes that went to Olmstead? Would they back turn to Batt now, in the race against John Evans, or had Olmstead planted doubts in their minds?

Batt jumped Evans on budgets and taxes. But these were not such sexy issues as in 1978 and 1980; those elections had defused their impact. Batt never learned how to appeal to voters' emotions, either. Late in the campaign a Canyon County group called BRIMSTONE (the acronym stood for nothing) published a cartoon book called Big John, critical of Evans' ties to education interests. Batt, who had nothing to do with the book, thought it hurt him and repudiated it. He had built a career on cooling heated situations rather than doing what candidates are supposed to do: riling people into crusades. Batt had no crusade. All he had left, in that arena, was Right to Work.

Batt considered it a matter for the back burner rather than a critical issue. "I never did want to make it a cornerstone of my campaign, and that's the way it evolved," he recalled. He talked Right to Work, unwisely, even around important union populations.

Despite Idaho's economic reversals, Evans personally stayed popular. He knew from the start how precarious was his footing and used his incumbency well. He spent a good deal of 1981 on a "Capital for a Day" program which took Evans and other officials to all 44 counties. It was a defensible state outreach but also a keen political move, putting the governor in an impressive light in home towns. (It had the same fanfare benefits as Symms' bus campaign in 1980.) Evans's 1982 campaign was not strong, but the governor was energetic and more polished than in 1978.

On election day Batt almost beat Evans. For most of election night Evans thought he was going the way of Frank Church.

He would have but for 4,208 votes and extraordinary Democratic effort in Pocatello and Lewiston, where the unions ran an all-out last-minute push, their strongest vote drive of the eighties.[94]

But this effort, a last gasp of real union power in Idaho, came to the edge of failure. The best they could do was barely re-elect a hard-campaigning, popular incumbent governor. Democratic state Auditor Joe Williams, who had been re-elected to that job since 1958, won by 6,078 votes against an understated political novice. Democrats did not lose ground in 1982, but their best efforts against less-than-usually hepped-up Republicans gave them no advances.

They had to do something. And they did.

In 1983 the Democrats elected as state chairman Pocatellan Mel Morgan, who first had run for the office a decade earlier. He was their best chairman in years, the first in decades to significantly strengthen the party structure.

"The party has always been in dire financial straits," Morgan recalled, but matters got especially serious in the early eighties. Morgan gradually improved them.

"It's always been a loose-knit organization out there in the counties," he said. "The counties feel they don't owe the state party. You'd hear a lot of hue and cry that's not true, but it is." Only Ada and Kootenai, and to a lesser extent Latah and Nez Perce, counties had truly coherent organizations by the mid-eighties – but that, too, was partly Morgan's doing.

Morgan was no cheery pep rally leader; he was a pragmatist, a cold slap in the face. He told the party what it needed, rather than wanted, to hear. His moves were not always popular. (He opposed detailed and highly partisan party platforms, correctly pointing out that such documents hurt Democrats in local elections.) But he did what had to be done, and by the time he resigned in 1988 Democrats had a much-improved organization.

Mel Morgan – *In my estimation, the day Frank Church got beat the party went downhill. It was a tough job to pull it up by its bootstraps.*

---

[94] Batt went on to win the governorship 12 years later, in the Republican landslide year of 1994. He was not only a beneficiary but also one of the architects of that landslide: state GOP chairman after the Republicans' bad year of 1990, he was the organizer of the Republican resurgence of 1992, and the unifier of what had been a fractured party. Batt's governorship started off a bit shaky, and Batt never seemed entirely comfortable in the office; but he grew and learned, became a strong and refreshingly independent thinker and leader, and finished well. By the time he announced he would not seek a second term, a wide range of Idahoans – probably a very large majority – were sad to lose him.

You have to remember what the process always was in those elections. No matter who the governor was, everything was built around Frank Church and his election. He would send his people out, and they were certainly great as far as everybody else running for office. Verda Barnes would move to Idaho and work like hell. And all they ever had was card indexes: a name, he's a Democrat, such and such an election. After every election those cards would mysteriously disappear. Or you'd find half of them. It got into too many hands, and cards are the worst things in the world to begin with. I can remember rummaging through people's basements in Bannock County because that's where the Church list was supposed to be ...

When he got beat in 1980, of course you saw a disintegration of the Frank Church organization, which in my estimation was the lifeblood of the party.

Morgan put high priority on the party developing its own voter identification list and keeping it up to date. By the late eighties it had that list – by itself a big organizational step.

So Close to Domination

In 1980 and 1984 Republicans were swept ashore by tidal waves of votes to the altar of Ronald Reagan. No sane Idaho politician in the eighties spoke ill of Reagan, and Democrats went out with the wash. But that had been less true in the off-year 1982. Some thought it might be even less true in 1986. (An irony developed here. The plan to elect governors on off-presidential years was developed by Republicans to help Republicans; but in the seventies and eighties it helped Democrats instead.)

As Democrats had coalesced and quit their fighting, so were Republicans getting better at controlling hostilities. Only some local organizations kept at it. (Bannock County Republicans, for example, went through nasty moderate- conservative Battles in the late seventies and early eighties.)

The Republicans also made shrewd choices for party chairman.

After the Andrus/Church wins – and Republican debacle – of the 1974 they chose ex-Democrat Vern Ravenscroft. He was an inspired choice: conservative enough to appeal across the board and – lacking a Republican history – not tied to any faction. He got them to work together, and they did much better in 1976.

When Ravenscroft quit to run for governor in 1978, the Republicans replaced him with Idaho Falls attorney Dennis Olson.

Olson had worked for the party for years but wasn't well known statewide. He had never run for office and had no plans to. His forte was organization. The Republicans under Olson – and it was his party; he controlled the machinery – were the most effective political organization in Idaho since Lloyd Adams and Tom Boise.

"Dennis wasn't at all times the greatest diplomat, and he wasn't afraid to tell you what he was thinking," organizer Richard Hendricks recalled. "There were a lot of people who didn't like Dennis. But they supported him because he produced. There was no question about that. Dennis, with the help of a lot of us, created a real organization, an in-depth organization."

Olson died in March 1985 while shoveling snow at his house. He had anointed a successor: Blake Hall, another Idaho Falls attorney. Hall's succession confirmed that Idaho Republican leadership had moved from Boise, its traditional base, to Idaho Falls.

Hall tried some different approaches to organization, and some of the long- timers grumbled.

Richard Hendricks – *Dennis was money-minded only to the point that he didn't believe in having $5,000 in the bank when the election ended. He wanted it spent to zero. He didn't want it one penny overdrawn, but if he had $100,000 in the bank to work with, he wanted $100,000 spent on the election.*

Now what I'm feeling – I bet I've had four or five letters in the last two, three months, asking for money. And then the other night I got a call saying, was I going to join the Century Club [for $100-and-up contributors]? And I said no, I'm not going to. Normally I would say, yeah, maybe I'll send $50 now and $50 later. But I'm not going to.

Uprooting the Fences

In 1984 Ronald Reagan beat Walter Mondale in Idaho almost three-to-one. He brought out the conservative Republicans as labor had Democrats in 1982, turning little Republican margins into big ones, winning two-thirds of both houses of the Legislature for the first time since 1952.

Reagan was one reason. Reapportionment was another.

For most of Idaho's history reapportionment was a minor task because the legislature was set up as Congress was: one senator for each of 44 counties and representatives based on population, each county getting at least one. Supreme Court decisions wiped out that system in the early sixties. So in 1965 the Legislature sliced nine House and nine Senate seats and split the state into legislative districts that didn't all match county lines. A few districts were a bit tortuous in dimension, but most made sense. Reapportionment in the early seventies was again agony - an extended lawsuit came of it - but the districts changed little.

Reapportionment barely affected the Legislature's balance of power; the same voters, after all, voted. State Sen. C.E. "Chick" Bilyeu, a Pocatello Democrat, would tell for years the story of how Republicans had figured out how to knock him out of his hard-won seat. Bilyeu ran for the Senate three times in the sixties and lost each time. His wife Diane ran in 1968 and won. When she decided not to run for a second term he ran instead, and won. Reapportionment came that term, and Bilyeu recalls the night a Republican senator told him it was all over. He would be tossed to the wolves, into the same district with popular American Falls Republican Sen. Joe Allen. It would be an easy Republican win, they thought – but they were wrong. Bilyeu won, and in 1986 he became the senior member of the Idaho Senate in either party.

After false starts and foul-ups, lawmakers drafted a new plan barely in time for the 1982 election. It was a patchwork no more gerrymandered than earlier plans – less so than the seventies model – but it fell under legal attack. Several Northern Idaho Democrats, aided by residents of the Coeur d'Alene Indian Reservation (which the plan split into three districts), said the legislature didn't have to abandon county boundaries to meet the Supreme Court's rules. District Judge Dar Cogswell agreed and adopted plan "14-B," later upheld by the state supreme court and put into effect. The logic behind it was more tortured than the old split-county districts ever were; it crafted districts for explicit political purposes, such as uniting the Hispanic vote in Canyon County by making the whole county one district. 14-B split Ada County into six districts but didn't split Canyon, Twin Falls or Kootenai counties, which could have been divided.

To smooth the population bulges that resulted from keeping county boundaries intact, 14-B gave two and three delegations (of one senator and two representatives each) to larger counties. It also added seven "floterial districts" which spanned the state, each including smaller regular districts. In all, it added 21 new legislative seats.

Democrats were delighted: it was a radical change and seemed to do nifty things with ethnic votes. Republicans said it was a mess but predicted they would win more seats under its terms.

They did.

The best case study is Canyon County. Before 14-B, the Hispanic vote was concentrated in one of three legislative districts, and there it had some clout. After 14-B that vote was diluted in the much larger Anglo population. In some counties like Canyon, Bonneville, and Bannock, voters filled 12 legislative seats at once, choosing between two dozen candidates. Voters knowing less about individual races were more inclined to vote party line; in most places that meant Republican. 14-B made counties more rigidly partisan than they had been in years.

Reapportionment, Reagan, and twists in a few close Senate races gave Republicans two-thirds of the state Senate. Evans' big red veto stamp, which two-thirds of both chambers together could override, lost its punch. In 1985 he helplessly vetoed Right to Work and only to see it become law. Labor got an initiative on the ballot and put it to the voters: do we keep Right to Work?

A Hard Turn to the Right

Voters also were asked: do we keep the Legislature?

Running against the mobocracy of Congress or Legislature is a time-honored campaign tactic that has impact if a Legislature outrages enough people. In 1986, the Idaho Legislature had.

The Legislature went through more changes over the decades than its stable party lineup indicates. The reapportionment of 1965 and gubernatorial election the next year changed the legislature as much as it did the party structure of Idaho. The reapportioned 1967 legislature was bereft not only of many of its old leaders but also of the old extremes. Its membership was middle-of-the- road and an odd contrast not only to its predecessors – the 1966 election was a clean break – but also to its governor. This session of new legislators ran head-first into rookie conservative Governor Samuelson. The result was an 89-day long session, second longest in Idaho history – and 39 vetoes, several times as many as the Democratic governors who would follow Samuelson ever stamped in a single session. It gave Samuelson a reputation for being unable to work well with the Legislature.

It also left legislators wanting to be more active in state government. They offered a constitutional amendment providing for annual sessions; in November 1968, the voters passed it. It was supposed to improve the legislative process. But in practice, it gave the system indigestion.

It created the high-speed turnover of legislators that began with the first annual session in 1969. People who could take three months or so out of every two years could less easily take that time every year. The number of successful businessmen and professionals in the Legislature fell: serving was too expensive. Increasingly farmers, who could still serve in the winter months, were joined by retirees and others with light personal responsibilities. Other candidates were zealots oblivious to financial loss or risk. Outstanding legislators could be found in any session, but their numbers began to fall.

It changed the tone of the legislature.

In the early seventies the Senate still was guided by old hands like Lt. Gov. Jack Murphy, President Pro Tem Jim Ellsworth and Majority Leader Phil Batt. After Batt the Senate was in effect led by Jim Risch, an exception to the rule since he was a successful attorney and a crisp professional who knew the written and unwritten rules.

In the House, moderate William Lanting of Twin Falls, who had held the job since 1967, had firm control for years. Change there came in 1974 when a conservative challenge to his speakership was imminent. Lanting retired from the House, and Blackfoot Republican Allan Larsen followed him as speaker. Larsen, a farmer who served in high offices in the Mormon church, was as conservative as the conservative wing of the House could have wanted. But he didn't take undue advantage. Larsen was a former chairman of the revenue and taxation committee and keenly interested in tax bills, but he didn't use a heavy hand in handling them.

When Larsen left in 1978 to run for governor, history repeated. Conservatism grew in the House to include members and close allies of the John Birch Society, and conservative Ralph Olmstead was the next speaker. He, too, kept his solidly conservative voting record but became even better liked by moderates.

The next speaker, also picked by conservatives, was different.

He was Tom Stivers, a Twin Falls businessman. As chairman of the Judiciary, Rules and Administration Committee he was thought to have done a solid job. (A harbinger of the future came during debate of a bill, backed by the odd couple of Risch and liberal Democratic Sen. Mike Black of Craigmont, to allow death row convicts the option to die by lethal injection. Stivers blasted it as "a slap on the wrist.") An energetic man with a lively sense of humor, he was expected to reach out to the House as Olmstead and Larsen had. Core conservatives knew better.

One knew where one stood with Stivers, and if one didn't know, Stivers would not hesitate to make it clear. Stivers, Evans, and Risch had royal set-tos in their weekly meetings. Stivers got into fights with the press, once ordering reporters off the House floor. (Desks are reserved there, as on the Senate floor, for the news media.) Stivers' conservatism was buttressed by the American Legislative Exchange Council, an organization he helped found as a meeting-point for conservative lawmakers; it pushed privatization of government services and a laundry list of other conservative ideas. Stivers chaired ALEC one year, and its ideas popped up regularly in the sessions that followed.

His stances led to a reaction among less conservative House Republicans. Led by relatively fearless freshmen like Reps. Dean Haagenson of Coeur d'Alene and Jerry Deckard of Eagle, they called themselves "Steelheads" after the fish that swim upstream. The Stivers crowd, they declared, were not conservatives – they reserved that word for themselves - but "flat-earthers."

They tried a coup in 1984, after Stivers' first term, and it showed how the House had changed. In 1980 conservatives revolted against a speaker who they felt gave too much aid and comfort to the moderates; now the moderates revolted against a speaker they felt was too conservative. The Steelhead candidate was Steve Antone, a Rupert farmer, the respected chairman of Revenue and Taxation. But he didn't win.

A politician with incumbency is a politician with a leg up, and seldom was that more true than in 1984, the election that led to both the boom and bust of the Stivers conservatives.

It was the first election after "14-B," expanding the legislature by 21 green lawmakers. The speaker, who makes committee assignments and appoints chairmen, is chosen by a vote within the majority party. An incumbent seeking re- election has enormous leverage with less-senior members: he can help get them elected and onto desired committees. And after 1984, the Republican House caucus was the most inexperienced in decades. Of 84 House members, 47 were new or had just one term under their belts. More strikingly, that was true of

40 of the 67 Republicans, who controlled the chamber. Easy re-election of Stivers was no surprise.

The 1985 and 1986 sessions weren't very productive. A pile of important legislation failed to get on track. Lawmakers fussed over taxes: increases came patch-n-scratch, and budget cuts were minor, putting off rather than resolving problems. The 1986 rejection of a constitutional amendment to allow a state lottery infuriated whole populations. Even disc jockeys who otherwise never talked politics rambled angrily about mossback legislators.

They were perceived as anti-education, rejecting improved spending for public schools, encouraging creationism, favoring home schooling. In 1986 Stivers bounced moderate Republicans Robert Fry of Horseshoe Bend (later a member of the state Tax Commission) and former Democrat Hilde Kellogg of Post Falls from the House Education Committee, which he then packed with conservatives. Fry and Kellogg, he said, were in the hip pocket of the Idaho Education Association – a top Stivers bugbear. The committee set to work on creationism and a bill intended to chase homosexual teachers out of schools.[95]

Stivers' anti-ed rap reached a pinnacle in 1986 when a teacher wrote him a thoughtful letter on the problems of Idaho education and concluded by saying she was leaving the state. Stivers' reply letter said simply: "Good-bye."

The last straw for some people was an offhand remark by Rep. Lyman Gene Winchester, a seven-term Kuna Republican. Winchester long was among the most conservative legislators but nothing he did in 14 years brought him as much attention as one offhand remark. While debating the homosexual teacher bill he said Stivers' ouster of Fry and Kellogg was a case of removing "queer lovers from the committee." The remark was taken as a measure of the House's mindset. Fry and Kellogg demanded apologies; Winchester gave none. Stivers caught heat for not pounding Winchester out of order. (Stivers said he didn't hear what Winchester said; he did in fact suffer hearing loss.)

It was one of the ugliest sessions ever. Stivers, who had never had trouble getting re-elected to the House, faced serious Republican opposition and decided to retire. He apparently read the tea leaves correctly. In the 1986 Republican primary, half a dozen of the most conservative House Republicans were defeated. Winchester lost to Deckard, whom Winchester had beaten in 1984.

The most telling primary race did not involve an incumbent.

Kootenai County had been electing some of the most conservative legislators Idaho ever saw. Rep. Cameron Fullmer of Post Falls proposed eliminating mandatory schooling above the sixth grade. Sen.

---

[95] Stivers bowed out of state government as of 1986, though he remained active in politics for some years. Fry and Kellogg were active in state government considerably longer. Fry became a member of the State Tax Commission, to 1993. Kellogg remained in the Idaho House up to the new millennium.

William Moore of Hayden Lake opposed a bill allowing for abortion in case of rape on grounds that a woman forced into sex probably couldn't become pregnant. In 1984 Moore lost to liberal Democrat Mary Lou Reed. That was the first big Democratic win in Kootenai in years, and Republicans wondered if it would take.

Ron Rankin, a veteran conservative activist in Kootenai, filed against her in 1986, and mobilized his organization. On the eve of the filing deadline a political unknown was recruited, by moderate state Republican vice-chairman Lee Shellman, to oppose Rankin. Rankin had support and he was articulate but he lost the primary, and Reed won re-election.

When the new House members arrived in November 1986 for the North Idaho tour at Coeur d'Alene, they had three candidates for speaker, all as easygoing as Stivers was abrasive. Robert Geddes was a Preston farmer and Mormon stake president entering his sixth term, as conservative as Stivers and presumed his heir apparent. John Sessions, a Driggs businessman, a shade less conservative, was a veteran (in his 11th term) in a House of newcomers. And moderate Tom Boyd was a Genesee farmer far geographically and philosophically from many of the Republicans. Boyd had never been a committee chairman or party leader. Even among moderates he was not a leader but one of the troops. Conventional wisdom suggested that the Battle was between Geddes and Sessions.

But Boyd outworked the others and had a sophisticated campaign led by Haagenson and Deckard. Boyd had a powerful case. Voters had tossed out the most vocal of Stivers' crew in the primary election, sending a message: If you don't want this happening to you, then vote for the greatest departure from Stivers. By the time the new House met in Coeur d'Alene and the members-elect compared notes, the race boiled down to Boyd and Geddes.

A month later when the voting came, Sessions lost on the first round. But for two tense hours Geddes and Boyd were locked in a dead heat: on two ballots, the 64 House members split evenly. On the third a couple of key votes went to Boyd and he became, strange as it might have seemed a year before, the new speaker -- the first speaker since Lanting not chosen by the conservatives.

The Turnaround That Didn't

1986 was supposed to be the strongest Democratic year since 1974. They had Andrus running for governor; the last time he was on the ballot, he won 70 percent of the vote. But that was the past. Since then he had been an unpopular interior secretary.

They had Evans running for Senate; after a decade as governor he had not turned off the voters and he undercut Symms' strength in Idaho while Symms was in Washington. But he didn't excite voters either. He lacked the groupies Andrus and Church had.

And they had Richard Stallings, the first Democrat to hold the second congressional district seat after 20 years of Republicans, who in 1984 barely beat a convicted felon who was, nevertheless, an incumbent. Stallings was still shy and was still a Democrat in one of the most conservative Republican districts in the nation.

These were the strongest candidates the Democrats could have fielded for those offices in 1986. And they all had problems.

That was one set of facts. Another had to do with who and what they were running with, and against.

Steve Symms had changed. In 1980 he had to work at appearing senatorial; now, after six years in the Senate, it came easily. He chaired a transportation budget subcommittee and got good marks for his work on it. He was less flamboyant and his speeches – unlike those in 1980 harping on federal spending almost to the exclusion of all else – covered a range of subjects.

So the fireworks came from stolid John Evans. Evans launched one torpedo after another in their debate that fall, and Symms looked shaken by the attack. He hadn't expected it; it seemed out of character for Evans. Legislators could have told him it wasn't. Evans was the same man who sniped with Senate Republican leaders when he was lieutenant governor and fought trench warfare with them while he was governor. Evans genuinely disliked Symms, didn't think he belonged in the Senate. If Symms had a similar attitude, he didn't let it show. (He was looking senatorial now.)

In the face of this, what was David Leroy to do?

Leroy, running for governor, was the Republicans' prototypical bright young candidate. He had both the skills - the smoothness and presentable appearance of the attorney he was – and the inclination to get ahead. It showed in his study of Idaho history; rare pictures and newspaper pages about early Idaho politicians covered his office walls. He was not an Andrus or Risch who happened to fall into politics. Leroy liked to say that he "fell into the bad crowd in the fifth grade, got elected to safety patrolman or something like that" – and never looked back. He was student president at the University of Idaho (his basic education in campaigning). He was an attorney in New York City for a while, but took a pay cut to return to Idaho, mainly to run for Ada County prosecutor.

David Leroy – *One thing that is eminently obvious in Idaho politics, Ada County politics included, is that a young person with a better mousetrap who's willing to work hard can actually get elected. If I had stayed in New York City and done everything right and worked and worked in the party and found benefactors and major donors who were inclined to support me through a series of minor offices and then public possibilities, if I had played my cards right, possibly this year I could be running for district attorney of Manhattan at the age of 40 (in 1988) instead of having done the kind of things I was able to do here in Idaho.*

Running against Andrus, the strongest Democrat in Idaho, he had to run his best campaign ever. But how to position himself? When he started in politics, as Ada County prosecutor in 1974, he sounded moderate. In 1976, when most Idaho Republicans backed Reagan against President Ford, Leroy was Ford's Idaho chairman. By 1980, two years after he was elected attorney general, he was solidly in Reagan's camp, moving away from his old crowd. And yet he didn't easily fit in. He was urban and a lawyer, and something about him made it obvious. (And he was from a Lewiston Democratic family. His brother Steve had been press secretary for Evans.)

His campaign was managed by Helen Chenoweth, a partner of Vern Ravenscroft who had helped engineer several of Symms' successful House races. But the campaign hit bumps in the spring of 1986. The previous fall state Sen. Skip Smyser of Parma, at Chenoweth's request, had released a poll Andrus had commissioned and Leroy's people had gotten; Smyser said it seemed designed to make Andrus look good. The pollster sued for libel, and in the spring Smyser retracted. Weeks later Chenoweth was out as manager.[96]

Her replacement was an odd choice: Chuck Lempesis of Coeur d'Alene, who had run a ferocious race for lieutenant governor against C.L. "Butch" Otter. Lempesis had enthusiasm, boundless energy and campaign experience. But now Leroy had a campaign manager sure to make his running mate – Otter – uncomfortable, and who would still have preferred to be running himself.

Andrus' campaign ran as smooth as a gyroscope, and was about as exciting to watch. He had presence, chemistry and messages that sounded good, and business experience and national ties that could help pull Idaho from its economic slump. He talked of getting support from Republicans more than of support from Democrats.

In November, the voters made no one comfortable. Symms beat Evans, but with just 52 percent of the vote. (Symms' campaign, with Reberger again at the helm, was the best-run of the bunch.) The Democrats regained their one-third- plus of the senate by winning a couple of races in Ada and Elmore Counties against weakened incumbent Republican senators; little changed in the other districts. Andrus beat Leroy by a margin so small as to be almost nonexistent – 3,635 votes. None of this showed great strength for either the Republicans or Democrats.

---

[96] But she was only beginning her major role in Idaho politics. She went back to work with Ravenscroft in consulting, and then eight years later ran for the first congressional district seat then held by a Democrat, Larry La Rocco, and like Steve Symms was at first thought likely to be the weak third-place finisher against two better-known candidates – one of them David Leroy, the other Ron McMurray, who the next year would become state Republican Party chair. Instead, those two tore each other apart and Chenoweth, with strong interest-group backing (especially from Sagebrush Rebel forces and some social conservatives), she took the nomination. And, in the 1994 Republican landslide (with some help from La Rocco mistakes) she won the general. She pledged to serve no more than three terms in the House, and unlike some others who made similar pledges, kept her word, and retired in 2000. She died in 2006.

More telling, Right to Work, after a bitter campaign, was affirmed. Its 31,179 margin signaled the passing of the era when the old Democratic formula, with labor as keystone, could win. It barely put Evans over in 1982; in 1986 it no longer could.

John Evans – *I really think that is a result of agriculture and the farmers' independence. Wanting to be left alone. I can do my own thing. I can work this land. I don't want any government involved in this - even though if we didn't have government in the agriculture subsidy area ...*

You've had a migration of that philosophy from the small communities to the larger communities and now that's the dominant philosophy in those communities. In a rural community, because of the Mormon influence and domination of the area, the families are very big. We don't think anything about having five, six, seven, eight, 10 children. That's the way of life in our area and philosophy and church. But they don't have opportunities to stay in those rural areas. There are not the jobs; you have to move to the cities, move to Pocatello, move to Boise, move to Twin Falls, to find jobs to stay in the area. So here's your philosophy being essentially bred in the very rural areas on the farms and then moving into the cities.

The Professor

Meanwhile in 1986, in the most Republican part of the state, a Democrat with a fraction of the experience of Andrus or Evans, a shy campaigner, won re-election to Congress by a solid 55 percent of the vote, outpolling Andrus and Evans in county after county.

He was Richard Stallings, the fluke congressman.

Stallings had lost to George Hansen in 1982, and in 1984 almost let victory slip away. Later, Republicans would say Stallings clawed his way to office by hammering at Hansen's criminal convictions. Not so; such aggressive campaigning would have been out of character for him. Stallings happily answered questions on Hansen's problems – with a low-key, chop-licking, tsk-tsk – but seldom brought up the issue himself. His prospects were fueled almost entirely by Hansen's problems, but he didn't structure his campaign around them. Stallings, like Hansen, did try to talk about national issues. None of it sank in. And on election day Hansen came within 170 votes of rebuilding his network. If the election had been held days later, he probably would have won.

So 1986 was the first crowded primary for a major race since the 1978 Republican fiasco. Five Republicans trampled all over each other, eager to get swoop in and collect the booty.

But no one knew who would best combat Stallings. Would it be J.F. "Chad" Chadband, a ferocious conservative who launched his campaign with some creative picture- cropping (in an attempt to link Stallings to Jane Fonda)? Or Connie Hansen, George's wife, trying to keep up the tradition while her husband was fending off prison? (She was no mere stand-in; she was a solid campaigner and had worked in

Hansen's Washington office.) Perhaps Dan Adamson, who barely lost the 1984 primary to Hansen? Or Dane Watkins, the conservative state senator from Idaho Falls appointed to the job by Cecil Andrus in 1971 and unshakeable from it ever since? (He was an incredibly easy-going person – his Statehouse nickname was "Cupcake" after the pastries he brought to committee meetings – but notorious for locking tax bills in his desk drawer.) Or Mel Richardson, the smooth-voiced Idaho Falls radio broadcaster unknown elsewhere?[97]

In such a crowded, all-conservative field, Richardson had the edge because Idaho Falls party leaders backed him. Not since the sixties had party leaders played so big a role choosing a candidate. Hall, the new state chairman, was determined the party not nominate a weak candidate or one open to attack. That left out the legislators, who had voting records and occasional absent-minded remarks to contend with, and Adamson, improved as a candidate since 1984 but still having a hard time making an impression. And Connie Hansen, of course, because of her husband's baggage. Democratic strategists thought she would run an energetic and skillful campaign and prayed she would win the primary; they fantasized about another Stallings-Hansen Battle.

Hall stacked the deck. He organized a straw poll at a Republican gathering, and saw to it that Richardson's win there was heavily publicized. Watkins' campaign, which started with the most money and organization, collapsed as Richardson's manufactured momentum built. Richardson's smashing win in the primary came mostly from party help. Bouyed by it, he followed advice that he could take it easy in the summer. After all, this was a Republican district and Stallings was a fluke, right?

The evidence of 1984 seemed to say so, but politicians can't go home again to the old battleground. Stallings knew this. He had not gone out of his way to protect himself on votes. He proclaimed himself conservative; his votes tended moderate. But Stallings did two things that were immensely helpful to him.

First, he bore down on constituent service. Stallings hired some Frank Church staffers and got advice from others. He learned, as Church had from Glen Taylor, and as Hansen knew, that meticulous attention to constituents made friends. Hansen had been overwhelmed in recent years with legal and financial problems; Stallings' operation now pleasantly surprised constituents.

Second, he asked for and got a seat on the House Agriculture Committee. That was nothing special in itself. Many Idahoans had served on it including, at different times, Symms and Hansen. Stallings had fewer ties to farming than Symms (whose family ran an orchard) or Hansen (a former grain elevator operator). But he saw the common denominator of Democrats who survived in conservative rural

---

[97] Watkins has a politically strong run during his years in the state Senate, but never regained his footing after he left. He ran unsuccessfully for Congress in 1988 (losing badly to Stallings), and sought the Republican nomination again in 1998 (losing distantly to Mike Simpson). He also failed in an attempt to return to the state Senate.

Republican districts: they were specialists in agriculture. Congressmen like Majority Whip Tom Foley of Washington and senators like Tom Harkin of Iowa took a populist pro-farmer approach and concentrated their time and their staffs' energies as publicly as they could on farm issues.

In 1986 crop prices sank, bankruptcies multiplied, and small farms consolidated. Not only farmers but merchants, implement dealers, and others in small rural towns were desperate. Farm influence in Idaho politics seemed on the wane: in the legislature farmers exerted less pull in the eighties. "It's inevitable," said farmer and state Sen. Laird Noh, "as people move off the farm and agriculture shrinks in relation to other sectors ... Agriculture is very sensitive to that. They often talk in terms of, we should get statutes in place now because in the years ahead it's going to be more difficult."

In 1985 and 1986, Stallings rained press releases on farm issues and held scads of meetings with farmers and farm leaders. He placed farm specialists, some Republicans, in his offices. In barely a year he built a network of farm support, centered in the Magic Valley, adding new Democratic votes. Considering the unusual nature of his incumbency, he got little press for his stands on national issues. That was blind luck. It meant many Republicans knew him as a congressman interested in agriculture.

Richardson put on a game effort toward the end. He held weekly press conferences, each dissecting Stallings' record. Stallings dismissed most of his charges as misleading. Richardson gave a respectable performance at the Pocatello debate, keeping the congressman on the defensive. None of it had much effect. Partly because of the Mormon influence (muted, since both Stallings and Richardson were Mormon) and partly because of the farm network, the second congressional district could be wired and votes locked in. Hansen wired it with a network that faltered only with his felony convictions. Now Stallings wired it a different way.[98]

The most successful Magic Valley Democratic politician was doing the same. State Sen. John Peavey, a rancher from Carey and a former Republican (his grandfather was U.S. Sen. John Thomas, a founder of the old Republican machine), switched parties in the seventies and returned to the Senate in 1980. He had solid opposition in the eighties but his margins grew, partly because of emphasis on rural issues. He linked with national farm groups and in 1987 brought Democratic Texas Agriculture Commissioner Jim Hightower, one of the best-known farm-government leaders, to Southern Idaho for a quick tour on behalf of a national farm bill. Hightower attracted hundreds of people.[99]

---

[98] Richardson, unlike so many congressional candidates, lowered his sights and ran for the Idaho Legislature. He was elected to the House in 1988, to the Senate soon after, and remained there for many years.

[99] Peavey almost ran for governor in 1994, then switched to lieutenant governor. He lost – in that Republican landslide year – to Republican Butch Otter. But of all the many major-office losing Democrats that year, Peavey came close to winning.

The farmers wanted to listen. In 1985 and 1986 devastating frost hit Eastern Idaho, followed by drought in 1987 and 1988.

Stallings won in 1986, without charisma or more than good campaigning.[100]

Jim Goller – *He's not a flaming liberal. He's not carrying a crusade. He admits to those people that he doesn't like too much government. He likes a balanced budget. I don't think people vote people out just on party lines. You've got to give people a reason why they should vote against him. If you run against an incumbent, you'd best give people reasons why. That's where you get into the real art of politics: How do you destroy that person without destroying yourself?*

Managed a little differently, he might have won and become a centerpoint for Idaho Democrats. But he has not run for another office since 1994, and now works at his sheep ranch near Carey.

[100] He would go on to win the seat twice more, in 1988 and 1990, in both of those elections by landslides. How he might have fared there in the Republican years of 1992 or 1994 is open to conjecture; but he ran for the Senate in 1992, and lost to Republican Dirk Kempthorne. In 1988 he ran again for the 2nd district seat, but lost to Republican Mike Simpson. Still later, though, after some years working on economic development in Pocatello, he was elected to the Pocatello City Council, and became chair of the Idaho Democratic Party.

12 | One-Percenters & Friends

In 1931 Idaho's Legislature set an income tax and, master of euphemism that it was, called it the "Property Tax Relief Act."

Income taxes - to back out property taxes - were popular. Farmers getting past the depression were crawling out from under, but still bartered or swapped where they could. Cash was scarce. Property taxes were a killer, income taxes easier to handle.

The old line goes that when people say, "It's not the money, it's the principle of the thing," it's the money. But Idahoans hate taxes not just because they have to pay them. Taxes are an intrusion. They would accept them under the right conditions, and Idaho has had one of the most balanced tax structures in the nation. But a balance of intrusiveness has to be struck.

If property taxes had not been the original fundraiser, they would have been hard to impose. Property taxes go back to territorial days; people saw them as a necessary evil handed down through generations. They were paid in lump sum, for one thing; sales taxes, paid in nibbles, seem less burdensome.

New Deal Democratic Gov. C. Ben Ross wanted more revenue to expand state government and match federal aid. He got his way with the 1931 income tax. In 1935 he called legislators into special session to pass a two-cent sales tax. The Federal Emergency Relief Act had spent $8 million in Idaho, the law said, "without cooperation from Idaho, [and] has to a large degree relieved actual distress among our indigent, aged, and unemployed ... Idaho must cooperate to the extent of its financial ability in the national recovery program, without which cooperation Idaho may not expect to receive further federal aid." It smacked of blackmail, and voters killed the sales tax in 1936.

For 30 years, Idaho Democrats wanted nothing to do with sales taxes. Burned once, they didn't intend to be burned again.

So stood the two-pronged tax system for decades, creaking under the weight of growing state government. It groaned in the late forties when Gov. C.A. Robins expanded services, relaxed in the early fifties when Gov. Len Jordan made cuts and racked up surpluses. Property taxes were phased out of state government and became, with federal funds, the local government money tree.

Then Robert Smylie expanded state government beyond Ben Ross' wildest dreams: the state budget went from $74.7 million in 1953 to $140.1 million in 1961. Since the Idaho constitution banned red ink, that meant creative financing.

Smylie did not specifically ask for a sales tax but did ask legislators to think about shaking up the system. After the 1955 session a committee on taxes was set up and Rep. Ralph Wickberg, a Kellogg Republican, was named chairman. The committee said the tax system was approaching burnout and needed a two-cent sales tax, like the one in Utah. "The sales and use tax is a dependable source of revenue and it secures revenue quickly," the committee report said. The report was scheduled for release on Oct. 15, 1956, then delayed a month until after the election. But word leaked. A week before the election Wickberg complained that "they're giving me a worse time on the sales tax issue now than they could if they had the report. I have absolutely no defense." He and the other Republican representative from Shoshone County, Norman Heikkila, were beaten by two Democrats.

(Perry Swisher said Wickberg later was appointed by Smylie to the Idaho Public Utilities Commission, where he served more than two decades, "in acknowledgement he was a sacrificial lamb.")

Wickberg's was a lesson taken to heart.

Democrats took over the Legislature in 1958. They, too, saw something had to be done about taxes but didn't intend to try sales taxes. Smylie would say later that most of the Democrats were less opposed to having a sales tax than to voting for one.

So in 1959 they passed a $10 head tax. Swisher called it "an abomination, a tax for being on earth." Apparently voters agreed: Democrats were mowed down in 1960 (one reason for the big freshman Senate class that year). It was a powerful lesson for those Democrats who opposed tax increases and to Republicans who regained control in 1961. Legislators danced around taxes, sometimes poking at them with a stick, knowing they had to do something but unwilling to take credit or blame.

Smylie said in 1964 that "the hallmark of the 10 years [he had been governor] has been an appetite for public expenditure that outran the will to pay. It has been a story of the people searching for the courage to meet their own aspirations."

He was elected in 1954 opposing the sales tax and spoke against it in his 1955 and (noting Wickberg's 1956 loss) 1957 state of state speeches. He was a brilliant improviser, finding stray cash, putting it where it wouldn't be disturbed. Instead of repealing the head tax he put the revenue into the state building fund. "He was very skilled at ratholing," Swisher said. "When he did get a tax, he knew how to hang onto it."

Years later Smylie said "one of their favorite things to criticize me about was that I didn't do it [pass a sales tax] sooner. Well, first off, I always operate on the basis that you did what you could get done; you moved to what ought to be through what could be. That was the nature of the legislative beast."

Making a Sales tax

The expansion of state government was financed by nickel-and-dime taxes, and some legislators foresaw passing a sales tax in return for repealing a bunch of others. But Northern Idaho opposed it because Washington had a sales tax and Idaho didn't, giving merchants an advantage. Southwest counties opposed it because Oregon had no sales tax, and if Idaho passed one they would be at a disadvantage. Farmers feared it, too. "They had a fear that it would pyramid," Vern Ravenscroft, then a member of the House Revenue and Taxation Committee, recalled. "That if they did have to pay sales tax on their production items [equipment], it would be a drastic tax because so much of their expense was for repairs and equipment and fertilizer and things of that kind. It's such a high-volume, low-margin business that if you pay a tax on that high volume, the expense will wipe you out."

These were Democrats, but they were not free spenders. "Some of them were much more conservative than some of the Republicans were," recalled Republican Allan Shepard, who served his first term in the House in 1959. "I think Clay Sutton, for example, from Washington County, is probably one of the most conservative people that ever sat in the Legislature from either party."

The House did pass a sales tax bill in 1963; the Senate killed it. Republicans barely controlled the House and Senate then (they had 23 R's to 21 D's in the Senate). Republicans made gains in 1964, and now Smylie figured the time had come.

Robert Smylie – *We had put off for so long so many of the things that needed doing, primarily in the field of education, both at the higher and lower level, that it was maybe true that the consequences of not doing these things were at least as politically dangerous as biting the bullet and doing it. So in October 1964 I started having meetings with the legislative leadership, with the exception of [Jim] McClure. We didn't ever invite McClure because he was from Payette County [on the Oregon border] and there was no way he could have been for it. He was assistant majority leader, and it [the sales tax] just made life miserable for him.*

These meetings started before the election of 1964. This was [Sen. George] Blick and [Senate President Pro Tem Jack] Murphy and [Rep. William] Lanting and [House Speaker Pete] Cenarrusa. The place we met was in Jack Murphy's house in Shoshone, where the press would never catch up with the fact that anything was going on. We had four or five meetings at which we talked about this. Finally in November I told them, this was about the 20th of November, "I have not yet reached a conclusion and you probably won't know until you hear the speech. But I would like a little show of hands. If I decide to go that way, will you go with me?" I got a unanimous vote [for it].

On New Year's 1965, Smylie was at his cabin near McCall when he decided to try writing the speech. In his fast two-fingered style he tapped out a pro-tax speech "to see how it wrote. It seemed to go together pretty good."

Smylie met again with the legislators. Murphy, who wanted to run statewide (and would in 1966, 1970, and 1974), urged putting it on the ballot. Smylie said that would kill the tax. "We're going to put the turkey on the table and then we're going to give them a knife," he said. "We're going to let it sit there until 18 months [after it became law] have gone by and they're going to be able to look at that turkey and know how good it's going to taste."

Murphy wasn't sure he could go along.

"Well, Jack," Smylie replied, "I think you ought to know that if you don't send that bill down here and send me an appropriations bill that's got all that money, I'll veto that appropriations bill and call you back."

Hardball

The Idaho constitution said tax bills had to start in the House, which was inclined toward a sales tax. Phil Peterson, dean of the law school at the University of Idaho, helped the House Revenue and Taxation Committee draft it. And redraft it. Opponents were bought off by a sheaf of tax relief bills, repealing taxes for the teacher retirement fund and other things, and a blanket prohibition on a statewide property tax for state government. The House passed the lot, with little anguish, 49-30. Democrats were split; about a third voted for the sales tax.

They were more unified in the Senate, where the numbers game came down to the crunch.

The Senate always was a tougher sell. (The House proposes, the Senate disposes.) There were 44 senators then, one for each county, giving border counties more strength than they would have two years later after reapportionment. They and some Easterners seemed enough to stop the sales tax. They were enough, the day it passed the House, to pass in the Senate the bill Murphy wanted, putting the sales tax to a vote before putting it into effect. But that plan folded, and the Senate was faced with the tax. The job of passing the House bill went to Sen. Swisher of Pocatello, a liberal Republican, the best vote-counter in the Senate.

Perry Swisher – *We didn't have enough votes. The governor thought I had enough votes. The press corps thought I had enough votes. Max Yost [Idaho's top tax expert] said there were enough votes. Everybody said we had enough votes except the senators.*

We needed Bill Young [the Canyon County senator] in the worst way. We wrote a school funding formula ... We had a group of counties that had a high tax base and a small population, and for as long as six or eight years had not received an additional nickel from the state ... This had gone on for so long these people [senators from those districts] couldn't vote for school funding. They couldn't go home and justify their votes, because they weren't bringing anything home. But you couldn't get the dominant forces in the Legislature - essentially, Ada County, Nez Perce County, Bannock County, Bonneville - to listen. Well, I had to listen. I was carrying the tax bill. So I wrote a separate [school funding] formula. It didn't take a lot of money – about $2 million – from the sales tax and moved it specifically to those counties. That way I got Sirloin Row [the rural senators]. I picked up Blaine

County. I picked up Owyhee County. I picked up Lemhi County. And of course Young, because those guys [in Canyon County] needed help and they needed to vote for the sales tax bill even though they didn't want to.

... At that time it was called scurrilous. Bribing. It was only fair. In fact, the education community by and large attacked me.

Swisher cut many deals; some have had more effect on Idaho than the sales tax itself. They still weren't enough when in late February the bill came to the Senate floor. The Democrats could still block it - unless some defected. Conservative Sen. Bill Dee and others worried about that young senator from Clearwater County, Cecil Andrus, who long had opposed the sales tax.

Cecil Andrus – *I'd go home at night and work the budget. I did not sit on the appropriations committee but I'd go home and work those [numbers], and I couldn't see where the revenue was going to come from unless we enacted a sales tax. Nobody knew, nobody could count me, but Swisher had me figured. He didn't divulge it. He came to me and I said, "Perry, I honestly don't know." They had everybody in that Senate figured except me.*

... I sat through that whole debate and didn't say anything. And then came the roll call and I said, "Mr. President, may I explain my vote?"

I heard Pops Murphy [Sen. Art Murphy of Shoshone County, a veteran of New Deal days], who sat beside me, go, "Now we know." You know how dear friends Pops and I were before he died. But they moved my chair out of the caucus room. They wouldn't speak to me. For the first couple of days Anita, Pops' wife, flat turned her nose up and wouldn't even talk to me.

On the first round of votes Andrus was the only Democrat to vote for the tax. The bill failed. Then Jack Murphy, who took to heart Smylie's warning, asked for another run, and four more Democrats switched to vote with Andrus.

Still not enough.

The session ran overtime. Tempers flared. Swisher hit on the Main Street merchants of Idaho, who weren't wild about a sales tax but badly wanted to be rid of the inventory tax. Merchants bore down hard on the legislators for the sales tax in return for getting the inventory tax lifted.

Swisher kept counting. On March 11, he saw a majority and struck. Six more senators, five Republicans and one Democrat, switched and it passed 26-18. Smylie was jubilant; he proclaimed "great new days ahead."

As legislators wondered how many they had left in office ...

Cecil Andrus – *The superintendent of schools in Orofino was a man by the name of Mike Cassetto. After the vote Mike and all the educators went, "Oh, Cece, you did the right thing, God, we love you."*

I said, "Don't give me that stuff, Cassetto. What you owe me" - I had letters from home, scathing stories in the newspapers ... They just worked my tail over like you wouldn't believe. And I told Cassetto, "you owe me one thing. Friday night at the auditorium at the elementary school, you set up the chairs, you put an ad in the paper that Andrus is there to discuss the legislative session, and give me a microphone. So we publicized it, that Andrus has been home a week, we've got a meeting at the schoolhouse to explain what's happened. And I'd lie there at night and I'd think about it, and see that room clear full of hundreds of angry people, my friends come to tear me apart.

The great night came and 11 people showed up. I think four of them were my relatives. And some of them were school teachers who came to thank me.

Idaho adjusted to the sales tax. In November 1966, more than 60 percent of the voters approved it.

Spinoffs

But it left aftershocks.

Such as repealing the inventory tax, which happened in 1967, after most of the key 1965 players had left the Legislature. Swisher recalled that "the Idaho retailers at that time were made up mainly of [locally-owned] Main Street stores, not Sears or Safeway. And they cut their own throat." Repealing the inventory tax, he said, encouraged national mass-retailers to pour into Idaho, wiping out Main Street businesses.

But the sales taxers would have been more alarmed at the consequences of another law they passed in 1965, one intended to take a bite out of property taxes.

That was dividing taxable property into three types: real, personal, and operating. The first two were to be assessed at 20 percent of value, but operating property - mainly owned by utilities and manufacturing businesses - at 40 percent. Many assessors had done that for years, unconstitutional though it was.

Don Loveland – *I told them at the time, fellows, that will not fly. When that issue goes to the court the court will say, you can't do that. You can't have 40 percent on utilities and 20 percent on others.*

Prior to that the ratio on utilities was, oh, it went between 34 and 35 percent. And this was one of the things that was causing a few aches and pains anyway. Hell, Bonner County up here, their residential property was only [assessed at] nine percent. Some counties were doing better than others.

In February 1967 the Idaho Supreme Court unanimously said all property had to be taxed equally, at 20 percent of value, and reappraised on a strict schedule by 1982. Aside from its clear legal reasoning, the decision was on solid ground politically. Its backers made the point that if legislators could single out utilities for high taxes, they could single out other groups too.

In the history of the Idaho Supreme Court only half a dozen, if that many, decisions changed Idaho so much as that one. In the next 10 years it led straight to the One Percent Initiative, ending the heady government growth that began in the mid-fifties.

It would have been hard to foresee then. The economic boom of the late sixties to mid-seventies created revenue surpluses. For many governments, the mid-seventies meant political moderation, planning, zoning, other services, and, of couse, rising budgets.

In that atmosphere county officials began to realize they were bumping up against the Court's deadlines. County assessors facing election hated to raise property values; then, like college students cramming before exams, they did rush work. Values on rural and residential property doubled or tripled. When that combined with increases in local government budgets, partly to meet demands imposed by state and federal governments, taxes soared.

The bomb was set; it needed only someone to light the fuse.

Agonizing Reappraisal

Don Chance, Kansas native and mustered-out Army sergeant, came to Idaho with his wife, an Idaho native, after World War II. Apart from a few years dealing in Angus cattle at Cambridge, he sold insurance until his retirement in 1975. Chance was interested in government but not in politics. He was appointed to the original Garden City council but quit after a few months when "it seemed like everyone owned slot machines but me." He wanted out and got out, and that was his only public office.

In 1976 Ada County was at a turning point. Two moderate Republicans had replaced two conservatives on the county commission in 1974. The third, conservative Gene Crawford, died as the 1976 election neared. Another Republican got the nomination against Democrat Linda Lund Davis. Crawford's widow, Darlene, ran a write-in campaign, and Chance helped. She got 11,665 votes, enough to split the Republicans and give the election to Davis. Davis and Gary Bermeosolo, another Democrat who also won that year, created the first Democratic Ada County commission in decades, and it yanked county government from its conservatism.

Bad timing for the Democrats. In April 1977 Republican Ada County Assessor J.L. "Mike" Clark was hit with a criminal charge of deliberately undervaluing property values. (The charge was dismissed in August.) The State Tax Commission ordered reappraisal and a firm, Max P. Arnold & Associates, was hired to do it. It worked at warp speed to meet the deadlines, and critics said that spawned a multitude of problems. When Arnold's people hit Boise they found appraisal records going back more than 30 years were flawed; the consultant had to backtrack before he could even begin what was originally assumed to be his work. "Directed to accomplish 25 appraisals a day," Chance wrote in a Statesman guest opinion, "the principal qualification of

Arnold's staff had to be the ability to run a hundred yards in nine seconds."

Don Loveland – *It increased the market value by 50 percent, in some instances as high as 100 percent. We'd have been all right if the commissioners had - see, they levied the levy [amount of tax collected per dollar of value] they used the year before, against this 50 to 100 percent increase in the base. If they had held their budgets - I said, "you fellows ought to hold that budget very close this year with the new appraisal that you had." And they didn't. They increased the amount by 56 percent. Why, God, people just come unglued.*

Just the reverse of this was Oneida County. [Gov.] John Evans and myself, we laughed about that. The Evanses were the largest property owners in Oneida County. They doubled their values but their tax bills that fall, I think John told me, was $75 or $100 [higher]. So they didn't complain.

In September the Ada County Commission certified new values 89 percent higher than the year before. About 15,000 Ada County property owners appealed those valuations; they included Chance, the owner of a five-acre agricultural parcel.

He was not new to watching county government. He had served on the board of Taxpayers' Voice, an anti-planning group. He had observed the We The People group (of which he wasn't a member) try unsuccessfully to recall pro-planning county commissioners. He looked north and saw property tax activism in Kootenai County, where a combination of reappraisal and fast growth led to higher taxes, and where Arth Day, a Coeur d'Alene realtor, formed the Kootenai County Property Owners Association.

Chance and a few others met at his house to set up public sessions to air grievances and share strategy. The idea took off. Chance said the first session, at the Boise Public Library, drew between 200 and 225 people. In April 1977 he and others formed the Ada County Property Owners Association. They did not create the tax revolt. But they accurately saw its inevitability.

Formal or informal groups sprang up in about 15 counties, including Canyon, Nez Perce, and Bannock, mostly where reappraisal led to higher taxes. In 1978 they formed the Idaho Property Owners Association, whose first order of business was getting the Legislature to cap property taxes at one percent of market value. (Taxes varied around Idaho but generally were higher than that.) The bill never left a House committee, which spent most of the session squabbling. Gov. John Evans and Republican leaders came up with conflicting ideas and blocked each other. The elderly and poor were given some relief, but legislators failed to act on the larger issues. It would pay dearly for that failure.

The Property Owners countered with two initiative petitions. One would make planning and zoning locally optional, allowing it if a popular vote gave thumbs up. The other would limit property taxes to one percent of market value. "Everybody knew it was a carbon copy of [California's] Proposition 13," Chance recalled. "It was intended to be ... We kind of tied our coattails to that." Thousands of copies of petitions were printed and sent around the state to people who often would photocopy them and get still more signatures. "We had an army of people out there working on this thing and didn't know it."

It was a hot issue in Idaho from the beginning, so hot that Chance maintains tax money was used at one point to hire a private detective to investigate him. A Statesman poll that spring said One Percent seemed headed for defeat (and may have been, until California's passage of Proposition 13 encouraged Idaho One-Percenters). The IPOA called petition carriers and asked them to drop the P&Z initiative, concentrating efforts on One Percent.

One Percent probably was better known in 1978 than any Idaho politician. For all its flaws, it was the only blunt weapon voters had at hand to lash out. And it was sufficiently powerful to satisfy them; for all the dissatisfaction, voters were kind to incumbents that year, including anti-One Percent Gov. Evans.

Attorneys questioned whether much of it could mesh with Idaho's constitution. That never was tested, but the initiative probably could not have worked as written: it would have made a hash of Idaho tax laws. Although passed by about 60 percent of the voters in November 1978, it never was enforced.

When the Legislature met in 1979 it had to tame the monster. Chance and the IPOA said the lawmakers should stand clear and let the initiative go into effect. But no one seemed to know exactly what it would do. State and local government officials said the initiative was inherently self-contradictory and couldn't be followed even with the best of intentions.

Don Loveland – *One Percent never was operative, never did work. There were some counties that [already] would have been at one percent [of market value], and there were some that were not [which created issues of fairness]. Then it got to the question of implementing One Percent. The initiative said that if you had a home and we had the same market value on our home, but you sell your home for $20,000 more than the market value of mine, then the new owner's market value would be $20,000 more than mine. Well, our constitution says you can't do that: like things have to be treated alike. So when the legislature looked at that, that's the reason they said, it's unconstitutional to start with.*

It was one of the toughest sessions ever for Idaho legislators: Should they go along with an unconstitutional law, ignoring the problems and lawsuits to come, or toss out the law and face public outrage, or what?

They went with what. The Revenue and Taxation Committee, so stymied a year before, rose to the challenge, writing a plan to freeze property taxes at 1978 levels while wiping out most of One Percent. The explanation was that this would move local taxes in the direction of One Percent. It didn't work quite that way. For the next several years legislators kept tinkering, eventually allowing small budget increases. Certain expenses – such as paying court judgements and some other costs – were taken out of One Percent restrictions. Eventually a third of property taxes were outside the state property tax restrictions. Before long little was left of the original initiative.

It still carried a wallop.

"It put the brakes on the growth of [government] budgets," Chance said. "I think it made people a little more conscious, especially politicians, as to what the people out there want. After all, they're supposed to be in charge." In the late seventies local governments made tremendous cuts in services, some wiping out whole departments. Maintenance of buildings and other services fell by the wayside. By the time the real effects of the initiative were felt in the early eighties, voter anger was spent. They were no longer threatened by the fluke of doubled or tripled property taxes. Now, in many places, they saw a slow death, by attrition, of government services. In other places, they saw services scaled back or cut off.

Charles Moss – *The cities that were leaner and meaner took the hits, because they didn't have any cash to fall back on. Part of it was that the so-called liberals [in the Pocatello city council] were such damn sticklers - if you didn't need it, you don't collect it. If you don't collect it, you don't have the tax base to build on in when One Percent was implemented, which was a freeze in the dollars. If we had been extravagant and hadn't been good stewards we would have had a much bigger base to build on and wouldn't have had to lay off 20 percent of the employees in 1979.*

We eliminated a bunch. Did a fairly good job, I think, which may have turned out to be a political mistake. What we kept we tried to do well. For example, we had a program to trim all the trees in the parks and get rid of dead trees and plant new ones that would replenish. We wiped out the whole forestry program. People did not see any of that, but it takes four or five years for a tree to get back, and now they're falling down. We didn't budget for things like that.

Library hours were cut, fire stations closed, and fire trucks took longer to get to the emergency. Fees for services were not covered by One Percent, and cities and counties imposed more of them. In Pocatello, councils experimented with street use fees.

Muddying Tax Waters

But voters also endorsed schemes to get around their own initiative. They passed increasing numbers of overrides and other tax issues not bound by budget restrictions. In 1978 they approved $28 million of these issues; in 1983, that was up to $51 million. New taxing districts could be created – and were – unfettered by the size of their budgets in past years, since there weren't any. Some were created with few people voting; fewer than one percent of eligible voters cast

IN THE HOUSE *House Speaker Tom Boyd (left) and key tax legislator Don Loveland talk over a point. (photo/Randy Stapilus)*

ballots in the election to create a new Ada County Rural Free Library District in 1985. Property owners startled by an unexpected tax increase – they apparently hadn't paid attention to the district's creation, though it was well-publicized – began a drive to wipe the district out of existence. But in November 1986, when voter turnout was large, county voters decided to keep the district.

That was notable. Idahoans showed that, skeptical as they were about taxes, they usually would sustain them once taxes and services were in place. The 1978 initiative was a reaction to an abrupt tax increase and to a perception of government bloat at federal and state as well as local levels. It was not a rejection of government services.

It was also a reaction to the idea of utilities and other big businesses getting tax breaks while residential taxes shot skyward. The One Percent initiative missed that: it kept constant the portion of taxes paid by various people and organizations.

In 1982 former state Sen. Ken Robison (later a state representative), a Boise Democrat and a former Idaho Statesman editorial page editor, seized on that discontent. He organized an initiative to exempt some value of residential property from taxation. The "50/50" homeowners exemption (it exempted 50 percent or the first $50,000 of value of a home, whichever was less) caught on fast, with little state organization help. Businesses bellyached and Republicans found themselves in the odd position of opposing a "tax cut" – actually a tax shift, since Robison wasn't trying to change the total. He maintained the new shift corrected the old shift of taxes paid by utilities and other businesses to homeowners. That was true. But "50/50" backers overlooked the fact that the original shift grew from a Court decision that businesses had been overtaxed.

Homeowners loved it and passed it into law.

Rhetoric of the time suggests that most voters thought local government services could be retained under One Percent laws, that the cut would just trim fat. It sliced away a lot of fat. But it also cut meat and muscle, and the Legislature had to step in and help.

The Upshot

What local governments asked for was either elimination of the post-One Percent budget restrictions, or authority for local option taxes (probably sales or income). The Legislature refused. The first would be construed as a slap in the face of the voters and the second was too – tricky. It was hypocrisy, of course, for legislators to deny local option to local governments when they spent so much time bellyaching about Big Brother in Washington. But they knew every scrap of taxing authority given to local government would be used, and the taxes blamed on the legislature. No, lawmakers thought, there had to be another way.

There was: pay local governments out of the state's till, making local governments ever more beholden to the legislature while giving them enough to get by.

That meant the state needed more money, so legislators started a series of state tax increases. They played around with small taxes – the old patch and scratch game – but big increases had to come from sales and income taxes. Fiddling with the income tax was too complicated; the state closely followed the federal format and changing it would be an accounting nightmare. They did start bumping the sales tax up and down to balance the budget. Most of those increases were supposedly temporary for a year or year-and-a-half only, but that fooled no one. In 1987 the Legislature ended the charade, setting the tax at five percent, a level it seemed likely to hold for a while.

Legislators earmarked part of those increases for local governments feeling withdrawal symptoms from losing federal revenue sharing money. By 1987, with the two cent sales tax increase permanent, local governments quit asking for local option tax authority. The annual handout from the state was more comforting than annually asking skeptical voters to buy proposals for more new, exotic taxes.

But the biggest beneficiaries were the school districts. State spending on schools – the sales and income tax money the legislature to gave school districts hit by the fallout of One Percent – increased from less than a third of the state budget in the mid-seventies to more than half in mid-eighties. It was the big boom item in the state budget through those recession years, and yet all those increases did little more than keep school districts even with where they were in pre-One Percent days.

School funding – how much was enough and would it be well spent? – had been an issue in Idaho since statehood. Now, with the economy stagnant, corporate and political leaders called for much more money for schools.

When Cecil Andrus ran for governor in 1986 that – and resurrecting the near-comatose Department of Commerce – keyed his campaign. He also supported repealing the investment tax credit (ITC) the legislature passed into law several years earlier at John Evans' urging. Andrus said it wasn't working, that only a few big businesses which weren't leaving Idaho anyway, such as utilities, used it much. Republican legislative leaders supported the ITC. Andrus got some corporate backers to support him, but some of the big ITC beneficiaries balked at losing it.

The Snap Point

A cautious legislature met in January 1987. The last one had been tagged as Neanderthal and buffoonish; the new one wanted a fresh image. But its members were almost as conservative as the year before, reluctant to become big spenders or end tax breaks to businesses. At the same time, legislators didn't want to seem unreceptive to ideas for improving education.

Andrus focused narrowly on education and Commerce budgets. He recommended increasing the Commerce budget from under a million dollars to $1.8 million, still diddly in the state spending picture. But he also asked for $342 million for public schools, compared to the $314 million the state then was spending. He suggested paying for it by keeping the nickel sales tax (scheduled to expire in midyear) in place and by repealing the ITC.

Conservatives thought his school figures were the stuff of dreams. And while most legislators conceded the nickel sales tax would stay, most were solidly against repealing the tax credit. Early in the session Risch even went public on that, telling a Republican luncheon that he had the votes in the Senate to block ITC repeal. All through the session House members pushed repeal bills to no avail.

That didn't bother Andrus. The repeal was one way to raise money, he said; if you can find another, that's okay, too. But he did insist his education and commerce budgets stay uncut. He proved more amiable and flexible than Evans in dealing with the legislators, but they sensed no less determination.

So they could try bucking him and risking a blowout at the Statehouse corral – which wouldn't look good in the wake of the 1986

– or caving in and giving him his budgets and then trying to find the money somehow. That's what they did.

It happened by the thinnest of margins and in improbable ways.

It meant making water run uphill.

Budgeting in the legislature means choosing whether the chicken or egg comes first. Do you decide how much you want to raise and then set the budget within that limit? Or, do you start with how much you want to spend, and then find the money to cover it?

At times, especially when tax revenue came in surplus, legislators went budget-first. When finances got tight in the late seventies they went the other way. They even institutionalized the change. Leaders weakened the Joint Finance-Appropriations Committee (JFAC), which wrote the budget. For years it had been a powerful committee; seats on it were prized and given to the brightest legislators who had time to spend on the budget. That changed in the late seventies. JFAC had fewer sharp operators. More members either were floor leaders or committee chairmen and had little time for budgeting or were easily led by floor leaders.

In the late seventies and for much of the eighties JFAC was dominated by the few members who studied the budget and orchestrated pro and con arguments. Through much of the eighties, that was Rep. Mack Neibaur, a conservative Republican farmer from Paul. He consistently put together budgets that carried JFAC, especially since it had so many conservatives distracted by other assignments. Until the late seventies the decisions on budget numbers were developed in the committee sessions, often with tightly-fought votes. Later, Neibaur usually put together winning conservative coalitions before the committee even met.

But in 1987, this changed as the membership on JFAC did. The 1986 elections wiped out conservatives like Sen. Dane Watkins and Rep. J.F. "Chad" Chadband, both of Idaho Falls and both of whom had run for the U.S. House. An upstart Republican Senate caucus wanted less powerful leadership and demanded that no floor leader also serve on JFAC. And Tom Boyd strengthened the moderate hand on JFAC. Conservatives had a clear majority on the committee in previous sessions; now JFAC was split down the middle. Budget battles returned to the committee floor and more members took more active and less predictable roles. They gave Andrus everything he wanted - more, in the case of public schools.

They could do that because the House, where all tax bills must be born, was unable to settle the tax issue. Boyd came to power under the presumption that he would not over-exercise it, and he was true to that. Now the House that had been so closely divided between he and Geddes for speaker had an almost impossible time coming to grips with taxes. Boyd tried herding Republicans into caucus sessions and schooling them on taxes. The legislators walked out more divided.

It was an overlong session which could have used just a touch of the old discipline. When JFAC passed a public school budget proposal of $343 million — $1 million more than Andrus suggested — a bolt of lightning seemed to hit. There was no running away. Yet run they did, for weeks, as tax bills poured like water through the Revenue and Taxation Committee. After approving the inevitable nickel sales tax, they still had to find $16 million. An investment tax credit repeal would have covered that, but GOP legislators had boxed themselves in as repeal opponents. So they scrambled.

Then, in the closing weeks of the session, a productivity dam broke. The legislature passed an astonishing number of important pieces of legislation that March, measures proposed for years and never passed. They approved a day care licensing law and telephone deregulation (vetoed by Andrus), put a state lottery on the 1988 ballot and raised the drinking age to 21. The 1987 session was the most productive since 1965, maybe ever. In that overheated atmosphere, by the narrowest of votes, legislators agreed to boost income tax rates enough to pay for the big public school budget. To get Democratic votes — essential, even in a House where few Democrats survived — Republican billcrafters had to shake down corporations for more tax money. Lawmakers who started the session determined not to send a negative signal to business by repealing the ITC raised business taxes almost as much anyway.

Andrus hailed the session as a good one, as well he might. He got what he wanted. But he got it by slim margins and the happenstance of a dozen factors in synchronicity; absent any of them, the session would have been radically different.

13 | At the Arid Club

The outer doors of the Arid Club are heavy and wooden, the gates of a medieval castle designed to keep out the Huns.

Like other gates, these keep some things in, others out. The Arid Club is as close as Idaho gets to an exclusive place for the rich and powerful. Not all the rich and powerful belong; some who do, seldom show up; some members are neither rich nor powerful but are given memberships by corporate employers or others.

The Arid men used to drink and dine on the 12th floor of a downtown tower. It gave them a clear view of downtown, but its space was limited. The new building, on Boise's Greenbelt about a mile from downtown, looks on the outside like an expansive golf clubhouse. Within, it is open and spacious, much like any of the better restaurants downtown. The river is hardly visible from the dining area where, at tables of four or five, members and guests quietly talk business, fishing, or whatever.

Boise is a small town to headquarter so many big corporations. The corporate kings know each other well. J.R. Simplot, possibly Idaho's wealthiest man, not only ran the J.R. Simplot Co. but served for decades on the board of Idaho Power Co. He helped set up Micron Technology Inc., and in 1986 three Simplot executives served on its board. William McMurren, many years the head of Morrison Knudsen Corp., was on the boards of Albertson's Inc. (supermarkets) and Idaho First National Bank. Former Albertson's executive Robert Bolinder was on Idaho Power's board; former Idaho Power Chairman James Bruce was on Albertson's.

Home Grown

Many western states complain of being fiefdoms of big eastern corporations. Idaho is more like a Third World country with home-grown businesses. So it is in the professions. Idaho has an unusual number of attorneys per capita, for example, but only a fraction earn more than a modest living.

Idaho does like business. It was less ravaged than other western states by booms and busts; it never had an Anaconda Copper, which for decades strangled an open society in Montana. Idaho has had company towns, but it is too diverse to be a company state.

More to the point, many businesses that cast big shadows in Idaho – Albertson's supermarkets, Boise-Cascade wood products, Simplot agriculture products, Morrison-Knudsen construction, and Moore Financial group (which includes Idaho First National Bank) - are home-grown and headquartered. (The two companies that were for

THE ARID CLUB *is located in central Boie on the Boise River, and remains a popular hangout for the corporate crowd. (One downtown wag likes to call it "The Arrogant Club.") (photo/Randy Stapilus)*

years the biggest in northern Idaho, Potlatch forest products and the Bunker Hill mine and smelter, were long based there too.) People in Boise pass corporate headquarters every day and accept them as a fact of life; in many cities the size of Boise, they would be considered remarkable. Idahoans see big business as a down-home thing, and politicians react accordingly.

The corporate types most often get into state policy-setting when their interests are on the line, which is why some corporate giants get more involved than others. Not all the big Idaho businesses have a large part of their operations in-state. Some of the largest, such as Albertson's and Morrison-Knudsen, are based in Boise but have national or world-wide operations.

They are still so big that influence is inevitable. M-K was a big factor in the Idaho Republican Party in the sixties. Since then, it has been less overtly involved in politics but remains important in many Idaho construction projects. (Idaho governments can feel hard put to turn down M-K.) In the mid- eighties, as independent groceries shut their doors, Albertson's gobbled up an enormous share of the supermarket market. Albertson's is bound to have terrific social and political impact in the nineties.

The Money Men

In 1920, Idaho, a state with more farm and resource products than currency, had 230 banks - one for every 1,900 people. Individually, these banks' decisions about money lending and investments shaped communities, but they had little impact on state policy because there were so many of them. Every settlement had a bank. In those days before cars and paved roads, travel from town to town made long-distance banking a tough proposition.

Idaho law then banned branch banking, though some banks were owned in common. Many, like the D.L. Evans and J.N. Ireland Banks, founded in Malad and spread to Albion and Aberdeen, were welcomed in bankless towns. But they could not pool assets. "Chain banking" was feared as oppression, compared to a crushing python.

Idaho's first big banker was the First Security Corporation of Ogden, Utah. Its ambitious founders, Marriner and George Eccles and Marriner Browning, bought Utah and Wyoming banks and stormed into Idaho in the twenties, buying banks in Idaho Falls, Nampa, and other places. In 1928 they hired Ralph Comstock, Sr., whose father Ross ran a pioneer bank in Rexburg, to head first its Nampa bank and then all their banks in eastern Idaho.

The Comstocks were friends of a young Sugar City newspaperman named Lloyd Adams; Adams had written that the Comstocks were the best bankers in the Snake River Valley, and that was the "plain, unvarnished truth." In 1909 Ross Comstock foreclosed on the failing *Rexburg Standard* newspaper and hired Adams to run it. While Adams was enmeshed in Republican politics, Ross Comstock schemed, intervened, and maneuvered to keep Adams from getting fired.

Ralph Comstock and Adams shared a lot of history and remained good friends and close allies. But the Adams-Republican-First Security ties were business ones too. In March 1928, First Security bought three Magic Valley banks – the First National Banks of Jerome and Gooding and the Shoshone National Bank - then under common ownership. But the ownership was uncommon. Frank Gooding, former governor and future senator, founded the Gooding bank between bouts of public office. When he was elected to the Senate in 1920, a stockholder, John Thomas, took over. Thomas, who during the twenties picked up the other banks, sold the batch to First Security in March 1928, three months before Gooding died. Adams then maneuvered Thomas into appointment to the Senate, replacing Gooding. Thomas became a member of the First Security Board and stayed on it until 1940. Not only Adams personally but the Gooding-Thomas machine were tied to First Security.

So First Security could and did seize the moment in 1933 when an opportunity came for branching. The farm depression of the twenties shut down dozens of banks; without branches, banking would be in trouble. That argument and political clout, along with changes in federal law to make chaining easier, allowed Adams and First Security to overcome the independents. In February 1933 the legislature passed a branch banking law, and in November First Security organized 15 Idaho branches. The First National Bank of Idaho (it became Idaho

First National Bank after 1936), which dated from 1867 and had bought other banks over the years, established seven branches.

For years they dominated Idaho banking. They divided the state between them, avoiding head-on competition in a single town. The field cracked open in December 1946 as Gov. Arnold Williams, defeated in the election the month before, prepared to leave office. Williams was from Rexburg, which had a First Security branch. A home town delegation asked him to charter the new Yellowstone Bank, led by S.M. Meikle, a banker in Ashton and Driggs. "They were loaning a lot of money to farmers in the area," newspaperman John Porter recalled. Meikle had been turned down once by the state bank commissioner. Now Williams went to bat, ordering the commissioner to charter the branch. When he refused, Williams fired him and hired a replacement who followed orders.

That was the turning point. Afterward, Lloyd Adams instigated a lawsuit challenging Williams' action, and the bank's opening was delayed. But the new policy carried through with the next governor, C.A. Robins, who didn't get along with Adams. Yellowstone Bank became the Idaho Bank of Commerce and, in 1972, Valley Bank, which grew into one of the largest in eastern Idaho.

In the seventies Idaho First was by far the largest in the state. By then branching had absorbed most of the small bankers, as they had feared. But some small banks remained, and branches did bring banking to small towns that had gone without.

Falling behind Idaho First, First Security's political clout eroded. Another lesson in economic politicking: Expanding concerns build confidence. Politicians who back a business in a controversy want to know they'll have a powerful friend for the long haul.

That was the story of Union Pacific.

UP, which runs the vital rail trackage in southern Idaho, once was as important in Idaho politics as it was in Wyoming – meaning, dominant. Pocatello, Shoshone, Glenns Ferry and Nampa developed Democratic constituencies because of rail workers there. The rails were arteries and veins to farm and other industries.

But railroads became regulated by the state utilities commission. More important, major rail carriers abandoned spur lines and concentrated on the few busy lines. Rail stops shut down or consolidated and scores of workers were laid off in the seventies and eighties. (That bit into the Democratic voting base.)

One reason was construction and improvement of major highways. In the early sixties the last obvious missing link was welded when the Lewis-Clark Highway from Missoula to Lewiston opened; from Orofino to Lolo, Mont., only primitive logging roads had existed before. In the mid-seventies the last heart-pounding switchbacks on Highway 95 were corrected with new White Bird Hill and Lewiston Hill roads. In the eighties both I-90 in Northern Idaho and I-84 and I-86 in the south approached completion. Trucking boomed and began to replace rails as prime commercial carrier.

The truckers' political clout has been delayed. On the occasional rail-versus- trucker issues such as ton-mile taxation, the railroad usually has prevailed. Union Pacific is a single business that runs most of the rail traffic, while no one trucking firm has such a grip. But if trucking follows the usual pattern of consolidation in what remains of the twentieth century, the big fish among the truckers could become powerhouses.

Potlatch

Timber followed a different pattern.

The first timber businesses in Idaho were one man operations. The next were branches of out-of-state companies. They began consolidating after 1900 with the Weyerhaeuser syndicate.

Great Lakes lumber man Frederick Weyerhaeuser created more than two dozen lumber companies even before he looked west. In 1899 he made one of the biggest real estate deals in American history, buying 900,000 acres of Pacific Northwest land once owned by Northern Pacific Railroad. The offspring of that deal would dominate Idaho's timber industry for the rest of the century, though not under the Weyerhaeuser name.

In 1901 Weyerhaeuser sent William Deary to Idaho to scout locations for timber production; Deary found useful sites in Latah County. Weyerhaeuser formed Potlatch Lumber Co. (later Potlatch Forests Inc., later still Potlatch Corp.) It built a sophisticated mill north of Moscow at Potlatch, a true company town: land, houses, even churches were owned by the company until Potlatch became an incorporated village in the fifties. Later the company built a massive paper mill at Lewiston and set up headquarters there.

It changed northern Idaho. Once the industry was run by scores of small mill operations – St. Maries or Orofino might have a dozen or more – but in time big operators like Potlatch bought mill after mill. "They did a pretty energetic job of it," Cecil Andrus (who helped run Orofino mills in the fifties) recalled.

Potlatch became a power in the Legislature. And the timber unions, along with miners' unions, were the spine of the northern Idaho Democratic Party. The timber industry became characterized more by unions and larger companies than by small operations.

After mid-century Potlatch's impact on Idaho diminished, but because of growth rather than decline. After World War II, Potlatch picked up vast properties nationally and turned its gaze away from Idaho. In 1965, company headquarters left Lewiston, where fast transit was hard to come by, for San Francisco, and soon lost touch with its roots. A semi-legendary story in northern Idaho in the seventies involved a San Francisco corporate executive curious whether the names of Potlatch, Idaho and the Potlatch Corporation were related.

Even while it was based in Idaho, Potlatch was quick to shut down operations at a sign of economic reversal. When recession hit in the seventies it let loose with a scarifying list of closures including, in March 1983, shutdown of the old Potlatch, Idaho operation. Even the Lewiston plant shut down in 1985 until a deal with unions allowed partial reopening. Potlatch stayed important to Northern Idaho but less overwhelming than it had been.

The Cascadeans

So it went with most timber companies. Collectively, they were a formidable lobby, but few had great individual clout on a statewide level.

Except for one that did retain Idaho heavyweight status.

Like Potlatch it started from Weyerhaeuser twigs: the Barber Lumber Co. on the Boise River (at Barber, a company town northeast of Boise) and the Payette Lumber and Manufacturing Co. on the Payette River. In 1957 they merged as the Boise Cascade Corp.

B-C's amazing run in the sixties from modest beginnings was even headier than Potlatch's. The critical difference for Idaho was that B-C kept to its roots - or rather, returned to them after developing a business version of homesickness.

The man in charge was Robert V. Hansberger, who by the late sixties seemed to have earned the right to do whatever he wanted. The $35 million-a-year lumber company he took over in the late fifties was a $1.8 billion conglomerate a decade later. He recruited a tribe of sharp young MBAs, many from prestigious eastern schools, and gave them unprecedented freedom – "free form management." Wall Street watched closely as B-C got into land development, recreational vehicles, and electric companies in Guatemala and Panama, and seemed to be running away from Idaho. But in 1970 the wrong sections of the economy – especially land development – turned sour and profits fell in half. The next year the former toast of Wall Street suffered $170.6 million in operating losses. The year after that Hansberger resigned and was replaced by one of his bright young proteges, John Fery.

Fery, company man that he was, never squabbled publicly with Hansberger. But he had favored dumping the peripheral stuff and concentrating on wood and paper products. By 1975 the sideshows were gone and Boise Cascade was riding high again, even upgrading forest products machinery and operations.

Both Hansberger and Fery, unlike many corporate leaders, encouraged employees to be active in community affairs. This led to an infusion of B-C people into Idaho politics.

In 1962, during Hansberger's uptick, his name was tossed about as a possible candidate for Senate or governor. He never ran. But in a newspaper column in 1964 then-state Sen. Perry Swisher of Pocatello warned that Boise Cascade seemed to have acquired the Idaho Republican Party as a wholly-owned subsidiary:

> *...The company first gathered ranking Republicans to its bosom, and only lately has begun to breed its own. While the national resurgence of business-into-politics is described as bipartisan, the major example is showering its talents almost exclusively on one party. As a result, when one Boise Cascade/ GOP leader makes a move, increasingly party officials and the press corps tend to see it as a planned effort by the entire knot hole gang. In August 1962, a planeload of B-C men set up headquarters in Pocatello four days ahead of the Republican convention, and directed the drive that nominated former Gov. Len Jordan and made him United States senator. No segment of the Idaho GOP had an organization that could come close to equalling that performance.*

Swisher also pointed out the Cascadeans in politics: former state House speakers Larry Mills (the 1951 session), W.D. Eberle (1961), and M.L. Horsley (1943; he had contractual ties to B-C), and state Rep. Charles McDevitt, a Boise Republican, a leading light in the 1963 session and a B-C general counsel.

Those days may have marked the peak of Boise Cascade's political clout, but it has never been slight. From its big brown office building four blocks from the Statehouse it overlooks the Capitol figuratively as well as literally. It is a steady contributor to political campaigns. It usually has at least one current or former or retired employee in the Legislature. In the seventies that was Larry Jackson, former major league baseball player and B-C government affairs officer. Jackson became co-chairman of the Joint Finance-Appropriations Committee, which writes the state budget, and ran for governor in 1978. His tenure in the House overlapped that of Rep. Larry Harris, a retired B-C executive. The chief of B-C's legal division, Randy Ayres, lost a race to replace Harris when he retired in 1986. But across town, that same year, one of Ayre's subordinates, Karl Brooks, became a Democratic state senator in a hitherto Republican part of southeast Boise.

Boise Cascade is liked and respected as a good corporate citizen, as active in civic affairs as any of the corporations. Its politicians tend to be solid office holders. But B-C did become controversial in the mid-eighties, because of local rather than state government.

Boise Urban Removal

In Hansberger's glory days, when Smylie was governor and Goldwater was about to be crushed by Lyndon Johnson, Boise's downtown had a string of venerable old buildings on Main Street. At least, some were venerable. Others were seedy. And Boiseans decided to fix it up in grand style.

A quarter-century later, one image of that effort stands out.

One morning in October 1970 the Boise Redevelopment Agency board was to accept the resignation of an executive director and hire a new one. Formalities were about to begin when the new director's wife called. She said that a car had crashed through their brick home. Its front end was resting in their bedroom.

It seems an omen of things to come.

Boise has no excuse for the apathy that so long clogged its drains. Yet for a while L.J. Davis, the New York writer and former Boisean, seemed correct in his prediction that Boise was about to become the first city ever to eradicate itself.

In mid-century Boise seemed merely in a slow lane to nowhere. The city proper grew little but its suburbs, eventually annexed, blossomed. Ada County's population edged to 100,000 by 1960 after growing 32.3 percent in the fifties, 40.2 percent in the forties.

Boise's downtown was built near mountains to the north and the Boise River to the south. Some desert land to the southeast could be developed, but less easily than to the south and west where land had been farmed for years, and where road and other services already existed. There development spread, far from downtown. As in so many cities, downtown slipped into decline.

Something had to be done.

An early stab at it came in 1949 when a women's group, the Columbian Club, collected 127 civic groups to push for a coliseum or auditorium building in Boise. A decade later, after rejecting it once, voters created the Boise Auditorium District. The next month voters turned down the new board's first proposal, a $2.4 million convention center. Five times more in the next 30 years, as the district's life flickered, glowed and faded, voters said no to convention center projects. (They did, however, vote in 1986 to retain the district, and the board then found a way to finance the center, allowing construction to begin in 1988.)

In the early sixties, a group of retailers, attorneys, land developers, and others declared, correctly, that downtown's problem was decentralization. They persuaded the activist 1965 legislature to rewrite Idaho's urban renewal law so cities could set up redevelopment boards with sweeping power to buy and sell property and raise money. The timing was flukey: the bill might not have passed a session less in ferment.

The Boise Redevelopment Agency was created in August 1965. Its first board was chaired by former Mayor Westerman Whillock, who ran a Boise broadcasting firm and in 1966 ran for governor.

The board put in for federal urban renewal money; it was given millions. The BRA used it for gobs of planning and for mass demolition, the "Boise urban removal" of nearly all the old Chinese district, saloons, and stores, all ripped down on the south side of Main Street. In their place stood gravel pits and parking lots, which would have extended north but for loud and timely complaints from historic preservationists.

"Actually, we didn't have a bad downtown before they started tearing it down," former Idaho Power Chairman Jim Bruce recalled.

The ambitious plans called for downtown as the regional retail center. Unlike many cities its size, Boise had no massive shopping center. With the 1967 inventory tax repeal, out-of-state retailers began knocking on Idaho's door. Karcher Mall in Nampa was built then; it would remain the area's biggest shopping center for 20 years, and Boisean insistence on building a dominant center was in part a reaction to it. The time was right, planners said, to build Idaho's biggest shopping center downtown. The plan was to bring in three or four major department stores to pull in smaller stores to pull in restaurants and night spots. This regional shopping center – the formal terminology – needed a half million or more square feet of space, which is why so many old buildings were bought and demolished by the BRA.

Maybe it could have happened. Retailers did want to come to Boise. Federal money flowed like the Salmon River – $16 million, eventually. Boise's environs were not yet too sprawled; retailers still could make believe downtown was near the center of population.

Or maybe not. Some say the interstate had settled it. In 1960, planners had to map the path of Interstate 84 through Boise. Some Boiseans said it should run close to the Union Pacific rail route, overlooking downtown and the river area. Others wanted it above and through the river area near downtown. But civic groups, the *Statesman*, and others proposed a desert route, south near the airport. It was a big civic fight and hearings were jammed. In the fall of 1960, a poll found overwhelming public support for the airport-desert route. There it was built, and so went the first step toward routing people away from downtown.

Two city policies intended to help downtown had the opposite effect. One was tearing down the old buildings without new construction, chasing away businesses and live bodies and hastening growth in the suburbs. City Hall also steered away much proposed downtown office construction, as it wouldn't leave room for retailers, while allowing office complexes elsewhere. In the eighties the largest and most attractive, in a park-like setting near the Boise River, was ParkCenter, where Albertson's, Ore-Ida and others occupied the equivalent of several urban towers. Morrison-Knudsen built a complex for itself nearby.

Of the big businesses only the banks, the J.R. Simplot Co., Mountain Bell, Idaho Power Co., and Boise Cascade stayed downtown. Downtown's working population was far lower than if the offices had been built there, rendering the area less attractive to retailers who want swarms of customers passing by.

These facts were not lost on retailers. Boise attracted interest from creative developers like the Rouse Co. of Baltimore, which worked miracles in downtown Boston and elsewhere – but in downtowns stuffed with offices and apartment buildings. Most mass retailers, especially the Big Two, the J.C. Penney Co. and Sears, Roebuck and Co., were inclined to build in fast growing suburbs and next to interstates or connectors. Downtown Boise was a couple of miles from the nearest freeway.

In the early seventies, California developer Harry Daum (Karcher Mall's builder) proposed redeveloping downtown on a smaller scale if the city would let him build a regional shopping center near the freeway connector. The city said no. Mayor Dick Eardley and the city council were committed to the idea that the next big retail development in Boise would happen downtown. Period.

At some point in the seventies, real hope for that plan died. The first smack of reality came in 1977 when Penney's, one of the key anchors for a large shopping area which had expressed interest in downtown, said it would not build a new store downtown. Eardley, furious, accused Penney's of leading the city down a "primrose path."

Eardley put a lot of himself into downtown development. He had been a newspaper reporter and ran the KBOI television news operation in the sixties, when it set the pace among Idaho broadcasters. In 1969, still news director at KBOI, Eardley ran for the council and outpolled the mayor, Jay Amyx, who won a second term that year. Eardley was one of a team of moderates who ran in part to help straighten out a city financial mess (and succeeded). In 1973 he was elected mayor and got a like-minded city council.

In his campaign for city council in 1977, Glenn Selander, a Boise State University professor, called for offering a referendum on downtown. He was elected, and once in office proposed it again. But the idea went nowhere, and Selander gradually joined Eardley's team.

But the BRA's progress was slight. It kept tearing down buildings, moving tenants, and trading developers (and was, in fairness, responsible for a few large building projects around downtown). Boise Cascade was master developer from 1970 to 1972, but quit when it got out of most of its non-lumber businesses. The BRA was a revolving door for developers; they'd show up, last a year or two, and quit.

Until Winmar.

The Seattle-based Winmar Co., a subsidiary of Safeco Insurance, became developer in October 1977. It brought in local businessmen, including the Futura Corp., operated by former B-C chief Hansberger. Within months Hansberger drew in one of the key figures in redevelopment: Floyd Decker, former Louisianan and former executive director of the Association of Idaho Cities.

Winmar's first plan model arrived in 1978. Key Boise business leaders were appalled – it was dull, flat, unexciting. When it was shown, Boise nearly turned into Winmar's lynch mob. A group of young businessmen formed Boise NOW to draft an alternate plan. They wanted to co-build downtown and a regional shopping center at Westpark, the old Daum site near the connector now controlled by developer Larry Leasure and allied Boise money men Allen Noble and Bill Moseley. NOW put Winmar on the defensive.

Decker suggested dumping the Winmar plan and setting up citizens committees to come up with something new. The committees crafted the "plan designed by 2,000" which got community support. But the retailers didn't like it. The years ahead were a round of lesser stores agreeing to go downtown, then pulling out, while Sear's and Penney's, the key players, folded arms across chests and said no way - it was suburban or nowhere. City Hall said the stores would go downtown or nowhere at all. Suburban would-be developers kept lining up locations. Every freeway interchange – or planned interchange – had one. Leasure kept working on Westpark; others hustled sites near Meridian west of Boise.

In July 1982 Penney's said it would build west of town at a site backed by Salt Lake City developer John Price, a heavy hitter who had built more malls in the Intermountain West – in Pocatello, Idaho Falls, and Twin Falls – than anyone else. It was a blow to Winmar; without Penney's, hope was all but gone.

Boise was getting impatient. Eardley set up a Blue Ribbon Committee which urged a new way of looking at downtown, and City Hall seemed about to change direction.

In 1981, Eardley ran for re-election against former Department of Law Enforcement Director Kelly Pearce, a Democrat who got bipartisan support for a suburban mall. In June the eight-block downtown core area owned by the BRA was sold to Winmar for $1.5 million, outraging many in town. Eardley said Winmar now had to perform or get out. Eardley had run City Hall well – he was a good manager – and was re-elected in a landslide. His opposition hadn't coalesced yet. The dead end of the downtown policy wasn't yet obvious. But it was about to be.

Winmar announced it was dropping out of the picture, and Decker went to work for Leasure, promoting Westpark. Then its executives said they had another nibble, and got back in. Winmar held on through 1984. But the stalemate continued as Eardley and the council held tough against a suburban mall.

Floyd Decker – *Dick Eardley is one of the most honorable, ethical, honest, straightforward people you'll ever meet. If he believes he's right, he'll die for it, politically, physically. He's not only tenacious, he's intelligent. And I just simply feel Dick Eardley did not feel he could hold his head up in the future if he did not stick with what was absolutely right ...*

The Citizens

A turning point for the voters came in the fall of 1983, when anti-City Hall rage reached the pressure cooker stage. Boise was stagnating now in the eighties; the heat was on for prosperity.

Incumbents usually have the edge in Idaho city council races. Until the eighties, state law made all council candidates run in a pack; the top three voter getters – or however many seats were up for grabs – won. Since incumbents usually were best known and they could not easily be targeted for defeat, they were shielded more than in head-to-head races.

But in 1983 the question of "which side are you on?" was on point. A group of young professionals, Democrats and Republicans with little in common but disgust at City Hall, hatched a scheme to butt heads. They formed Citizens for Progressive City Government, headed by attorneys Jim Harris (a conservative Republican) and Paul Buser (a liberal Democrat), banker Brent Robinson, and surgeon Dean Sorensen (a Republican later elected to the Idaho House). Their platform: Allow a suburban mall and build a "mixed-use" downtown. The Citizens developed an incredible network of alliances, from some of the most conservative Republican legislators to the AFL-CIO. (Arrayed against them were corporate executives and much of the more upscale Democratic organization.) On election day they swept out the one incumbent council member who dared run for re-election (long-time Councilman Fred Kopke, who finished a dismal sixth) and swept in the Citizens' endorsees: Ron Twilegar, Brent Coles, and Mary Tate.

Tate wound up siding with Eardley on key downtown votes. But Twilegar and Coles spent the next two years waging legislative guerrilla warfare against Eardley and the downtown crowd. Coles had been a city planner in the Eardley Administration, and Twilegar had as fine a sense of political tactics as anyone in Idaho.

Twilegar was one of the few Democrats ever elected to the Legislature from Ada County, and - with his Senate successor Gail Bray - the only one to easily win re-election. (Even Frank Church could not win an Ada County legislative seat.) Schooled as an attorney, he quit the law to form from scratch a business amalgam called First Idaho Corp. Twilegar had the quick eyes that betrayed mental machinery constantly in motion. His minority years in the Senate, and now on the council, gave him the look of a caged animal who had just concocted a brilliant escape.

He had little interest in any city business but downtown.

But he always had something up his sleeve.

Eardley, a meticulous manager, genuinely disliked Twilegar. The new council member took time meeting after meeting, peering over at Eardley from the end of the council bench, raising the subject of downtown like a cat pawing an object to the table's edge for the interest of watching it fall over the side. He exasperated Eardley, who sometimes blew his stack. Eardley had enjoyed his first ten years as mayor, he said, but the last two were no fun at all.

The mayor did keep downtown policy on track most of that time. Winmar finally was replaced in March 1984 by The Taubman Co. of Troy, Mich., which had done some of the classiest developments in the nation. Boise's problem, President Robert Larson said, lay with the details of Winmar's plan; a better one would bring in stores. Give us time, he said, and you'll get your regional center downtown. And Taubman went to work.

In 1984 a Decker-inspired ad hoc group spent several days at the Western Idaho State Fair, easily rounding up 10,000 signatures for a referendum on downtown. The Ada County Commission refused to put it on the ballot. Two Citizens-backed Ada Commission candidates, conservative Republicans, were elected in November 1984.

By 1985, the heat was on high; plotting, counter-plotting and counter-counter- plotting was epidemic. As Taubman's backers, including City Hall, pleaded for peace and unity, the rumbling and skepticism would not be quelled. This was a job for -

Uptown's Downtown

Uptown Boise?

The working-class mayor had won allies in the corporate crowd that sipped drinks in the quiet of the Arid Club, people familiar with other downtowns. In Boston and San Francisco and Seattle, where they did much of their shopping, downtowns seemed like artwork. Why, on a small scale, couldn't Boise's? Coming from a different world view than the mayor, they reached the same conclusion. Downtown needed unity; maybe they could give it that. John Fery of Boise Cascade led the way in forming Uptown Boise, and Eugene Thomas, head of one of Idaho's top law firms (and a future president of the American Bar Association), was co-chairman. Members included Jim Bruce of Idaho Power, James Phelps of First Security, and Gary Sherlock, publisher of the Statesman. The Statesman's editorials, long critical of the BRA, abruptly switched to cheery optimism.

But Uptown gave Twilegar, Decker, Harris, and the rest wonderful ammunition. What was Uptown up to, they wondered? Uptown's goals were philanthropic, but it was also a player in a big-money-versus-young professionals conflict; some may have been concerned about the prospect of Twilegar and his group running Boise. The Twilegar/Citizens crowd painted dark scenarios of robber barons and power brokers, conveying a feeling that money people had lined up with City Hall to thwart the will of the people. The voters sensed oppression; the result was predictable.

Things moved fast in the summer of 1985 as the next city election approached. Taubman's Larson dramatically flew into Boise and quit. The B.R.A. board, chaired by ex-Boise Cascadean Peter O'Neill, changed course toward a smaller shopping center downtown. Eardley, while maintaining that he could be re- elected if he ran, decided not to run for a fourth term. The three council members up for election that year – Eardleyites all – decided likewise. One, Selander, bravely ran for mayor.

The Progressive Citizens, quietly aided by suburban developers, were back in force. They got behind council candidates Democrat Mike Wetherell (a former Frank Church staffer), Republican Jay Webb (a lobbyist and former legislator), and city planner Sara Baker, mirroring their winning formula of two years before. (They had a Democrat, a Republican, an unknown; one woman; and a city planner.) They also backed mayoral candidate Dirk Kempthorne, a legislative lobbyist who had run Republican state Sen. Phil Batt's campaign for governor in 1982. That did not stop Democrats from jumping on his bandwagon. Kempthorne was the inevitable winner from the day he announced early in the spring.

Floyd Decker – *A guy who I knew from his days in the Idaho Conservation League, Mark Ingram, brought this tall, good-looking young guy to my office. He said, "I want you to meet a guy named Dirk Kempthorne. He's thinking about running for mayor." I looked at him and I thought, this guy looks like a Sunday School teacher, Mr. Goody Goody Two Shoes. The guy is too good to be true. I met with Dirk several times and he grilled me, just like a newspaper reporter, boom, boom, boom, which surprised me.*

He had a mustache then. I remember telling him, you've got to get rid of that mustache. He said, "I intend to."

When the dust settled in November 1985, the Citizens made a clean sweep. Kempthorne, Wetherell, Webb, and Baker won. In just two years, the mayor's office and six city council positions had been taken over by the anti-City Hall crowd.

In a sense the revolution had already been won by then. When Taubman withdrew, machinery was set in motion by the Eardley Administration and the old council to allow a suburban mall. The new Kempthorne administration simply kept that policy in effect and goosed it along. Twilegar became co-chairman of the BRA board with O'Neill – an uneasy but effective partnership – and construction got underway both downtown and in the suburbs.[101]

---

[101] It seems such a long time ago. By 1988, Boise seemed to be recovering somewhat from its downer days, but the future still was a little shaky. Perched in the 00s, we can see that from 1986 on, the city has had spectacular growth – maybe too much growth – and its downtown has rebounded nicely. New tower buildings have been built, and downtown is in general livelier than it had been in decades. All this while the regional mall shopping area (the "mall" itself is the lesser part of it) has continued to go great guns, and develop into a huge traffic morass (a problem for which no one has found a solution yet). All of this is more or less, though, from the perspective of 2008; the economic tremors of late '08 and into '09 raise some real questions about where Boise goes from here. But downtown has retained, so far, at least most of its prosperity. As for some of the key players. Dick Eardley has not returned to electoral politics; he was for a time an executive in the state Department of Employment. Ron Twilegar ran for the U.S. Senate in 1990, losing to Larry Craig; he has pursued various business interests since; in 2008, he was elected prosecutor at Boise County. Dirk Kempthorne was re-elected as mayor in 1989, then elected to the U.S. Senate in 1992 and governor in 1998 and 2002; he resigned in early 2006 to become secretary of the interior, a position that (at this writing) he has just departed. Brent Coles followed Kempthorne as mayor, winning election but eventually resigning under an ethical cloud.

Floyd Decker – *The results of that convinced me that there is no power structure in Boise. There are power clusters, and the Arid Club is one. But it convinced me they didn't control the vote in the street. They would have lost if they had taken it to the street.*

Tour | Magic Valley

The Magic Valley is the endless farm field so many out-of-staters imagine Idaho to be.

It rises far above the Snake River, which cut a deep gorge in the landscape. Farming means irrigation here; yet farming barely existed here before the water was first diverted around the turn of the century. Even then the water did not go far, and the people are huddled within a few miles of the Snake.

While dry-land farmers to the north split their votes, irrigation farmers in the south almost always are Republicans who see themselves as rugged individualists. Perhaps a belief that they have a greater physical investment in the land, compared to dry-land farmers, built a stronger self-image as businessmen. Twin Falls County last elected a Democratic legislator in 1936.

But Democrats did scratch together a voting base in some places. In the fifties and sixties the other counties elected some conservative Democrats. But when the conservative wing collapsed so did the Magic Valley's Democratic Party.

Shoshone, seat of little Lincoln County, is the closest to an exception. Lincoln was the last Valley county settled by the usually-Republican Mormons, and remained lightly populated by them into the twentieth century. More important, Shoshone is as much a rail stop as a farm community, and rail votes can be enough to give a strong Democrat an even break.

Gooding is also less Republican than some neighbors. Conservative Democrats like Vern Ravenscroft once had a strong base here. Gooding had a Methodist College early in the century. It still has the State School for the Deaf and Blind, placed there in 1910 during the term of Gov. James Brady, a close friend of Frank Gooding, who founded the town and gave it his political spin. But this farming town has grown more Republican with the years.

Even solidly Republican Jerome County once had a Democratic base. Some of that came from the big Tupperware plant. This base vanished when the plant closed in the mid-eighties.

Magic Valley Republicans are mixed moderates and conservatives. The rugged individualists depended on cooperation on water and rail services and on federal reclamation projects. T.W. "Tom" Stivers, the conservative House speaker who enraged so many Idahoans not enamored with his world view, was elected easily for years from Twin Falls. But so was state Sen. Laird Noh, a Kimberly farmer and one of the most scholarly, articulate, and urbane – his rural background notwithstanding – of legislators.

254

Twin

Magic Valley towns rise or fall on the farm economy. During the hard-luck eighties, most grew little or not at all.

Twin Falls, the valley's center, did grow; its population increased about a third, to 28,000, by the mid-eighties. Twin Falls' politics are strikingly like Boise's. Republicans win partisan offices almost without exception. But Democrats and independents can get, and have gotten, elected to city hall, and statewide Democratic candidates can take the county on occasion.

Twin has a moderate Republican tradition; in the fifties and sixties it was a bastion of Smylie support.

City leaders were wise enough to know Twin could not live on agriculture alone, and worked to attract manufacturing plants and other business. This is an innovative place. Twin was the first Idaho city (in 1949) to adopt council- manager government. Boise instigated Idaho's urban renewal law but Twin first used it successfully. Boise made no progress until long after Twin finished its project. (For that matter, Idaho Falls and Lewiston also completed their projects before Boise did.)

The moderation here comes partly from a settled farm and business community led by established downtown merchant families. But Noh said the strongest base of moderation is the Republican women's organization. "There have always been a number of [volunteers] who were willing to not only participate but get the work done. And very quietly. They didn't want a lot of credit, but they were always there to do the work. They were also there to ensure that the more radical elements of the party didn't take control of the central committee."

The key figure has been Oriette Sinclair, also a top state Republican leader. In the eighties she was the local field representative for both senators McClure and Symms.

These centers of influence were being transformed in the eighties as older members dropped out. Twin Falls probably never will change radically, but some change, maybe meaning a larger role for an active Democratic Party, could be in the wind.

Twin Falls has had powerful state legislative delegations. In the early seventies it included House Speaker William Lanting and both budget committee co-chairmen, Sen. Richard High and Rep. William Roberts. All were moderates. When a couple of conservatives, farmer Ralph Olmstead and former county clerk Stivers, ran in 1972 and 1974 and won by dint of energetic campaigning, they were seen as interlopers. Noh, then county Republican chairman, recalled "very hard feelings between Ralph and Tom and the rest of the Twin Falls delegation, to the point that they would not even communicate with one another. I used to, as county chairman, just get them in the same room to talk over their differences and work for the common interest of Twin Falls County. Very awkward situation. Very intense personal feelings ... They perceived of themselves as the two outs, and the others were ins."

That changed. Four years after Lanting retired from the House in 1974, Olmstead became speaker. He was followed by Stivers, who became the best-known speaker Idaho had in years. But in 1986, when Stivers retired, Twin swung back to traditional moderation.[102]

South of town is intensive cattle country dominated by the "71 Association," conservative old-line cattlemen. The small towns here are more solidly conservative than Twin Falls.

East Valley

East of Twin's orbit, beyond Eden, Kimberly, and Murtaugh, is Magic Valley's second constellation of farm towns: Burley, Rupert, Heyburn, Paul, Declo. But if Twin is marked by stable moderation, Burley-Rupert has variety.

Unlike most Southern Idaho farmers, many here are powered by public electric cooperatives. Rupert, population about 5,600, has been from its inception - aside from a brief flirtation with socialism early in the century - a quiet farm town which has an ancestral Democratic history. It turned Republican by mid-century, but moderate Republican, much like Twin Falls. The food processing plant work force is a counterpoint to the farmers.

Burley, with 9,100 residents the largest of these communities, was an important rail crossroads, and a wild town once.

Robert Smylie — *When I was attorney general [1947-55] there were three houses of ill repute all located in buildings that belonged to one of the saints in the Mormon Church, and I mean a high-placed saint. We couldn't get anybody to do anything about it. The county and public health people were concerned about it because by this time there were trace-and-treat techniques, and they found these were pretty good centers of VD infestation.*

So we got to looking at the communicable disease statute one day ... The public health people went down there and quarantined the place for communicable diseases. Boy, that brought that to a screeching halt.

More established and stodgy forces clamped down. Burley has become rock-hard conservative since.

Rupert and Minidoka County are sometimes vote for Democrats but next-door Burley and Cassia County seldom do. Aside from state Sen. Robert Saxvik, a popular radio station manager (later on the Northwest Power Planning Council), Cassia last elected a Democrat to

---

[102] In the 90s and into the 00s, the leading Twin Falls area legislator was Laird Noh, relatively moderate and widely regarded as thoughtful, even scholarly in his approach. Noh retired from the Senate in 2004; his successor, Charles Coiner, has been described as of a similar mold.

the Legislature in 1950. The cities' and counties' economic rivalry can be a philosophical rivalry as well.

"People tend to turn to the Democrats when things are not going well. When everybody is fatcatting and doing well, then you have all these Republican farmers," Cecil Andrus said. "Take a look at the depth of the loam of the soil and where they get their water. I can get 300 sacks of spuds to the acre south in Cassia County, and out on the Minidoka flats you can get only 180 acres. The soil is different. The water delivery systems are different. The payment schedules are different. No mystery to it."

South of the Snake River, down to Declo and Malta and the remote mountain town of Albion, water is sparse and farming developed accordingly. But this is deeply Republican territory.

The most distinctive town is Albion, a former county seat which once had a strong non-farming element in its population: a state teacher's college located there for several decades. For a time the school provided a broader mix in local politics. It was shut down in 1951; a private school replaced it in 1957 but closed after a decade. The campus has been deserted since, and the town run mainly by conservative farmers.

14 | The Rise & Swan Falls
of Idaho Power

If politics is the distribution of resources, then nowhere in Idaho is politics plainer than in the Snake River plain.

This was the scene of the most startling political reversal in Idaho history – of no mere politician, but of Idaho Power Company. In the fifties Idaho Power was the center of the struggle of the decade. A generation later, it anchored a conflict even more sweeping in scope – but friends and enemies had switched sides and made strange partners. The Swan Falls clash, which has stretched through the eighties, unmade and remade politics in Idaho.

Reclamation

The Snake came first, ripping a thousand-mile trench through the desert of Southern Idaho. Then came settlers, Mormons to the east, miners to the west, making arable land where none had been.

The Mormons of the Upper Snake knew from their Utah years all about canals and ditches, and by the 1890s they had irrigated vast tracts. Boise was a rowdy supply center for the mountain mining towns. Nearby, farmers grew crops for the miners; they, too, built irrigation systems, but in more chaotic fashion.

Irrigation populated the Magic Valley, which was desert before the turn of the century. It created networks of personal and political power based on water agreements, the only important link between farmers and between them and society at large.

The key group for decades has been the Committee of Nine, nine water districts above Milner Dam, from Filer to Ashton. The Committee for decades has been respected throughout southern Idaho and has tied farmers together, transcending differences of crop or acreage. Turnover on the committee was low, and its members became quiet regional leaders. The Nine kept a low profile, but its thoughts spread fast and deep. No sane Southern Idaho politician intentionally would get on their wrong side.

Others also influence how water is used, and so how Idaho grows, especially water law attorneys like Kent Foster of Idaho Falls, Ray Rigby of Rexburg, J.D. Williams of Preston, Roger Ling of Rupert and Ben Cavaness of American Falls, and the Nelson, Rosholt, Robertson, Tolman and Tucker firm of Twin Falls.

Reclamation packed the Twin Falls area with farms, but for years Burley and Rupert farmers still couldn't manage. Then the 1902

Reclamation Act, which brought the feds into dam-building, gave them lots of water and electric power.

One of Idaho's first federal dams was the Minidoka Dam Project completed in 1909. Minidoka was Idaho's first big electric power producer, and the Rupert-Burley area became thoroughly electrified. Half a century later, juice from the Palisades Dam would help local irrigators and electric co-ops. But most power from federal projects in Idaho left the state and, by the late thirties, flowed west to the Bonneville Power Administration.

Juice

The BPA, set up in 1937, was supposed to be a "temporary" New Deal experiment marketing power from federal projects in the Northwest. To most Idahoans public power meant damming Idaho streams and extracting juice for export. No wonder private power companies became so popular.

The first electric power in Idaho, in Ketchum and Hailey in the 1880s, came from string, glue, and bailing wire operations. The first electricity in Twin Falls, in 1905, came from a threshing machine engine in the back of the Hotel Perrine. But the mom-and-pop companies died out. Idaho's population quadrupled from 1890 to 1910, and electric companies frantically gobbled up each other like corporate raiders to combine power lines and production capacity. In the Upper Snake River Valley and near Utah, each county once had its own power company; by 1913 they were sucked up into Utah Power and Light. Most of the score or so of other private companies in southern Idaho were reduced to five by 1914, and by 1916 to just one – Idaho Power Co.

Instead of hotel turbines, IPCo used hydropower dam plants, many on the Snake River: American Falls in Eastern Idaho, Shoshone Falls in the Magic Valley, Swan Falls in the Southwest, and others. (Swan Falls was built by the Trade Dollar Consolidated Mining Co. for the mining community of Silver City. By the time it fired up, Silver City was becoming a ghost town. The dam came to Idaho Power in the consolidations of 1915.)

Hydro is cheap power, and Idaho Power's rates have always been among the lowest in the nation. While utilities elsewhere would be blasted by politicians as a matter of course, Idaho Power was for years loudly defended by them.

Eastern Idaho was served partly by Utah Power and Light, which relied on coal-fired plants and charged higher rates. Resentment simmered but did not boil; religious folk may have been reluctant to criticize a utility from Utah. (Although, in the mid-eighties community leaders and legislators did start militating for a takeover of their region by Idaho Power.)

A Game of Checkers

But Idaho Power's dams also meant conflict in the making. Idaho had far more water resources than any of the other interior western states, but it was still limited.

The Depression that spurred so many federal hydro projects also slowed Idaho Power's growth. World War II slowed both of them. Post-war, Idaho Power and the feds – urged on by a pro-public power Truman Administration – played a gigantic board game, each picking off dam sites the other had not yet claimed.

Ed Emerine, one of the few frankly liberal editors in Idaho then, described it in 1952 in his *Idaho Farm Journal*. "Let's look at the pattern," he wrote. "The Bureau of Reclamation had a 'drawing board' dam at Bliss. Idaho Power rushed in and built a dam there. The Bureau contemplated, at some future time, a multiple-purpose dam farther down the Snake River. Idaho Power effectively blocked it with the C.J. Strike Dam. The Bureau of Reclamation wants to build a dam at Hell's Canyon, power revenues of which would ultimately be used to bring water to Mountain Home desert. Idaho Power now rushes in and wants to kill a Hells Canyon Dam forever by asking for Oxbow. A few months ago the Bureau of Reclamation stated it wanted to build a power dam at Eagle Rock below American Falls to pump Snake River water to 10,000 acres on Michaud Flats. A few weeks later the Idaho Power Co. filed for a damsite at Eagle Rock."

The game meant, for one thing, BPA's inclusion of Northern but not Southern Idaho in its marketing area. Inclusion of the South, in 1963, was bitterly fought by Idaho Power and its allies. Frank Church said that "Southern Idaho was excluded because too many of our politicians were men, not as big as Borah, who were afraid to face the wrath of the private utilities." Since BPA did not serve the south, it got no sympathy there.

Idaho Power did get sympathy for being ahead of most private utilities in electrifying remote areas. Idaho Power President C.J. Strike, who came from the Dakotas, saw the spread of public power there and shrewdly countered it in Idaho. IPCo was an enormously effective lobby; water lawyer Ray Rigby described it as "always subtle, yet always so effective."

But the company, the BPA, and public officeholders realized the Snake River was not inexhaustible: when enough dams are built along a river, they slow it to the point of making it useless.

Hells Canyon

The scramble was for Hells Canyon, a true scenic spectacle and, Rigby suggested, "the most advantageous power site on the North American continent." In this deepest gorge in North America, water could be dammed to tremendous depths.

The stakes were high. In 1950 private utilities nationally went on a building binge as the United States entered the Korean war. A new federal tax code allowed fast tax writeoffs for "defense-oriented" private investments. Electric power facilities qualified, and power companies scrambled to take advantage.

In the late forties the Army Corps of Engineers and Bureau of Reclamation had surveyed the Columbia River system for new dam sites and fastened on Hells Canyon. In 1950 Idaho Power, faster than a sluggish fed, slipped an application to the Federal Power Commission for a dam called Oxbow, with plans to build four nearby dams later. (IPCo later changed the five dams to three.) Two years later the Department of Interior asked that the IPCo request be set aside and that the utility instead build one mega-dam at Hells Canyon – what would be the second biggest dam in the world. These ideas were not compatible; Oxbow would have been underwater if the federal Hells Canyon Dam were built.

Jim Bruce – *There was a tremendous amount of argument about it. I think in retrospect a lot of people would agree the three dams we have is better. You take that big high dam up there, when you have to draw it down you have mud banks along a [huge] area, you have a lot of problems with it. But we use Brownlee for flood control and then we have almost level flow off Oxbow and Hells Canyon, so we get better power production out of those.*

There was hardly any debate that wasn't virulent ... It got so bad over in Oregon that I was the only officer of the company that could go over there. They said they were going to throw all the officers of the company in jail. So they'd send me over. I was a young attorney, assistant secretary of the company, and they reckoned I was expendable.

Voices were shrill as well as loud: Idaho Power was driven solely by greed and was selling out Idaho, Federal dam backers were socialists wanting federal control of Idaho's precious water. Rumors – inaccurate – said Idaho Power could not finance the dams. "Idaho Power Co. has set out to kill forever any and all future reclamation projects in the state of Idaho," editor Emerine fumed. "If Oxbow Dam is built by Idaho Power, then kiss good-bye to that great future for Idaho you dreamed about."

Actually, reclamation was in the contracts. In the early fifties, as planners saw increasing strain on the Snake, the state and the Federal Power Commission put "subordination" clauses into water use licenses. Subordination of Idaho Power's water rights meant rights of upstream users such as farmers would take precedence. When the FPC wanted to subordinate at C.J. Strike Dam, Idaho Power fought and in 1951 compromised: the rights were subordinated, but the feds had to pay damages or buy the dam if federal irrigation projects cut power production.

Len Jordan became governor that year and planned a similar deal, pressuring Idaho Power into subordination of its Hells Canyon licenses. Jordan's support for the application was crucial, and Idaho Power gave in, guaranteeing irrigators their water. At the Federal Power Commission hearing in July 1953, Idaho Power Chairman Tom Roach said that Snake River water was crucial for agriculture. He said that for at least 37 years his company "has followed the policy of always placing the use of that water for irrigation in a prior position to the use of the water for hydroelectric development ... Currently all of our state permits in the state of Idaho carry in them a specific provision which preserves for irrigation not only now but at all times in the future a prior claim on the water with the claim for hydroelectric energy being secondary to that of the irrigator or farmer."

Water lawyer Rigby said, however, that in the case of Swan Falls Dam that provision somehow never did get into the permit.

Jordan kept up his end, going all out for Idaho Power's three-dam plan. For that as in so much else in his contentious governorship, he was loudly praised and damned.

Robert Smylie – *Ever see the old cartoon? Here's this great square-jawed fellow sitting there with two flashing light bulbs for eyes, Reddy Kilowatt eyes. And the caption on it is, "That's ol' Clem Gordon. He just sits there, but damn, he do sit good."*

The turning point came with Dwight Eisenhower's election in 1952. He wanted to change the course of Democratic policies, including those on public power, and said he would not interfere with private utilities' development plans. In 1955 the Federal Power Commission gave Idaho Power all it wanted - an incredible win by a small utility over powerful national forces.

The case dragged on. Hells Canyon was a partisan issue, a big national issue, and when Congress went Democratic in 1955 IPCo's position was tenuous. In 1956 a federal Hells Canyon bill died in the Senate. The next year Sen. Frank Church's first major speech supported a new dam bill, which the Senate passed. It died in the House, beaten to death by the White House and skillful IPCo lobbying. Persistence paid off: The utility got its dams. Brownlee Dam began producing power in 1958, Oxbow Dam in 1961 and Hells Canyon Dam in 1967.

Idaho Power was growing fast. Brownlee alone doubled IPCo's capacity. The utility went from generating 100,000 kilowatts in the early forties to more than 1.5 million by 1970. By the late seventies it served more than half of Idaho and produced more than 60 percent of the juice generated in the state. It was a political powerhouse, too, sending top lobbyists (in the seventies and eighties, Vice President Logan Lanham) to the Statehouse and to Washington when need be. Hells Canyon had proved the value of keeping tabs on government.

For a while, that seemed to end Idaho Power's growth. Speculation about Hells Canyon dams ended when much of the region became a national recreation area. The proposed Guffey Dam became part of the Snake River Birds of Prey area. The unpopularity and high cost of nuclear power plants made them an unlikely prospect for new power. Until 1971, when it began importing coal-fire electric power from Rock Springs, Wyo., Idaho Power was the biggest all-hydro utility in the nation, and its power rates stayed low.

Controversy returned when Idaho Power inched away from hydro production – and again when it lurched back.

The Commission

In the seventies Idaho's politics changed. Democrat Cecil Andrus was governor now, and he began appointing new members to the Idaho Public Utilities Commission.

The PUC was created in 1913, as Mom & Pop Power died out. But for decades its clout – sweeping control over electric, gas, telephone, railroad and other utilities – went unrealized. Universal phone service waited for years. And as long as Idaho Power gave good service and kept rates low, the PUC left it alone and gave it what it wanted. The three-member commission was by law bipartisan, but it veered conservative. A few PUC staffers – the staff was small until the seventies – would sit down with utility spokesman and settle rate increases. Public hearings were held, but few people showed up. Idaho Power didn't abuse the quiet: from 1960 to 1970 the biggest electric company in Idaho asked for a grand total of $31.6 million in rate increases – a pittance. The PUC granted about two-thirds of that.

In the early seventies the commission had two Republicans, Ralph Wickberg – the former legislator defeated in 1956 after proposing a sales tax – and Burns Beal, a former state senator. The Democrat, Harry Nock, was so conservative that in the fifties he had supported McCarthyite Republican Sen. Herman Welker.

In 1973 Andrus replaced Beal, changing the commission with a vengeance by appointing Robert Lenaghen, a former Pocatello labor leader then running the state Department of Administration. He was a former state legislator, but people more easily envisioned the man with the gravelly voice and manner in the tougher world of labor organizing. When he came to the PUC, utilities saw this tough labor leader becoming one third of their government. They flew into a panic, and thus commenced six years of warfare.

Lenaghen had eight months in the job before facing confirmation by the Republican state Senate. That didn't ease the bloody process. Lenaghen's PUC confirmation hearings in 1973 and 1979, were among the most emotionally charged the Idaho Legislature ever had. (Some utilities, such as Intermountain Gas Co., did endorse him.) He appeared twice before the Senate State Affairs Committee and was boisterously opposed. When the battle went to the Senate floor it was fought to a draw. On the first run of votes, five moderate Republicans joined the dozen Democrats for a 17-17 tie. Then Republican Sen.

Lyle Cobbs of Boise, who passed on the first round, said that "innuendoes and heresay I cannot accept," and voted for Lenaghen.

For all that, the changes on the PUC during the next five years, and there were many, were less due to Lenaghen than to changing times. PUC staff became a stronger counterpoint to utilities. Ratepayers organized and appeared at hearings. Rate hearings got far more complicated (sometimes exciting) because more people got involved. Lenaghen boosted all this by attracting interest in the PUC. And when Nock was replaced by attorney Karl Shurtliff, and after Shurtliff was followed by PUC staff attorney Conley Ward, the Democratic commission became more aggressive.

Its record was not so different on rate increases. Though Idaho Power asked for much higher rate increases in the seventies than before, it still got most of what it wanted. But the PUC did change course in other areas.

Witness Pioneer.

In the early seventies Idaho Power began importing small amounts of coal-generated electric power. Now IPCo execs wanted to build their own coal-fired plant.

Jim Bruce – *It's cyclical; if you stay around, the cycle comes around. Right after World War II, there was a large influx of people into Idaho. In the middle fifties through the middle sixties it was pretty steady, not a large influx. And then I guess, more in the seventies. At Idaho Power Co., that's where we got caught in a lot of problems with Pioneer. We had 10,000 to 11,000 new customers being hooked on, and it looked as though that was going to keep on. It didn't. The cycle turned, and I guess those are the things you're going to have to remember.*

For a time planners thought of building near Bliss – they considered 21 sites – at a site Bruce personally favored. But in November 1974 IPCo asked the PUC for permission to build a coal-fired power plant in the desert 26 miles southeast of Boise, near a wide spot in the road called Orchard. It was near the Union Pacific rail, which would haul in coal, and the Snake River, which would supply water. Two 500-megawatt generators would burn coal shipped from Western Wyoming. Idaho Power planned to crank up one unit in 1980, the other in 1981. Those were boom days in Idaho. Farms were growing; acreage increased 10 percent in 1975 and 1976, reflecting increases in wheat prices. IPCo handed the PUC convincing data on the need to expand; even a PUC study showed Idaho Power needed 500 new megawatts of electric power by 1981. Pioneer would be located out in barren desert where few people lived. Surely no one would object to a plant way out there ...

They did. The Pioneer case Idaho Power executives thought would get snap PUC approval became the longest utility case the PUC had considered until then. It lasted nearly two years.

The myth that would grow around it, as around the 1970 Andrus-Samuelson gubernatorial faceoff, was that Idahoans turned down a big, ugly development purely because they wanted a pristine environment. Even Idaho Power's semi-official history, Hydro Era, said that a "high pitch" of environmental concern killed Pioneer. The reality is murkier. Concerns about air quality did arise, although studies showed air pollution would not have been severe. A group called the Idaho Environmental Council stood up to Pioneer even before plant plans were announced, and Ada County doctors mobilized against it too.

But much of the discussion centered around money.

Pioneer was a precursor to the Washington Public Power Supply System fiasco, which gave the Northwest five hideously expensive nuclear plants and some of the biggest and least serviceable debt outside the Third World.

IPCo first figured Pioneer's cost at $400 million. At the first of nine PUC hearings in January 1975, that was up to $600 million; by August, $800 million. As the PUC said later, "This is a staggering investment for a company of Idaho Power's size. By way of comparison, at the end of 1974 the Company had a net plant in service valuation of only $648 million. But the Pioneer plant, if approved, would not be the only construction undertaken by the applicant during the next decade. Adding the cost of existing construction commitments to the cost of Pioneer results in projected construction expenditures of $1.8 billion within the next 10 years." IPCo officials admitted they would need "substantial and frequent rate increases" for the plant. Others calculated that every man, woman and child in Idaho Power's territory would pay $4,000 in the next 20 years for IPCo's building plans.

That was where many Idahoans got off Idaho Power's boat. In July 1975 environmental and consumer activists called Citizens for Alternatives to Pioneer (CAP) looked into the finances and ran devastating ads on the project. If Pioneer was built, CAP said, power rates would double in four years. (The PUC estimated doubling in seven years.) By the early eighties, CAP said, the average annual power bill would rise from $240 to $611.

It pointed out even worse effects on agriculture. IPCo had argued that making more power available would allow farmers to pump water to remote land. The catch was that taking more water out of the Snake for irrigation would reduce water available for cheap hydro, forcing Idaho Power to rely more on expensive coal-fired power, thus increasing rates. CAP said rates for pump irrigators would rise from $45 to $112 an acre. Existing irrigators would be victimized by efforts to add competing cropland. It was a bitter scenario, and many farmers would not swallow it.

In 1976 another group, The Committee to Put Pioneer on the Ballot, got commissioners in Elmore and Canyon counties to agree to a vote on Pioneer. The Ada County Commission first said no; when the Committee supplied 15,000 names on petitions, the commissioners gave in. The vote came on the May 1976 presidential primary ballot. The results may have been skewed, since Frank Church was on that ballot for president and Democrats were out in force. But clearly, Pioneer was unpopular. Its opponents won all 91 precincts of Ada and 56 percent of the vote. In Canyon they got 60 percent, and in Elmore 80 percent.

The PUC decision four months later to reject Pioneer was based mostly on environmental concerns and partly on the enormous costs. It did say Idaho Power needed new generating facilities, so it wasn't a complete defeat for the company. It was signed by all three commissioners, so it was not a partisan decision. And Lenaghen wasn't commission president then.

But Idaho Power and its friends were upset. The PUC came under microscopic legislative scrutiny. When Shurtliff resigned to become U.S. district attorney for Idaho, Andrus and, later, John Evans fought with the Idaho Senate over the new commissioner. Finally Conley Ward, a PUC staff attorney, was confirmed.

The big fight came in 1979, when Lenaghen was up for re-appointment. IPCo officials said they weren't out to "get" anybody; their friends, at least, certainly were. Jim Risch, who was majority leader and whose law firm did heavy business for Idaho Power, orchestrated much of the questioning. Emotions again built to a high pitch, and this time the Senate unseated Lenaghen.

Evans then made two of the shrewdest appointments of his career. He wanted independent souls who would not reverse the strides toward independence the PUC made in the seventies - and he got them. He called on Perry Swisher, then a Democrat (elected as such to the Idaho House in 1974) and working as night managing editor of the *Lewiston Morning Tribune*. Swisher was confirmed almost without debate by a Senate weary of bloodletting. To replace Wickberg, Evans named Republican Richard High, a Twin Falls farmer and former state senator as independent as Swisher. Ward, Swisher and High were one of the premier PUCs in the country, and both utilities and consumer groups worked with it smoothly. Ward and Swisher later were reappointed without much opposition.

Their political success lay in adroit and unpredictable moves. (Swisher liked to say in his early days on the commission that he didn't consider himself a consumer advocate, because he wasn't a fan of mass consumption.) They seemed to delight in solutions that were not compromises between utility Position A and opponent Position B, but a completely different Position C.

One early and controversial example was pay phone rates. The toll in 1979 was a dime. Mountain Bell wanted 20 cents; consumer groups opposed the increase. The PUC increased the rate to 25 cents, requiring Bell to provide new services and give customers a break in other areas. The state rumbled for days; newspapers hooted down the "two-bit" decision. But Bell was satisfied; it got most of what it wanted, while the new services helped rank the Idaho telephone system among the best in the nation. Early in the eighties the commissioners were regarded less as partisans in a utility-consumer war than as activist "social engineers."

Idaho Power began to lean for help on the Idaho Supreme Court, to which PUC decisions could be appealed. For a time in the early eighties the court became so deeply enmeshed in the PUC that Swisher went public with criticism, saying the court could not do the detailed study the PUC did and that it shouldn't try to become a "super-PUC." But the years of Democratic governors changed the court as it had on the PUC. By 1988 either Andrus or Evans had appointed every appellate judge in Idaho except Supreme Court Chief Justice Allan Shepard. The court seemed more likely in the late eighties to accept PUC reasoning.

Idaho Power was losing clout. It lacked the comfortable base on the PUC, the Supreme Court, among farmers, and in other quarters it once could take for granted.

Jim Bruce – *I don't think that Idaho Power is probably as powerful now as it might have been in past years, for several reasons. Number one, you take 20 to 30 years ago, Idaho Power Co. was probably the biggest business we had. Now you've got Albertson, you've got Hewlett-Packard, you've got Morrison-Knudsen, Boise-Cascade -*

J.R. Simplot, for example, has 7,500 employees. Idaho Power has less than 1,500. When you take in assets, because of the dams and power plants and things of that nature, Idaho Power Co. is probably the largest in terms of assets. But assets don't necessarily relate to power.[103]

Swan Falls

Even before the Pioneer decision, some people at Idaho Power realized they would have to keep relying heavily on hydropower.

In June 1976, three months before the Pioneer decision, Idaho Power's Bruce was handed a detailed interal memo on the "possibility of using the Swan Falls water right to stop upstream depletion of the Snake River." The possibility of doing that came up in the Pioneer debate. Now, this internal analysis of the legal issues concluded, "the Idaho Power Co.'s water rights for its Swan Falls plant cannot be used to prevent consumptive uses from depleting the flow of the Snake River above Swan Falls."

Or could they?

The next year, as Pioneer cooled off, 32 Idaho Power ratepayers filed a lawsuit to block future big power plants.

The state water plan, which governed flows of the Snake River, was nearing legislative approval. (It would be approved in 1978). The plan

---

[103] Fast-forward to 2009: Albertson, M-K, B-C and other top corporate players are gone or a shadow of their former selves. Idaho Power in some ways looms larger again. But Idaho watchers have been on the lookout for possible efforts from outsiders to buy the company once the last paperwork is done on the utility's Hells Canyon dam relicensing.

allowed drawing down the Snake to 3,300 cubic feet per second near Swan Falls Dam. The ratepayers said Idaho Power hadn't protected its water rights and that the failure squandered water and cost ratepayers money. (Swan Falls produced about 10.3 megawatts of juice, enough to power Eagle or Ketchum or Gooding.) In mid-summer 1977, in a drought season, water levels at the dam dipped to two-thirds of the plant's generating capacity. The 32 ratepayers said that meant Idaho Power had to buy more expensive out-of-state coal power than it should have. If IPCo had demanded its Swan Falls water, they said, rates would be lower. They insisted Idaho Power insist on its rights. But these ratepayers, many of them farmers, also had in mind a court ruling protecting their own water rights, and were confident they would get it.

Laird Noh, making his first race for the state Senate in 1978, was a friend of some of the key plaintiffs. "I used to go to lunch with them and say, But what if the decision [on that lawsuit] goes this way [in your favor]? And they would all say, there's no way in the world, no reasonable people could ever rule in that fashion, just don't waste your time worrying about it."

IPCo executives tried to get the complaint dismissed. Failing that, and realizing that not acting meant stockholders could hold the company legally liable, they did two things. First, they got the PUC to stop new electric hookups for irrigation; at a stroke, that froze farm expansion in southern Idaho. Second, IPCo sued to get the Fourth District Court to say its Swan Falls rights were not subordinated - that no one had rights superior to Idaho Power's – and the state water plan was a "taking" of rights.

District Judge Jesse Walters ruled Idaho Power subordinated at the Hells Canyon Dams in the early fifties (to curry favor with Len Jordan and the irrigators). He reasoned that the Snake and the dams on it were one system, and that when Idaho Power subordinated at the end of the system at Hells Canyon, it had agreed to subordinate the whole works. Since Idaho Power had agreed to all that, it could not argue that the state water plan took away its assets; the utility, Walters said, had already signed them away. His ruling was the conventional wisdom of the time.

But in November 1982 the Supreme Court overturned him in a unanimous decision that threw Idaho into turmoil. The supremes said that the federal Hells Canyon license referred to Hells Canyon as "one complete project," not Swan Falls or anything else. "We find therefore no intent to subordinate water rights at other projects," the court said. Idaho Power, the court said, had the right to 8,400 cubic feet per second at Swan Falls Dam (subject to some continuing court action on related issues).

"It came as a real shock to everyone," Noh recalled.

Now the moratorium on irrigation power hookups expanded to a third of the state: all of the Snake River drainage east of Swan Falls. State officials worried farmers might have to quit irrigating 200,000 acres to free enough water for IPCo's water rights. Hundreds of water permits issued since 1919 were at risk.

Early in 1983 IPCo President Jim Bruce warned that "if we ... don't file a suit to uphold the decision granted to us by the Supreme Court of the state of Idaho, I would have a serious question in my mind that we might be subject to a number of suits." That meant suing individual water right owners. In March 1983, IPCo did sue 7,500 of them. Farmers stared down the barrel of an Idaho Power lawsuit and no longer saw a friend on the other side. The area hardest hit was the Magic Valley, where irrigation came later than in the East and Southwest.

The shape of things took focus when Ken Dunn, director of the state Department of Water Resources, went on the road to explain Swan Falls in rural communities. If Idaho Power won, critics said, it could decide who and what could have water. Evans, scion of a ranching family, backed subordination, warning the Snake was Idaho's "jugular vein" and Idaho Power might clamp it.

Evans had an ally in Jim Jones, the attorney general elected in 1982. Jones was a protege and former staffer of Idaho Power's old friend, Len Jordan. But Jones came from a farm family and knew well that side of the picture.

Their point may have been put best in a letter by Kent Foster, a water law attorney and member of a Swan Falls task force Evans set up, written when he resigned from it at the end of 1983:

> *Whether there should be any future irrigation development in the Snake River basin is, of course, the underlying policy issue. We have invested a lot of time, expense and effort as a state to establish a constitutional and statutory mechanism for addressing such an issue. Our Idaho Water Resource Board spent several years going through the required procedures and did in fact formulate and implement a policy calling for future irrigation development in the Snake River basin until a minimum of 255,000 presently farmed acres receive supplemental water, 850,000 new acres are brought into production and flows at Murphy (near Swan Falls) dropped to 3,300 cubic feet per second. I am satisfied that this established policy is basically correct, but right or wrong it ought not to be, and I think legally cannot be, modified or revoked without at least the use of the constitutional and statutory mechanism which already exists.*

But there was another side. Idaho Power did not need all its water to keep Swan Falls at full steam. The year 1977 brought drought; July and August – the months the 32 ratepayers complained about – were its pits, and even then water levels did not fall drastically short. Not much of the water farmers had been using really needed be at risk. More to the point was water sought by new developers - and the water which would be used at the Hells Canyon dams, which produced four-fifths of IPCo power. Although water rights there technically were subordinated to irrigation and other use, in practice once water got past Swan Falls little was used for other purposes until it got to Hells

Canyon. The reality was that a water right at Swan Falls was almost the same as a water right at Hells Canyon. At moments that long-term impact seemed less important that the immediate situation, but precedent was highly valued in Idaho.

Legislators started questioning the precedent: if the Legislature erased Idaho Power's water rights, whose were next?

The most potent point, though, was again economic.

Idaho Power's rates would rise if it lost hydropower water, a prospect increasingly significant as more water was diverted for irrigation. A PUC study said customers could wind up paying $54 million above normal rate increases, or $200 per customer per year. That was especially poignant for farmers. Consumer groups said the higher rates would hurt senior citizens and others on fixed incomes; business groups said they would hurt the economy. Al Fothergill, executive director of the Idaho Citizens Coalition, argued that "the question is whether we want to irrigate more land at the expense of all power consumers in the Idaho Power service area."

The coalitions were bizarre. Idaho Power, which had fought so hard to go coal-fired, now defended cheaper hydro with all its might. The PUC was on its side. So were the conservation and consumer groups who so often fought the utility.

Many farmers bought their logic for a time. Jones recalled that when he traveled the Magic Valley and Eastern Idaho in 1983, "I had numerous people saying, 'You're cutting your throat politically, because you're not going to get anywhere on this'." Jones worked with the Committee of Nine and other farm groups and hammered subordination into the public's consciousness. He crusaded and made it a powerful political issue, frequently sniping at the utility and pushing hard-line subordination positions.

And in the next two years Southern Idaho public opinion changed in favor of subordination, and so against Idaho Power.

The first skirmish came in the 1983 legislative session. A thick stack of Swan Falls bills and resolutions was proposed, most of it aimed at subordinating. That session was the longest in Idaho history; Swan Falls was one reason.

But the votes weren't there. The anti-IPCo crowd got behind a bill that subordinated IPCo water, protected the utility from lawsuits for failure to protect water rights, and allowed anyone with a big investment in irrigation wells or equipment to file for a water right. Idaho Power's odd coalition barely prevailed. The Legislature passed an IPCo-backed plan allowing the state and utility to sign a contract protecting 5,000 water right holders, leaving the larger subordination question unsettled.

The contract, negotiated by Idaho Power and the Department of Water Resources, was released in July 1983. In return for immunity from lawsuits, water used by farmers and businesses was severely restricted.

The contract barely preceded a followup court case on whether Idaho Power had forfeited some of its water rights by not protecting them over the decades.

Jim Jones – *It was only after we were requested to do an attorney general's opinion on the legislation that was produced in 1983 – the bill that authorized the contract between the state and Idaho Power – that we started looking at it and really became quite concerned. [Deputy Attorney General] Pat Kole came in and said, "Lord, this litigation was handled very poorly" [by the state], the litigation that led to the 1982 decision. He said it looked like the power company was headed to another big victory, which essentially undercut the state's litigating position. So we started looking at it [the contract] and decided that somehow the thing was going to have to be stopped.*

We actually talked to some private counsel and suggested that maybe it would be a nice idea to bring a suit which would give us the ability to write the governor and say, well, this suit is pending, you better not sign the contract until the suit is taken care of. And we found accommodating counsel.

Reed Hansen, an Idaho Falls farmer on the Water Resources Board, later a legislator, warned Evans in October 1983 that "the contract will give the impression to the legislature and the general public that the problem is solved and the issue will no longer be of public concern, and will delay the tough decisions that must be made to provide for Idaho's future growth. I sincerely hope that a way can be found to delay or not sign so we can concentrate the public's attention on the main issue."

Idaho Power put on heat, too. A September 1983 letter signed by Senior Vice President Tom Spofford, mass-mailed to ratepayers, said that "if Gov. Evans signs the contract, your water right identified at the top of this letter will be protected and we will dismiss any challenge to that water right from our lawsuit. If the governor does not sign the contract, however, Idaho Power will have no choice but to proceed."

Evans killed the contract, hinting he would keep trying for subordination. IPCo officials said they were "very disappointed."

In the 1984 legislature, Evans, Jones, Senate Resource Committee Chairman Noh, and House Resources Chairman Vard Chatburn of Albion backed a new bill to "reinstate Idaho's long-standing policy of subordinating hydropower usage of water to consumptive uses for industry, agriculture and drinking."

So a range of industry and farm forces roared for subordination. "I never saw as many people come to a hearing as came when that legislation, subordination legislation, was here in the Legislature," Jones said. "Lord, they had busloads of people coming in from Aberdeen, American Falls, Idaho Falls. It really put the pressure on the Legislature."

Fothergill, arguing the water was needed to hydro production to keep power rates down, blasted back that if the subordination bill passed, "in a few years the dams will be sitting high and dry, monuments to folly and greed." The bill failed, foiled by energetic resistance led partly by Reps. Gordon Hollifield of Jerome and John Brooks of Gooding, both Idaho Power stalwarts.

Jim Jones – *We got wind that the power company was cranking up a few candidates [for the Legislature], and so we got a few candidates of our own. I talked my second cousin, Waldo Martens, into running against Gordon Hollifield. I called around trying to find a candidate and finally got hold of Waldo and twisted his arm a little bit, and he agreed to run. And Gary Robbins [of Dietrich] was running against Brooks ...*

We told Gary we'd give him any help possible; he had been a client of mine previous to that. We also gave a couple of incumbents a little surreptitious help. The guys that had hung in with us we tried to help, in sort of a targeted way. We couldn't help everybody. But with those that were friends in the Legislature. And those that were not, we targeted for trouble.

Jones and Idaho Power swapped public barbs, too, especially over a $115,000 Idaho Power advertising campaign decrying subordination – timed just before the primary election.

"I had a great big advertising campaign ready to go myself. I was going to call a press conference and announce it," Jones said. "he defendants in the suit [brought by Idaho Power] financed it, and it consisted of a bumper sticker which says, 'Support Idaho Power, Send a Kilowatt to California' ... We were going to get bumper stickers on every car in Idaho."

Brooks and Hollifield lost. Rep. Gene Winchester of Kuna won a tough primary campaign against another incumbent legislator who had opposed subordination. In fact, Idaho Power lost wherever Swan Falls was a key issue. Subordination also launched another legislator, Bruce Newcomb of Burley, elected to the House in 1986; in 1984 he was an organizer of a political action committee backing pro-subordination candidates.

The election probably was the most decisive political reversal Idaho Power ever had and undercut its bargaining strength. Idaho Power had come to the bargaining table early on; now it was eager to arrive at a settlement before it lost still more strength.

In the summer of 1984 Evans, Jones, and Bruce signed a 32-page compromise: Idaho Power would drop demands for 8,400 cubic feet per second and be guaranteed 3,900 in the summer and 5,600 from November 1 to March 31. The state agreed that the effect of new water permits on hydropower had to be considered. IPCo's lawsuit against water right holders would be dropped. Jones almost pulled out because of a provision saying Idaho Power could keep its water until the state issued permits for it, but returned to the fold when Rexburg attorney Rigby crafted a plan for putting IPCo water rights in trust by the state for the near term.

It was a complex settlement – so complex no one knew what it would do. The agreement seemed to lift most restraints on irrigation, but no one knew how much agriculture in Southern Idaho would grow. Two University of Idaho economists guesstimated 195,000 acres by the year 2000. Ken Robison, the conservationist publisher of the *Idaho Citizen*, said it could free water to irrigate 600,000 acres. A lot of the water rights situation would be hammered out in bits and pieces. A special Snake River water rights adjudication court was set up in Twin Falls and energetic young Judge Daniel Hurlbutt assigned to preside.

But there was a snag. The Federal Energy Regulatory Commission (FERC), successor to the Federal Power Commission, kept the issue on its calendar ... and kept it there. Evans and Jones asked the congressional delegation to step in. With Sen. McClure taking the lead in the Senate and Rep. Richard Stallings in the House – each in the majority party – a bill shoving the agreement down FERC's throat cleared Congress in mid-1986. It had the bad luck to be tied to another bill President Reagan disliked. A few days after Reagan stopped in Twin Falls to do a song and dance for Steve Symms, then running for re-election, he vetoed the bill.

When a new federal bill emerged in 1987 Jones was convinced a report attached to it could lead to a federal water grab. "The House language in the bill itself was designed to be ambiguous in certain areas: number one, what control FERC may have over the river, and number two, what the studies that were going to be conducted pursuant to the legislation would be used for," Jones said. "The committee report caused real problems, tipping the balance in favor of federal control."

McClure and Stallings agreed to revisions. The bill got through Congress in December 1987, and Reagan signed it.

It will shape the future of Idaho.

Idaho Power's clout was diminished, maybe permanently. The network of community leaders and the raw money stayed. But, as Noh said, before Swan Falls, "the legitimate political interests of the irrigators and agriculture and Idaho Power were one and the same. Now, they aren't always ... As the Swan Falls issue unfolded, we would find that Idaho Power employees had roles as secretaries or treasurers of agricultural or irrigation organizations, and suddenly they had to get out of those positions."

Swan Falls ended the era of the sodbuster, the new farmer who comes on to the desert, sprinkles water, and makes things grow. The farm lobby, weakened in part by low prices, was not as strong as it once was. Swan Falls may condemn it to continuing weakening. And the federal government's move out of reclamation, after decades as an eager dam-builder, is bound to change farmers' political attitudes.

Jack Peterson – *I think that the full result of that disinclination of the federal government to be the major player in reclamation and irrigation is that marginal farmers will cease to exist on irrigated land, because the subsidies they* *enjoyed are rapidly disappearing. Concomitant with the decline of the Bureau of Reclamation and the decline of interest in the federal government in opening new lands for reclamation has been the rise in power rates irrigators have had to pay ...*

When we opened some of these formerly dry lands to pressure irrigation up the big canyons of the Snake River, up 700 feet and back five to 10 miles, we added great pumping costs to agricultural costs. That was okay when electricity was 2.3 mills per kilowatt hour. Then it was three, and 3.4. I can remember when it went to four in the early seventies, and people were hollering. It's 23 and 24 now.

If crop prices and demand rise, pressure will grow to reopen the Swan Falls compact. If Idaho Power becomes more reliant on coal-fired power, raising rates, pressure will rise from the other direction. That could happen, too, if irrigated land increases little but need for power for more industries or homes increases more. Speculation in the mid-eighties was that, given a sluggish farm economy and hopes for bringing small businesses to the state and expanding existing ones, that will happen.[104]

Subject, as ever, to change ...

---

[104] And it has been changing, and the fallout is continuing well into the new millennium. The Snake River Basin Adjudication has become the largest lawsuit in Idaho history, affected people across 87 percent of the state's land mass, with more than 150,000 claims and endless large and complex legal issues. It has become a political football, returning for consideration back to the Idaho Legislature. At this writing, the case is on its fourth judge. For all that, this adjudication has been proceeding remarkably well, and could wind up toward the end of the first decade of this new century. (That may not sound especially speedy, but compared with adjudications in most other western states, it is.) Ridenbaugh Press has, since 1993, published the monthly *Snake River Basin Adjudication Digest.*

| Epilogue

In January 1988 a large man sat uneasily on a metal folding chair, back to the wall. He looked out a window into the gray sky from a meeting room on the fourth floor of the Idaho State Capitol. The other people who waited with him, also seated against the walls, tried not to pay too much attention to him

Larry Jackson was on trial today. His jury would be the Senate Local Government and Taxation Committee.

In the summer of 1987 Gov. Andrus had appointed him to a State Tax Commission seat that traditionally went to a Republican.

Jackson was a Republican. He was elected to the Legislature four times and ran for governor as a Republican, and he had been executive director of the state Republican Party.

Jackson was qualified. He had run a small business, worked as an executive for a large corporation, co-chaired the legislature's budget committee, and earned respect in each place. To top it off, he had been a respected major league baseball player.

But what Jackson had also done was openly support Democrat Cecil Andrus for governor in 1986. And therein lay problems.

The committee members walked in, one by one, some pausing to shake hands with Jackson. As they questioned him about his background and plans for the tax commission, and his support for Andrus, no one seemed angry. The proceedings stayed polite, perhaps because everyone knew the results were foreordained. The committee Republicans – th majority – votd to recommend Jackson be denied the commission job. And so it went on the Senate floor. Only two Republicans voted to support Jackson.

And so was fired the early warning flare that the 1988 session of the Idaho Legislative would not be like the 1987 session.

The Senate Republicans took a lot of heat for rejecting Jackson. In fact they had turned down a qualified and skilled appointee. But there were other truths too.

Andrus got everything he wanted out of the 1987 session. By demonstrating no successful opposition to him, the Legislature's Republicans had given no reason Andrus ought to be opposed at all. And Jackson's confirmation would show that Republicans who supported Andrus could do so with impunity. Republicans needed to draw a line in the sand - and where better than over a Republican who had supported Andrus for governor?

Every major event of the session to follow, and the political combat in Idaho in 1988, stemmed from that carefully-drawn line.

So Andrus got little from the Legislature that year. The Republicans turned thumbs down on all of Andrus' major tax and budget plans. Andrus, Senate pro tem Risch and House Speaker Boyd negotiated settlement after settlement in 1987; in 1988, Andrus and the Republican leaders barely spoke. One night Andrus vetoed two big education appropriations and went on live television to explain why; Risch and Boyd followed with a segment of their own.

This was part of the natural swing and sway of Idaho politics.

Idaho easily could tear itself apart. It doesn't because no one is allowed to get too uppity. In Idaho, a Mayor Daley would be tossed out of office. Too arrogant, too cocky, voters would say. Too capable of intruding on my homestead. Idahoans distrust winning streaks, in sports or in politics. In time, unless the politicians are very, very careful, the voters will snap them.

So the honeymoon Andrus enjoyed in 1987 had to end. Technically, the Legislature stuck it to him; but legislators tend to act, on the big issues, based on what they hear from back home.

Yet balance is ever-present, as the other high-wire act under the Capitol dome also discovered.

In the spring of 1988 Risch lined up with the primary opponent of fellow Republican Sen. Rachel Gilbert of Boise. Gilbert could be abrasive, but she was also smart and had a keen wit - and knew how to use it. She launched a ferocious counterattack aimed less at her opponent ("a nice young kid," she said) than at Risch. The pro tem, she suggested, was trying to quash independent thought in the Senate. Gilbert beat her opponent almost three to one. Risch, unopposed in the primary, got fewer votes than any other unopposed Republican running countywide.

He too was given bounds beyond which he ought not to tread.

In the nineties much may hinge on Idaho's two top politicians, Republican Sen. Jim McClure and Democratic Gov. Andrus.[105]

Andrus' third term expires after the 1990 election. But as of 1988, he appeared ready for another run, and in a strong position to keep his job. Idaho Democrats' problem is that as of 1988 no strong new Democrats were moving up the ranks behind him to step into his shoes in 1994. (His most probable successor, as of 1988, was Republican Lt. Gov. Butch Otter.) Developing a second tier of talent will be the Democrats' biggest challenge.

The Republicans, on the other hand, have in McClure a bottleneck. A herd of ambitious elephants are eager to follow him into the Senate. If McClure, who will be 66 at the end of 1990, young enough to serve another term, runs again, he would win big again. Just as important, for the long haul, much of the Republicans' top talent will be

[105] Less, though, than I thought in 1988. McClure decided to retire in 1990, and that Senate spot went (for the next 18 years) to Republican (then-Representative) Larry Craig. McClure has spent much of his time since in Idaho, but his direct involvement in the state's politics has been limited. You could say (reasonably) that McClure played a big role in laying groundwork for the conservative Republican dominance that would follow him. But what then to say about Andrus, who was re-elected in 1990 and a leading figure in the state early in the decade, but who retired from office in 1994 at the same time his party crashed to the ground all around him?

frustrated, and some may get out of politics. McClure's retirement would – as Len Jordan's did in 1972 – inspire a complicated, crowded and expensive race. It could turn into a pivotal year.

But Idaho politics will always go where voters want it to ...
Which is?

Well, demographics favor the Republicans. With the union vote in decline, the number of small farmers (who would be the most likely Democratic converts) shrinking, much of the traditional Democratic base will continue to slip. Meanwhile, the numbers of small businesses and of conservative Mormons will grow. The only long-term signs of demographic hope for Democrats lie in isolated areas, notably Bonneville, Ada and Canyon Counties, where larger manufacturing or other companies may bring in more workers with Democratic backgrounds from out of state.

But cycles favor the Democrats. Republicans had a time of enormous power in the Reagan eighties, and Idahoans rebel against absolutes. Emerging from that period, more Idaho votes may be up for grabs than at any time since the Watergate era of the mid-seventies, or since the early sixties.

A lot will depend on national economic trends and national political leadership.

But more will depend on what those iconoclastic Idahoans decide to do about it.[106]

---

[106] Wishy-washy, but from the standpoint of mid-1988, reasonable. That year would be – for a presidential year – not bad for Idaho Democrats; they would pick up legislative seats. Two years later, in 1990, they would do very well indeed, winning a string of statewide offices and half the congressional delegation (which they had not had since 1966) and drawing to a tie in the Idaho Senate (broken for the Republicans by Lieutenant Governor C.L. "Butch" Otter), their best legislative showing since 1958. Republicans were in disarray. But the tide turned in a big way in 1992, throwing lots of Democrats out of office, and in 1994 the party was decimated, brought down to levels not seen since the 1920s. And, with a handful of asterisks, that is where matters have stayed to the time of this writing (2009). The story of Idaho politics in the years since Paradox was published is radically different from the story of the decades preceding. Sounds like the subject for another book ... albeit a book of a different sort.

Appendix | The Winners

1890 House/At Large - Willis Sweet (R) 55.8% Governor - George L. Shoup (R) 56.3% Legislature - Senate 18/House 36 (Party affiliation not provided)

1892 President - James B. Weaver (Populist) 54.2% House/At Large - Willis Sweet (R) 44.1% Governor - William J. McConnell (R) 40.7% Legislature - Senate 18/House 36 (Party affiliation not provided)

1894 House/At Large - Edgar Wilson (R) 43.4% Governor - William J. McConnell (R) 41.5% Legislature - Senate: 10 R, 2 D, 5 Populists, 1 Independent/House: 25 R, 1 D, 8 Populists, 1 Independent

1896 President - William Jennings Bryant (D) 78.1% House/At Large - James Gunn (People's Democratic) 46.5% Governor - Frank Steunenberg (D, SilverR) 79.8% Legislature - Senate: 7 R, 7 D, 7 Populists/House: 17 R, 15 D, 16 Populists

1898 House/At Large - Edgar Wilson (D, SilverR) 45.3% Governor - Frank Steunenberg (D, SilverR) 48.8% Legislature - Senate: 9 R, 3 D, 7 Fusion Party, 2 Populists/House: 14 D, 12 R, 17 Fusion Party, 6 Populists

1900 President - William Jennings Bryant (D) 51% House/At Large - Thomas Glenn (D-Pop-SilverR) 51.1% Governor - Frank Hunt (D-SilverR) 50.8% Legislature - Senate: 10 D, 7 R, 3 Populists, 1 SilverR/House: 20 R, 16 D, 7 SilverR, 6 Populists

1902 House/At Large - Burton French (R) 54.3% Governor - John Morrison (R) 52.9% Legislature - Senate: 14 R, 6 D, 1 ind/House: 35 R, 11 D

1904 President - Theodore Roosevelt (R) 65.8% House/At Large - Burton French (R) 63.9% Governor - Frank Gooding (R) 58.8% Legislature - Senate: 19 R, 2 D/House: 48 R, 2 D

1906 House/At Large - Burton French (R) 58.6% Governor - Frank Gooding (R) 52.2% Legislature - Senate: 15 R, 6 D/House: 38 R, 12 D, 1 ind

1908 President - William Taft (R) 54% House/At Large - Thomas Hamer (R) 52.6% Governor - James Brady (R) 49.6% Legislature - Senate: 13 R, 10 D/House: 44 R, 9 D

1910 House/At Large - Burton French (R) 55.4% Governor - James Hawley (D) 47.4% Legislature - Senate: 14 R, 9 D/House: 35 R, 24 D

1912 President - Woodrow Wilson (D) 32.1% House/At Large - Burton French (R) 27.4% House/At Large - Addison Smith (R) 22.4% Governor - John Haines (R) 33.2% Legislature - Senate: 21 R, 3 D/House: 56 R, 4 D

1914 Senator - James H. Brady (R) 43.9% House/At Large - Robert McCracken (R) 21.9% House/At Large - Addison Smith (R) 22.6% Governor - Moses Alexander (D) 44.1% Legislature - Senate: 19 R, 11 D, 2 Pr, 1 Soc/House: 32 R, 28 D, 1 Pr

1916 President - Woodrow Wilson (D) 52% House/At Large - Burton French (R) 25.4% House/At Large - Addison Smith (R) 25% Governor - Moses Alexander (D) 47.5% Legislature - Senate: 21 R, 16 D/House: 36 D, 29 R

1918 Senator - John Nugent (D) 50.5% House/1st District - Burton French (R) 63.3% House/2nd District - Addison Smith (R) 63.2% Governor - D.W. Davis (R) 59.9% Legislature - Senate: 29 R, 12 D/House: 46 R, 18 D

1920 President - Warren Harding (R) 65.6% Senator - Frank Gooding (R) 54% House/1st District - Burton French (R) 59.3% House/2nd District - Addison Smith (R) 63% Governor - D.W. Davis (R) 53% Legislature - Senate: 39 R, 5 D/House: 51 R, 3 D

1922 House/1st District - Burton French (R) 46.8% House/2nd District - Addison Smith (R) 47.8% Governor - Charles C. Moore (R) 39.5% Legislature - Senate: 25 R, 14 D, 5 Pr/House: 37 R, 22 D, 6 Pr

1924 President - Calvin Coolidge (R) 47.3% Senator - William E. Borah (R) 79.5% House/1st District - Burton French (R) 61.8% House/2nd District - Addison Smith (R) 54.6% Governor - Charles C. Moore (R) 43.9% Legislature - Senate: 32 R, 5 D, 7 Pr/House: 45 R, 5 D, 12 Pr

1926 Senator - Frank Gooding (R) 45.4% House/1st District - Burton French (R) 66.3% House/2nd District - Addison Smith (R) 60.6% Governor - H.C. Baldridge (R) 50.2% Legislature - Senate: 29 R, 11 D, 4 Pr/House: 52 R, 7 D, 8 Prog, 1 ind

1928 President - Herbert Hoover (R) 64.2% Senator - John Thomas (R) 62.6% House/1st District - Burton French (R) 68.9% House/2nd District - Addison Smith (R) 64.1% Governor - H.C. Baldridge (R) 57.8% Legislature - Senate: 31 R, 12 D, 1 ind/House: 50 R, 9 D

1930 Senator - William E. Borah (R) 72.4% House/1st District - Burton French (R) 64.9% House/2nd District - Addison Smith (R) 63.2% Governor - C. Ben Ross (D) 56% Legislature - Senate: 23 R, 21 D/House: 43 R, 27 D

1932 President - Franklin D. Roosevelt (D) 58.7% Senator - James P. Pope (D) 55.6% House/1st District - Compton White (D) 54.9% House/2nd District - Thomas Coffin (D) 55% Governor - C. Ben Ross (D) 61.7% Legislature - Senate: 35 D, 9 R/House: 59 D, 4 R

1934 House/1st District - Compton White (D) 61.9% House/2nd District - D. Worth Clark (D) 60.5% Governor - C. Ben Ross (D) 54.6% Legislature - Senate: 36 D, 8 R/House: 53 D, 6 R

1936 President - Franklin D. Roosevelt (D) 62.9% Senator - William E. Borah (R) 63.4% House/1st District - Compton White (D) 70.2% House/2nd District - D. Worth Clark (D) 60.5% Governor - Barzilla Clark (D) 57.2% Legislature - Senate: 33 D, 11 R/House: 50 D, 9 R

1938 Senator - D. Worth Clark (D) 54.7% House/1st District - Compton White (D) 62.8% House/2nd District - Henry Dworshak (R) 53.6% Governor - C.A. Bottolfsen (R) 57.3% Legislature - Senate: 27 R, 17 D/House: 39 R, 20 D

1940 President - Franklin D. Roosevelt (D) 54.4% Senator (2 yr) - John Thomas (R) 53% House/1st District - Compton White (D) 62% House/2nd District - Henry Dworshak (R) 53.1% Governor - Chase Clark (D) 50.5% Legislature - Senate: 23 D, 21 R/House: 38 D, 26 R

1942 Senator - John Thomas (R) 51.5% House/1st District - Compton White (D) 54.1% House/2nd District - Henry Dworshak (R) 54.8% Governor - C.A. Bottolfsen (R) 50.1% Legislature - Senate: 31 R, 13 D/House: 32 R, 27 D

1944 President - Franklin D. Roosevelt (D) 51.6% Senator - Glen Taylor (D) 51.1% House/1st District - Compton White (D) 56.6% House/2nd District - Henry Dworshak (R) 52.3% Governor - Charles Gossett (D) 52.6% Legislature - Senate: 24 R, 20 D/House: 30 R, 29 D

1946 Senator (2 yr) - Henry Dworshak (R) 58.6% House/1st District - Abe McGregor Goff (R) 50.6% House/2nd District - John Sanborn (R) 60.7% Governor - C.A. Robins (R) 56.4% Legislature - Senate: 31 R, 13 D/House: 42 R, 17 D

1948 President - Harry Truman (D) 50% Senator - Bert Miller (D) 50% House/1st District - Compton White (D) 51.7% House/2nd District - John Sanborn (R) 50.7% Legislature - Senate: 24 D, 20 R/House: 35 R, 24 D

1950 Senator (6 yr) - Herman Welker (R) 61.7% Senator (4 yr) - Henry Dworshak (R) 51.9% House/1st District - John T. Wood (R) 50.5% House/2nd District - Hamer Budge (R) 57.1% Governor - Len Jordan (R) 52.6% Legislature - Senate: 29 R, 15 D/House: 36 R, 23 D

1952 President - Dwight Eisenhower (R) 65.4% House/1st District - Gracie Pfost (D) 50.3% House/2nd District - Hamer Budge (R) 66.2% Legislature - Senate: 33 R, 11 D/House: 45 R, 14 D

1954 Senator - Henry Dworshak (R) 62.8% House/1st District - Gracie Pfost (D) 54.9% House/2nd District - Hamer Budge (R) 60.8% Governor - Robert Smylie (R) 54.2% Legislature - Senate: 24 R, 20 D/House: 36 R, 23 D

1956 President - Dwight Eisenhower (R) 61.2% Senator - Frank Church (D) 56.2% House/1st District - Gracie Pfost (D) 55.1% House/2nd District - Hamer Budge (R) 60% Legislature - Senate: 19 R, 25 D/House: 32 R, 27 D

1958 House/1st District - Gracie Pfost (D) 62.4% House/2nd District - Hamer Budge (R) 55% Governor - Robert Smylie (R) 51% Legislature - Senate: 27 D, 17 R/House: 35 D, 24 R

1960 President - Richard Nixon (R) 53.8% Senator - Henry Dworshak (R) 52.3% House/1st District - Gracie Pfost (D) 60.4% House/2nd District - Ralph Harding (D) 51.1% Legislature - Senate: 23 R, 21 D/House: 31 R, 28 D

1962 Senator (6 yr) - Frank Church (D) 54.7% Senator (4 yr) - Len Jordan (R) 50.1% House/1st District - Compton White, Jr. (D) 53% House/2nd District - Ralph Harding (D) 52.8% Governor - Robert Smylie (R) 54.6% Legislature - Senate: 23 R, 21 D/House: 34 R, 29 D

1964 President - Lyndon Johnson (D) 50.9% House/1st District - Compton White, Jr. (D) 51.7% House/2nd District - George Hansen (R) 52.2% Legislature - Senate: 25 R, 19 D/House: 42 R, 37 D

1966 Senator - Len Jordan (R) 55.4% House/1st District - James McClure (R) 51.8% House/2nd District - George Hansen (R) 70.3% Governor - Don Samuelson (R) 41.4% Legislature - Senate: 22 R, 13 D/House: 38 R, 32 D

1968 President - Richard Nixon (R) 56.8% Senator - Frank Church (D) 60.3% House/1st District - James McClure (R) 59.4% House/2nd District - Orval Hansen (R) 52.6% Legislature - Senate: 20 R, 15 D/House: 38 R, 32 D

1970 House/1st District - James McClure (R) 58.2% House/2nd District - Orval Hansen (R) 65.7% Governor - Cecil Andrus (D) 52.2% Legislature - Senate: 19 R, 16 D/House: 41 R, 29 D

1972 President - Richard Nixon (R) 64.2% Senator - James McClure (R) 52.3% House/1st District - Steve Symms (R) 55.6% House/2nd District - Orval Hansen (R) 69.2% Legislature - Senate: 23 R, 12 D/House: 51 R, 19 D

1974 Senator - Frank Church (D) 56.1% House/1st District - Steve Symms (R) 58.3% House/2nd District - George Hansen (R) 55.7% Governor - Cecil Andrus (D) 70.9% Legislature - Senate: 21 R, 14 D/House: 43 R, 27 D

1976 President - Gerald Ford (R) 60% House/1st District - Steve Symms (R) 54.6% House/2nd District - George Hansen (R) 50.6% Legislature - Senate: 20 R, 15 D/House: 48 R, 22 D

1978 Senator - James McClure (R) 68.4% House/1st District - Steve Symms (R) 59.9% House/2nd District - George Hansen (R) 57.3% Governor - John Evans (D) 58.8% Legislature - Senate: 19 R, 16 D/House: 50 R, 20 D

1980 President - Ronald Reagan (R) 66.5% Senator - Steve Symms (R) 49.7% House/1st District - Larry Craig (R) 53.7% House/2nd District - George Hansen (R) 58.8% Legislature - Senate: 23 R, 12 D/House: 56 R, 14 D

1982 House/1st District - Larry Craig (R) 53.7% House/2nd District - George Hansen (R) 52.3% Governor - John Evans (D) 50.6% Legislature - Senate: 21 R, 14 D/House: 51 R, 19 D

1984 President - Ronald Reagan (R) 72.4% Senator - James McClure (R) 72.2% House/1st District - Larry Craig (R) 68.6% House/2nd District - Richard Stallings (D) 50.0% Legislature - Senate: 28 R, 14 D/House: 67 R, 17 D

1986 Senator - Steve Symms (R) 51.6% House/1st District - Larry Craig (R) 65.3% House/2nd District - Richard Stallings (D) 54.3% Governor - Cecil Andrus (D) 49.9% Legislature - Senate: 26 R, 16 D/House: 64 R, 20 D

1988 House/1st District - Larry Craig (R) 65% House/2nd District - Richard Stallings (D) 63% Legislature - Senate: 23 R, 19 D/House: 64 R, 20 D

| Notes

The biennial Idaho Blue Books, 1969-70 to 1987-88, are fine general-purpose sources, as were the 1963 and 1977 Idaho Almanacs.

The Frank Church and Len Jordan Senate papers are kept at the special collections section of Boise State University Library; indexing still was underway in 1988. The papers of Govs. Williams, Robins, Jordan, Smylie, Samuelson, Andrus and Evans are in the archives of the Idaho Historical Society, based in the state historical library in Boise. Many thanks are due both staffs.

Sources on elections included Blue Books, records in Idaho's secretary of state office, and Idaho Voting Trends (1975), the massive study of votes for Idaho statewide and congressional offices, 1890-1974, developed by Boyd Martin of the University of Idaho's Bureau of Public Affairs Research and Idaho Research Foundation. Results of the 1976 Pioneer Power vote and 1985 and 1986 Ada County Rural Free Library District votes came from the Idaho Statesman. One fine analysis of vote patterns was a doctoral thesis, "Voting Behavior in Idaho 1950-62, A Study of Party Predisposition at the Precinct Level," by Herman Damien Leilehua Lujan (1964), University of Idaho.

Population figures come from the Blue Books and Almanacs.

Names and dates for key interviews are in "Acknowledgements."

BIBLIOGRAPHY

Barrett, Glen. *Idaho Banking, 1863-1976.* Boise State University Press, Boise. 1976.

Barrett, Glen. J. Lynn Driscoll, *Western Banker.* 1974.

Church, F. Forrester. *Father and Son.* Harper and Row, New York, 1985. Reminiscence of a son's life with Frank Church.

Conley, Cort. *Idaho for the Curious.* Backeddy Books, Cambridge, Idaho. 1982. Idaho guidebook.

David L. Crowder. Rexburg, Idaho, *the First 100 Years.* (no publisher indicated) 1983.

Davis, L.J. *Bad Money.* St. Martin's Press, New York. 1982.

Ghazanfar, S.M. *Idaho Statistical Abstract,* Third Edition. University of Idaho. 1980.

Hansen, George, and Anderson, Larrey. *To Harrass Our People.* Positive Publications, Washington, D.C. 1980.

Hyman, Sidney. *Challenge and Response, the First Security Corporation, First 50 Years.* First Security Foundation/University of Utah, Salt Lake City. 1978.

Johnson, Claudius O. *Borah of Idaho.* Longmans, Green & Co., New York. 1936. An early biography of Sen. William Borah.

Jordan, Grace. *The Unintentional Senator.* Syms York Co., Boise, Idaho. 1972.

Lamm, Richard D., and McCarthy, Michael. *The Angry West, a Vulnerable Land and Its Future.* Houghton Mifflin Co., Boston. 1982

Malone, Michael. *C. Ben Ross and the New Deal in Idaho.* University of Washington Press, Seattle. 1970.

McKenna, Marian C. *Borah.* The University of Michigan Press, Ann Arbor. 1971. A revisionist look at the senator.

Newquist, Jerreld. *Prophets, Principles and National Survival.* Publishers Press, Salt Lake City. 1964. Quotes on Mormon doctrine.

Peirce, Neal. *The Mountain States of America, People, Power and Politics in the Eight Rocky Mountain States.* W.W. Norton & Co., New York. 1972.

Petersen, Keith. *Company Town: Potlatch, Idaho, and the Potlatch Lumber Co.* Washington State University Press, Pullman, Wash. 1987.

Peterson, Ross. *Prophet Without Honor.* University Press of Kentucky, Lexington, Ky. 1974. Biography of Glen Taylor.

Reeves, Thomas C. *The Life and Times of Joe McCarthy.* Stein & Day, New York. 1982.

Taylor, Glen. *The Way It Was With Me.* Lyle Stuart, Inc. Secaucus, N.J. 1979. Autobiography.

Young, George, and Cochrane, Frederic. *Hydro Era, the Story of Idaho Power Company.* Idaho Power Co, Boise. 1978.

CHAPTER ONE/Combatants

AT THE RESORT - Articles, in *Idaho Statesman* Nov. 10, 11, 1986; "Risch Expects," Stapilus in *Statesman*, Nov. 8, 1986.

RISCH'S BACKGROUND - Interview: Risch. Campaign biographies. Letter, Don Samuelson to Risch, Aug. 28, 1970; reply, Risch to Samuelson, Sept. 10, 1970, both from Samuelson papers. Article, "Risch ... Reputation," Charles Etlinger in *Idaho Statesman*, Jan. 27, 1983.

1982 "COUP" - Interviews: Risch, Budge (in 1983 and 1984). Article, "Risch Unseats," Stapilus in *Idaho State Journal*, Dec. 2, 1982.

ANDRUS IN OROFINO - Interviews: Andrus, McLaughlin, Inscore. Articles, *Intermountain Observer*, Jan. 2, 1971; *Clearwater Tribune*, April 14, 1960.

SEN. ANDRUS - Interviews: Andrus, Ravenscroft. Articles, "Making of a Governor," Sam Day in *Intermountain Observer*, Jan. 2, 1971; "If Carter Picks Andrus," David Morrissey in *Idaho State Journal*, Dec. 14, 1976.

ANDRUS LATER - Column, "Is Cecil, Cecil?" Steve Ahrens in *Idaho Statesman*, Nov. 27, 1977.

TOUR/The North Country

THE PANHANDLE - Interviews: Leroy, Tucker, Goller, Hawkins, Magnuson, Swisher, Drummond, Reed, Stacy, Jack Peterson, Smylie.

LATAH COUNTY - Interviews: Hall, Inscore, Andrus.

LEWISTON - Interviews: Hall, Andrus, Swisher.

CAMAS PLAIN - Article, "Idaho County," Kathy Hedberg in *Lewiston Morning Tribune*, Dec. 1, 1986.

CHAPTER TWO/Wild Lands

HARRIMAN PARK OFFER - Interview: Smylie. Column, "Harriman Park," Smylie in *Idaho Statesman*, Sept. 7, 1986. Articles, "Railroad Ranch," *Ashton Herald*, Dec. 28, 1961; "Governor Hints," Statesman, Dec. 6, 1961; "Harriman Land," Jerry Gilliland in *Idaho Statesman*, Dec. 2, 1976.

PARKS BEFORE 1965 - Idaho...Curious, Conley. Undated memo, "Parks," Smylie papers. Smylie campaign report (undated). Letter, James Donart to Frank Church, Jan. 14, 1963, Church papers.

CHURCH AND HELL'S CANYON - Articles, "Battle of the River," Sam Day in *Intermountain Observer*, Aug. 23, 1969; "Congressional Infighting," Chris Carlson-Robert Smith, in *Observer*, July 3, 1971; "Hell's Canyon," John Simonds in *Idaho Statesman*, Sept. 27, 1974. Letter to members, Hell's Canyon Preservation Council, Inc., Richard Farman, President, Aug. 17, 1973.

1962 HEARINGS - *Idaho Statistical Abstract*, 3rd Edition (1980), on land use. Campaign booklet, "Frank Church Story," Volunteers for Church Committee, 1962, Church papers. Column, Corlett in *Idaho Statesman*, Nov. 2, 5, 1961. Dispatch, Associated Press, on wilderness, Earle Jester, Nov. 5, 1961. Articles, *Idaho Statesman*, Nov. 9, 11, 12, 17, 26, 1961.

WHITE CLOUDS - Interviews: Andrus, Samuelson, Ravenscroft. Articles, "Silent Mountain Peak," *Intermountain Observer*, Dec. 27, 1969; "Whose Wilderness?," Donald Jackson in *Life* magazine, Jan. 9, 1970. Cut-out labels, Samuelson papers. Paper by state Inspector of Mines, O.T. Hansen, "White Clouds," October 1970, Samuelson papers. Form response and letter to Mr. and Mrs. James E. Brown, Sept. 15, 1970, Samuelson papers. Letter, McClure to Hartzog, Oct. 15, 1970, Samuelson papers. TV ad script, Circuit & Eddington Inc., Salt Lake City, Samuelson papers.

CHAPTER THREE/Sagebrush Rebels

RAVENSCROFT - Interview: Ravenscroft. Article, "Ravenscroft," Steve Ahrens in *Idaho Statesman*, May 29, 1978.

FARM COMMUNITY AND CATTLEMEN - Interviews: Ravenscroft, Jack Peterson, Lundberg. Address, "Visions of the Future," Jack Peterson, Snake River Regional Study Center, College of Idaho, and Idaho Department of Water Resources, Boise, March 26, 1986.

FEDS AND THE LAND - Interviews: Egbert, Hendricks. Letter, Burns to Evans, Oct. 1, 1984.

SODA SPRINGS MEETING - The author attended the 1978 meeting.

SAGEBRUSH REBELLION - Interviews: Ravenscroft, Burke, Jack Peterson. Idaho for Church brochure, 1980, "Quality of Life," Church papers.

PAYETTE COUNTY - Interview: Smylie. 1950, 1954, 1956 and 1960 editions, *Payette Independent-Enterprise.*

MCCLURE - Interviews: Goller, Loveland. Articles, *Idaho Observer.*

TOUR/The Southwest Valleys
RIGGINS - "Riggins," Kathy Hedberg in *Lewiston Morning Tribune*, May 2, 1983.

PAYETTE - Interview: Smylie.

CANYON COUNTY - Interviews: Batt, Goller.

OWYHEE COUNTY - Interview: Yarbrough. Promotional brochures.

BOISE - Interviews: Goller, Williams, Decker. Letter, Richard Bauer to Ravenscroft, March 29, 1977, state Republican papers.

CHAPTER FOUR/Use it and/or ...
PLANNING - Interview: Andrus.

PLANNING IN ADA COUNTY - Interview: Risch. Article, "Crowd of 200," David Zarkin in *Idaho Statesman*, July 7, 1967.

COEUR D'ALENE - Interviews: Stacy, Reed. Article, "Coeur d'Alene's Endangered Beaches," Stacy in *Intermountain Observer*, Sept. 2, 1972.

CHAPTER FIVE/ Democrats: Boom and Bust
SLOTS IN IDAHO - Interviews: Smylie, Egbert, Evans, Schweibert, Chance, Williams. Article, "Gaming Issue," Ken Robison for the Associated Press, in *Idaho State Journal*, Sept. 17, 1962.

ANTI-GAMBLING LEGISLATION - Interview: Smylie, Schweibert, Swisher, Walker. Master's thesis, Mike W. Hatch, "Extremism in Idaho Politics," University of Utah at Ogden, August 1966.

DERR RUNS - Interviews: Ravenscroft, Samuelson, Williams, Max Hanson. Letter, Delbert G. Taylor to Robert Smylie, Oct. 8, 1958, Smylie papers. Memo, John Martin to "the governor, congressional delegation, officers of the state central committee and state candidates," July 15, 1958, Smylie papers. Hatch's thesis. Letter, Evan Kackley to Smylie, Aug. 14, 1958, Smylie papers. Campaign flyers: John Glasby, Max Hanson.

SMITH RUNS - Letter, Schweibert to Dworshak, June 17, 1962, Jordan papers. Memorandum to Vice President, from Frank Church, Oct. 8, 1962, Church papers.

ROSS - Interviews: Corlett, Williams, Egbert. Ross, Malone. Article, "Storm Warnings," Walter Davenport in *Collier's* magazine, April 4, 1936.

JAMES POPE - Article, "James P. Pope," Robert Sims, in *Idaho Yesterdays*, Fall 1971.

CLARK FAMILY - Interviews: Corlett, Egbert. Malone on Ross. Official biographies of Barzilla and Chase Clark, Idaho Historical Society. Articles, "Clark and the Japanese-American Relocation," Robert C. Sims in *Pacific Northwest Quarterly*, April 1979; Steve Crump in *Idaho State Journal* "Enjoy," Oct. 25, 1974; "Clark's Life," Bob Lorimer in *Idaho Statesman*, Dec. 31, 1966. Column, Corlett, "Clark for Judge," in *Idaho Statesman*, February 1943.

TAYLOR - Interviews: Corlett, Swisher, Goller, Inscore. Peterson, "Prophet." Taylor's autobiography. Article, "Coulter Overcomes," Ernest Hood in *Idaho Statesman*, Aug. 29, 1942. Ads, Taylor in *Idaho Statesman*, Aug. 6, 1950; Taylor's backers in *Idaho Statesman*, Aug. 8, 1950.

TOM BOISE - Interviews: Andrus, Corlett, Porter, Burke, White, Inscore, Williams, Egbert, Martin Peterson, Reid, Smylie, Ravenscroft, Greenfield. Obituary, *Lewiston Morning Tribune*, Oct. 10, 1966.

GRACIE PFOST - Interview: Schweibert, White. Article, "Hell's Belle," Sam Day in *Intermountain Observer*, May 5, 1973.

TAYLOR IN 1954 AND 1956 - Prophet, Peterson; Taylor autobiography.

CHURCH'S BACKGROUND - Interviews: Burke, Greenfield, Inscore, Hawkins. Ad, "Are You Sick of Smears?," in *Idaho Statesman*, Nov. 4, 1956. Campaign finances in letter, Church to Maurice Rosenblatt, National Committee for an Effective Congress, Nov. 24, 1956, in Church papers. Father, Forrester Church.

MOUNTAIN HOME PRECINCT - Interviews: Swisher, Corlett, former Sen. Albert Gore, Sr. (December 1987). Taylor's autobiography.

IDAHO LIBERALS - Interviews: Schweibert, Ravenscroft, White. Article, "What is a 'Liberal?'," Church in *U.S. News and World Report*, May 6, 1963.

CHAPTER SIX/ Republicans: Sorcerers' apprentices
THE BOY AND BORAH - Church at a Borah Foundation lecture, University of Idaho, March 1964; text in *Idaho Yesterdays*, Summer 1964.

BORAH - Interview: Williams. "Borah the Statesman," Church speech. Article, "William E. Borah, Political Thespian," John Milton Cooper, Jr., *Pacific Northwest Quarterly*, October 1965.

SUPPORT FOR WHEELER - William Hutchinson, International News Service, a friend of Borah, wrote of his politics in News Articles on the Life and Works of Honorable William E. Borah, printed by the U.S. government, 1940. "Hoover statement" from Church's Borah speech.

GOODING - Obituary, June 25, 1928, in *Idaho Statesman*. Editorial, the *Idaho Statesman*, June 26, 1928. Ross, Malone.

LLOYD ADAMS - Interviews: Porter, Corlett, Smylie, Swisher, Egbert, Ricks. Article, "W. Lloyd Adams," by then-Idaho State University President William "Bud" Davis, in *Idaho Yesterdays*, summer 1968.

JOHN THOMAS - *Idaho Banking*, Barrett, and Challenge, Hyman.

BERT MILLER - Article, "Glen Taylor," Richard Neuberger in *Collier's*, May 20, 1950.

GOSSETT AND ADAMS - Interviews: Corlett, Porter, Swisher. Article, "Kingmaker," Davis; articles, editorials in *Idaho Statesman*, November 1945.

HERMAN WELKER - Interviews: Corlett, Hendricks. Dispatch, on Bing Crosby, Associated Press, Aug. 6, 1950. "Weakling" line, in *Idaho Statesman*, Aug. 2. Column, John Corlett in *Idaho Statesman*, Nov. 9, 1950. Reeves, "McCarthy." Taylor autobiography. *Time* magazine, July 13, 1953. Dworshak on McCarthy, in *U.S. News and World Report*, June 4, 1954.

JOHN WOOD - Interviews: Schweibert, Corlett, Smylie. Articles, *Coeur d'Alene Press*, Oct. 16, 18 and 28 and Nov. 6, 1950, obituary Nov. 2, 1954. Paper, "Building Socialism in One City," Stanley Phipps, excerpted in Museum of Northern Idaho newsletter, winter 1986. Columns, John Wood, Mondays in the Press 1953-54; his last (Oct. 4, 1954) said the U.S. entered World War II not because of foreign aggression but because of American interventionists. Associated Press dispatches, Oct. 26, 1952. Column, Corlett in *Idaho Statesman*, Nov. 9, 1952. "Doc Quack" quote from editorial in *Boise Bench Journal*, Oct. 31, 1952.

ROBINS ADMINISTRATION - Interviews: Shadduck, Smylie, Corlett, Swisher. Article, Smylie in *Intermountain Observer*, Sept. 26, 1970.

JORDAN ADMINISTRATION - Interviews: Corlett, Evans, Swisher. Article, "Twilight," Sam Day in *Intermountain Observer*, Jan. 1, 1972.

1954 PRIMARY ELECTION - Interviews: Smylie, George Hansen. Columns by Corlett in *Idaho Statesman*, Aug. 2 and 3, 1954.

SMYLIE ADMINISTRATION - Interviews: Smylie, Loveland, Swisher.

SUCCESSION/LCSC DEAL - Interviews: Porter, Hall, Swisher.

HAMER BUDGE - Interviews: Hendricks, Goller, Corlett, Smylie. Letter, Frank Church to Ralph Harding, Aug. 29, 1960, in Church papers. Column, Drew Pearson, "Know the Crowd" (in *Washington Post*), Oct. 16, 1960.

CHURCH AND BIRCH - Interviews: George Hansen, Shepard. Articles, "Mormons," Stapilus in *Lewiston Morning Tribune*, Sept. 17, 1978; *Idaho State Journal*, "John Birch Society," Nov. 1, 1963. Master's thesis, "Extremism," Hatch, University of Utah, 1966. *Congressional Record*, Sept. 25, 1963, speech by Ralph Harding, with quoted material. Letters, Ezra Taft Benson to Jordan, April 13, 1964, in the Jordan papers; Joseph Fielding Smith, LDS Council of the Twelve, to Ralph Harding, Dec. 23, 1963.

GEORGE HANSEN - Interviews: George Hansen, Hendricks, Egbert, Corlett. Author attended Pocatello homecoming Oct. 17, 1987.

REPLACING DWORSHAK - Interviews: Smylie, Goller, Corlett, Samuelson. Articles, "Jordan Nominated," Corlett in *Idaho Statesman*, Aug. 5, 1962; "Jordan Strength," Jensen in *Idaho Observer*, Aug. 9, 1962. Letters, mass mailing by Jordan, July 29, 1962, in Smylie papers; Swisher to Smylie, July 26, 1962, in Smylie papers.

JORDAN/SMYLIE - Interview: Smylie. Letters, Jordan to Smylie, Sept. 26, 1963, in Jordan papers; Smylie to Jordan, Oct. 10, 1963, in Jordan papers. Column, Corlett in *Idaho Statesman*, Sept. 18, 1963.

REPUBLICAN CONFLICT - Interviews: Smylie, Corlett, George Hansen, Hall. Article, "GOP Giant-Killer," Bill Hall in *Intermountain Observer*, June 26, 1971. Article, "Republicans Select Four," Corlett in *Idaho Statesman*, June 14, 1964.

CHAPTER SEVEN/ Painful Realignment

SALTER PROGRAM - Transcripts of Dec. 20, 27 and 28, 1965, Bob Salter KATN programs, prepared for Smylie, in his papers.

SMYLIE AND THE JBS - Article, *Los Angeles Times*, Dec. 7, 1965; Dec. 16, 1965 Associated Press dispatch. Letter, Benson to Smylie, Dec. 9, 1965, from Smylie papers.

SMYLIE AND THE REPUBLICANS: Interviews: Smylie, Samuelson, Shepard.

SAMUELSON BACKGROUND - Interviews: Samuelson, Smylie, Hall, Egbert. Article, "Big Don," *Idaho Observer*, Oct. 15, 1966. Samuelson to Smylie letter, Jan. 10, 1966 in Smylie papers. Details on announcement: undated clipping, *Idaho Statesman*, 1966, in Smylie papers.

SAMUELSON'S CAMPAIGN - Interviews: Samuelson, Andrus, Yarbrough, Ravenscroft. Article, Bruce Biossat in the *Washington Daily News*, July 28, 1966.

MATTMILLER - Interviews: Goller, Schweibert, Hawkins. Dispatch, Associated Press, Feb. 3, 1966. Column, Corlett in *Idaho Statesman*, Feb. 3, 1966.

FIRST DISTRICT PRIMARY - Interviews: Goller, Schweibert. McClure release on candidacy, March 10, 1966, Smylie papers. Purcell release on candidacy, March 17, 1966, same source. Letters, Smylie to McClure, Purcell and Schweibert, March 21, 1966, same source. Columns, Dwight Jensen in *Idaho Observer*, Feb. 17, 1966; Corlett in *Idaho Statesman*, Feb. 3, 1966. Editorial, Bill Hall, *Lewiston Morning Tribune*, March 17, 1966.

BILL DEE - Interviews: Evans, Ravenscroft, Corlett, Swisher. Articles, "Dee," in *Idaho Observer*, June 4, 1966; "Dee Tosses Hat," in *Idaho Statesman*, March 28, 1965; "Art Lessons," Dwight Jensen in *Observer*, Jan. 7, 1965. Editorial, *Idaho Observer*, April 8, 1965.

ANDRUS-DEE RELATIONS - Interviews: Andrus, Swisher, Ravenscroft. Article, "Andrus," in the *Idaho Observer*, June 4, 1966.

WALKER AND BOISE - Interview: Walker.

HERNDON CAMPAIGN - Interviews: Andrus, Williams, Walker, Max Hanson. Article, *Idaho Observer*, Sept. 1966. Column, Corlett in *Idaho Statesman*, Sept. 18, 1966.

DEMOCRATIC CONVENTION - Article, *Idaho Observer*, June 18, 1966.

SWISHER'S ANNOUNCEMENT - Interviews: Swisher, Andrus. Article, *Idaho Observer*, Aug. 20, 1966. Column, Corlett in *Idaho Statesman*, Sept. 16, 1966.

JUNGERT - His statement in *Idaho Statesman*, Nov. 6, 1966. Editorial, Bill Hall in *Lewiston Morning Tribune*, Oct. 23, 1966. Article, "Second Coming," in the *Idaho Observer*, Oct. 8, 1966. Also pp. 74-76 of master's thesis, "The Ideological Predisposition of the Swing Voter," James Ullman Hamersley, University of Denver, Denver, Colo., 1968.

HERNDON'S DEATH - Interview: Swisher. Article, *Idaho Statesman*, Sept. 15, 1966. Article, "Death on Elk Mountain," *Idaho Observer*, Sept. 17, 1966.

CENTRAL COMMITTEE FIGHT - Interviews: Andrus, Burke, White, Max Hanson, Walker, Johnson, Williams, Park, Sasser, Hall. Articles, Idaho Statesman,

Sept. 18, 20 and 21, 1966. Columns, Corlett, *Idaho Statesman*, Sept. 18 and 21, 1966; Bill Hall, "Andrus," Sept. 23, 1966, *Idaho Observer*. Article, "The Candidate," in *Idaho Observer*, Sept. 24, 1966. Letters, Frank Church to Jim Suffridge, Retail Clerks International Association, Sept. 21, 1966; Verdie Chase to Church, Sept. 21, 1966; William Hawkins to Church, Sept. 22, 1966; Gilbert Larsen to Church, Sept. 23, 1966, all from Church papers.

SWISHER STAYS IN - Interviews: Swisher, Andrus. Article, *Idaho Observer*, Oct. 24, 1966.

HEATH'S CONCERNS - Letters, Tom Heath to Samuelson, Sept. 29, 1966, and Smylie, Oct. 1, 1966, both in Smylie papers.

JORDAN BACKGROUND - Article, "Twilight," Sam Day in *Intermountain Observer*, Jan. 1, 1972. Unintentional Senator, Grace Jordan.

JORDAN-HARDING - Letter, Harding to Jordan, April 25, 1964, and reply, Jordan to Harding, April 29, 1964, both in the Jordan papers. Column, "Jordan and Harding Still Slugging," Bill Hall in *Lewiston Morning Tribune*, Oct. 23, 1966. Harding campaign ads, *Idaho Observer*, October 1966. News release Oct. 26, 1966 from Samuel Archibald, executive director, Fair Campaign Practices Committee, Inc., in Jordan papers.

CHURCH-HANSEN - Interviews: Burke, George Hansen, Hendricks. Letters, Burke to Church, Nov. 15 and 16, 1966, in Church papers. Letter, William Hawkins to Frank Church, June 19, 1967, Church papers.

SAMUELSON ADMINISTRATION - Interviews: Samuelson, Loveland, Yarbrough. Letters, Noel Meyer to Samuelson, Jan. 22, 1967; Samuelson to Meyer, Jan. 27, 1967; Hansen to Samuelson, May 11, 1967; Samuelson to McClure, May 31, 1967; all from Samuelson papers. Article, "Samuelson Drops Fault at State Board's Feet," *Coeur d'Alene Press*, Jan. 8, 1969.

SAMUELSON CAMPAIGN FINANCES - Interview: Samuelson. Internal memo (Smylie staff), Tom Hazzard to John Cobley, July 20, 1966, Smylie papers.

SAMUELSON AS SPEAKER - Column, Dwight Jensen in *Intermountain Observer*, Sept. 6, 1969. Article, Sam Day in *Observer*, July 25, 1970.

SMITH - Letters, Samuelson to Smith, July 10, 1968; Eugene Halstrom to Samuelson, Feb. 3, 1969; Smith to Samuelson, March 30, 1970; Samuelson's reply, April 8, 1970; all in Samuelson papers. Articles, "The Long Shot," Sam Day, in *Intermountain Observer*, April 4, 1970; Day in *Observer*, June 27, 1970. Columns, "Smith vs. Samuelson?", Bill Hall in *Lewiston Morning Tribune*, June 22, 1969; Hall in *Observer*, Oct. 18 and Dec. 13, 1969.

AGNEW DINNER - Letters, Douglas Bean to Jack Linkletter, May 4, 1970; Samuelson to Richard Chastain, May 15, 1970; Grant Kilbourne to Art Linkletter, May 29, 1970, all in Samuelson papers; Evan Kackley to Jordan, April 6, 1970, in Jordan papers. News release, Tribute to our Governor Committee, March 28, 1970, Samuelson papers.

SMITH SURVEY - Copy, in Jordan papers.

DEMOCRATS LINE UP - Interviews: Andrus, Ravenscroft, Walker. Column, "Lloyd Walker," Sam Day in *Intermountain Observer*, May 7, 1970. Articles, "Choice," Day in *Observer*, July 25, 1970.

SAMUELSON-ANDRUS '70 - Interviews: Andrus, Samuelson, Jack Peterson, Hall. Copy, TV script, Circuit and Eddington, start date July 21, 1970. Letter, Mike Ripley, KOFE radio, to Lee Craig Felt, Oct. 15, 1970. Columns, "Big Don Writes Them Off," Oct. 17, 1970 and "It Looks Like a Close One," Oct. 31, 1970, Bill Hall in *Intermountain Observer*. Memo, Doug Bean to Samuelson, Oct. 14, 1970, on Salter's poll; Samuelson papers.

ROBSON'S LETTER - June 3, 1971, in Jordan papers.

TOUR/East in Zion
MORMONS - Interviews: Hendricks, Ricks, Egbert. Master's thesis, Ronald Walter Campbell, May 1970, University of Idaho graduate school.

SOUTHEAST IDAHO - Interviews: Evans, Hendricks. Article, "Two Montpeliers," A. McKay Rich in *Idaho Yesterdays*, winter 1959.

POCATELLO - Interviews: Moss, Evans, Hendricks.

INEL - Interviews: Jack Peterson, Moss, Porter. Presentation materials, DOE, Idaho Falls.

IDAHO FALLS - Interviews: Rigby, Porter, Hendricks, Evans, Egbert. Editorial, Perry Swisher in *Intermountain Enterprise*, Nov. 5, 1958.

REXBURG AND THE CHURCH - Interviews: Porter, Ricks, Rigby. Crowder, "Rexburg." Excerpts, *Memoirs of W. Lloyd Adams* (unpublished, dated April 21, 1960), in Smylie papers. Editorials, *Rexburg Standard*, Nov. 5, 12 and 19, 1958.

ST. ANTHONY - Interview: Johnson.

ISLAND PARK - Article, "Island Park," Idaho Falls *Post-Register*, Sept. 30, 1956. Letter, Willard Burton to C.A. Robins, June 25, 1947. Brochure, "Island Park," 1963.

CHAPTER EIGHT/Out of Control

LEN JORDAN - Unintentional, Grace Jordan. Article, "Twilight," Sam Day, in *Intermountain Observer*, Jan. 1, 1972. Letter, Church to Jordan, Nov. 8, 1971, Church papers.

SENATE SCRAMBLE - Interviews: Park, Johnson, Goller. Articles, "Bombshell," *Intermountain Observer*, Sept. 2, 1971; "Park," Bill Hall in *Observer*, Oct. 2, 1971; "McClure," Chris Carlson in *Observer*, Oct. 2. 1971.

DAVIS - Interviews: Morgan, Goller, Park. Articles, Corlett in *Idaho Statesman*, Aug. 10, 1972; "Combinations," Bill Hall in *Lewiston Morning Tribune*, August 1972.

HANSEN'S CHARGES - Interviews: Goller, George Hansen. Columns, "Political Arrangers," Corlett in *Idaho Statesman*, September 1972; "Fat Cats," Bill Hall in *Lewiston Morning Tribune*, September, 1972.

POTATO BOYCOTT - Interviews: Park, Morgan, Shelledy, Williams. Letter, Kackley to Church, Oct. 2, 1972, Church papers. Associated Press dispatch, Oct. 24, 1972, on McClure and Davis farm policies. Column, "McClure-Davis gap," Corlett in *Idaho Statesman*, Oct. 26, 1972. Davis ad in *Statesman* Nov. 6, 1972. Article, Steve Guerber in *Statesman*, Nov. 30, 1972.

PARK'S NARCS - Interviews: Park, Morgan, Andrus, Shelledy. Column, "Hallucinations," Swisher in *Lewiston Morning Tribune*, Sept. 21, 1973. Editorial, "Park's Mistake," Bill Hall in *Tribune*, Sept. 21, 1973. Dispatches, Richard Charnock, United Press International, "Political Career," in *Idaho Statesman* Dec. 3, 1974; Articles, "Drug Agency Probe," Ken Matthews in *Statesman*, Sept. 14, 1973; "Morgan Blasts Allegatons," Paul Smith in *Idaho State Journal*, Sept. 14, 1973; "Morgan: Vindicated," Dwight Jensen in *Journal*, Sept. 14, 1973; "Tony Park," Ed Mohler in Statesman, Oct. 30, 1974; "Drug Files Leaked," *Statesman*, Sept. 19, 1973; "Drug Issue," Nov. 7, 1974, *Statesman*; drug inquiry $30,000, *Tribune*, Sept. 29, 1973; narcs "call off," *Statesman*, Oct. 25, 1973; Caldero shooting, Jay Shelledy in *Tribune*, Nov. 18, 1973.

BENDER - Interviews: Park, Andrus. Articles, Ken Matthews in *Idaho Statesman*, Sept. 20 and 21, 1973; Mindy Cameron in *Statesman*, Oct. 2, 1972; "Wallace Houses Close," Jay Shelledy in *Lewiston Morning Tribune*, Oct. 1, 1973. Editorial, "Idiotic Fuss," in *Intermountain Observer*, October 1973. Dispatches, Associated Press, Caldero-Shelledy trial, Sept. 10-12, 1980.

ORVAL HANSEN - Interviews: Corlett, Shadduck, Loveland. Hansen letters to "My Fellow Republican," April 15, 1968, in Samuelson papers. Article, "Who Will Win?," Dwight Jensen, in *Idaho Observer*, Nov. 1, 1962. Editorial, "Idaho GOP," in *Idaho Statesman*, Aug. 9, 1968. Column, Corlett, "GOP Heirarchy," in *Idaho Statesman*, Nov. 23, 1969. Letter, James Musser, Twin Falls, to Orval Hansen, Sept. 14, 1970, in Samuelson papers.

ORVAL HANSEN'S DEFEAT - Interview: Shadduck. Articles, "Orval Hansen," John Simonds (Gannett News Service) in *Idaho Statesman*, Dec. 22, 1974; "Hansen Defends Stand," in *Idaho State Journal*, Aug. 15, 1971.

GEORGE HANSEN'S FINANCIAL TROUBLES - Interviews: Hendricks, Hansen, Jones, Shelledy. A greatly abridged list of written sources:

Hansen/Anderson, *To Harrass Our People*.

Letter, John Runft (Hansen's attorney) to Congressman William Dickinson, R-Alabama, Nov. 13, 1975; Hurley Hamilton to Andrus, April 21, 1975, Andrus papers.

Articles, "Sunshine," Jay Shelledy in *Lewiston Morning Tribune*, Sept. 15. 1974; "Two-Month Term," David Pike in *Washington Star*, July 18, 1975; "Hansen

Chronically Tardy," Shelledy in *Tribune*, Oct. 15, 1976; "Hansen- Kress Debate," David Morrissey, Dan Flynn in *Idaho State Journal*, Oct. 22, 1976; "Mrs. Hansen," Steve Ahrens in *Idaho Statesman*, June 4, 1977; "Campaign Aide," Stapilus in *Idaho State Journal*, May 11-12, 1978; "Second Fight," Stapilus in *Journal*, Sept. 9, 1978; "Credit Report," Stapilus in *Journal*, June 13, 1980; "Links to Bunker Hunt," July 27, 1982, and "$135,000 Sum Owed to Bank Swindler," Dec. 2, 1982, Edward T. Pound/Brooks Jackson in *Wall Street Journal*; 1984 Hansen trial, Robert Rose, Spokane *Spokesman-Review*, March 18-30, 1984; "Hansen Bank Records," Rick Ripley, *Statesman*, Aug. 5, 1984.

Congressional Record (reprimand), July 31, 1984, pp. H8050 to H8063.

Criminal information, U.S. District Court, criminal case 75-124, District of Columbia, Feb. 19, 1975; Presentence Memorandum on Behalf of George Hansen, U.S. District Court for the District of Columbia, Jan. 10, 1975. "Report of Special Counsel Upon Completion of Preliminary Inquiry," pp. 1- 51, Stanley Brand-Abbe David Lowell, released June 14, 1984. Defendant's Memorandum of Law in Opposition to the Prosecution's Notice of Intent to Use Evidence, U.S. District Court, District of Columbia, criminal case 83- 75, Feb. 9, 1984; Federal Election Commission report, MUR347(76), on Barlow deposits in Hansen bank account, Nov. 26, 1976. Investigative report, Idaho Attorney General's office, on 1984 voting in Blaine County, March 8, 1985.

Ad, "Open Letter," signed by Anderson, Eden, Idaho, paid by Citizens for Truth in Politics, Oct. 28, 1976.

News Releases, "Big Labor Takes Aim at Hansen," Hansen office, Oct. 4, 1978; Stallings campaign, on Hansen's records, July 6, 1984.

Fundraising letter, Connie Hansen, Arlington, Va., 1977.

Cartoon book, "George the Dragon Slayer," Dick Hafer, March 19, 1984.

CHAPTER NINE/ Sunnyslope and the Supply Side

SYMMS IN POLITICS - Interviews: Noh, Park. Articles, "Symms Formally Enters," Steve Ahrens in *Idaho Statesman*, Jan. 17, 1980; Church-Symms backgrounds, Stapilus in *Idaho State Journal*, Sept. 17, 19 and 23, 1980. Letters, Symms to Robert Smylie, June 11, 1966, Smylie to Symms, June 16, 1966, both from Smylie papers; Symms to Church, Feb. 23, 1970, and reply, March 18, 1970, both from Church papers.

SYMMS IN 1972 ELECTION - Articles, "Jeffersonian Republican," Diane Simmons in *Intermountain Observer*, Nov. 11, 1972; "Apple Theme," Tim Woodward in *Idaho Statesman*, July 22, 1972. Column, "GOP Vote," John Corlett in *Statesman*, Aug. 10, 1972. Letter, Ed Williams to Frank Church, Aug. 29, 1972, Church papers. Copy, the *Idaho Compass*, Vol. 1, No. 1, June, 1969.

SYMMS IN CONGRESS - Articles, "Symms Files," Jan. 4, 1973, "Original Idea of Congress," Jan. 7, 1973, by William Ringle, Gannett News Service; "Congressman," Stapilus in *Idaho State Journal*, Sept. 25, 1980.

SMITH RUNS - Interview: Martin Peterson. Column, "Symms' Alter Ego," Corlett in *Idaho Statesman*, July 9, 1973. Dispatch, Associated Press, Nov. 8, 1973. Editorial, "Memory," *Twin Falls Times-News*, June 23, 1974.

JBS - Articles, "Church and the Birchers," Loch Johnson in *The Nation*, Oct. 19, 1974; "Chameleon in the Senate," Alan Stang in *American Opinion*, March 1974; "Birch Contribution," Sylvia Harrell in *Tribune*, June 25, 1974. Columns, "Smith Punts," Bill Hall in *Tribune*, June 27, 1974; "Smith's Retort," Sept. 24, 1974, Corlett, reprinted in *Tribune*. Letter to editor, "A Reply from the Congressman," Symms in *Tribune*, Sept. 29, 1974.

SYMMS' ELECTIONS - Interview: Goller.

OTTER - Article, "Success Story," Stapilus in *Idaho State Journal*, Aug. 2, 1978.

ANDRUS AND EVANS - Interview: Rigby. Letters, Andrus to Church and Carter, both Aug. 18, 1975, in Andrus papers. Evans often repeated the story about the gas station. Letter, Evans to Cecil Andrus, March 17, 1977.

1978 REPUBLICANS - Interviews: Ravenscroft, Ricks.

OTTER-LEMPESIS - Articles, "Lempesis Pulls up to Otter," Rod Gramer in *Idaho Statesman*, May 17, 1986; "Lempesis Maintains His Attack," Dean Miller in *Times-News*, April 2, 1986.

CHAPTER TEN/Showdown in 1980
CHURCH IN PRESTON - Article, Stapilus in *Idaho State Journal*, Oct. 20, 1980.

TAYLOR AND CHURCH - Taylor said in an interview with biographer Ross Peterson (*Intermountain Observer*, Nov. 11, 1967), "I'm glad Church beat me," and praised Church's stand on Vietnam. But in his 1979 autobiography: "By his deeds and actions, Frank Church has contributed to the erosion of the public's faith and confidence in politics and politicians."

CHURCH IN 1958 - Letter, Evan Kackley to Robert Smylie, Aug. 14, 1958, in the Smylie papers.

CHURCH AND 1962 RACE - Letters, Wynne M. Blake to Church, Aug. 31, 1960, and reply, Sept. 21, 1960, in Church papers; Lloyd Adams to Smylie, April 10, 1962, Smylie papers. Field report, Blaine Bailey to Victor Johnson, Dec. 10, 1961-Jan. 8, 1962 year summary, from Jordan papers.

1974 ELECTION, CHURCH CONSTITUENT SERVICE - Interviews: Corlett, Goller, Sasser, Martin Peterson, George Hansen.

VERDA BARNES - Interviews: Sasser, Burke, Williams, Martin Peterson.

CHURCH'S START - Interview: Burke, Sasser, Martin Peterson, Lundberg. Letters, George Smathers to Church, Nov. 1, 1960; Harry Wall to Paul Butler, Chairman, Democratic National Committee, Oct. 7, 1959, Church papers. Article, "The Liberals," Stapilus in *Idaho State Journal*, Sept. 18, 1980.

CIA INVESTIGATION - Interview: Sasser. Article, "Sherlock Holmes," Stapilus in *Idaho State Journal*, Sept. 29, 1980. Dispatch, Associated Press, Oct. 7, 1980, on Church "losing sleep" over CIA criticism.

CHURCH AS CHAIRMAN - Article, "Mr. Chairman," Stapilus in *Idaho State Journal*, Oct. 9, 1980.

RACE BEGINS - Letter, Jill Buckley to Peter Fenn, Oct. 25, 1979, in Church papers. Article, "ABC Charges," in *Idaho State Journal*, Sept. 23, 1980. Dispatches, Associated Press, Sept. 25, Oct. 9, 1980. NCPAC script, aired 1979, in Church papers.

SYMMS ANNOUNCEMENT - Author present at Sunnyslope.

DEBATE - Leroy's advice, from a copy of the "Confidential Memorandum Prepared for Congressman Steve Symms and Campaign Manager Phil Reberger." Articles, "The Old Symms," Rod Gramer in *Idaho Statesman*, Oct. 25, 1980; "Neither Scores Win," Stapilus in *Idaho State Journal*, Oct. 24, 1980; "Church-Symms Round 2," Stapilus in *Journal*, Oct. 27, 1980.

SYMMS CAMPAIGN BUS - Article, "On the Bus," Stapilus in *Idaho State Journal*, Oct. 23, 1980.

THE PRESS - Article, "Endorsements," Stapilus, *Idaho State Journal*, Oct. 29, 1980.

SYMMS PROBLEMS - Bad Money, Davis. News release, Dennis Olsen, Idaho GOP chairman, Aug. 28, 1980.

AN ASIDE/Mountains in the Middle
MOUNTAIN COUNTRY - Interviews: Johnson, Lundberg, Yarbrough.

CHAPTER ELEVEN/ Back to the future?
THE J-J - The author attended. Articles, "Hart Predicts," "He'll Veto," Steve Ahrens in *Idaho Statesman*, Jan. 31, 1982.

RIGHT TO WORK - Interview: Evans. Columns, Steve Ahrens in the *Idaho Statesman*, Feb. 7 and 14, 1982.

MORMONS AND RIGHT TO WORK - Prophets, Newquist. Article, "Church Disclaims," *Idaho State Journal*, June 22, 1984.

UNIONS IN DECLINE - Article, "Declining Unionization," Jim Wilterding, professor, Boise State University, in Idaho's Economy, BSU periodical, Spring 1987. Article, "Unions Still Linked to Democrats," Harry Bernstein, *Los Angeles Times*, in *Lewiston Morning Tribune*, March 10, 1985.

RIGHT TO WORK REVIVED - Telegram, Lawrence Gold, General Counsel AFL-CIO, to James Kerns, Idaho AFL-CIO, Jan. 23, 1985. Booklet, "Right to Work," by Idaho Freedom to Work Committee, January 1985. Veto message, John Evans of House Bill 2, Jan. 31, 1985. Complaint for Injunctive Relief and Declaratory Judgement, Sixth Judicial District Court of Idaho, Case 39414- 8, Plaintiffs Proposed Findings of Fact and Conclusions of Law, Sixth Judicial District Court of Idaho, Case 87674, April 8, 1985, on legal issues.

BUNKER HILL - Interviews: Magnuson, Jack Peterson. Dispatches, Associated Press, in *Idaho Statesman*, Aug. 23, 1981; United Press International, in *Statesman*, "Workers Worry," Aug. 26, 1981. Articles, "Bunker Hill to Close," Larry Swisher in *Statesman*, Aug. 26, 1981; "Bunker Deserves Break," Steve Ahrens in *Statesman*, Sept. 26, 1981; "Valley Residents," Swisher in *Statesman*, Dec. 12, 1981; "Labor Agreement," Doug Barker in *Kellogg Evening News*, Jan. 15, 1982; "Pact in Limbo," Barker in *News*, Jan. 18, 1982; "Battle of Airwaves," Jim Fisher in *News*, Jan. 18, 1982; "Steelworkers Remove Officers," Fisher in *News*, Jan. 19, 1982; "Purchase Falls Through," Barker in *News*, Jan. 20, 1982; "Legal Hassle," Barker in *News*, Jan. 21, 1982. Columns, "Who's Serving Whom Here?," Fisher in *News*, Jan. 19, 1982. Letters to editor in *News*, August 1981-February 1982.

DEMOCRATS: Interview: Morgan.

BATT - Interview: Batt.

OLMSTEAD - Articles, "Olmstead," Stapilus in *Idaho State Journal*, May 3, 1982; "Olmstead Steps Down," Stapilus in *Journal*, Dec. 2, 1982.

EVANS' 1982 WIN - Interviews: Batt, Evans. Article, "Evans Wins," Stapilus in *Idaho State Journal*, Nov. 3, 1982.

OLSON - Interview: Hendricks.

COGSWELL'S PLAN - Editorial, *Idaho State Journal*, Sept. 4, 1983.

SYMMS IN THE EIGHTIES - Article, "Highway Funding," *Idaho Statesman*, May 15, 1981; "Symms Humor," Chris Collins, Gannett News Service, Aug. 16, 1981. News release, Symms on Reagan programs, May 18, 1981.

SYMMS-EVANS - Articles, "Idaho Donnybrook," *National Journal*, Nov. 9, 1985; "Union Campaign Role," T.R. Reid in Washington Post, Oct. 30, 1986; "Senate Race," Reid in *Post*, Oct. 13, 1986. Symms and Evans releases, 1986. Evans address, Idaho Press Club, Oct. 5, 1986.

ANDRUS-LEROY - Interviews: Andrus, Leroy. Articles, "Waiting in the Wings," Kit Miniclier in Denver Post, Feb. 20, 1983; Article, "Andrus Campaign Poll," Rod Gramer in Idaho Statesman, Nov. 26, 1985; "Leroy, Wetherell," Stapilus in *Idaho State Journal*, Nov. 3, 1978. News Release, Skip Smyser, Nov. 25, 1986. Andrus speech, March 10, 1986. Leroy speech, Sept. 11, 1985.

STALLINGS - Articles, "Democrats," Stapilus in *Idaho State Journal*, April 26, 1982; "Stallings," Chuck Malloy in *Post Register*, July 14, 1985.

FARM POLITICS - Interview: Noh.

STALLINGS 1986 RACE - Interview: Goller, Ricks. Articles, "Vote Differences," Rod Gramer in *Idaho Statesman*, Aug. 16, 1985; "Idaho's Great Divide," Gramer in *Statesman*, Sept. 1, 1985.

CHAPTER TWELVE/ One Percenters and Their Friends
ROSS' SALES TAX - Malone, "Ross." Bill, Idaho Session Laws 1935. Barrett, "Driscoll." Article, "Lion Triumphant," Orde Pinckney in *Idaho Yesterdays*, summer 1959.

BUDGETS - Interviews: Smylie, Loveland, Swisher. *Idaho Almanac*, 1963.

HEAD TAX - Interviews: Andrus, Swisher.

1956 SALES TAX REPORT - Interviews: Swisher, Smylie, Loveland, Magnuson. Articles, *Idaho Statesman*, Oct. 31, Nov. 5, 15 and 16, 1956.

LEGISLATURE, LATE FIFTIES: Interviews: Shepard, Smylie, Swisher.

1965 SALES TAX - Interviews: Smylie, Loveland, Swisher, Andrus, Reid. Columns, Corlett in *Idaho Statesman*, Feb. 3, 4, 12, 26, March 4, 1965. Articles, "Bitter Fight," Corlett in *Statesman*, Feb. 4, 1965; "Senators Discuss," Corlett in *Statesman*, Feb. 5, 1965; "Sales Tax Passes Senate," Corlett in *Statesman*, March 12, 1965.

INVENTORY TAX - Interview: Swisher.

SUPREME COURT PROPERTY TAXES - Interview: Swisher. Idaho Supreme Court decision, Idaho Telephone Co. et al vs. E.D. Baird et al., Feb. 2, 1967.

DON CHANCE - Interview: Chance. Articles, "1 Percent Man," Charles Etlinger in *Idaho Statesman*, June 4, 1978; "Rift in 1 Percent," Paul Brinkley-Rogers in *Statesman*, Aug. 8, 1978.

REVALUATION - Interviews: Loveland, Chance. Articles, "Assessor," Charles Etlinger in *Idaho Statesman*, April 14, 1977; "Tax Burden Shift," Rick Ripley in *Statesman*, May 22, 1977. Guest Opinion, "Valuation Methods," Don Chance in *Statesman*, Sept. 4, 1977. Case file 75C-985, Idaho vs. J.L. Clark, complaint and dimissal, 1977, Ada County Magistrate Court.

ONE PERCENT - Interviews: Chance, Loveland, Moss. Articles, "1 Percent Drive," Steve Ahrens in *Idaho Statesman*, July 23, 1978; "Undecided Voters," Rod Gramer in *Statesman*, Nov. 3, 1978; "Property Tax Relief," Gramer in *Statesman*, Nov. 4, 1978; "Fallout," Tom Grote in *Statesman*, Aug. 24, 1980. Dispatch, Associated Press, on districts created, Nov. 22, 1979.

'87 SESSION - Columns, Stapilus, *Idaho Statesman*, Jan. 13-April 2, 1987.

CHAPTER THIRTEEN/ At the Arid Club
BANKING - Interview: Porter. Challenge, Hyman. Banking, Barrett. Driscoll, Driscoll. Article, "Kingmaker," Davis.

TIMBER BUSINESS - Interview: Andrus. Company, Petersen.

BOISE-CASCADE - Reports, 1971-1986. Column, Perry Swisher, 1964, state Republican files. Articles, "Tighter Control," *Business Week*, May 15, 1971; "Buckles Down," BW, March 11, 1972; "Manageable Size," BW, Feb. 10, 1973; "John Fery," BW, June 1, 1974; "Bob Hansberger," *Dun's*, September 1974.

INTERSTATE - Articles, *Idaho Statesman*, Sept. 10, Oct. 7, 30, Nov. 15, Dec. 23, 1960.

URBAN RENEWAL - Interviews: Decker, Bruce. Booklet, *BRA Years, A Dateline History, 1964-1982*, by the BRA. Press releases, BRA, "Penney's Decision," Aug. 4, 1977; J.C. Penney Co., Aug. 5, 1977. Articles, "Tearing Down Boise," L.J. Davis in *Harper's* magazine, November 1974; "New Downtown - Dream or Reality?", Tom Knappenberger in *Idaho Statesman*, June 24, 1984; "Car Through House," in *Statesman*, Oct. 28, 1970.

AN ASIDE/The Magic Valley
TWIN FALLS - Interviews: Noh, Walker, Evans, Lundberg.
BURLEY-RUPERT - Andrus.

CHAPTER FOURTEEN/The Rise and Swan Falls of Idaho Power
RECLAMATION DAYS - Article, "Water Use, Energy, and Economic Development," W. Darrell Gertsch in *Idaho Yesterdays*, summer, 1979.

EARLY ELECTRIC POWER - Young/Cochrane, Hydro. Columbia, BPA.

COMMITTEE OF NINE - Interviews: Jones, Noh.

HELL'S CANYON - Interviews: Bruce, Rigby. Official Stenographer's Report, testimony of Tom Roach before the Federal Power Commission, July 8, 1953, pp. 1416-1421. Article, "The Shifting Battles of Hell's Canyon," James Weatherby in *Intermountain Observer*, April 18, 1970. Newsletter, Frank Church, spring, 1962, Church papers. Letter, Abe McGregor Goff to Len Jordan, July 17, 1952, Jordan papers. Idaho Power on BPA marketing, "making a door to door canvass of all their customers to fight BPA," memo to Church from staffers, July 15, 1963, Church papers.

ROACH-EMERINE - Column, "Comments," Ed Emerine in *Idaho Farm Journal*, July 24, August 7, 1952. Letters, T.E. Roach, Idaho Power Co., to Emerine, July 31, 1952, in Jordan papers.

JORDAN'S STAND - Interviews: Bruce, Rigby, Smylie (cartoon quote). Jordan to House subcommittee on reclamation, 1952, in Jordan papers.

CONGRESSIONAL DEBATE - Campaign booklet, "The Frank Church Story," 1962, Volunteers for Church Committee, Boise, in Church papers.

PIONEER PLANT - Interview: Bruce. Order No. 12663, the Idaho Public Utilities Commission, Sept. 17, 1976. Hydro, Young/Cochrane. Articles, "PUC Rejects Pioneer," Paul Flanders in *Idaho Statesman*, Sept. 18, 1976; "Pioneer Controversy," Jerry Gilliland in *Statesman*, Sept. 18, 1976. Newspaper ad, "Planning Our Future," Citizens for Alternatives to Pioneer, in *Statesman* Dec. 21, 1975. Guest opinion, "Citizens' Organization," by William Smallwood of CAP, in *Statesman* Jan. 15, 1976. Editorial, "Decisive Vote on Pioneer," in *Statesman*, May 27, 1976.

LENAGHEN ON PUC - Articles, "Heart-Stopper 18-17 Vote," Corlett in *Idaho Statesman*, Feb. 2, 1974; "PUC-Utility Struggle," Earl Dunn in *Statesman*, Nov. 27, 1977; "Lenaghen Says Witnesses Gave Misinformation," Steve Hallock/Stapilus in *Idaho State Journal*, Feb. 7, 1979.

THE NEW PUC - Article, "Interesting Sort of Thing," Stapilus in *Idaho State Journal*, April 1979.

SWAN FALLS - Interviews: Bruce, Jones, Rigby, Noh, Evans, Jack Peterson. 1982 opinion 96, Idaho Supreme Court, Case No. 13794, Nov. 19, 1982.

Dispatches, United Press International, Bruce on power rates, March 19, 1983; Associated Press, on Swan Falls, April 18, 1983.

Articles, "Ward Backs Swan Falls Compromise," Paul Beebe in *Idaho State Journal*, March 20, 1983; "Swan Falls Questions," Ron Zellar in *Statesman*, July 1, 1983; Swan Falls series, Zellar in *Statesman*, Aug. 14-16, 1983.

Memorandum, from Thomas G. Nelson to James Bruce, "Possibility of using the Swan Falls Water Right to stop upstream depletion," June 22, 1987.

Letters, Logan Lanham to Stivers, March 21, 1983; Sherl Chapman, Idaho Water Users Association, to Evans, July 18, 1983; Evans to Bruce, Sept. 16, 1983; Reed Hansen to Evans, Oct. 26, 1983; Scott Reed to Swan Falls Task Force, Sept. 7, 1983; mass mail to water users, Tom Spofford, Idaho Power, Sept. 15, 1983; Kent Foster to Evans, December 1983. All in Evans papers.

News releases, Evans, on settlement, July 25, 1983; Evans and Jones, on resolution, Jan. 23, 1984; Evans, on proposals, Jan. 10, 1984.

Guest opinions, Jones and Al Fothergill in *Statesman*, Aug. 5, 1984.

Ad, Idaho Power on subordination, in *Statesman*, May 15, 1984.

Memo, Robert Lenaghen to Evans, April 26, 1983, Evans papers.

Governor's Swan Falls Task Force minutes, Evans papers.

Confidential draft, "An Investigation into the Economic Impacts of Subordinating the Swan Falls Hydroelectric Water Right to Upstream Irrigation," Joel Hamilton/R. Ashley Lyman, Department of Economics, to Swan Falls Interim (legislative) Study Committee, December, 1983, Evans papers.

THE FUTURE - Interviews: Ravenscroft, Jones, Jack Peterson, Swisher.

NEED MORE?

Additional copies of this book are available from Ridenbaugh Press, and so is the *Idaho Public Affairs Digest* – keeping you up to date on Idhao.

PARADOX POLITICS: People and Power in Idaho

_____ copy/copies, $16.95 each from Ridenbaugh Press
plus $2.50 shipping and handling

IDAHO PUBLIC AFFAIRS DIGEST

Keep up with Idaho every month with the *Idaho Public Affairs Digest*, the independent review since 1990 of key developments in the state.
_____ Subscriptions: e-mail $58/year. Print, first class mail $62/year.
Would you like to see a copy? Ask for a sample at
watkins@ridenbaugh.com

Name _____

Address _____

City _____ State _____ Zip _____

Email _____

Ridenbaugh Press
Box 843, Carlton OR 97111.
Order by phone (503) 852-0010.
Order by e-mail stapilus@ridenbaugh.com
World Wide Web at http://www.ridenbaugh.com

CPSIA information can be obtained
at www.ICGtesting.com
Printed in the USA
LVHW081526190220
647491LV00035B/912